8 00
med
8/20

D0805186

APHA MISSION STATEMENT

The American Public Health Association is an association of individuals and organizations working to improve the public's health. It promotes the scientific and professional foundation of public health practice and policy, advocates the conditions for a healthy global society, emphasizes prevention, and enhances the ability of members to promote and protect environmental and community health.

American Public Health Association
800 I Street, NW
Washington, DC 20001–3710
www.apha.org

© 2005 by the American Public Health Association

All rights reserved. No part of this publication may be reproduced, stored in a retrieval system, or transmitted in any form or by any means, electronic, mechanical, photocopying, recording, scanning, or otherwise, except as permitted under Sections 107 and 108 of the 1976 United States Copyright Act, without either the prior written permission of the Publisher or authorization through payment of the appropriate per-copy fee to the Copyright Clearance Center [222 Rosewood Drive, Danvers, MA 01923 (978) 750-8400, fax (978) 750-4744, www.copyright.com]. Requests to the Publisher for permission should be addressed to the Permissions Department, American Public Health Association, 800 I Street, NW, Washington, DC 20001-3710; fax (202) 777-2531.

Georges C. Benjamin, MD, FACP
Executive Director

Burton W. Wilcke, PhD, APHA Publications Board Liaison

Printed and bound in the United States of America

Cover Design: Orin Buck and Marianne Irmler

Cover Photo: © Lannis Waters/The Palm Beach Post

Typesetting: Sue Westrate and Michele Pryor

Set in: New Baskerville and Gill Sans

Printing and Binding: Automated Graphic Systems, Inc., White Plains, MD
ISBN: 0-87553-045-1

Second Edition

2C 10/04
2M 2/05

This book was printed on recycled paper.

Library of Congress Control Number: 2005921111

PUBLIC HEALTH MANAGEMENT OF DISASTERS

THE PRACTICE GUIDE

2nd Edition

Linda Young Landesman, DrPH, MSW

This book is dedicated to my husband Paul as a thank you for his understanding and patience, and to my son Andy—for he is our future.

Table of Contents

Foreword

BY

ERIC K. NOJI, M.D., M.P.H.

CENTERS FOR DISEASE CONTROL & PREVENTION (CDC)

With both disasters and the number of people affected by such events on the increase, the importance of disasters as a public health problem is now widely recognized. The last quarter century has witnessed a heightened recognition of the role of the health professional in managing disasters. For example, in the early 1970s, health personnel working in disaster situations observed that the effects of disasters on the health of populations were amenable to study by epidemiological methods and that certain common patterns of morbidity and mortality following certain disasters could be identified. Subsequently, post-disaster evaluations of the effectiveness of the health management of disasters have provided critical lessons for improving preparedness and mitigating the human impact of these events. Furthermore, government officials and other decision-makers have increasingly acknowledged the importance of collecting relevant health data that can be used as a scientific basis for taking action on a myriad of problems facing a disaster-affected community (i.e., recovery and reconstruction).

During the past 15 years, the medical and public health impact of disasters have been reviewed in a number of publications with periodic updates on the "state of the art" appearing every few years. As a result, a considerable body of knowledge and experience related to the adverse health effects of disasters is now accumulating that requires regular updating so that we can apply the lessons learned during one disaster to the management of the next. This book, Public Health Management of Disasters: The Practice Guide, does exactly that and more. With years of experience, Dr. Landesman gives the reader ample technical descriptions of each kind of disaster, the structural and organizational makeup of emergency management particularly those related to the role and responsibilities of health professionals, and copious information useful for management practices in the disaster setting (e.g., risk assessment, surveillance, communications and environmental issues). In addition, always emphasizing the use of proven management methods and practices, Dr. Landesman challenges public health professions with questions that must still be answered to respond effectively in emergency situations.

All disasters are unique because each affected region of the world has different social, economic, and baseline health conditions. Public Health Management of Disasters: The Practice Guide will serve as the essential desk reference not only for health professionals responsible for preparing for and responding to disasters, but for emergency managers, government officials and other decision-makers charged with ensuring that limited resources of the affected community are well managed.

AUTHOR REFLECTIONS AND ACKNOWLEDGEMENTS

On September 11, 2001, I realized that a second edition was required—even before the first book was on the shelf. Because of the expansion of disaster-related resources available, the need for a book which consolidates important information into one source is even more crucial than it was in 2001. In the second edition, by including sections such as setting up a reception center, point of dispensing sites, provider credentialing, and the application of GIS to the public health response, I am hopeful that our profession can plan for tasks for which "on the job" has been the chief teacher.

Initially, I thought that the edition you are holding would just need an update to the organizational response sections. However, my vision for the book broadened while observing the dramatic changes in local and federal activities. This changed scope reflects striking improvements in disaster readiness in the United States. Inter-organizational cooperation and planning among response agencies are now the norm. Through technology, the capability for monitoring and response has been maximized. Even if the next catastrophic incident taxes our systems, we have made important enhancements that will be evident in avoided morbidity and mortality.

As always, my colleagues have been a wonderful source of knowledge, tips, and resources. Rick Bissell and Eddie Gabriel, always current, provided important direction for the sections describing the organization of the emergency management response.

The expanded mental health chapter was possible because of the generous sharing of Anita Appel, Jack Hermann, Jeannie Straussman, and Joyce Wale. During the response following 9/11, my valued colleague Joyce helped define new principles in the management of mental health issues during disasters and I am fortunate to be able to learn from her.

In San Francisco, dinner with June Kailes and Brenda Premo was invaluable, as we talked about disaster preparedness for those with disabilities. June has cleared the path for those of us who want to develop ways to improve response to these communities and I am grateful that she helped shape the disability chapter in this book. I also want to thank my sister, Pam Holmes, one of the country's leading advocates for the deaf, for her support and the important direction that she provided on the ADA and the FCC rules.

The innovators at the Greater New York Hospital Association, Susan Waltman and Doris Varlese have led the hospital preparedness effort in the metropolitan New York City Region. Their briefings, website, and personal guidance were valuable resources and provided important direction to many of the topics in this book.

Many thanks to Burt Wilcke, Terence Mulligan, Ellen Meyer, and Georges Benjamin at APHA for their roles in making this book a reality.

Finally, a round of applause to my dear colleagues at the New York City Department of Health and Mental Hygiene and the New York City Health and Hospitals Corporation. I have learned by example and hopefully have incorporated the spirit of their important efforts into this work.

ABOUT THE AUTHOR

Dr. Linda Young Landesman, a native of Michigan, has almost 30 years of experience in social services, health care and emergency preparedness. She earned Bachelors of Arts and Masters of Social Work degrees from the University of Michigan and practiced clinical social work for 10 years before pursuing a DrPH in health policy and management from the Columbia School of Public Health. Her doctoral dissertation focused on hospital preparedness for chemical accidents and won the Doctoral Dissertation Award from the Health Services Improvement Fund in 1990.

Since 1996, Dr. Landesman has been an assistant vice president at the New York City Health and Hospitals Corporation where she is responsible for $600 million in programmatic contracts. In 2004, Dr. Landesman received a national award for Business Process Improvement from the Technology Managers Forum for the development of a web-based tracking system for medical resident work hours. She was elected President of the Public Health Association of New York City (PHANYC) and under her leadership this APHA Affiliate's visibility has been advanced through the development of the PHANYC agenda for a Healthy New York.

She has promoted an increased public health role in disaster preparedness and response since 1982, through the development of national EMS response standards and national APHA policy, conducting research, organizing meetings, teaching, publishing, and consulting. She is an Assistant Clinical Professor at the Mailman School of Public Health, Columbia University and visiting faculty at the University of Massachusetts-Amherst Public Health Practice Program where she teaches online. Dr. Landesman has been appointed to numerous disaster related advisory boards including the WMD Committee of the New York City Department of Health and Mental Hygiene, the Mailman School Center for Public Health Preparedness and the Mailman School World Trade Center Evacuation study. In addition, she is a member of the editorial board of the American Journal of Public Health and the Commissioner's Community Advisory Committee for the New York City Department of Health and Mental Hygiene. Dr. Landesman led the initial CDC-ASPH sponsored effort to develop a national curriculum in the public health management of disasters. Her course is now being used nationwide.

Chapter 1

Types of Disasters and Their Consequences

A disaster can be defined as an emergency of such severity and magnitude that the resultant combination of deaths, injuries, illness, and property damage cannot be effectively managed with routine procedures or resources. These events can be caused by nature, equipment malfunction, human error, or biological hazards and disease. Public health agencies must be concerned about the universal risk for disaster, the increase in natural disasters across the United States, the negative impact of disasters on public health, and the likely increase of actual and potential effects of manmade disasters.

A significant proportion of Americans are at risk from only three classes of natural disasters: floods, earthquakes, and hurricanes. Twenty-five to 50 million people live in floodplains that have been highly developed as living and working environments. Another 110 million people live in coastal areas of the United States, including the Great Lakes region. By the year 2010, 60 percent of the US population may be living within 50 miles of the East or West Coast. A category 4 hurricane has an 80 percent chance of hitting the coastal area from Maine to Texas.

Disasters pose a number of unique problems not encountered in the routine practice of emergency health care. Examples include the need for warning and evacuation, widespread urban search and rescue, triage and casualty distribution, and coordination among multiple jurisdictions, government offices, and private sector organizations. The effective management of these concerns requires special expertise.

However, hospitals and other health care agencies must be able to address these situations quickly and effectively to meet the standards of the Joint Commission on Accreditation of Healthcare Organizations and the regulations of the Occupational and Safety Health Administration.

NATURAL AND TECHNOLOGICAL DISASTERS

Natural disasters can be categorized as "acute" or "slow" in their onset. They are predictable because they cluster in geographic areas. Natural hazards are unpreventable and, for the most part, uncontrollable. Even if quick recovery occurs, natural disasters can have long–term effects. Natural disasters with acute onsets include events such as earthquake, flood, hurricane or typhoon, tornado, fire, tsunami or storm surge, avalanche, volcanic eruption, extreme cold or blizzard, and heat wave. Natural hazards with a slow or gradual onset include drought, famine, desertification, deforestation, and pest infestation. The most important natural disasters and examples of their environmental effects are listed in Table 1.

Technological or manmade disasters include nuclear accidents, bombings, and bioterrorism. Increasingly, agencies involved in disasters and their management are concerned with the interactions between man and nature, which can be complex and can aggravate disasters.

TABLE 1. NATURAL DISASTERS AND THEIR ENVIRONMENTAL IMPACT

Natural Disaster	Environmental Effects
Blizzard/Coldwave/Heavy Snowfall	Avalanche, erosion, snow melt (flooding), loss of plants and animals, river ice jams (flooding)
Cyclone	Flooding, landslide, erosion, loss of plant and animal life
Drought	Fire, depletion of water resources, deterioration of soil, loss of plant and animal life
Earthquake	Landslide, rock fall, avalanche
Flood/Thunderstorm	Heavy rainfall, fire, landslide, erosion, destruction of plant life
Heatwave	Fire, loss of plants and animals, depletion of water resources, deterioration of soil, snow melt (flooding)
Lightning	Fire
Thunderstorm/Heavy Rainfall	Flooding, fire, landslide, erosion, destruction of plant life
Tornado	Loss of plant and animal life, erosion, water disturbance
Tsunami	Flooding, erosion, loss of plant and animal life
Volcanic Eruption	Loss of plant and animal life, deterioration of soil, air and water pollution
Wildfires	Destruction of ground cover, erosion, flooding, mud slides, long-term smog, and tainted soil

The severity of damage caused by natural or technological disasters is affected by population density in disaster-prone areas, local building codes, community preparedness, and the use of public safety announcements and education on how to respond correctly at the first signs of danger. Recovery following a disaster varies according to the public's access to pertinent information (e.g., sources of government and private aid), pre-existing conditions that increase or reduce vulnerability (i.e., economic or biological factors), prior experience with stressful situations, and availability of sufficient savings and insurance.

BLIZZARD/COLDWAVE/HEAVY SNOWFALL[1]

A major winter storm can be lethal. Winter storms bring ice, snow, cold temperatures, and often dangerous driving conditions in the northern parts of the United States. Even small amounts of snow and ice can cause severe problems for southern states where storms are infrequent.

Familiarity with winter storm warning messages, such as wind chill, winter storm watch, winter storm warning, and blizzard warning can facilitate quick action by public health. "*Wind chill*" is a calculation of how cold it feels outside when the effects of temperature and wind speed are combined. On November 1, 2001, the National Weather Service (NWS) implemented a replacement Wind Chill Temperature (WCT) index for the 2001/2002 winter season. The reason for the change was to improve upon the current WCT Index which was based on the 1945 Siple and Passel Index. A *winter storm watch* indicates that severe winter weather may affect your area. A *winter storm warning* indicates that severe winter weather conditions are definitely on the way and emergency preparedness plans should be activated. A *blizzard warning* means that large amounts of falling or blowing snow and sustained winds of at least 35 miles per hour are expected for several hours.

Risk of Morbidity and Mortality

Transportation accidents are the leading cause of death during winter storms. Preparing vehicles for the winter season and knowing how to react if stranded or lost on the road are the keys to safe winter driving. Morbidity and mortality associated with winter storms include

---

1 Sections on Blizzards and Heatwaves reprinted with permission from Landesman LY and Veenema TG. Natural Disasters. In Veenema TG(ed), *Disaster Nursing and Emergency Preparedness for Chemical, Biological, and Radiological Terrorism and Other Hazards*. New York: Springer Publishing Company, 2003: 270-274.

frostbite and hypothermia, carbon dioxide (CO) poisoning, blunt trauma from falling objects, penetrating trauma from the use of mechanical snow blowers, and cardiovascular events usually associated with snow removal. Frostbite is a severe reaction to cold exposure that can permanently damage its victims. A loss of feeling and a white or pale appearance in fingers, toes, or nose and ear lobes are symptoms of frostbite. Hypothermia is a condition brought on when the body temperature drops to less than 90 degrees Fahrenheit. Symptoms of hypothermia include uncontrollable shivering, slow speech, memory lapses, frequent stumbling, drowsiness, and exhaustion.

Water has a unique property in that it expands as it freezes. This expansion puts tremendous pressure on whatever is containing it, including metal or plastic pipes. No matter the "strength" of a container, expanding water can cause pipes to break causing flooding. Flooding creates a risk for drowning and electrocution. Pipes that freeze most frequently are those that are exposed to severe cold, like outdoor hose bibs, swimming pool supply lines, water sprinkler lines, and water supply pipes in unheated interior areas like basements and crawl spaces, attics, garages, or kitchen cabinets. Also, pipes that run against exterior walls that have little or no insulation are also subject to freezing. Pipe freezing is a particular problem in warmer climates where pipes often run through uninsulated or underinsulated attics or crawl spaces. A secondary risk is the loss of heat due to freezing pipes.

COLD WEATHER AND THE DISABLED

Individuals who are particularly vulnerable to exposure from freezing temperatures, such as the elderly and those with disabilities, should organize activities outside of their home so that they go out in the warmest part of the day (usually noon to 2 pm). Those paralyzed from the chest or waist down and individuals who have difficulty sensing and maintaining heat in their extremities are at risk for severe frostbite and need to protect their feet, pelvic areas, and hands because of circulation problems. It is important to dress for the weather by wearing several layers of clothes, keeping one's head, neck, and chest covered with scarves, and wearing two pairs of thick socks under lined boots. Those in a wheelchair should wrap a blanket over their pelvic region and limit their amount of time outside.

To enable the full functioning of driving adaptation equipment in motor vehicles, these vehicles have to warm up before the person gets in them. Service animals should wear a coat or cape underneath their regular harness and should sit or lay on a blanket in the vehicle. Dog's paws should be protected with boots.

Pneumatic tires provide better traction for wheelchairs on icy surfaces. Tires for dirt bikes (sold through bicycle shops) can be used as an alternative on icy surfaces. Ramps should be cleared of ice by using standard table salt or cat litter, as rock salt is poisonous to service dogs. Rock salt can also be slippery for certain types of mobility aides. Freezing rain will stick to canes, walkers, fore arm cuffs, and wheelchairs making the metal parts slippery and cold to touch. Driving gloves which grip can be helpful. When returning wheelchairs to vehicles, it is important to first remove the tires and shake the debris and ice off of them. The tire rims, and other metal parts that may have any salt or other de-icing chemicals on them need to be wiped off to avoid rust on the metal parts.

Public Health Interventions

Educating communities about preventive steps that they can be taken both in advance of winter and once a storm has begun will help reduce the impact. Winter storm preparation activities should include:

- Home winterization activities (insulating pipes, installing storm windows).

- Collect winter clothing and supplies such as extra blankets, warm coats and clothes, water-resistant boots, hats and mittens.

- Assemble a disaster supplies kit containing a first aid kit, battery powered weather radio, flashlight, and extra batteries.

- Stock canned food, non-electric can opener, and bottled water.

- Winterize vehicles, keep gas tank full, and assemble a disaster supplies car kit.

- In heavy snow, stay away from downed power lines.

CYCLONE

Cyclones are large-scale storms characterized by low pressure in the center surrounded by circular wind motion (counter clockwise in the Northern Hemisphere, clockwise in the Southern Hemisphere). Severe storms arising in the Atlantic waters are known as hurricanes, while those developing in the Pacific Ocean and the China seas are called typhoons. The precise classification (e.g., tropical depression, tropical storm, hurricane) depends on the wind force (Beaufort scale), wind speed, and manner of creation.

Hurricanes are powerful storms that form at sea with wind speeds of 74 miles per hour or greater. They are tracked by satellites from the moment they begin to form, so warnings can be issued three to four days before a storm strikes. A hurricane covers a circular area between 200 and 480 miles in diameter. In the storm, strong winds and rain surround a central, calm "eye," which is about 15 miles across. Winds in a hurricane can sometimes reach 200 miles per hour. However, the greatest damage to life and property is not from the wind but from tidal surges and flash flooding. Hurricanes are rated on a 1 to 5 scale, known as the Saffir-Simpson Scale. Category 3, 4 and 5 hurricanes are considered major storms. See Table 2 for the Saffir-Simpson Scale.

TABLE 2 SAFFIR-SIMPSON HURRICANE SCALE

Category	Damage	Winds	Storm Surge
1	Minimal	74-95 mph	4-5 ft.
2	Moderate	96-110 mph	6-8 ft.
3	Extensive	1111-130 mph	9-12 ft
4	Extreme	131-155 mph	13-18 ft
5	Catastrophic	156 mph	18 ft. +

Owing to its violent nature, its potentially prolonged duration, and the extensive area that could be affected, the hurricane or cyclone is the most devastating of all storms. The hurricane season lasts from June 1 through November 30, but most occur in August and September. Scientists have developed a relatively good understanding of the nature of hurricanes through observation, radar, weather satellites, and computer models.

A distinctive characteristic of hurricanes is the increase in sea level, often referred to as the storm surge. This increase in sea level is the result of the low-pressure central area of the storm creating a vaccuum, the storm winds piling up water, and the tremendous speed of the storm. Rare storm surges have risen as much as 14 meters (45.9318 feet) above normal sea level. This phenomenon can be experienced as a large mass of sea water pushed along by the storm with great force. When it reaches land, the impact of the storm surge can be exacerbated by high tide, a low-lying coastal area with a gently sloping seabed, or a semi-enclosed bay facing the ocean.

The severity of a storm's impact on humans is exacerbated by deforestation, which often occurs as the result of population pressure. When trees disappear along the coastlines, the winds and the storm surges can enter the land with greater force. Deforestation on the slopes of hills and mountains increases the risk of violent flash floods and landslides caused by the heavy rain associated with tropical cyclones. At the same time, the beneficial effects of the rainfall—replenishment of the water resources—may be negated due to the inability of a forest ecosystem to absorb and retain water.

Risk of Morbidity and Mortality

Deaths and injuries from hurricanes occur because victims fail to evacuate or take shelter, do not take precautions in securing their property despite adequate warning, and do not follow guidelines on food and water safety or injury prevention during recovery. Morbidity during the storm itself results from drowning, electrocution, lacerations or punctures from flying debris, and blunt trauma from falling trees or other objects. Heart attacks and stress-related disorders can arise during the storm or its aftermath. Gastrointestinal, respiratory, vector-borne, and skin disease as well as accidental pediatric poisoning can all occur during the period immediately following the cyclone. Injuries from improper use of chain saws or other power equipment, disrupted wildlife (e.g., bites from animals, snakes, or insects), and fires are common. Fortunately, the ability to detect and track storms has helped reduce morbidity and mortality in many countries.

Injury Prevention

Public health professionals work with local emergency management agencies to prepare people to evacuate and to turn off their utilities. To avoid injury, residents should be advised to use common sense and wear proper clothing, including long sleeved shirts, pants, and safety shoes or boots. Furthermore, they should learn proper safety precautions and operating instructions before operating gas-powered or electric chainsaws. People should use extreme caution when using electric chainsaws to avoid electrical shock and should always wear gloves and a safety face shield or eyeglasses when using any chainsaw. Evacuees should be advised against wading in water as there may be downed power lines, broken glass, metal fragments, or other debris beneath the surface.

When returning to their dwellings after a disaster, residents should check for structural damage and electrical or natural gas or propane tank hazards. They should return to homes during the daytime and only use battery-powered flashlights and lanterns to provide light rather than candles, gas lanterns, or torches.

During the recovery period, public health and local emergency management officials must ensure an adequate supply of safe water and food for the displaced population. In addition to offering acute emergency care, community plans should provide for the continuity of care for homeless residents with chronic conditions.

Public Health Interventions

- Conduct needs assessment for affected communities, including a review of public health infrastructure.

- Establish active and passive surveillance systems for deaths, illness, and injuries.

- Educate the public about maintaining safe and adequate supplies of food and water.

- Establish environmental controls.

- Monitor infectious disease and make determinations about needed immunizations (e.g., tetanus).

- Institute multifaceted injury control programs.

- Establish protective measures against potential disease vectors.

- Monitor potential release of hazardous materials.

- Assure evacuation plans for people with special needs in nursing homes, hospitals, and home care.

- Work with local communities to improve building codes (e.g., developing improved designs for wind safety).

DROUGHT

Drought affects more people than any other environmental hazard, yet it is perhaps the most complex and least understood type of all environmental hazards. Drought is often seen as the result of too little rain and used synonymously with famine. However, fluctuation in rainfall alone does not cause a famine. Drought often triggers a crisis in the arid and semi-arid areas, since rain is sparse and irregular, but alone does not cause desertification. The ecosystem changes leading to desertification are all attributed to human activities, such as overcultivation, deforestation, overgrazing, and unskilled irrigation. Each of these activities is exacerbated by increasing human populations. The first three activities strip the soil of vegetation and deplete its organic and nutrient content. This leaves the soil exposed to the eroding forces of the sun and the wind. The subsoil that is left can become so hard that it no longer absorbs rain, and the water flows over the surface, carrying away the little topsoil that might have remained.

Risk of Morbidity and Mortality

Displaced populations suffer high rates of disease due to stress of migration, crowding, and unsanitary conditions of relocation sites. Morbidity and mortality can result from diarrheal disease, respiratory disease, and malnutrition. Mortality exceeding a baseline rate of one death per 10,000 people per day is the index of concern. Low weight to height is identified through the percentage of children two or more standard deviations (z-score) from the reference median compared with mean z-scores; children with edema are severely malnourished.

Public Health Intervention

- Monitor health and nutritional status by assessing weights and heights.

- Assess and ensure food security, including availability, accessibility, and consumption patterns.

- Monitor death rate.

- Ensure safe water, sanitation, and disease control.

EARTHQUAKE

Earthquakes are sudden slippages or movements in a portion of the earth's crust accompanied by a series of vibrations. Aftershocks of similar or lesser intensity can follow the main quake. Earthquakes can occur at any time of the year. An earthquake is generally considered to be the most destructive and frightening of all forces of nature. Earthquake losses, like those of other disasters, tend to cause more financial losses in industrialized countries and more injuries and deaths in undeveloped countries.

The Richter magnitude, used as an indication of the force of an earthquake, measures the magnitude and intensity or energy released by the quake. This value is calculated based on data recordings from a single observation point for events anywhere on earth, but it does not address the possible damaging effects of the earthquake. According to global observations, an average of two earthquakes of a Richter magnitude 8 or slightly more occur every year. A one digit drop in magnitude equates with a tenfold increase in frequency. Therefore, earthquakes of magnitude 7 or more generally occur 20 times in a year, while those with a magnitude 6 or more occur approximately 200 times.

Earthquakes can result in a secondary disaster, catastrophic tsunami. Tsunami, a series of waves of very great length and period, are usually generated by large earthquakes under or near the oceans, close to the edges of the tectonic plates. These waves may travel long distances, increase in height abruptly when they reach shallow water, and cause great devastation far away from the source. Submarine landslides and volcanic eruptions beneath the sea or on small islands can also be responsible for tsunami, but their effects are usually limited to smaller areas. Volcanic tsunami are usually of greater magnitude than seismic ones; waves of more than 40 meters (131.234 feet) in height have been witnessed.

Geologists have identified regions where earthquakes are likely to occur. With the increasing population worldwide and urban migration trends, higher death tolls and greater property losses are more likely in many areas prone to earthquakes. At least 70 million people face significant risk of death or injury from earthquakes because they live in the 39 states that are seismically active. In addition to the significant risks in California, the Pacific Northwest, Utah, and Idaho, six major cities with populations greater than 100,000 are located within the seismic area of the New Madrid fault. Major Third World cities in which large numbers are forced to live on earthquake-prone land in structures unable to withstand damage include Lima, Peru; Santiago, Chile; Quito, Ecuador; and Caracas, Venezuela.

Risk of Morbidity and Mortality

Deaths and injuries from earthquakes vary according to the type of housing available, time of day of occurrence, and population density. Common injuries include cuts, broken bones, crush injuries, and dehydration from being trapped in rubble. Stress reactions are also common. Morbidity and mortality can occur during the actual quake, the delayed collapse of unsound structures, or clean-up activity.

Injury Prevention

Public health officials can intervene both in advance of and after earthquakes to prevent post-earthquake injuries. The safety of homes and the work environment can be improved by building standards that require stricter codes and use of safer materials. Measures to prevent injuries include securing appliances, securing hanging items on walls or overhead, turning off utilities, storing hazardous materials in safe, well-ventilated areas, and checking homes for hazards such as windows and glass that might shatter.

Public health workers should follow the recommendations listed previously for *Cyclone*.

Public Health Interventions

- Encourage earthquake drills to practice emergency procedures.

- Recommend items for inclusion in an extensive first aid kit and a survival kit for home and automobile.

- Teach basic precautions regarding safe water and safe food.

- Ensure the provision of emergency medical care to those who seek acute care in the first three to five days after an earthquake.

- Ensure continuity of care for those who have lost access to prescriptions, home care, and other medical necessities.

- Conduct surveillance for communicable disease and injuries, including location and severity of injury, disposition of patient, and follow-up contact information.

- Prepare media advisories with appropriate warnings and advice for injury prevention.

- Establish environmental controls.

- Facilitate use of surveillance forms by search and rescue teams to record type of building, address of site, type of collapse, amount of dust, fire or toxic hazards, location of victims, and nature and severity of injuries.

FLOOD

Global statistics show that floods are the most frequently recorded destructive events, accounting for about 30 percent of the world's disasters each year. The frequency of floods is increasing faster than in any other type of disaster. Much of this rise in incidence can be attributed to uncontrolled urbanization, deforestation, and, more recently, the effects of El Niño. Floods may also accompany other natural disasters, such as sea surges during hurricanes and tsunamis following earthquakes.

Except for flash floods, flooding causes few deaths. Instead, widespread and long-lasting detrimental effects include mass homelessness, disruption of communications and health care systems, and heavy loss of business, livestock, crops, and grain, particularly in densely-populated, low lying areas. The frequent repetition of flooding means a constant, or even increasing, drain on the economy for rural populations.

Risk of Morbidity and Mortality

Flood-related mortality varies from country to country. Flash flooding, such as from excessive rainfall or sudden release of water from a dam, is the cause of most flood-related deaths. Most flood victims become trapped in their cars and drown when attempting to drive through rising or swiftly moving water. Other deaths have been caused by wading, bicycling, or other recreational activities in flooded areas.

The stress and exertion required for clean up following a flood also cause significant morbidity (mental and physical) and mortality (e.g., myocardial infarction). Fires, explosions from gas leaks, downed live wires, and debris can all cause significant injury. Water-borne diseases (e.g., enterotoxigenic *Escherichia coli*, *Shigella*, hepatitis A, leptospirosis, giardiasis) become a significant hazard, as do other vector-borne disease and skin disorders. Injured and frightened animals, hazardous waste contamination, disruption of sewer and solid-waste collection systems, molds and mildew, and dislodging of graves pose additional risks in the period following a flood. Food shortages due to water-damaged stocks may occur due to flooding and sea surges.

Injury Prevention

Educating the public about the dangers of floods and about avoiding risky behaviors may prevent deaths. Since most flood-related deaths are due to drowning in motor vehicles, educational campaigns can discuss how cars do not provide protection from moving water and that as little as two feet of water is capable of carrying vehicles away.

Even more important to injury and disease prevention is education regarding clean up procedures and precautions. Rubber boots and waterproof gloves should be worn during cleanup. Walls, hard-surfaced floors, and many other household surfaces should be cleaned with soap and water and disinfected with a solution of one cup of bleach to five gallons of water. Surfaces on which food may be stored or prepared and areas in which small children play must be thoroughly disinfected. Children's toys must be disinfected prior to use or discarded. All linens and clothing must be washed in hot water or dry cleaned. Items that cannot be washed or dry cleaned, such as mattresses and upholstered furniture, should be air dried in the sun and then sprayed thoroughly with a disinfectant. All carpeting must be steam cleaned. Household materials that cannot be disinfected should be discarded.

Residents must understand that flood water may contain fecal material from overflowing sewage systems as well as agricultural and industrial byproducts. Although skin contact with flood water does not by itself pose a serious health risk, there is some risk of disease from eating or drinking anything contaminated with flood water. Anyone with open cuts or sores that could be exposed to flood water must keep these areas as clean as possible by washing with soap to control infection. Wounds that develop redness, swelling, or drainage require immediate medical attention.

Routine sanitary procedures are essential for disease prevention. Hands must be washed with soap and water that has been boiled or disinfected before preparing or eating food, after toilet use, after participating in flood clean up activities, and after handling articles contaminated with flood water or sewage. Children's hands should be washed frequently, and children should not be allowed to play in previously flooded areas.

Public Health Interventions

- Conduct needs assessment to determine the status of public health infrastructure, utilities (e.g., water, sewage, electricity), and health, medical, and pharmaceutical needs.

- Conduct surveillance of drinking water sources, injuries, increases in vector populations, and endemic, water-borne, and vector vector-borne disease.

- Organize delivery of health care services and supplies and continuity of care.

- Educate public regarding proper sanitation and hygiene.

- Educate public regarding proper clean up.

HEAT WAVE

Over time, populations can acclimatize to hot weather. However, mortality and morbidity rise when daytime temperatures remain unusually high for several days in a row and nighttime temperatures do not drop significantly. Because populations acclimatize to summer temperatures, heat waves in June and July have more of an impact than those in August and September. There is often a delay between the onset of a heat wave and adverse health effects. Deaths occur more commonly during heat waves where there is little cooling at night and taper off to baseline levels if a heat wave is sustained. Table 3 lists common terms associated with heat related conditions.

TABLE 3. HEATWAVE TERMS

Heat Wave: A prolonged period of humidity. The National Weather Service steps up its procedures to alert the public during heat and humidity.

Heat Index: A number in degrees Fahrenheit that tells how hot it really feels when relative humidity is added to the actual air temperature. Exposure to full sunshine can increase the heat index.

Heat Cramps: Heat cramps are muscular pains and spasms due to heavy exertion, usually involving the abdominal muscles or legs. It is generally thought that the loss of water from heavy sweating causes the cramps.

Heat Exhaustion: Heat exhaustion typically occurs when people exercise heavily or work in a warm place where body fluids are lost through heavy sweating. Blood flow to the skin increases, causing blood flow to decrease to vital organs. This results in a form of mild shock. If not treated, the victim's condition will worsen. Body temperature will keep rising and the victim may suffer heat stroke.

Heat Stroke: Heat stroke is life-threatening. The victim's temperature control system, which produces sweating to cool the body, stops working. The body temperature can rise so high that brain damage and death may result if the body is not cooled quickly.

Sunstroke: Another term for heat stroke.

Risk of Morbidity and Mortality

Heat waves result in adverse health effects in cities more than in rural areas. Those at greatest risk of adverse health outcomes include older adults, infants, those with a history of prior heatstroke, and those who are obese. Drugs that may predispose users to heatstroke include neurolepics and anticholinergics. Heat-related morbidity and mortality come from heat cramps, heatstroke, heat exhaustion, heat syncope, myocardial infarction, loss of consciousness, dizziness, cramps, and stroke.

Injury Prevention

Residents at greatest risk must be moved to air-conditioned buildings for at least a few hours each day. All residents must maintain adequate hydration and reduce outdoor activity levels. Education campaigns should concentrate on protecting older adults and helping parents of children under five years of age understand how to protect their children from heat and prevent heat disorders.

Public Health Interventions

- Develop an early warning surveillance system that triggers the mobilization of prevention and intervention activities.

- Identify the location of residents who might be at risk due to age, pre-existing conditions, lack of air conditioning, and other environmental or health factors.

- Work with utilities to educate the public about preventive actions when energy blackouts might be anticipated.

THUNDERSTORMS

A thunderstorm is formed from a combination of moisture, rapidly rising warm air, and a force capable of lifting air such as a warm and cold front, a sea breeze or a mountain. All thunderstorms contain lightning. Thunderstorms may occur singly, in clusters, or in lines. Thus, it is possible for several thunderstorms to affect one location in the course of a few hours. Some of the most severe weather occurs when a single thunderstorm affects one location for an extended time. Thunderstorms can bring heavy rains (which can cause flash flooding), strong winds, hail, lightning, and tornadoes. Severe thunderstorms can cause extensive damage to homes and property.

Lightning is a major threat during a thunderstorm. Lightning is an electrical discharge that results from the buildup of positive and negative charges within a thunderstorm. When the buildup becomes strong enough, lightning appears as a "bolt." This flash of light usually occurs within the clouds or between the clouds and the ground. A bolt of lightning reaches a temperature approaching 50,000 degrees Fahrenheit in a split second. The rapid heating and cooling of air near the lightning causes thunder.

Risk of Morbidity and Mortality

In the United States, between 75 to 100 Americans are hit and killed each year by lightning. Morbidity is reduced if, when caught outdoors, individuals avoid items which act as natural lightning rods, such as tall isolated trees in an open area or the top of a hill, and metal objects such as wire fences, golf clubs, and metal tools. It is a myth that lightning never strikes twice in the same place. In fact, lightning may strike several times in the same place in the course of one discharge.

While thunderstorms and lightning can be found throughout the United States, they are most likely to occur in the central and southern states. The state with the highest number of thunderstorm days is Florida.

TABLE 4. SEVERE WEATHER WATCHES AND WARNINGS: DEFINITIONS

Flood Watch: High flow or overflow of water from a river is possible in the given time period. It can also apply to heavy runoff or drainage of water into low-lying areas. These watches are generally issued for flooding that is expected to occur at least 6 hours after heavy rains have ended.

Flood Warning: Flooding conditions are actually occurring or are imminent in the warning area.

Flash Flood Watch: Flash flooding is possible in or close to the watch area. Flash Flood Watches are generally issued for flooding that is expected to occur within 6 hours after heavy rains have ended.

Flash Flood Warning: Flash flooding is actually occurring or imminent in the warning area. It can be issued as a result of torrential rains, a dam failure, or ice jam.

Tornado Watch: Conditions are conducive to the development of tornadoes in and close to the watch area.

Tornado Warning: A tornado has actually been sighted by spotters or indicated on radar and is occurring or imminent in the warning area.

Severe Thunderstorm Watch: Conditions are conducive to the development of severe thunderstorms in and close to the watch area.

Severe Thunderstorm Warning: A severe thunderstorm has actually been observed by spotters or indicated on radar, and is occurring or imminent in the warning area.

Tropical Storm Watch: Tropical storm conditions with sustained winds from 39 to 73 mph are possible in the watch area within the next 36 hours.

Tropical Storm Warning: Tropical storm conditions are expected in the warning area within the next 24 hours.

Hurricane Watch: Hurricane conditions (sustained winds greater than 73 mph) are possible in the watch area within 36 hours.

Hurricane Warning: Hurricane conditions are expected in the warning area in 24 hours or less.

TORNADO

Tornados are rapidly whirling, funnel-shaped air spirals that emerge from a violent thunderstorm and reach the ground. Tornados can have a wind velocity of up to 200 miles per hour and generate sufficient force to destroy even massive buildings. The average circumference of a tornado is a few hundred meters, and it is usually exhausted before it has travelled as far as 20 kilometers (12.4274 miles). Severity is rated on the Fujita Scale according to wind speed. The Fujita Scale uses a scoring system of F0 (no damage) to F5 (total destruction). The extent of damage depends on updrafts within the tornado funnel, the tornado's atmospheric pressure (which is often lower than the surrounding barometric pressure), and the effects of flying debris.

Risk of Morbidity and Mortality

Approximately 1,000 tornadoes occur annually in the United States, and none of the lower 48 states is immune. Certain geographic areas are at greater risk due to their recurrent weather patterns; tornados most frequently occur in the midwestern and southeastern states. Although tornadoes often develop in the late afternoon and more often from March through May, they can arise at any hour of the day and during any month of the year.

Injuries from tornados occur due to flying debris or people being thrown by the high winds (i.e., head injuries, soft tissue injury, secondary wound infection). Stress-related disorders are more common, as is disease related to loss of utilities, potable water, or shelter.

Injury Prevention

Because tornadoes can occur so quickly, communities should develop redundant warning systems (e.g., media alerts and automated telephone warnings), establish protective shelter to reduce tornado-related injuries, and practice tornado-shelter drills. In the event of a tornado, the residents should take shelter in a basement if possible, away from windows, while protecting their heads. Special outreach should be made to people with special needs who can make a list of their limitations, capabilities, and medications and have ready an emergency box of needed supplies. People with special needs should have a "buddy" who has a copy of the list and who knows of the emergency box.

Other precautions include those listed under *Cyclone*.

Public Health Interventions

- Work with emergency management on tornado shelter drills for vulnerable communities.

- Conduct needs assessment using maps that detail pre-existing neighborhoods, including landmarks, and aerial reconnaissance.

- Ensure the provision of medical care, shelter, food, and water.

- Establish environmental controls.

- Establish a surveillance system based at both clinical sites and shelters.

VOLCANIC ERUPTIONS

Volcanic activity involves the explosive eruption or flow of rock fragments and molten rock in various combinations of hot or cold, wet or dry, and fast or slow. Extremely high temperature and pressure cause the mantle, located deep inside the earth between the molten iron core and the thin crust at the surface, to melt and become liquid rock or magma. When a large amount of magma is formed, it rises through the denser rock layers toward the earth's surface. Magma that has reached the surface is called lava. Volcanic hazards vary in severity depending on the size and extent of the eruption and whether the eruption is occurring in a populated area. Volcanos are classified by similar characteristic behavior, and have been called "Strombolian," "Vulcanian," "Vesuvian," "Pelean," "Hawaiian," and others. When active, volcanoes may exhibit only one characteristic type of eruption or a sequence of types.

A volcano may begin to show signs of unrest several months to a few years before an eruption. Accurate long-term predictions, specifying when and where an eruption is most likely to occur and what type and size eruption should be expected are not possible. Warnings that an eruption is hours to days away are possible because eruptions are preceded by such changes in a volcano's earthquake activity, ground deformation, and gas emissions over a period of days to weeks.

In the United States, volcano warnings are made through a series of alert levels that correspond generally to increasing levels of volcanic activity. Each increase in the alert level helps authorities gauge and coordinate their response to a developing volcano emergency.

Depending on the location of the volcano (California, Alaska, Pacific Northwest or Hawaii), different alert levels[2] are used to provide volcano warnings and emergency information regarding volcanic unrest and eruptions. Different alert levels are used because volcanoes exhibit different patterns of unrest in the weeks to hours before erupting, volcano hazards differ requiring a warning scheme that addresses specific volcano hazards, and there is variability in the intensity of monitoring U.S. volcanoes. The Volcanic Explosivity Index or VEI is the eruption magnitude scale used to rate the eruption. The VEI considers the plume height, the volume of magma, the classification, and how often it erupts. The VEI ranges from VEI 0 to VEI 8. Any eruption that occurs anywhere will rate at least a VEI 0 on the scale and have less than 10,000 cubic meters of ejecta, which includes lava and ash. VEI 3 volcanoes have as much as 100 million cubic meters of ejecta. A VEI 8 volcano must spew out a minimum of one trillion cubic meters of ejecta.

Morbidity and Mortality

Many kinds of volcanic activity can endanger the lives of people and property located both close to and far away from a volcano. The range of adverse health effects is quite broad and extensive. Immediate, acute, and nonspecific irritant effects have been reported in the eyes, including corneal abrasions, nose, skin, and upper airways of persons exposed to volcanic dusts and ash particles. Victims can have exacerbation of their asthma symptoms and can asphyxiate due to inhalation of ash or gases. There is the potential of injuries from blasts and projectile of rock fragments. Lacerations can occur if sound waves shatter windows and break glass. Volcanic flow can set homes on fire causing thermal injuries including death. Victims can experience trauma due to fallen trees or rocks or the collapse of buildings under weight of the ash. Foraging animals may be unable to find adequate supply of food or water. Indoor air radon levels may be elevated. Flooding and pooling of water secondary to debris or obstruction of waterways can lead to spread of infectious disease. Finally, victims can experience anxiety, depression, or post traumatic stress disorder.

---

2 Also referred to as status levels, condition levels, or color code.

Public Health Interventions

- Collaborate with emergency-management specialists to develop effective warning schemes.

- Participate in volcano-emergency planning workshops and emergency-response exercises.

- Prepare educational materials, including fact sheets, booklets, video programs, and maps.

- Designate areas for evacuation and evacuate when indicated.

- Provide emergency air-monitoring equipment for detecting toxic gases.

- Stockpile and distribute masks and eye shields or goggles, where indicated.

- Prepare for breakdown of water systems.

- Encourage protection by remaining inside sturdy houses with shuttered windows when evacuation not indicated or possible.

- Strengthen roofs of building with supports or take shelter in most resistant part of the building.

- Stay indoors during worst conditions.

WILDFIRES

More and more people are building their homes in woodland settings in or near forests, rural areas, or remote mountain sites. As residential areas expand into relatively untouched wildlands, these communities are increasingly threatened by forest fires. Protecting structures in the wildland from fire poses special problems, and can stretch firefighting resources to the limit. Wildfires often begin unnoticed. They spread quickly, igniting brush, trees, and homes.

There are three different classes of wildfires. A "surface fire" is the most common type and burns along the floor of a forest, moving slowly and killing or damaging trees. A "ground fire" is usually started by lightning and burns on or below the forest floor in the human layer down to the mineral soil. "Crown fires" spread rapidly by wind and move quickly by jumping along the tops of trees. Depending on prevailing winds and the amount of water in the environment, wildfires can quickly spread out of control causing extensive damage to personal property and human life. If heavy rains follow a fire, other natural disasters can occur, including landslides, mudflows, and floods. Once ground cover has been burned away, little is left to hold soil in place on steep slopes and hillsides. A major wildland fire can leave a large amount of scorched and barren land and these areas often do not return to prefire conditions for decades. If the wildland fire destroyed the ground cover, then erosion becomes one of several potential problems. Danger zones include all wooded, brush, and grassy areas—especially those in Kansas, Mississippi, Louisiana, Georgia, Florida, the Carolinas, Tennessee, California, Massachusetts, and the national forests of the western United States.

Risk of Morbidity and Mortality

Morbidity and mortality associated with wildfires include burns, inhalation injuries, respiratory complications, and stress-related cardiovascular events (exhaustion and myocardial infarction from fighting or fleeing the fire).

Public Health Interventions

More than four out of every five wildfires are started by people. Negligent human behavior, such as smoking in forested areas or improperly extinguishing campfires, is the cause of many forest fires. Another cause of forest fires is lightning. Prevention efforts include working with the fire service to educate people to:

- Build fires away from nearby trees or bushes. Ash and cinders lighter than air float and may be blown into areas with heavy fuel load, starting wildfires.

- Be prepared to extinguish the fire quickly and completely. If the fire becomes threatening, someone will need to extinguish it immediately.

- Never leave a fire—even a burning cigarette—unattended. Fire can quickly spread out of control.

- Encourage the development of a family wildfire evacuation plan if the area in your community is at risk for wildfire.

MANMADE AND TECHNOLOGICAL DISASTERS

Manmade or technological disasters are unpredictable, can spread across geographical boundaries, may be unpreventable, and may have limited physical damage but long-term effects. Some disasters in this class are entirely manmade, such as terrorism. Other technological disasters occur because industrial sites are located in communities affected by natural disasters, equipment failures occur, or workers have inadequate training or fatigue and make errors. The threat of terrorism is categorized as a potential technological disaster and includes bioterrorism, bombings, civil and political disorders, riots, and economic emergencies.

Technological disasters include a broad range of incidents. Routes of exposure are water, food and drink, airborne releases, fires and explosions, and hazardous materials or waste (e.g., chemical, biological, or radioactive) released into the environment from a fixed facility or during transport. Fires, explosions, building or bridge collapses, transportation crashes, dam or levee failures, nuclear reactor accidents, and breaks in water, gas, or sewer lines are other examples of technological disasters.

Risk of Morbidity and Mortality

Communities in which industrial sites are located or through which hazardous materials pass via highway, rail, or pipeline are at risk for technological disasters. Injuries can occur to workers at the site, to responders bringing the incident under control and providing emergency medical care, and to residents in the community. Those with pre-existing medical conditions, such as lung or heart disease, could be at increased risk for negative health outcomes if exposed to toxic releases. Burns, skin disorders, and lung damage can result from exposure to specific agents. Table 5 lists the health consequences of several classes of toxins.

TABLE 5. HEALTH EFFECTS OF CHEMICAL AGENTS

Chemical Agent	Health Effects
Nerve agents	Miosis, rhinorrhea, dyspnea
Vesicants	Erythema, blisters, eye irritation, cough, dyspnea
Cyanide	Loss of consciousness, seizures, apnea
Pulmonary CG (phosgene)	Dyspnea, coughing

Injury Prevention

Ensuring that local industry implements basic safety procedures can significantly reduce negative health outcomes from accidental releases of toxins. Emergency preparedness—including the ability of prehospital and hospital systems to care for patients exposed to industrial agents, the training of medical personnel to work in contaminated environments, and the stockpiling of personal protective equipment for responders—is key to providing care following industrial accidents or acts of bioterrorism. Government agencies, in coordination with hospitals and public health, should conduct computer simulations or field exercises to test the community's ability to evacuate those at risk and the ability of the health sector to provide care to those exposed to accidental releases. Information about the clinical management of exposure to toxins can be provided by poison control centers, CHEMTREC, and industry databases.

Public Health Interventions

- Take a visible role in community planning.

- Conduct hazard assessments.

- Review Material Safety Data Sheets for agents produced, stored, or used locally and regionally to evaluate range of potential adverse health effects.

- Conduct vulnerability analyses to identify target populations and potential adverse public health consequences.

- Conduct risk assessment to determine if specific agents will reach toxic levels in the vicinity of vulnerable populations.

- Determine minimal thresholds of exposure for specific agents that would trigger evacuation.

- Gather information on chemical neutralization, estimation models of plume-dispersion, and appropriate antidotes.

- Work with local hospitals to stockpile appropriate antidotes, medications, and supplies.

- Stockpile two pills per person of potassium iodide in communities located within ten miles of nuclear reactor sites.

- Provide emergency services and medical care to victims.

- Activate the health alert network.

BLAST INJURIES

Explosions can inflict multi-system life-threatening injuries to many persons simultaneously. Multiple factors contribute to the injury patterns which result from blasts. Contributing factors include the composition and amount of the materials involved, the environment in which the event occurs, the method of delivery, such as a bomb, the distance between the victim and the blast, and the absence/presence of protective barriers or environmental hazards in the area of the blast. To predict subsequent demand for medical care and resources needed, it is useful to remember that post-blast, half of the initial casualties will seek medical care over the first one-hour period. Those with minor injuries often arrive before the most severely injured, because they go directly to the closest hospitals using whatever transportation is available. Further, where the explosion has resulted in a structural collapse, victims will be more severely injured and their rescue can occur over prolonged time periods.

The two types of explosives, high-order explosives (HE) and low-order explosives (LE), cause different injury patterns. Injury patterns also differ whether the bombs are manufactured or improvised. HE devices, such as TNT, C-4, Semtex, nitroglycerin, dynamite, and ammonium nitrate fuel oil, produce a defining supersonic over-pressurization shock wave. LE devices, such as pipe bombs, gunpowder, and pure petroleum-based bombs (AKA Molotov cocktails), create a subsonic explosion and lack the over-pressurization wave. Manufactured explosives are usually those used by the military, are mass produced, and quality-tested as weapons. Improvised explosives and incendiary (fire) bombs are often individually produced in small quantities and include devices used differently than their initial purpose.

Morbidity and Mortality

The most common injury for survivors of explosions is penetrating and blunt trauma. Table 6 describes the four basic mechanisms of blast injury. Blast lung is the most common fatal injury among initial survivors. Explosions in confined spaces (mines, buildings, or large vehi-

TABLE 6 THE FOUR BASIC MECHANISMS OF BLAST INJURY.

Category	Characteristics	Body Part Affected	Types of Injuries
Primary	Unique to HE, results from the impact of the over-pressurization wave with body surfaces.	Gas filled structures are most susceptible—lungs, GI tract, and middle ear.	• Blast lung (pulmonary barotrauma) • TM rupture and middle ear damage • Abdominal hemorrhage and perforation • Globe (eye) rupture • Concussion (TBI without physical signs of head injury)
Secondary	Results from flying debris and bomb fragments.	Any body part may be affected.	Penetrating ballistic (fragmentation) or blunt injuries Eye penetration (can be occult)
Tertiary	Results from individuals being thrown by the blast wind.	Any body part may be affected.	Fracture and traumatic amputation Closed and open brain injury
Quaternary	All explosion-related injuries, illnesses, or diseases not due to primary, secondary, or tertiary mechanisms. Includes exacerbation or complications of existing conditions.	Any body part may be affected.	Burns (flash, partial, and full thickness) Crush injuries Closed and open brain injury Asthma, COPD, or other breathing problems from dust, smoke, or toxic fumes Angina Hyperglycemia, hypertension

Source http://www.cdc.gov/masstrauma/preparedness/primer.htm August 8, 2003

cles) and/or structural collapse are associated with the greatest morbidity and mortality. Blast injuries can occur to any body system: audi-
tory, digestive, circulatory, central nervous system, extremities, renal,
and respiratory. Up to 10 percent of all blast survivors have significant
eye injuries. These injuries can occur with minimal discomfort initially
and patients can come for care days, weeks, or even months after the
event. Symptoms include eye pain or irritation, foreign body sensation,
altered vision, periorbital swelling, or contusions. Clinical findings in
the gastrointestinal tract may be absent until the onset of complications. Victims can also experience tinnitus, and/or temporary or permanent deafness from blasts.

Public Health Interventions

- As part of a community preparedness plan, identify the medical institutions and personnel who can provide the emergency
  care that will be required, including otologic assessment and
  audiometry, burn and trauma centers, hyperbaric oxygen
  chamber, etc.

- Ensure that the community preparedness plan includes structure for surge capacity. To estimate the "first wave" of casualties, double the number appearing for care in the first hour.
  Prepare written communications and instructions for victims
  who may experience temporary or permanent deafness.

- Work with the regional Emergency Management Organization,
  police, fire, and EMS, to have a plan in place to identify potential toxic exposures and environmental hazards for which the
  health department will need to help protect responders in the
  field and the community.

- With the hospital community, establish a victim identification
  registry.

- With the mental health community, plan for the reception and
  intervention with family and friends.

EPIDEMICS

The spread of infectious disease depends upon pre-existing levels of the disease, ecological changes resulting from disaster, population displacement, changes in density of population, disruption of public utilities, interruption of basic public health services, and compromises to sanitation and hygiene. The risk that epidemics of infectious disease will occur is proportional to the population density and displacement. A true epidemic can occur in susceptible populations in the presence or impending introduction of a disease agent compounded by the presence of a mechanism that facilitates large-scale transmission (e.g., contaminated water supply or vector population).

Quick response is essential because epidemics, which result in human and economic losses and political difficulties, often arise rapidly. An epidemic or threatened epidemic can become an emergency when the following characteristics of the events are present. Not all of these characteristics need be present and must be assessed with regard to relative importance locally:

- risk of introduction to and spread of the disease in the population;

- large number of cases may reasonably be expected to occur;

- disease involved is of such severity as to lead to serious disability or death;

- risk of social or economic disruption resulting from the presence of the disease;

- authorities are unable to cope adequately with the situation due to insufficient technical or professional personnel, organizational experience, and necessary supplies or equipment (e.g., drugs, vaccines, laboratory diagnostic materials, vector-control materials);

- risk of international transmission.

The categorization of "emergency" differs from country to country, depending on two local factors: whether the disease is endemic and a means of transmitting the agent exists. Table 7 describes epidemic emergencies for particular diseases listed in endemic and nonendemic areas.

TABLE 7. EPIDEMIC EMERGENCIES DEFINED

Disease	Nonendemic areas	Endemic areas
Cholera	One confirmed indigenous case	Significant increase in incidence over and above what is normal for the season, particularly if multifocal and accompanied by deaths in children less than 10 years old
Giardiasis	A cluster of cases in a group of tourists returning from an endemic area	A discrete increase in incidence linked to a specific endemic place
Malaria	A cluster of cases, with an increase in incidence in a defined geographical area	Rarely an emergency; increased incidence requires program strengthening
Meningococcal meningitis	An incidence rate of 1 per 1000 in one week in a defined geographical area	The same rate for two consecutive weeks is an emergency
Plague	One confirmed case apparently linked by domestic rodent or respiratory transmission or by a rodent epizootic	A cluster of cases
Rabies	One confirmed case of animal rabies in a previously rabies-free locale	Significant increases in animal and human cases
Salmonellosis	A large cluster of cases in a limited area, with a single or predominant stereotype (e.g., specific event or restaurant), or a significant number of cases occurring in multiple foci, apparently related by a common source (e.g., specific food product)	
Smallpox (a)	Any strongly suspected case	Not applicable
Typhus fever/rickettsia	One confirmed case in a louse-infested, nonimmune population	Significant increase in number of cases in a limited period of time
Viral Encephalitis	Cluster of time- and space-related cases in a nonimmune population (a single case should be regarded as a warning)	Significant increase in the number of cases with a mosquito-borne single, identified etiological agent in a limited period
Viral hemorrhagic fever	One confirmed indigenous or imported case with an etiological single agent with which person-to-person transmission may occur in a limited period of time	Significant increase in the number of cases with an identified etiological agent
Yellow fever	One confirmed case in a community	Significant increase in the number of cases in a population and an adequate/limited period of time for vector population to increase

TABLE 8 NATURAL DISASTER EFFECTS MATRIX – MOST COMMON EFFECTS OF SPECIFIC EVENTS ON ENVIRONMENTAL HEALTH

1- Severe possible effect;

2 -Less severe possible effect;

3- Least or no possible effect

	Earthquake	Hurricane	Flood	Tsunami	Volcanic Eruption
WATER SUPPLY AND WASTE DISPOSAL					
Damage to civil engineering structures	1	1	1	3	1
Broken mains	1	2	2	1	1
Damage to water sources	1	2	2	3	1
Power outages	1	1	2	2	1
Contamination (biological or chemical)	2	1	1	1	1
Transportation failures	1	1	1	2	1
Personnel shortages	1	2	2	2	1
System overload (due to population shifts)	3	1	1	2	1
Equipment, parts, and supply shortages	1	1	1	2	1
SOLID WASTE HANDLING					
Damage to civil engineering structures	1	2	2	3	1
Transportation failures	1	1	1	2	1
Equipment shortage	1	1	1	2	1
Personnel shortage	1	1	1	3	1
Water, soil, and air pollution	1	1	1	2	1
FOOD HANDLING					
Spoilage of refrigerated foods	1	1	2	2	1
Damage to food preparation facilities	1	1	2	3	1
Transportation failures	1	1	1	2	1
Power outages	1	1	1	3	1
Flooding of facilities	3	1	1	1	2
Contamination/degradation of relief supplies	2	1	1	2	1
VECTOR CONTROL					
Proliferation of vector breeding sites	1	1	1	1	3
Increase in human/vector contacts	1	1	1	2	1
Disruption of vector-borne disease control programs	1	1	1	1	1
HOME SANITATION					
Destruction or damage to structures	1	1	1	1	1
Contamination of water and food	2	2	1	2	1
Disruption of power, heating, fuel, water or supply waste disposal services	1	1	1	2	1
Overcrowding	3	3	3	3	2

REPRINTED FROM NATURAL DISASTERS- PROTECTING THE PUBLIC'S HEALTH, SCIENTIFIC PUBLICATION #575, PAN AMERICAN HEALTH ORGANIZATION, 2000, PAHO PUBLICATIONS (WWW.PAHO..ORG) 525 23RD ST., NW, WASHINGTON DC 20037

Public Health Interventions

- Control or to prevent epidemic situations.

- Conduct surveillance to identify when an epidemic is likely to occur.

- Ensure that items requiring refrigeration, such as vaccines, are kept refrigerated throughout the chain of distribution.

- Monitor the maintenance of immunization programs against childhood infectious disease (e.g., measles, mumps, polio).

Chapter 2

Role and Responsibility of Public Health

Public health professionals must take responsibility for community health in both disaster preparedness and response. This chapter outlines in detail action plans, personnel requirements, applicable laws, and the functional model of public health response.

PUBLIC HEALTH ROLE

- Identify community resources applicable to the physical, social, and psychosocial effects of disaster.

- Identify groups most at risk from disaster (i.e., children, older adults, homeless, chronically ill, homebound, physically or mentally disabled).

- Provide disaster education both in advance of (i.e., what to expect in a disaster) and after (i.e., how to deal with effects) event.

- Take responsibility for the health of a community following a disaster.

- Use such resources as assessment, epidemiology, and data analysis to make and implement recommendations for limiting morbidity and mortality following disaster.

- Cooperate and collaborate with the broadest range of community agencies to ensure that primary health, public health, mental health, and social impacts are adequately addressed in disaster planning.

- Prevent disease by providing health advisories on injury prevention, food and water safety, and vector control.

- Assure that health services continue post impact, including acute care, continuity of care, primary care and emergency care.

- Inspect Red Cross shelters and feeding operations.

- Request volunteers from the American Red Cross to supplement medical and nursing needs.

- Communicate with government officials about the public health effects of potential disasters and provide expert assistance during and after disasters.

- Develop and advocate public policies designed to reduce the public health impact of potential disasters.

- Collaborate with other health and human service professionals to rigorously evaluate intervention outcome.

Local public health authorities have the primary responsibility for the health of a community following a disaster. These professionals bring unique resources to the emergency management community that can limit morbidity and mortality caused by both natural and technological disasters. In fact, the contributions of public health authorities to community disaster preparations and response represent an extension of their normal activities. Public health officials are knowledgeable about the prevention of infectious disease and injury, routinely conduct surveillance for infectious disease, maintain working relationships with other agencies within the health sector, have governmental jurisdiction for overseeing the public's health, can draw from the expertise of multidisciplinary members, and use triage skills that can easily be adapted for use following a disaster.

The responsibilities of public health agencies in disaster preparedness and response are more complicated than in a typical public health activity. In preparedness activities, public health professionals must participate as part of a multiagency team, some members of which have little or no knowledge of public health. Public health and other human service departments (aging, disability, and mental health, etc.) are often organized as separate governmental units. As such, careful advance coordination of preparedness efforts is an essential part of community planning. Further, public health practitioners must work with multiple bureaucratic layers of infrastructure in a condensed time frame and interact with personnel with whom they normally do not have contact and whose lexicon and methods may be different. Since the sectors involved in the Incident Command System have already trained together, public health must integrate itself into this established response, particularly where there is a Unified Command.

Public health workers can conduct assessments and epidemiological studies and can make and implement appropriate recommendations based on data analysis. Such data collection is critical before disaster occurs so as to ensure that potential social impacts are adequately addressed in disaster planning and that emergency, public, and mental health needs are met in the community. Maintenance of continuity of care is especially important for older adults, those with chronic disease, and those in long-term care facilities. Health advisories on injury prevention, food and water safety, and disaster-specific precautions should be developed in advance and available for immediate distribution when needed. Public health officials should regularly communicate with elected officials about the likely impact of potential disasters for which the community is at risk and help develop policies and regulations that can prevent or reduce morbidity and mortality following disaster.

ACTION PLAN

The health sector is responsible for ensuring the continuity of health care services. Resource problems following disasters in the United States have resulted from poor planning in the use or distribution of assets rather than a deficiency of those assets. Public health works with health sector agencies in the community to coordinate planning for the continued delivery of services both during and after the disaster. This interagency coordination includes the development of an action plan to address community health needs. Components of the plan include:

- ensuring continuity of health care services (acute emergency care, continuity of care, primary care, and preventive care);

- monitoring environmental infrastructure (water, sanitation, and vector control);

- assessing the needs of the elderly and other special populations;

- initiating injury prevention programs and surveillance;

- ensuring that essential public health sector facilities will be able to function post–impact (hospitals, health departments, physicians' offices, storage sites for health care supplies, dispatch centers, paging services, and ambulance stations); and

- allocating resources to ensure that the above responsibilities can be accomplished.

PERSONNEL

The responsibility of disaster preparedness should be assigned to someone who has the organizational authority to ensure an adequate level of preparation. Otherwise, the effort may be less than optimal because the designated individual lacks authority to delegate tasks to the proper offices and personnel. In addition, such a decision creates the false impression that an effective program exists because someone has been assigned to disaster preparedness.

Both the lead individual and all those involved in disaster preparedness and response must have a well–grounded understanding of the public health consequences of disaster and human response to disaster on the part of both victims and responders. Public health practitioners must recognize how the health sector fits into the emergency management model of disaster preparedness and response, including components of a typical response and team–based, interdisciplinary problem solving. Those involved in disaster response must have both the expertise and ability to access state–of–the–art resources to provide technical assistance to communities and to collect and analyze data as quickly as possible. Through such data collection, epidemiological methods can be applied to develop the best disaster response both to prevent morbidity and mortality and to mitigate medical or public health problems. Public health officials also help blend public health approaches with clinical practice. Likewise, they provide direction to the American Red Cross to ensure the provision of appropriate care and resources and inspect Red Cross shelters and feeding operations.

PUBLIC HEALTH LAW AND EMERGENCIES

As part of public health disaster preparedness, health departments must review state and local laws to understand the nuances of their authority in these circumstances and to prepare a legal plan of action for times of emergency. While universal generalities form the under-pinnings of emergency authority, operational authority will vary among jurisdictions. Indeed, the Centers for Disease Control and Prevention have developed a public health law program whose mission is to articulate the connection between law and public health for public health practitioners, including during emergencies. As of this writing, local health department heads do not have the necessary authority to declare a health emergency, an issue of national concern.

The authority to protect the health of the public in emergencies is not assigned in a single law, but generally requires a chain of events. For example, a Board of Health could declare an emergency, allowing the Commissioner of Health to modify requirements set forth in the health code. A mayor could declare an emergency, which would in turn allow the mayor's office to modify provisions of local laws and regulations or the health code. Similarly, if a governor declares an emergency, the governor can modify applicable provisions of state and local laws and regulations, including the health code. However, again, each public health department must research in advance which procedures for declaring emergencies and altering health codes apply to each jurisdiction.

FUNCTIONAL MODEL OF PUBLIC HEALTH RESPONSE

The functional model summarizes a typical disaster response within the public health field and categorizes the cycle of activities. The model identifies tasks assigned to each of the core areas of public health in the context of emergency management activities. The functional model expands traditional public health partnerships with other disciplines and agencies and emphasizes collaboration to ensure competence in disaster preparedness and response.

The functional model outlined below and on the pages following comprises seven phases that correspond to the type of activities involved in preparing for and responding to a disaster: planning, prevention, assessment, response, surveillance, recovery and evaluation. The model additionally delineates the responsibilities of the various disciplines of public health.

Planning

- Apply basic concepts of local public health to disaster management

- Conduct hospital disaster planning and coordinate with hospitals

- Help community develop plan with public health focus

- Develop health promotion and disease prevention protocols and motivate use through education campaign

- Conduct needs assessments and analyze hazards and vulnerability

- Work with other health professionals to write a disaster plan specifically for public health and health concerns

- Train workforce on public health responsibilities

- Inventory supplies, equipment, communications, and people available for response

- Develop mutual aid agreements in advance

- Conduct facility–wide/agency–wide exercises to stress organizational mobilization, coordination, and communication

Prevention

Primary Prevention (before event)

- Immunization

- Control/prevent outbreaks

- Protect against risks identified in hazards, vulnerability, and needs assessments

- Conduct community education in first aid, personal hygiene, and injury prevention

- Protect and distribute safe food and water

- Protect or reestablish sanitation systems

Secondary Prevention (response to event)

- Detect and extricate victims

- Provide emergency medical care

- Organize services and treatment

- Conduct case identification and surveillance

- Establish infectious disease control

- Conduct short–term counseling/intervention

- Manage bystander response

Tertiary Prevention (recovery from event)

- Provide long–term counseling and mental health intervention

- Manage emergency services

- Manage injuries and clean-up behavior

- Reestablish health services

- Use records from response to update action plan

Assessment

- Identify potential outbreaks

- Identify potential medical, behavioral, social, and political effects of event

- Assess potential effect of loss of infrastructure on health and mental health

- Identify potential hazards and levels of acceptable exposure

- Determine incidence of disease and causal factors

- Understand mechanics of hazardous agents (i.e., radiation, toxins, thermal and water pollution, landmines, weapons)

- Determine vulnerability, level of risk, and requirement for rapid needs assessment

- Identify appropriate data to collect for decision making

- Summarize damage to health care infrastructure

- Establish continuous data monitoring

Response

Service

- Conduct "quick and dirty" assessments on which to base initial decisions

- Administer logistics

- Organize services (casualty management and behavioral health)

- Communicate plans and needs (internal and external)

- Identify need for and provide emergency treatment, resources, and equipment

- Institute unified command and control

- Continue provision of primary care

- Coordinate with emergency management response structures (incident command, federal response plan, international disaster relief, UN agencies, International Committee of the Red Cross, Non-Governmental Organizations)

Education

- How long foods can be stored in a refrigerator or freezer after the power goes off

- When the water is or is not safe to drink

- How long water should be boiled before drinking

- Whether mass immunizations are needed

- When it is safe to reenter homes or eat food after a toxic cloud has dissipated

- What is risk of delayed effects (i.e., cancer, birth defects) from the chemical or nuclear mishap to the average citizen and to those who are pregnant

Management

- Dispose of waste, debris, human and animal bodies, and biologic hazards

- Control disease vectors

- Monitor water, sanitation, food, and shelter

- Control infection

- Control clean–up injuries (i.e., chainsaw accidents, electrocution, fire, unsafe structures)

- Coordinate delivery of mental health services

- Communicate health information and risks via media outlets

- Control disease and issue quarantines where necessary

- Provide interventions to large groups

Surveillance

- Establish syndromic information systems for disaster

- Conduct sentinel surveillance, using active or passive systems, of disease and public health conditions

- Use data to recognize acute disease states and high risk groups

Recovery

- Determine present level and extent of patient care capability

- Interpret data to influence deployment of resources

- Work with community agencies to mitigate long–term impact on public health

- Conduct evaluations (structured, semi–structured, qualitative)

- Plan and direct field studies

- Manage media

- Use principles of capacity building

- Mobilize resources

- Use techniques for supplemental and therapeutic food distribution and feeding

- Organize and conduct large–scale immunization and primary health care

- Ensure maintenance of mental health program

- Establish and operate special needs shelters

- Sheltering—provide basic medical care and referral services for those requiring medical attention; staff 24 hours, consider 12 hour shifts

- Set up emergency public health hotline which is staffed 24 hour/day for medical issues and another for mental health issues with workers speaking the major languages of the community

Evaluation

- Use information revealed through evaluation to make decisions about a community's emergency management needs or improving future response

- Conduct assessments of planning and emergency response to provide continuing feedback which can improve an organization or community's preparedness

- Determine whether emergency plans and disaster response are effective and efficient

Chapter 3

Structure and Organization of Health Management in Disaster Response

L ocal response to disaster situations requires extensive planning, organization, and coordination with other regional, state, and federal officials. Since the federal response has been reorganized after 2001, this chapter starts with the new organization of the federal agencies and response systems, the responsibilities of local responders and health providers (including public health incident command), interactions with other responders, and costs and reimbursement sources for disaster response and relief.

PUBLIC HEALTH ROLE

- Participate with other professionals who engage in emergency preparedness and response.

- Activate public health emergency operations centers (EOC) and participate in community–wide EOC.

- Assess medical, public health, and mental health needs, prepare recommendations on clinical aspects of emergency, and assure provision of services.

- Assess viability of health care infrastructure.

- Conduct health surveillance, detect, identify and verify individual cases through laboratory sciences, and institute measures to control infectious disease.

- Provide expert assistance in responding to chemical, radiological, or biological hazards.

- Staff public health clinics involved in emergency

- Supplement clinical back–up to school health program sheltering activities

- Assure potable water supply, food safety, and sanitation.

- Assure worker safety.

- Educate about vector control and implement appropriate measures.

- Provide public health information.

- Work with voluntary organizations (i.e., American Red Cross) to provide emergency shelter.

- Identify victims and manage corpses.

- Be able to respond 24 hours a day, 7 days a week.

- Coordinate with other sectors on long–term consequence management.

STRUCTURE AND OPERATION OF THE FEDERAL RESPONSE

The Department of Homeland Security was established by the President and Congress (Homeland Security Act of 2002) to coordinate federal programs and to assist state and local governments in responding to terrorist attacks and disasters. To provide guidance to federal, state, and local agencies regarding a national response to a potential or actual terrorist threat, the Department of Homeland Security created the National Response Plan (NRP) and National Incident Management System (NIMS). These plans provide a mechanism to implement and coordinate the federal response in support of state and local officials. The NRP, with an all hazards approach, provides national direction for managing and responding to domestic disasters and combines fundamental principles from existing federal response plans (i.e., Federal Response Plan (FRP), National Contingency Plan (NCP), Federal Radiological Emergency Response Plan (FRERP), and the Domestic Terrorism Concept of Operations Plan (CONPLAN)). The final NRP will supersede the interim NRP, interim FRP, CONPLAN, and FRERP[1] and provide annexes on response to incidents involving biological, cyber, radiological, and other terrorism.

Under the NRP and NIMS, the President will designate a Principle Federal Official to coordinate activities of all Federal agencies during an incident of national significance. For example, the Environmental Protection Agency will provide technical personnel and supporting equipment and the Department of Health and Human Services, with its own Counter–Terrorism Concept of Operations Plan, has lead responsibility for the medical response to national emergencies in support of local authorities. The Centers for Disease Control and Prevention (CDC) maintains its separate responsibilities.

The interim Federal Response Plan (FRP), updated in January 2003 and described below, provides that to the maximum extent possible, internal state and local resources should be used as the first line of support in response to a disaster. This principle drives all preparedness at the state and local level, since states must pay a share of the costs of federal response and recovery, and an efficient use of local resources can reduce that additional cost. Once state resources and capabilities are exhausted, federal assistance may be provided to support state operations. While several of the current Presidential Decision Directives for disaster response are relevant,[2] particular attention should be paid to

[1] As the development of these frameworks are in process, descriptions of the existing plans are provided for the reader to be able to locate current policy.
[2] The full list is available at http://www.fas.org/irp/offdocs/direct.htm

PDD #39 (see chapter 11), PDD#62, and Homeland Security Presidential Directive HSPD#5 (28 Feb 2003).

In order to receive federal funding, state and local governments and nongovernmental agencies need to modify existing incident management plans to conform to the operational principles of the NRP/NIMS within one year of its implementation.

DISASTER DECLARATIONS AND FEDERAL ASSISTANCE

In the event of a natural disaster, the Robert T. Stafford Disaster Relief and Emergency Assistance Act, PL 92–388 amended by Disaster Mitigation Act 2000 PL 106–34042 (U.S. Code 5121, et seq.), provides for "an orderly and continuing means of assistance by the Federal government to state and local governments in carrying out their responsibilities to alleviate the suffering and damage which result from major disasters and emergencies." Under the Stafford Act, the President may provide federal resources, financial assistance, services, medicine, food, and other consumables through what is known as a presidential declaration.

Prior to the passage of the Homeland Security Act of 2002, Federal assistance was initiated in one of three ways: states request federal assistance in advance of the disaster to activate a declaration when the threat is imminent and warrants limited predeployment actions to lessen or avert a catastrophe; governors submit requests after the disaster has struck; or the President exercises primary authority, as was done following the bombing at Oklahoma City. With the passage of the Homeland Security Act, the Secretary of Homeland Security has a lot of discretion in the deployment of federal resources. Homeland Security can activate the Federal Government's resources if and when any of the following four conditions applies:

- A Federal department or agency, acting under its own authority, has requested the assistance of the Secretary.

- The resources of state and local authorities are overwhelmed and Federal assistance has been requested by the appropriate state/local authorities (ie. through the Stafford Act).

- More than one Federal dept/agency has become substantially involved in responding to the incident.

- The Secretary has been directed to assume responsibility for managing the incident by the President.

Once there has been a presidential declaration, the Federal Emergency Management Agency (FEMA), now part of the Emergency Preparedness and Response Directorate of the Department of Homeland Security (DHS), is tasked with its traditional role of coordinating the response, though DHS is by law the responsible manager.[3] FEMA performs many of the same functions as a local emergency management agency but can also directly utilize federal resources and money toward the preparation for, response to, and recovery from larger emergencies and disasters. If there is no presidential declaration, communities/agencies providing mutual aid to one another should execute interagency agreements, as mutual aid will be voluntary without the authority of the Stafford Act.

More than 27 other federal agencies and the American Red Cross provide personnel, technical expertise, equipment, and other resources to state and local governments, and they assume an active role in managing the response. To coordinate the federal efforts, the Secretary of DHS, on behalf of the President, appoints a Federal Coordinating Officer (FCO), who is responsible for coordinating the timely delivery of federal disaster assistance to the affected state and local governments, and disaster victims. In many cases, the FCO also serves as the Disaster Recovery Manager (DRM) who administers the financial aspects of assistance authorized under the Stafford Act. The FCO works closely with the State Coordinating Officer (SCO), appointed by the Governor to oversee disaster operations for the state, and the governor's authorized representative (GAR), empowered by the governor to execute all necessary documents for disaster assistance on behalf of the state. At the FCO and SCO, federal and state personnel work together to carry out their response and recovery responsibilities. Requests for assistance from local jurisdictions are channeled to the SCO through the designated state agencies in accordance with the state emergency operations plan and then to the FCO or designee for consideration. When resources from the federal government are required, states must complete a purchase order, blanket purchase agreement, contract, or cooperative agreement. Additionally, DHS may use a mission assign-

---

[3] Under the Stafford Act and Executive Orders 12148, Federal Emergency Management, and 12656, Assignment of Emergency Preparedness responsibilities, DHS has been delegated primary responsibility for coordinating Federal emergency preparedness, planning, management, and disaster assistance functions. DHS also has been delegated responsibility for establishing Federal disaster assistance policy. In this stewardship role, DHS has the lead in developing and maintaining the FRP.

ment, (a work order issued to another Federal agency directing completion of a specific task or provision of a service in anticipation of, or in response to, a Presidential declaration of a major disaster or emergency).

In addition to their Washington, DC headquarters, FEMA operates a number of regional offices (see Appendix Q for list). Other agencies, such as the US Department of Health and Human Services and the National Disaster Medical System (NDMS) described below, use the same geographic zones to organize personnel and resources throughout the nation.

HOMELAND SECURITY

The Department of Homeland Security (DHS) provides a unifying core for the vast national network of organizations and institutions involved in preparedness efforts. The Department of Homeland Security assumes primary responsibility in the event of a terrorist attack, natural disaster, or other large–scale emergency. DHS is responsible for developing and implementing preparedness plans; developing procedures and policies to guide response to a terrorist attack; conducting training and exercises for first responders, enhancing partnerships with state and local governments, private sector institutions and other organizations; and funding the purchase of equipment for first responders, states, cities, and towns.

DHS is comprised of five major divisions or directorates:

- Border & Transportation Security responsible for maintaining the security of our nation's borders and transportation systems. The largest of the Directorates, it is home to agencies such as the Transportation Security Administration, the former U.S. Customs Service, the border security functions of the former Immigration and Naturalization Service, Animal & Plant Health Inspection Service, and the Federal Law Enforcement Training Center;

- Emergency Preparedness and Response ensures that our nation is prepared for, and able to recover from, terrorist attacks and natural disasters;

- Science & Technology coordinates DHS's efforts in research and development, including preparing for and responding to the full range of terrorist threats involving weapons of mass destruction;

- Information Analysis & Infrastructure Protection (IAIP) merges the capability to identify and assess a broad range of intelligence information concerning threats to the homeland under one roof, issue timely warnings, and take appropriate preventive and protective action; and

- Management is responsible for budget, management and personnel issues in DHS.

Besides the five Directorates of DHS, other agencies are being folded into the new department or are being newly created (U.S. Coast Guard, U.S. Secret Service, Bureau of Citizen and Immigration Services, Office of State and Local Government Coordination, Office of Private Sector Liaison; and Office of Inspector General). The following figure provides the organization or DHS.

FIGURE 1 DEPARTMENT OF HOMELAND SECURITY

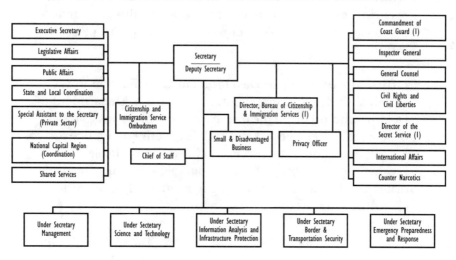

Note (1): Effective March 1, 2003

In disasters of the magnitude requiring a presidential declaration, public health resources may be deployed by the Department of Health and Human Services (HHS) through its executive agent, the Assistant Secretary for Public Health Emergency Preparedness (ASPHEP). ASPHEP coordinates interagency activities between HHS, other federal departments, agencies, offices and state and local officials responsible for emergency preparedness, acts of bioterrorism and other public health emergencies. Three offices are part of ASPHEP: the Offices of Planning and Emergency Response Coordination, Research and Development Coordination, and State and Local Preparedness.

- **Offices of Planning and Emergency Response Coordination—** HHS emergency response operations are now coordinated in the Secretary's Command Center (SCC) where U.S. Public Health Service commissioned officers monitor and report year round on evolving worldwide situations. Equipped with state of the art communications, data processing and graphics capabilities the SCC provides a centralized location to coordinate the federal response to public health emergencies and is the focal point of HHS incident management activities. The SCC is also responsible for planning and exercises, such as "Top Officials" (TOPOFF 2). With the Department of Homeland Security, the SCC coordinates the public health and medical response aspects for all federal government planning and response.

- **Office of Research and Development Coordination** works closely with the National Institutes of Health, Department of Defense and other medical research organizations to quickly procure vaccines needed in a public health emergency such as for smallpox and anthrax. RDC also works on Project Bioshield to develop and make available modern, effective drugs and vaccines to protect against attack by biological and chemical weapons or other pathogens.

- **Office of State and Local Preparedness** (SLP) works closely with the Centers for Disease Control and Prevention (CDC) and Health Resources and Services Administration (HRSA) to coordinate HHS activities related to bioterrorism and public health preparedness.

HOMELAND SECURITY ADVISORY SYSTEM

The Department of Homeland Security established a color–coded system to alert the public about threat conditions which indicate an increasing risk of terrorist attacks. For each threat condition, Federal departments and agencies are responsible for developing and implementing appropriate agency–specific protective measures. The colors, in ascending order of threat are green, blue, yellow, orange and red. Public health agencies should develop a checklist of activities that they would undertake with each changing level of threat. The checklist should include: 1) Informational gathering—check information from CDC, State DOH, OEM, others; 2) Surveillance system—check emergency/ambulatory admissions for patients who may have conditions/illness suggestive of any nuclear, biological or chemical (NBC) exposure; 3) Security—enhance security measures with each level of threat; 4) Staffing—assess staffing patterns and determine what to do for coverage; 5) Communications—check availability of systems, including state information systems; and 6) Supplies and equipment—assure availability and accessibility. Appendix R describes the 5 DHS color–coded threat levels.

FEDERAL RESPONSE PLAN

The interim Federal Response Plan (FRP) provides guidance for the coordination of federal assistance following natural disasters, provides the mechanism for coordinating delivery of Federal assistance and resources to augment efforts of state and local governments, supports implementation of the Stafford Act, as well as individual agency statutory authorities, and supplements other federal emergency operation plans developed to address specific hazards. The FRP employs a multiagency operational structure that uses the principles of the Incident Command System (ICS), based on a model adopted by the fire and rescue community

The emergency management community uses the term "function" to describe each of 12 responsibilities within the FRP. These responsibilities are grouped into 12 Emergency Support Functions (ESFs), each headed by an agency with the support of the others. See Table 9. All of the ESFs directly or indirectly affect efforts to protect the health and welfare of disaster victims. However, federal response to the specific health needs of disaster victims is primarily contained in ESF 8: Health and Medical Services. Roles maintained through this function include:

- Assessment of health and medical needs

- Health surveillance

- Medical care personnel

- Medical equipment and supplies

- Patient evacuation

- In-hospital care

- Food/drug/medical device safety

- Worker health/safety

- Radiological, chemical, and biological hazards

- Mental health

- Public health information

- Vector control

- Potable water/wastewater & solid waste disposal

- Victim identification/mortuary services

- Veterinary services

TABLE 9. THE 12 EMERGENCY SUPPORT FUNCTIONS

Emergency Support Function	Responsibility	Lead Agency
ESF 1: Transportation	Providing civilian and military transportation	Department of Transportation
ESF 2: Communications	Providing telecommunications support	National Communications System
ESF 3: Public Works and Engineering	Restoring essential public services and facilities	US Army Corps of Engineers, Department of Defense
ESF 4: Fire Fighting	Detecting and suppressing wilderness, rural, and urban fires	US Forest Service, Department of Agriculture
ESF 5: Information and Planning	Collecting, analyzing, and disseminating critical information to facilitate the overall federal response and recovery operations	Federal Emergency Management Agency
ESF 6: Mass Care	Managing and coordinating food, shelter, and first aid for victims; providing bulk distribution of relief supplies; operating a system to assist family reunification	American Red Cross
ESF 7: Resource Support	Providing equipment, materials, supplies, and personnel to federal entities during response operations	General Services Administration
ESF 8: Health and Medical Services	Providing assistance for public health and medical care needs	US Public Health Service, Department of Health and Human Services
ESF 9: Urban Search and Rescue	Locating, extricating and providing initial medical treatment to victims	Federal Emergency Management Agency
ESF 10: Hazardous Materials	Supporting federal response to actual or potential releases of oil and hazardous materials	Environmental Protection Agency
ESF 11: Service, Food	Identifying food needs; ensuring that food gets to areas affected by disaster	Food and Nutrition US Department of Agriculture
ESF 12: Energy	Restoring power systems and fuel supplies	US Department of Energy

CDC

Through CDC's recent reorganization, preparedness from the impact of infectious, environmental, and terrorist threats is now one of the agency's two overarching health protection goals. Multiple Centers, Institutes and Offices (CIOs) perform preparedness and response activities to optimize the assets and expertise available across the agency. CDC established the Office of Terrorism Preparedness and Emergency Response (OTPER) within the Office of the Director. OTPER coordinates and supports the preparedness and emergency response efforts of the agency while the CIOs are responsible for providing technical and scientific expertise. CDC interacts closely with partners in the public health and healthcare communities, coordinates across multiple professions and communities and the breadth of federal and state agencies involved in preparedness and response including law, forensics, public safety, and national security. As example, CDC has collaborated with the American Medical Association to strengthen planning for emergencies. The CDC program focuses on a number of critical aspects of public health infrastructure. It seeks to improve disease surveillance and epidemiology, assure readiness at the state and local level for distribution of pharmaceuticals and vaccines, expand laboratory capacity, strengthen the Health Alert Network and risk communication, enhance education and training programs, and support planning for infectious disease, such as smallpox. During an emergency, CDC provides information for clinical diagnosis and medical management, as guidance to first responders, to inform the public health response, to facilitate the utilization of clinical and reference laboratory protocols, and to educate the public. Federal assistance may be provided directly to the states by the Epidemic Intelligence Service officers from the Centers for Disease Control and Prevention or by experts from the Agency for Toxic Substances Disease Registry, among others. These federal public health personnel, stationed at regional offices of the US Department of Health and Human Services, can quickly get into the field to conduct surveillance and rapid needs assessments. Table 10 lists the programs within CDC which have a role in emergency preparedness and response.

TABLE 10. CDC PROGRAMS FOR PREPAREDNESS AND RESPONSE

ATSDR	Agency for Toxic Substance Disease Registry
EPO	Epidemiology Program Office
NCEH	National Center for Environmental Health
NCID	National Center for Infectious Diseases
NCIPC	National Center for Injury Prevention and Control
NIOSH	National Center for Occupational Safety and Health
NIP	National Immunization Program
OC	CDC Director's Office of Communication
PHPPO	Public Health Program Practice Office

NATIONAL INCIDENT MANAGEMENT SYSTEM (NIMS)

The goal of Homeland Security Presidential Directive 5 (HSPD—5, February 28, 2003) is to enhance the ability of the U.S. to oversee response to domestic incidents by establishing a single, comprehensive model for the national management of major incidents. The National Incident Management System (NIMS) was developed through a collaborative effort by the users of the plan and completed March 1, 2004. In a unified structure and standardized management plan, NIMS uses common terminology, concepts, principles, and processes so execution during a real incident will be consistent and seamless. Key elements and features of NIMS include:

- Incident Command System (ICS). NIMS establishes ICS as the standard incident management model with five functional areas—command, operations, planning, logistics, and finance/administration. NIMS operates through unified command to coordinate the efforts of many jurisdictions, and to provide for and assure joint decisions on objectives, strategies, plans, priorities, and public communications. An example of public health incident command is described later in this chapter.

- Preparedness. To enhance responder readiness to carry out their functions, NIMS defines activities of advance preparedness such as planning, training, exercises, qualification and certification, equipment acquisition and certification, and publication management. Preparedness also incorporates mitigation activities such as public education, enforcement of building standards and codes, and preventive measures to deter or lessen the loss of life or property.

- Communications and Information Management. NIMS prescribes interoperable communications systems for both incident and information management in order to standardize communications during an incident. Interoperable communication is described in Chapter 6.

- Joint Information System (JIS). To ensure that all levels of government are releasing the same information during an incident, the Joint Information System provides the public with timely and accurate incident information and unified public messages. This system employs Joint Information Centers and brings incident communicators together during an incident to develop, coordinate, and deliver a unified message.

- NIMS Integration Center (NIC). The NIMS NIC will be established by the Secretary of Homeland Security to evaluate how NIMS is working and to propose any changes to NIMS. The NIC will provide strategic direction and oversight of the NIMS, will develop and facilitate national standards for NIMS education and training, first responder communications and equipment, typing of resources, qualification and credentialing of incident management and responder personnel, and standardization of equipment maintenance and resources.

INCIDENT COMMAND

In the United States, the response to disasters is organized though multiple jurisdictions, agencies, and authorities. The term "comprehensive emergency management" is used to refer to these activities. The emergency management field organizes its activities by sectors, such as fire, police, and emergency medical services. Because disasters, regardless of magnitude, require a coordinated response from a number of different agencies, the emergency management community uses standard methodology referred to as the Incident Command System (ICS)—alternatively called Incident Management System (IMS)—for organizing the delivery of services in disaster response. While the ICS was originally developed in the 1970s as a way of responding to fires in Southern California, this methodology now applies to all disaster situations. The ICS organizes its responses with a single person in charge and divides the tasks, functions, and resources into manageable components. Table 11 identifies some of the agencies involved in the incident command system and the resources that they bring.

The ICS organization is constructed with five major components: command, planning, operations, logistics, and finance/administration. Whether there is a routine emergency, a major event, or a catastrophic disaster, the management system employs all five components. The management system expands or contracts depending on the size of the event. An incident commander is responsible for on-scene management, regardless of the size or complexity or the event. Incident management encompasses:

- Establishing command

- Ensuring responder safety

- Assessing incident priorities

- Determining operational objectives

- Developing and implementing an Incident Action Plan (IAP)

- Developing an appropriate organizational structure

- Maintaining a manageable span of control

- Managing incident resources

- Coordinating overall emergency activities

- Coordinating the activities of outside agencies

- Authorizing the release of information to the media

- Monitoring and recording costs

ICS is used to respond to all types of incidents, including hazardous material incidents, fires, transportation accidents, mass casualty incidents, search and rescue operations, and natural or technological disasters. The sector responsible for public health services (including non-EMS health care providers, such as hospitals, urgent care centers, and health departments) faces several challenges when integrating their efforts into this coordinated response. First, until recently, the ICS was a pre-existing management structure that may have planned and practiced for incidents without any input from the broader public health community. Public health agencies must continue to find a "fit" with this pre-existing response structure. Second, since health care systems draw patients from broader geographic areas than the political jurisdiction in which they are located, coordination is required between the prehospital system, which uses the ICS, and the public health delivery system, which may have a broader authority.

TABLE 11. AGENCIES INVOLVED IN THE INCIDENT COMMAND SYSTEM

Agency	Resources
American Red Cross	Shelter personnel Road signs, blockades Communications equipment
Electric company	Repair personnel Trucks Repair equipment Communications equipment
Emergency management	Emergency Operations Center (EOC) Equipment
Fire	Fire fighters Fire apparatus
Law enforcement	Police officers Flares, blockades Communications equipment
Public Health	Surveillance systems Public health personnel
Public works/ Highway department	Repair personnel Trucks Repair equipment Communications equipment

Source: Basic Incident Command System (ICS) Independent Study Course, Federal Emergency Management Agency, Emergency Management Institute, IS-195/Jan 1998.

ICS CONCEPTS AND PRINCIPLES

Many jurisdictions establish and maintain an emergency operations center as part of their community's emergency preparedness program. The ICS and emergency operations center function together but at different levels of responsibility. The ICS is responsible for on–scene activities, while the operations center is responsible for the community–wide response.

The organization of ICS response is modular and develops from the top–down structure at any incident. See Table 12. Several communications networks may be established, depending on the size of the incident, but all communication is integrated. ICS employs a unified command whereby all agencies with responsibility for the incident, including public health, establish a common set of objectives and strategies. All involved agencies help to determine overall objectives, plan for joint operational activities, and maximize the use of assigned resources. Under unified command, the incident functions under a single, coordinated plan.

Effective response depends on all personnel using common terminology, as defined by the ICS. The Incident Commander will give a specific name to the incident (i.e., Ground Zero for the bombing at this location). All response personnel use the same name for all personnel, equipment, and facilities. Radio transmissions should not use agency specific codes or terms but rather the language that everyone will understand.

PREPAREDNESS

Public health professionals work with many community agencies in a multidisciplinary effort. In a local operation, the American Red Cross has a credentialing system for those who respond in the field. The Red Cross provides sheltering, feeding, emergency first aid, family reunification, and distribution of emergency relief supplies to disaster victims. They also feed emergency workers, handle inquiries from concerned family members outside the disaster area, provide blood and blood products to disaster victims, and help those affected connect with other resources. Faith–based affiliated groups provide meals, clothing, or assistance during recovery and reconstruction efforts. Public works departments manage the water supply and clean up. Social services agencies work with the displaced, deliver psychosocial services, and assure that special needs populations (i.e., elderly, children, disabled)

TABLE 12. THE INCIDENT COMMAND ORGANIZATION

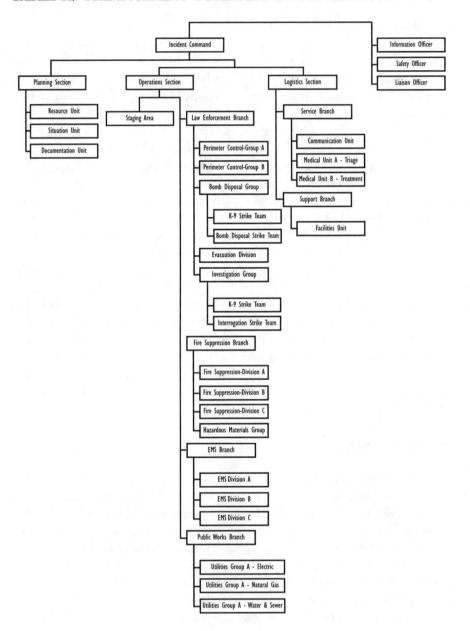

receive needed care. Importantly, if an agency's staff are not prepared, they will not be able to work at optimum performance. As part of your agency's preparedness, ask all staff to develop a personal preparedness plan for themselves and their families, so when they function as part of your organization's response they will not need to put these plans in place during an emergency.

STRATEGIC NATIONAL STOCKPILE

The Strategic National Stockpile (SNS) Program, formerly the National Pharmaceutical Stockpile Program (NPS), is now managed under the new Department of Homeland Security through the Surgeon General's Office of Emergency Preparedness with the logistics cared for by FEMA personnel. The purpose of the SNS Program is to maintain a stockpile of pharmaceutical agents, vaccines, medical supplies, and equipment to augment state and local resources during a large–scale disaster or bioterrorism event. Each stockpile is under the care of the state in which it resides. The State Emergency Management Office (SEMO) is responsible for both warehousing and the logistics of distribution, in partnership with DOH. Each state has a stockpile officer who is responsible for coordination with SEMO. The actual logistics for distribution within a state are the responsibility of SEMO. Relationships have also been worked out with private companies regarding the warehousing and distribution. Requests for predeployment of full or modified push packs can be considered in advance if a community is anticipating a major event, such as the requests made by Boston and New York City in advance of the Democratic and Republican National Conventions in 2004.

The push packs are located in 12 sites around the U.S. Each one weighs over 50 tons and fills seven 53–foot trucks. The contents occupy 130 cargo containers and include pharmaceuticals, antibiotics, antitoxins, nerve agent antidotes, and other emergency medications, intravenous supplies, airway equipment, etc. Additional vendor–managed inventory (VMI) is stored at pharmaceutical companies. which have the experience and manpower to deliver supplies quickly. Upon request, the SNS Program will deliver materials anywhere in the United States within 12 or fewer hours. DOH can contact CDC and request that only certain medications be delivered. In an emergency DOH should refer to CDC's response program for guidance.

NDMS

The National Disaster Medical System (NDMS) is currently a section within the Department of Homeland Security, Federal Emergency Management Agency, Response Division, Operations Branch. It serves as the lead Federal agency for managing and coordinating the federal medical response to major emergencies and federally declared disasters under the National Response Plan. NDMS works in partnership with the Departments of Health and Human Services (HHS), Defense (DoD), and Veterans Affairs (VA). The NDMS establishes the national capability of an integrated medical response to 1) help state and local authorities address the medical and health effects of major peacetime disasters and 2) provide support to the military and medical systems of the Department of Veterans Affairs in caring for casualties evacuated to the United States from overseas armed conflicts.

NDMS has three components:

- Medical response to a disaster area in the form of teams, supplies, and equipment,

- Patient movement from a disaster site to unaffected areas of the nation, and

- Definitive medical care at participating hospitals in unaffected areas.

There are multiple teams within the NDMS including the Disaster Medical Assistance Teams (DMATs), Disaster Mortuary Operational Response Teams (DMORTs), Veterinary Medical Assistance Teams (VMATs), National Pharmacy Response Teams (NPRT), and National Nursing Response Teams (NNRTs). Members of these teams are required to maintain appropriate certifications and licensure within their discipline and are activated as federal employees with their licensure and certification recognized by all states. Additionally, they are paid while serving as part–time federal employees and have the protection of the Federal Tort Claims Act in which the Federal Government becomes the defendant in the event of a malpractice claim.

Disaster Medical Assistance Teams (DMAT)

Disaster Medical Assistance Teams (DMAT) are self–sustaining squads of licensed, actively practicing professional and paraprofessional medical personnel who function as a rapid–response medical team to supplement local medical care during a disaster or other event. These teams include a cadre of logistical and administrative staff and all the equipment needed to set up ambulatory clinics and remain self–sustaining for 72 hours. In mass casualty incidents, their responsibilities include triaging patients, providing austere medical care, and preparing patients for evacuation. In other situations, they may provide primary health care or assist overloaded medical staffs. Additionally, they are prepared to provide patient care during evacuation to definitive care sites.

Each team has a sponsoring organization, such as a major medical center, public health or safety agency, nonprofit, public, or private organization that signs a Memorandum of Agreement (MOA) with the Department of Homeland Security. The DMAT sponsor organizes the team of local reservists and recruits members, arranges training, and coordinates the dispatch of the team. State DOHs issue their identification credentials so DMATs are credentialed in advance of activation. In addition to standard DMATs, there are highly specialized DMATs that deal with specific medical conditions such as crush injury, burn, and mental health emergencies. The Commission Core Readiness Force, described below, is another group of volunteer clinicians who can be activated to practice as federal providers to augment federal assets. They are pulled from their regular jobs for a two–week course of duty.

Management Support Teams

Management Support Teams provide field command and control for federal medical assets that are deployed post–impact. These units can provide and coordinate communications, transportation, a medical cache, and other logistical support to disaster medical assistance and other specialty teams.

Federal Coordinating Centers

Federal coordinating centers recruit hospitals and maintain local nonfederal hospital participation in the NDMS; assist in the recruitment, training, and support of DMATs; coordinate exercises and emergency plans with participating hospitals and other local authorities to develop patient reception, transportation, and communication plans; and coordinate the reception and distribution of patients being evacuated to the area.

Where the need for hospital beds exceeds local capacity, patients will be stabilized by DMATs or other specialty teams and then evacuated to hospitals that are part of the NDMS system, either by the Department of Defense aeromedical system or by contracts with reconfigured commercial carriers. At the airport of the NDMS reception area, patients will be met by a local medical team who will assess patients and transport them to participating hospitals according to procedures developed by local authorities and the local area's NDMS federal coordinating center. Patients will be transported to participating hospitals using locally organized ground and air transport.

Hospitals become part of the NDMS by signing a Memorandum of Agreement between the Chief Executive of the hospital and the Director of the Federal Coordinating Center in their locale. As of this printing, NDMS reimburses those hospitals up to 110 percent of the Medicare rate and is secondary to the primary carrier. Hospitals should assume that comprehensive and complete documentation will be required to receive reimbursement and must establish information systems necessary to comply.

In the event of a Federally declared natural or technological disaster, the Global Patient Movement Requirements Center (GPMRC) will be tasked to deploy the Immediate Response Assessment Team (IRAT) along with other elements of the federal response system to determine the need for the evacuation of patients. Once a mission tasking order is issued to DOD, the NDMS Federal Coordinating Centers (FCC) will be activated for patient movement. The GPMRC will issue instructions to the FCCs for the reporting of available beds. Simultaneously, patient information will be gathered at the disaster site and forwarded to GPMRC through the IRAT. GPMRC will determine to which FCCs the patients will be moved based on the victims' needs, beds available, and transportation availability. GPMRC will coordinate with the IRAT and other deployed DOD transportation elements at the disaster site to ensure smooth air operations.

Disaster Mortuary Operational Response Teams (DMORT)

Disaster Mortuary Operational Response Teams (DMORTs) were developed to fulfill the responsibilities outlined for NDMS in the National Response Plan under Emergency Support Function #8 (ESF #8). DMORTs are composed of private citizens who work under the guidance of local authorities whose function is to augment the capacity of the local coroner. They provide technical assistance and personnel in the recovery, identification, and processing of deceased victims during an emergency response. Teams are composed of funeral directors, medical examiners, coroners, pathologists, forensic anthropologists, medical records technicians and transcribers, finger print specialists, forensic odontologists, dental assistants, x–ray technicians, mental health specialists, computer professionals, administrative support staff, and security and investigative personnel. The team members are skilled in identifying victims and working with relatives of victims. They bring their own equipment and are self–contained.

These responsibilities include:

- temporary morgue facilities

- victim identification

- forensic dental pathology

- forensic anthropology methods

- processing

- preparation

- disposition of remains

FEMA maintains two Disaster Portable Morgue Units (DPMUs). The DPMU is a depository of equipment and supplies for deployment to a disaster site, containing a complete morgue with designated workstations for each processing element and prepackaged equipment and supplies. Both DPMUs are staged at FEMA Logistics Centers, one in Rockville, MD and the other in San Jose, CA.

Veterinary Medical Assistance Teams (VMAT)

The Federal Response Plan provides that Veterinary Medical Assistant Teams (VMATS) provide veterinary medical treatment and address animal and public health issues resulting from disasters when the local veterinary community is overwhelmed. VMATs are teams of veterinarians, technicians, and support personnel established and sponsored by the American Veterinary Medical Association. VMATs can be deployed only if a state or the federal government requests a VMAT following a presidential disaster declaration. Once the state determines that its local veterinary community is overwhelmed, the state submits a Request for Federal Assistance (RFA Form) through FEMA and, once approved, the request is forwarded to the United State Public Health Service for approval. If a state alone requests a VMAT, the state must fund the response. If a Federal Disaster is declared, the Federal Government covers a large part of the cost.

VMAT team members triage and stabilize animals at a disaster site, such as search and rescue dogs, and provide austere veterinary medical care. These teams are mobile units that can deploy within 24–48 hours when their assistance is requested by the state officials from the affected state. The members carry a 3–day supply of food, water, personal living necessities, and medical supplies and equipment, if needed. Each team is capable of establishing a veterinary field hospital and can provide any other veterinary services needed to support a complete disaster relief effort. VMAT responsibilities during disasters include:

- Humane Euthanasia

- Epidemiology

- Assessment of medical needs of animals

- Medical treatment and stabilization of animals

- Animal disease surveillance

- Zoonotic disease surveillance and public health assessment

- Technical assistance to assure food and water quality

- Hazard mitigation

- Biological and chemical terrorism surveillance

- Animal decontamination

National Pharmacy Response Team (NPRT)

The National Pharmacist Response Teams (NPRTs) are located in each of the ten Department of Homeland Security Regions, and will be used to assist in chemoprophylaxis or the vaccination of Americans, or other scenarios requiring hundreds of pharmacists, pharmacy technicians, and students of pharmacy. NPRTs are sponsored by the "Working Group" of the Joint Commission of Pharmacist Practitioners in a cooperative undertaking with the Department of Homeland Security. NPRT members are asked to complete web–based training programs, stay current in treatment recommendations for diseases compatible with weapons of mass destruction, participate in training, and be available to deploy if needed.

National Nurse Response Team (NNRT)

Nursing Response Teams (NNRTs) are available for situations specifically requiring nurses but not full DMATs. The National Nurse Response Team is a specialty DMAT that will be used in any scenario requiring hundreds of nurses to assist in chemoprophylaxis, a mass vaccination program, or a scenario that overwhelms the nation's supply of nurses. The National Nurse Response Teams are directed by the NDMS in conjunction with a Regional Team Leader in each of the ten standard federal regions. The NNRTs are composed of approximately 200 civilian nurses. National Nurse Response Team members are required to:

- Maintain appropriate certifications and licensure within their discipline;

- Stay current in treatment recommendations for diseases compatible with weapons of mass destruction;

- Complete web–based training courses in disaster response, humanitarian relief, bioterrorism, and other relevant training;

- Participate in regular training exercises; and

- Be available to deploy when needed.

COMMISSIONED CORE READINESS FORCE (CCRF)

The CCRF was created by the Office of the Surgeon General (OSG) in 1994 to improve the DHHS ability to respond to public health emergencies. Operational management for the CCRF was transferred to the Office of Emergency Preparedness (OEP) in October 1997, at which time a CCRF Workgroup was established to develop a mission statement and operations plan. Following the 9/11 terrorist attacks and the anthrax attacks, OEP became the Office of Emergency Response (OER) and was transferred to the Department of Homeland Security. CCRF was concurrently transferred back to OSG in March 2003.

Operations/Deployment

The Surgeon General considers requests for CCRF assistance in response to public health emergencies exceeding the capabilities of local or state resources, public health requirements under the Federal Response Plan, Department of State and/or Agency for International Development, or during other declared emergencies, or critical technical public health requirements outside normal agency activity. Once the mission requirements and the category, discipline, and/or specialty of CCRF members are determined, CCRF will match the requirement against the qualifications of officers on that month's rotational "ready roster." Table 13 summarizes the activation and deployment process.

TABLE 13. CCRF ACTIVATION AND DEPLOYMENT PROCESS

Activation Process	Request for Activation	Identification of Assets	Deployment
Request for Assistance	CCRF staff submits formal request for activation of CCRF to the Surgeon General (SG)	Needs of the mission are matched with the skills and qualifications of officers on the rotational ready roster	Agencies are informed when officers from the roster are needed
CCRF staff receive request	The SG is briefed regarding the situation	Officers are identified	Officers are contacted
Evaluation of need - appropriate utilization of CCRF	If the SG concurs; CCRF is activated		Supervisory release is obtained
			Travel orders and arrangements prepared; Officer is deployed

CCRF members are on active duty in the U.S. Public Health Service Commissioned Corps, have updated their officer summary information regarding deployability with CCRF, and have joined the CCRF Listserv (the primary mechanism that CCRF communicates with its members). To remain in an active status these potential responders must complete Basic Life Support (BLS) for Healthcare Providers (or Cardio Pulmonary Resuscitation (CPR) for the Professional Rescuer) and continue to login at least once every three (3) months.

Other Deployment

In incidents involving weapons of mass destruction, Health and Human Services officials provide both technical and operational support. The agency assists with identification of agents, sample collection and analysis, on–site safety and protection, and medical management. Operational activities may include mass immunizations, mass prophylaxis, mass fatality management, pharmaceutical stockpiling, patient tracking, contingency medical records, patient evaluation, and provision of definitive medical care. The Substance Abuse and Mental Health Services Administration (including the Center for Mental Health Services and the Emergency Services and Disaster Relief Branch) also plays a key role in responding to the social and psychosocial impacts of disaster as the lead mental health services agency of the Department of Health and Human Services. SAMHSA helps assess mental health needs and mental health training for disaster workers. SAMHSA also helps arrange training for mental health outreach workers, assesses the content of applications for federal crisis counseling grant funds, and addresses worker stress issues and needs.

STRUCTURE AND OPERATION OF THE STATE AND LOCAL RESPONSE

Every state has an emergency management agency, alternately called an office of emergency preparedness. Under the authority of the governor's office, the emergency management agency coordinates the deployment of state resources used in an emergency or disaster. This includes the resources of the many agencies of state government, such as health, public safety, and social services.

Mutual Aid

When the resources of the local jurisdiction are insufficient to respond to a given disaster, additional resources are requested from surrounding jurisdictions, a process commonly referred to as mutual aid. Additional resources may also be requested from the state, regional, or federal level. This is called "escalating a response." States can receive aid from neighbors through regional mutual aid compacts, or they can request federal resources, as described above. States in many regions of the country have formed regional agreements. Due to geographic closeness to disaster sites, these regional consortia enable neighboring states to respond rapidly. Intra–state and inter–state mutual aid can be executed prior to a Presidential disaster declaration or when a declaration is not necessary, providing both timely and cost–effective support. One lesson from the response to the World Trade Center bombings was that while collaboration with one's neighbors is necessary, it may not be sufficient to respond to the most far–reaching disasters. Communities need to increase mutual aid by broadening their geographic and traditional partnerships through cross–jurisdictional collaboration and regional consortia extending to agencies and organizations that were not previously linked. In some communities, there may be multiple mutual aid agreements within the public health and medical community. Working with the local OEM, public health could serve as a clearinghouse and help coordinate mutual aid pacts which impact on the health of the community.

EMERGENCY AND DISASTER RESPONSE COMPONENTS

While public safety agencies (i.e., emergency management, sheriff's office/police department, fire department) are usually the local lead for the overall disaster response, optimally local health departments coordinate the many health related agencies. The health department plans in advance how personnel will carry out their emergency response functions and assigns tasks to appropriate divisions within each department. Health departments work with the emergency management sectors, local hospitals, and other health care providers to develop a public health emergency response plan. A well–designed preparedness program will include a hazard and vulnerability analysis, a risk assessment, a forecast of the probable health effects, a list of the resources needed, an analysis of resource availability, and the identification of vulnerable individuals in the community who will require additional assistance (i.e., elderly, homebound, disabled).

EMERGENCY MEDICAL SERVICES

Throughout most of the United States, Emergency Medical Services (EMS) are provided by local agencies with oversight at the regional or state level. In most states, EMS is not provided directly by the state health department but is under its authority. The health department or other duly appointed governmental agency has training and regulation jurisdiction over all EMS personnel regardless of their organizational affiliation. Some EMS systems are based in local fire departments, with ambulance and fire services operated side by side. Medics based in fire departments are often cross–trained in both fire fighting and victim extrication. Some cities and counties operate independent EMS systems. In some parts of the United States, particularly the east coast and in many rural areas, EMS is provided by volunteer independent rescue squads or volunteer ambulance squads, which may be connected with a volunteer fire department. Finally, some EMS services are operated from local hospitals.

The EMS system includes both pre–hospital and in–hospital components. The pre-hospital components start with a public access system through which a resident notifies authorities that a medical emergency exists. Where available, the 911 emergency telephone system is used for this access. A dispatch communications system is then used to dispatch ambulance personnel or other emergency first responders to respond to the person(s) in need.

Emergency medical technicians (EMTs) and paramedics (EMT–Ps), who are trained to identify and treat medical emergencies and injuries, provide medical support while transporting patients to hospitals or other sources of definitive care. The medical care delivered by EMS is classified as basic or advanced life support. Most EMS providers are trained to provide care at the basic life support level (i.e., noninvasive first aid, stabilization for a broad variety of emergency conditions, and defibrillation for cardiac arrest victims). Paramedics provide more sophisticated diagnosis through advanced life support, with treatment following medical protocols both in the field and while being transferred to the hospital. Ground ambulances are the vehicle of choice for most transports, but helicopters, boats, or snow cats may be used under specific circumstances.

When planning for the delivery of disaster care through EMS, officials must consider response patterns that commonly occur. Initially, units can be dispatched in an atypical fashion. Often they will hear about the disaster on police scanners or via the news media rather than through normal dispatch. Assuming that too much help is better than too little, emergency units may respond on an unsolicited basis, sometimes from tens or even hundreds of miles away. In widespread disasters such as earthquakes, floods, tornadoes, and hurricanes, there may be no single site to which trained emergency units can be sent. Similarly, hospitals may obtain their initial information about what has happened in an unplanned way from the first arriving casualties or the news media.

Based on state–identified response requirements and FCO or designee approval, those responsible for the FRP ESFs coordinate with their counterpart state agencies or, if directed, with local agencies to provide the assistance required. Federal fire, rescue, and emergency medical responders arriving on scene are integrated into the local response.

PUBLIC HEALTH INCIDENT COMMAND

Departments of Health are organizing their internal emergency response structure around incident command principles. The cornerstone of a Public Health Incident Command System (PHICS) is to define the role, responsibility, chain of command and job title of the person(s) carrying out each function that will be necessary to manage an incident. Table 14 lists the types of roles and responsibilities that might be pre–defined in Departments of Health. The goals are to: 1) provide direct public health services as required by the emergency, 2) support the response of federal, state, local, and international health systems in public health emergencies, 3) support the deployment of health assets in response to or anticipation of a public health emergency, and 4) provide real–time situational information to and from federal, state, local, and international agencies, organizations, and field teams. The operationalization of the PHICS includes the establishment of an agency Emergency Operations Center and each of the supporting units. The specific components of the Emergency Operations Center may vary from agency to agency. On a local level, typical units may include operations (including alert, notification, and escalation), epidemiology and surveillance, medical/clinical response teams, specialized laboratories and subject matter experts, environmental consultation and response, management information services, and administration.

TABLE 14. ROLES, RESPONSIBILITIES, AND CHAIN OF COMMAND FOR DEPARTMENTS OF HEALTH

Function	Role	Responsibility	Chain of Command
Health Commissioner or Departmental Director	Incident Commander responsible for overall agency response	Declares emergency	Reports to Mayor/Governor
		Authorizes DOH EOC activation	Report to Commissioner
		Authorizes allocation of resources	
		Communicates with Mayor/Governor and OEM EOC Coordinator	
		Principal Departmental Spokesperson to media	
		Identifies need for consultants on technical issues	
		Authorizes requests to CDC for assistance	
		Authorizes requests for mutual aid from other DOH jurisdictions	
Senior Manager Descriptions below:	Counsel and assist Commissioner and/or DOH EOC members	Respond to request for assistance from Commissioner and DOH EOC	
Deputy Commissioner		Senior Advisor to Commissioner on policy decisions Reports to	Commissioner
	Senior Advisor to EOC Coordinator on operational decisions		
		Assumes Commissioner's role in Commissioner's absence	

TABLE 14. ROLES, RESPONSIBILITIES, AND CHAIN OF COMMAND FOR DEPARTMENTS OF HEALTH (CONTINUED)

Function	Role	Responsibility	Chain of Command
Public Affairs		Liaison with press offices of Mayor, OEM, and other agencies	Commissioner or Deputy Commissioner
		Coordinates press and public requests for information	
		Drafts press releases	
		Assists in creating and disseminating public information and educational messages	
		Monitors press coverage of emergency	
		Compiles/prepares material for website posting	
Governmental and Community Affairs		Liaison with non-DOH governmental and community agencies/parties	Commissioner or Deputy Commissioner
		Notifies these agencies/parties of new developments or responses to emergency	
		Assists in gaining cooperation of local officials for DOH activities	
Legal Affairs		Monitors Departmental activities and advises re. legal issues	Commissioner
		Reviews documents related to emergency activities (e.g. Declaration by Commissioner)	

TABLE 14. ROLES, RESPONSIBILITIES, AND CHAIN OF COMMAND FOR DEPARTMENTS OF HEALTH (CONTINUED)

Function	Role	Responsibility	Chain of Command
Incident-specific experts		Provide expertise and advice to guide policymaking around emergencies: Exposure, vector and disease specific knowledge Training Health and safety Mental health	Commissioner or deputy commissioner
DOH Emergency Operations Center (EOC) Coordinator:	Coordinates DOH response during emergency. Responsible for all operational aspects of the response. Oversees EOC during activation	Directs the DOH EOC	Reports to Commissioner Receives input from Senior Emergency Managers, Committee representatives and Senior Managers
		Oversees Emergency Committees	
		Oversees response to OEM activity requests	
		Maintains documentation of key elements of the response and compiles final report	
		Assesses need to request outside assistance (e.g. CDC)	
		Responds to requests and needs of senior managers	
		Synthesizes data from all sources	
		Raises policy issues to Commissioner	
Senior Emergency Manager	Coordinates administrative and logistical operations of the DOH EOC	Communicates with DOH EOC Coordinator	Reports to EOC Coordinator Receives input from Committee representatives and EOC liaison

TABLE 14. ROLES, RESPONSIBILITIES, AND CHAIN OF COMMAND FOR DEPARTMENTS OF HEALTH (CONTINUED)

Function	Role	Responsibility	Chain of Command
		Coordinates committee activities	
		Communicates with DOH liaison at OEM EOC (report and job requests, transmits information and dispositions)	
		Assures ongoing rotation of staff at DOH EOC and OEM EOC	
		Assists/Coordinates mobilization of staff to carry out Committee activities	
		Compiles and distributes manual of operations to EOC participants (staffing schedule, contact numbers, protocols, etc.)	
EOC Liaison	DOH representative at OEM EOC	Staffs DOH work station at OEM EOC	Reports to Senior Emergency Manager Receives input from OEM and Senior Emergency Managers
	Liaison between OEM EOC and DOH EOC	Follows developments in emergency situation and in city-wide response and provides briefing to DOH EOC	
		Receives OEM requests for DOH activities and transmits to Senior Emergency Manager (at DOH EOC)	
		Informs OEM of DOH activities/ responses/recommendations	
		Interacts with other agency representatives at OEM	

TABLE 14. ROLES, RESPONSIBILITIES, AND CHAIN OF COMMAND FOR DEPARTMENTS OF HEALTH (CONTINUED)

Function	Role	Responsibility	Chain of Command
Emergency Committee Representatives	Represent Emergency Committees at DOH EOC	Staff DOH EOC	Report to EOC Coordinator and Senior Emergency Manager Receive input from Committee Response Coordinators
		Provide policy guidance from OEM via Senior Emergency Manager	
		Accept action requests from OEM via Senior Emergency Manager	
		Accept request for data or activity orders from EOC Coordinator	
		Transmit information/requests for data or activity orders from EOC Coordinator	
		Report Committee activities and information to EOC Coordinator and Senior Emergency Manager	
Committee Response Coordinators	Coordinate the Emergency Committee activities that comprise the DOH response to emergencies	Oversee activities of Emergency Committees	Report to committee representatives at DOH EOC Receive input from Committee members
		Mobilize necessary workforce	
		Receive information and job requests from Committee representatives at DOH EOC	
		Regularly report data and developments to Committee Representatives at DOH EOC	

TABLE 14. ROLES, RESPONSIBILITIES, AND CHAIN OF COMMAND FOR DEPARTMENTS OF HEALTH (CONTINUED)

Function	Role	Responsibility	Chain of Command
		Report needs to Committee Representatives at DOH EOC	
Epidemiology Surveillance		Research specific topic	
		Provide background information	
		Conduct field epidemiological investigations	
		Identify and monitor existing surveillance and data systems	
		Establish new surveillance systems	
		Assemble field teams;	
		Develop question-naires/abstraction forms/information sheets;	
		Liaison with hospital or other field personnel;	
		Collect data; establish databases; analyze data; develop recommendations for policy	
Medical Clinical		Research specific topic	
		Provide background information	
		Prepare recommendations/advice on clinical aspects of emergency: • Public safety issues • Worker safety issues • Disinfection and/or decontamination issues • Clinical information and training of community physicians • Development of prevention and treatment messages	

TABLE 14. ROLES, RESPONSIBILITIES, AND CHAIN OF COMMAND FOR DEPARTMENTS OF HEALTH (CONTINUED)

Function	Role	Responsibility	Chain of Command
		Establish and staff prophylaxis or treatment distribution centers	
		Staff DOH clinics engaged in clinical activities related to emergency	
		Liaison with Office of Chief Medical Examiner	
		Provide clinical back-up to Shelter Committee activities	
Environmental		Research specific topic	
		Provide background information	
		Prepare advice/recommendations re public health threat, sample collection, evacuation. reoccupation	
		Collect samples	
		Collaborate with Fire, HAZMAT, DEP, etc.	
Shelter		Mobilize nurses to staff ARC clinics	
		Provide MD back-up to clinics	
Operations		Provide resources to facilitate Emergency Committee Activities: • Transportation • Communication • Facility issues • Security • Human Resources remobilizing work force • Printing	
		Coordinate telephone hotlines for public and provider information	

TABLE 14. ROLES, RESPONSIBILITIES, AND CHAIN OF COMMAND FOR DEPARTMENTS OF HEALTH (CONTINUED)

Function	Role	Responsibility	Chain of Command
MIS		Facilitate computing issues during emergency: Website posting Field to HQ data transmission Database management Mapping/GIS	
Laboratories		Provide recommendations re. specimen types and handling	
		Accept specimens for testing	
		Ensure rapid transport to reference labs if testing not available at DOH lab	
		Perform testing	
		Coordinate with epi/surveillance re data entry	
		Liaison with outside labs re testing and data reporting	
DOH Emergency Operations Center (EOC)	Integrated operations center for organizing and facilitating DOH response activities during emergencies	Provides accurate, timely information concerning the emergency to policymakers and public affairs officials	Staff: EOC Coordinator;Senior Emergency Managers; Emergency Committee Representatives Support staff, as needed Senior managers and consultants as needed
		Mobilizes DOH resources to respond to emergencies	
		Communicates with and receives requests from OEM regarding data and activities	
		Serves as a forum for integrating and synthesizing data as it comes in from the Emergency committees, OEM, EOC, senior managers, etc.	

When a PHICS is activated, personnel must know what their role is and what they will be asked to do. Often, much of a disaster response is maintaining the daily functions of an agency. Most personnel will be doing their same job, though possibly at a different time of day, in a different location, and/or with different people. The tasks and required skills will be more specific as the responsibilities become more administrative. Agency administration should ensure that each staff know what task group they are assigned to and the responsibilities of that group, and how and where they get information about their responsibilities during an emergency. While many skills are translatable (i.e., clerical personnel can answer phones and provide directions as instructed and drivers can transport people and materials), some require additional training (i.e., chart abstractors who need specific skills in identifying disease specific indicators).

HOSPITAL EMERGENCY INCIDENT COMMAND SYSTEM (HEICS)

Hospital Preparedness

Earlier, we discussed the pre–hospital component of an emergency medical system. The in–hospital system components include definitive care, usually delivered in the emergency department of a hospital, often by emergency physicians and certified emergency nurses who specialize in emergency medical care. Hospitals face challenges similar to public health in becoming integrated within the community's incident command system.

As of 2001, hospitals must meet expanded standards for comprehensive emergency management as part of their accreditation by the Joint Commission on Accreditation of Healthcare Organizations (JCAHO). JCAHO standards mandate that hospitals marry the range of activities regularly conducted by the emergency management community with the traditional tasks of providing health care. Hospital disaster plans must be applicable to all hazards.

Hospitals are required to establish a hospital emergency incident command system (HEICS). HEICS focuses on how a hospital organizes internally by establishing a chain of command with one person in charge, while using job action sheets with pre–defined responsibilities. HEICS requires that hospitals conduct a hazard analysis (as discussed in Chapter 5 and Appendix H); establish mutual aid; coordinate with the local office of emergency management; and maintain comprehensive documentation on how decisions were made, where patients went, how patients were tracked, and how reimbursement was obtained. The new standards help to protect hospitals from claims of liability after a disaster. Further, the National Fire Protection Association, NFPA 99 and 1600 establish minimum criteria for health care facilities and standardize the coordination of disaster management and business continuity within communities. Hospitals must follow federal procedures to be reimbursed for disaster-related response, and administrators should review the requirements of the Stafford Act, JCAHO, and NFPA 1600. The applicable 2004 JCAHO standards are provided in full in Appendix G.

In addition to the JCAHO requirements, hospitals have to meet other regulations. To fulfill requirements of the U.S. Occupational Safety and Health Administration (OSHA), hospitals have to develop and implement an emergency action plan (EAP) to report fires and other emergencies. An EAP must include 1) evacuation policy and procedures, including emergency escape procedures and routes (floor plans, maps, and areas of refuge), 2) name, title, and contacts for additional information, 3) procedures to shut down the clinical operation, 4) fire–fighting or other essential services, and 5) rescue and medical duties. OSHA also recommends the assignment of an area to assemble, procedures for accountability, establishing an alternative communications center and system for document management and data back–up. OSHA recommends that hospital staff be trained on the types of emergencies that could occur and the proper course of action; a review of who is in charge and the process of incident command; staff roles and responsibilities; the process of notification, warning and communication; emergency response procedures; evacuation, shelter and accountability; the location and use of emergency equipment; emergency shut–down procedures; first aid and cardio–pulmonary resuscitation; respiratory protection; and methods to prevent unauthorized access.

When patients go directly to hospitals, rather than being evaluated by first providers in the field, hospitals have to consider decontamination of patients (gross or secondary) in the event that the incident involves hazardous materials or WMD. Preparedness requires the purchase and stocking of personal protective equipment (PPE) so that providers can perform patient care. PPE must be appropriate to the risk and be accepted by the users and hospitals have to provide training on the use of PPE so that providers are familiar with it in advance. Hospitals have to establish a mechanism for medical surveillance and fit testing so that all personnel are ready to use the PPE quickly in an emergency.

The ability to respond to a large influx of patients is a challenging one for U.S. hospitals, most of which operate daily with a thin margin of staff and supplies. One surge capacity model developed for calculating the resources needed in a bioterrorist incident or epidemic outbreak is the Weil/Cornell Bioterrorism and Epidemic Outbreak Response Model (BERM). BERM is available on download from the American Hospital Association website.

VOLUNTEERS

The Medical Reserve Corps

The Medical Reserve Corps (MRC) is a federally sponsored program of the Office of the Surgeon General. The MRC provides an organized way for medical and public health volunteers from the community to supplement existing local emergency plans by offering their skills and expertise during local emergencies. The MRC is designed to provide the needed organizational structure and promote appropriate training of these community volunteers. The MRC can also be activated for nonemergency public health services, such as immunization or blood drives. MRC units have been organized through governmental offices, faith–based groups, public health offices, hospitals, and other nongovernmental organizations.

Unlike the 23 DMAT teams in the United States, which can be deployed anywhere in the U.S. during large–scale emergencies, MRC units are created by communities for local use, and can only be activated for local use. The coordination of the MRC with other response groups occurs at the community level. Most MRCs are integrated with local health care, public health, or emergency management organizations. In communities which have established Citizen Corps Councils (which organize programs of volunteerism at a community level) it is important that the planners and managers of a local MRC Unit have a working relationship with this Council.

Liability is an issue that each locality must investigate thoroughly. All states have some form of "good Samaritan legislation," although this legislation may be limited in its protections. Further protection is found through the Volunteer Protection Act ("VPA") (codified at 42 U.S.C. § 14501 et. Seq.). The VPA, which provides qualified immunity from liability for volunteers, is helpful because it provides baseline legal protection where there is a wide variety of state laws. A number of health profession organizations and the U.S. Congress are exploring appropriate liability protection for health providers during public health emergencies.

HOSPITAL CREDENTIALING OF VOLUNTEERS

The CCRF and DMAT are two systems where the process of credentialing medical volunteers is "federalized," whereby the federal government waives state licensing procedures and also assumes liability. However, until those resources are in place, hospitals and public health agencies might have to credential staff in a rapid manner. Experience shows that following a disaster, the community is deluged with calls from volunteers, many of whom are physicians and nurses looking to help. As part of their overall disaster plan, hospitals and public health agencies should have a procedure to manage and verify the credentials of professional volunteer staff. Coordinate planning with your state licensing boards, professional societies, and regional hospitals as they may have developed a uniform way to verify current licensure, specialty, and hospital status of professionals. Medical staff bylaws should also be amended to allow for emergency credentialing in disaster situations, and should designate who will be responsible for credentialing and overall clinical direction and supervision of volunteers. Keep in mind that practitioners should not be granted emergency privileges for procedures that they are not credentialed to perform at the hospitals where they are fully credentialed and that emergency privileges terminate on their own when the disaster is under control and the emergency management plan is no longer activated.

In July, 2002 the JCAHO approved Medical Staff Standard 5.14.4.1 (MS.5.14.4.1) which provides for the granting of emergency privileges when a hospital's emergency management plan has been activated and the organization is unable to handle patient needs.

To grant emergency (or disaster) privileges to licensed independent practitioners who are not members of that hospital's medical staff, the following is necessary:

- The emergency management plan has been activated.

- The hospital is unable to manage its patients' immediate needs.

- The individual(s) responsible and alternatives for granting emergency privileges are identified (chief executive officer or medical staff president or his or her designee(s)), as are the responsibilities of the individual(s) accountable for granting emergency privileges.

- Mechanisms to manage the activities of individuals who receive emergency privileges and to allow staff to readily identify these individuals are developed.

- A privileging process, identical to the process established under the medical staff bylaws for granting temporary privileges, is established with a verification procedure.

- The chief executive officer or president of the medical staff or his or her designee(s) *may* grant emergency privileges upon presentation of any of the following:

  1. A current picture hospital identification (ID) card.

  2. A current license to practice and a valid picture ID issued by a state, federal, or regulatory agency.

  3. Identification indicating that the individual is a member of a DMAT.

  4. Identification indicating that the individual has been granted authority to render patient care in emergency circumstances, such authority having been granted by a federal, state, or municipal entity.

  5. Presentation by current hospital or medical staff member(s) with personal knowledge regarding practitioner's identity.

The plan for credentialing physicians in an emergency should provide for clear identification of these practitioners. Identification should be easily legible, including a picture, their name and service and the words "Disaster Privileges" in a different color. In the event of a power outage, a Polaroid camera and a label maker can be used, as can wrist bands.

The management plan should provide precise recordkeeping of who was credentialed and their profession/specialty. Employees from the medical staff office should be identified to manage the emergency credentialing, and to orient the volunteers and familiarize them with hospital operations and the nature of the emergency services needed.

Verify and check the following, or similar agencies and databases which operate in your state:

- National Practitioner Data Bank

- State medical license

- Office of Professional Medical Conduct

- Office of Inspector General

- Photo identification

Finally, request the hospital where current privileges are held to confirm current active membership and privileges, the American Medical Association profile, and require a signed statement from the "non" staff physician attesting to the facts and allowing the hospital to obtain the necessary documents.

COSTS, FUNDING, REIMBURSEMENT FOR DISASTER PREPAREDNESS AND RESPONSE

For public and nonprofit entities, the Stafford Act provides for federal reimbursement of some expenses associated with the effects of the disaster and disaster response. This funding is known as public assistance. Title 44 of the Code of Federal Regulations (Emergency Management and Assistance) contains the rules, policies, and procedures regarding the administration of federal disaster assistance programs by FEMA. Part 206 of the 44 CFR, Subparts G, H, and I contain most of the regulations applicable to FEMA's disaster assistance program. FEMA coordinates that process and provides the forms that must be submitted for reimbursement. When local governments receive the support of any federal assets, the federal government absorbs the costs in the initial hours of the response. However, local governments are expected to reimburse the federal government for assets provided thereafter through a cost–sharing formula. In extraordinary cases, the President may choose to adjust the cost share or waive it for a specified time period. The Presidential declaration notes any cost–share waiver, and a DHS–State Agreement is signed further stipulating the division of costs among Federal, State, and local governments and other conditions for receiving assistance.

Public assistance will reimburse for damage to infrastructure, for equipment, and for overtime for personnel. It will not reimburse for providing patient care as part of the normal course of doing business. The usual cost sharing formula provides for the federal government to reimburse 50.0 percent of the costs, for states to provide 12.5 – to 25.0 percent of the costs, and for the local entity to absorb the remaining expenses. Public assistance will not reimburse for service eligible for funding under another federal program, such as the Veterans Administration. All public health agencies should obtain a copy of the rules, including the details of documentation necessary for reimbursement. Local agencies should identify what aid is available through their state. Some have a state–funded reimbursement mechanism, similar to the federal assistance program, which may reimburse local health departments for a percentage of costs for medical emergencies through public health law. However, total reimbursement from state and federal sources cannot exceed 100 percent. Importantly, ensure that there is no duplication, as disaster victims are responsible for repayment of Federal assistance duplicated by private insurance or other Federal programs. Finally, if an event is declared a terrorist attack, localities should realize that commercial insurance policies may deny reimbursement because care was required due to "an act of war."

Currently, there are a variety of funding opportunities to help communities prepare for disasters. DHS recently formed the Homeland Security Funding Task Force to facilitate the funding process. Grant listings have been integrated at [**www.dhs.gov/grants**] and the application process has been streamlined. Another example is the Catalogue of Federal Domestic Assistance [**http://12.46.245.173/cfda.html**] which links to a variety of federal funding programs. Table 15 summarizes other federal funding opportunities.

TABLE 15. FEDERAL FUNDING OPPORTUNITIES

SOURCE	WEBSITE
Government funding	[www.grants.gov]
Office of Justice Planning	[www.ojp.usdoj.gov/fundopps.htm]
Federal Domestic Assistance Programs	[http://12.46.245.173/servlet/page?_pageid=316&_dad=portal30&_schema=PORTAL30]
Institute of Justice	[www.ojp.usdoj.gov/nij/funding.htm]
CDC	[www.cdc.gov/od/pgo/funding/grantmain.htm]
The CDC ATSDR Federal Assistance Funding Book	[www.cdc.gov/od/pgo/funding/FAFBG.pdf]
FEMA Fire Service	[www.usfa.fema.gov/fireservice/grants/federal/g_assist.shtm]

Chapter 4

Disaster-Related Surveillance and Emergency Information Systems

Surveillance and exchange of gathered information guides emergency response as well as long-term planning. This chapter examines disaster epidemiology, emergency information systems throughout the disaster event, and public health surveillance in response to disaster.

PUBLIC HEALTH ROLE

- Develop, apply and evaluate tools, methods, guidance and protocols to improve investigation of public health emergencies at the federal, state and local levels:

  - Describe and monitor medical, public health, and psychosocial effects of disaster.

  - Identify changes in agents and host factors.

  - Detect changes in health practices.

  - Detect illness or injuries, including sudden changes in disease occurrence.

- Detect, investigate and analyze collected data to identify necessary interventions.

- Monitor long-term disease trends.

- Provide evidence for establishment of response protocols

- Provide information about probable adverse health effects for decision making.

- Investigate rumors.

- Determine needs and match resources in affected communities.

- Evaluate how personnel and partners are conducting surveillance activities for effective practice and the improvement of surveillance activities.

- Inform the evaluation of the effectiveness of response activities.

DISASTER EPIDEMIOLOGY

Epidemiology can be used to investigate the public health and medical consequences of disasters. The aim of disaster epidemiology is to ascertain strategies for the prevention of both acute and chronic health events due to the occurrence of natural or technological hazards. Primary prevention seeks to prevent disaster–related deaths, injuries, or illness before they occur (i.e., evacuate residents prior to landfall of a hurricane). With secondary prevention, the goal is to mitigate the health consequences of a disaster by providing education about injury control during the clean–up and recovery period. Tertiary prevention minimizes the effects of disease and disability among those already ill by setting up evaluation units where the chronically ill can obtain access to short–term pharmaceuticals when their usual source of care has been disrupted.

Disaster epidemiology includes rapid needs assessment, disease control strategies, assessment of the availability and use of health services, surveillance systems for both descriptive and analytic investigations of disease and injury, and research on risk factors contributing to disease, injury, or death.

EMERGENCY INFORMATION SYSTEMS

Emergency Information Systems (EIS) collect data about the effects of a disaster during the impact phase, the response phase, and the early stages of recovery. EIS consist of integrated sets of files, procedures, and equipment for the storage, manipulation, and retrieval of information. Data must be collected rapidly, sometimes under adverse circumstances, and the analysis must be processed and interpreted cohesively yet ensure a timely flow of information to inform an appropriate response.

The data collected through EIS are used to make decisions about the services that are needed post–impact. EIS personnel examine how the everyday relationship between people and their physical and social environments has been disrupted by disasters, such as lost productivity, as well as emerging problems or problems under control. Surveillance, defined by CDC, is the ongoing and systematic collection, analysis, interpretation and dissemination of data on health problems that affect or threaten the general population. Surveillance concentrates on the incidence, prevalence, and severity of illness or injury due to ecological changes, changes in endemic levels of disease, population displacement, loss of usual source of health care, overcrowding, breakdowns in sanitation, and disruption of public utilities. Surveillance also monitors increases in communicable diseases, including vector–borne, water–borne, and person–to–person transmission. EIS data provides accurate and reliable information needed to make decisions about emergency and short–term relief as well as long–term planning for recovery and reconstruction. Table 16 summarizes the types and uses of data collected through EIS.

PUBLIC HEALTH SURVEILLANCE

Before initiating an EIS, managers assess concern about public health issues and the necessity of monitoring disaster–related morbidity and mortality to determine actions important for a public health response. Considerations include whether existing systems could be used (preferable due to the level of resources required for active surveillance); sufficient personnel are available, including volunteers such as medical, nursing, or public health students; the data are needed to influence the public health response; and data collection can be funded, either by the participating institutions or externally, such as funding through the Stafford Act.

TABLE 16. EIS DATA COLLECTION

Type of Data	Uses of Data
Deaths	Assess the magnitude of disaster
	Evaluate effectiveness of disaster preparedness
	Evaluate adequacy of warning system
Casualties	Estimate needs for emergency care
	Evaluate pre-impact planning and preparedness
	Evaluate adequacy of warning systems
Morbidity	Estimate type and volume of immediate medical relief needed
	Evaluate appropriatenes of relief
	Identify populations at risk
	Assess needs for further planning
Health needs	Prioritize services delivered
	Prioritize groups most affected
	Evaluate adequacy of resources
Public health resources	Estimate the type and volume of needed supplies, equipment, and services
	Evaluate appropriateness of relief
	Assess needds for futher planning
Donated goods	Estimate the type and volume of needed supplies, equipment, and services
	Evaluate appropriateness of relief[1]
	Assess needs for further planning
Hazzards	Monitor health events, disease, injuries, hazards, exposures, or risk factors
	Support early warning sysem to forecast occurance of a disaster event by monitoring conditions that may signal the event[2]

[1] For example, the Pan American Health Organization's supply management program (SUMA) facilitates the sorting, classifying, and inventorying of the supplies sent to a disaster-stricken area.

[2] An example is the Famine Early Warning System, whih predicts the occurence of famine by monitoring meteorological data, availability of food, and mobidity related to nutrition.

When using existing systems, such as those established to track reportable diseases, EIS personnel must ensure they have the capacity to provide information that is both adequate and timely. Existing hospital–based data may provide an accurate representation of morbidity related to the disaster. Data can be obtained from mobile care sites and clinics. All health care facilities may be asked to participate in a syndromic surveillance system, or, given finite resources, selected sites may be chosen to provide a reasonable representation of the health effects being monitored. At a minimum, hospitals should report on surge capacity (beds, staffing, supply needs, and availability), event–related data (numbers of patients seen, waiting to be seen, unidentified or deceased) and patient locator information (name, sex, and date of service for patients seen as a result of the disaster).

Community clinicians play a key role in identifying and reporting cases, educating patients about infectious risks and preventing the spread of infections. Interventions to improve detection and to ensure that information is reported quickly and correctly include outreach to both hospital–based and community providers through educational forums for clinicians, laboratorians, and trainees, health department mailings, health alerts by broadcast fax and email, a provider portal, the Health Alert Network, and a public website. While the ability to collect surveillance information has expanded tremendously in the past few years, if existing systems do not meet the adequate and timely standard, temporary systems can be organized for the duration of the emergency period or at any point before, during, or after the disaster. To initiate an EIS, epidemiologists need portable computers with access to other data reporting systems, such as the National Electronic Disease Surveillance System (NEDSS), and existing electronic disease reporting. Data should be collected using standardized protocols, including veterinary inputs. The information should be presented in a simple format, in a manner easily understood by both public and emergency management officials.

ESTABLISHING A POST–IMPACT SURVEILLANCE SYSTEM

Outcomes anticipated from a specific disaster must be identified (i.e., crush injuries from earthquakes, diarrheal diseases from floods). The incidence of diseases endemic to an area prior to the disaster event would be expected to rise due to population displacement, increased population density, the interruption of existing public health programs, and breakdown in sanitation and hygiene. From a sample of the disaster–affected population, epidemiologists determine associations between exposure and outcome (disease variables) by identifying demographic, biological, chemical, physical, or behavioral factors associated with outcomes of death, illness, or injury. Examples of exposure–outcome relationships in disaster settings are included in Table 17.

To ensure uniformity, case definitions must be established in advance for the outcomes that will be measured. Without standard case definitions and data, unusual occurrences of diseases might not be detected, trends cannot be accurately monitored, and the effectiveness of intervention activities cannot be easily evaluated. Within the definitions, detection thresholds must be flexible enough to respond to changing risk levels and priorities of detection. Criteria for evaluating morbidity include clinical signs and symptoms, results from laboratory tests that confirm a diagnosis, and epidemiological limits on person, place, and time. Four case classifications are used: confirmed, probable,

TABLE 17. EXPOSURE-OUTCOME RELATIONSHIPS

Timing	Disaster	Exposure	Outcome
Pre-impact	Cyclone Tornado	High winds Presence of functioning warning system	Injury Evacuate or not, injury, death
Impact	Flash flood Volcanic eruption	Motor vehicle occupancy Ash particulate of respirable size	Death by drowning Silicosis
Post-impact	Earthquake Cyclone	Building type, flood level, age Outdoor cleanup activity	Injury, death Injury during cleanup activity, death by electrocution

suspect, or not a case because it failed to fulfill the criteria for confirmed, probable, or suspect cases. In addition, sources of comparison data, such as incidence of a disease in the same month or time period during prior years, should be identified for use in analysis. CDC/ATSDR, collaborating with the Council of State and Territorial Epidemiologists (CSTE) has published and distributed standard case definitions to states and jurisdiction enabling the collection of uniform national data sets.

Appropriate methods for analysis must be considered and applied. Examples include descriptive (age, gender, ethnic group), geographic location, rates of disease or death, secular trends, and an analytic time series defining the total number of cases and trends over time.

Possible reporting units for data collection include all the institutions that provide information for the surveillance system (i.e., hospital, clinic, health post, mobile health unit, Nongovernmental Organizations, health care facility, temporary shelters, first responder logs).

DATA COLLECTION USED FOR DECISION MAKING

Since response activities and planning for relief and recovery are based on the data collected, the information should reflect as accurate and reliable a picture of the public health needs as possible. Hazard mapping and vulnerability assessments can provide useful background information about the disaster event that can be used for planning disaster preparedness programs, response activities, and evacuation plans.

While this information is usually available from the local emergency management office, geological institutions, or departments related to natural resources and the environment, public health can work with these groups to create assessments which highlight public health concerns.

Information about the incident itself includes:

- Demographic characteristics of affected areas;

- Assessment of casualties, injuries, and selected illness;

- Numbers and characteristics of displaced populations;

- Coordination of volunteers, categorized by type needed (i.e., medical, mental health, search and rescue, etc.);

- Management of healthcare infrastructure;

- Storage and distribution of relief materials, including food, water, medical supplies;

- Public information and rumor control.

Information can often be obtained from existing data sets (census, state hospitalization data), hospitals and clinics (emergency departments, patient medical records, e–codes), health maintenance organizations and insurance companies, private providers, temporary shelters (daily shelter census, logs at medical facility in shelter), first responders (Disaster Medical Assistance Team patient logs), and mobile health clinics, such as those run by the military, Nongovernmental organizations, and volunteer medical groups (patient logs, records of prescription medications dispensed).

Due to time constraints and adverse environmental conditions, use of rigorous epidemiological methods may not be feasible in the post–impact phase. In disaster situations, assessment team members often use "quick and dirty" methods. "Quick" in that they are simple, flexible, and can be used under difficult circumstances. "Dirty" in that numerator and denominator data may be rough estimates that are subject to bias, although they serve to answer immediate questions whose answers are needed for the response.

DATA COLLECTED DURING A DISASTER

To enhance data collection during a disaster, it is important to identify the elements in advance. The public health and responder community will be interested in hospital capacity, such as bed, staffing and
supply needs and availability; event related visits; and information from
the patient locator system. A web–based collection system is best, but
alternative collection through fax and phone should be established.
Business rules need to be defined, such as who gets access to hospital
specific, aggregate information. If a pre–existing system is not in place
when a disaster hits, an interim system should be developed. Where
hospitals are using radio–frequency identification chips (RFID chips
are placed inside patient wristbands) in lieu of traditional medical
records, health departments can have instant access to hospital databases that can be uploaded through the use of personal data assistants
(PDAs) or notebooks with RFID readers.

UNIFORMITY IN DATA COLLECTION

Traditional public health surveillance is dependent on medical
providers reporting unusual diseases or unusual patterns of disease and
laboratorians reporting unusual clinical isolates or unusual patterns of
routine isolates. The establishment of national standards for electronic
data interchange can facilitate communication and integration with a
breadth of information systems if the data definitions, coding conventions, and other specifications are identical. To ensure that data can be
compared across jurisdictions by reducing incompatibilities across data,
a number of efforts are being made to establish uniform definitions for
data capture. As example, the National Center for Injury Prevention
and Control (NCIPC) at CDC is coordinating a national effort to develop uniform specifications for data entered in emergency department
(ED) patient records. The initial product, Data Elements for
Emergency Department Systems, Release 1.0 (DEEDS), is for use by
individuals and organizations responsible for maintaining record systems in 24–hour, hospital–based EDs throughout the United States.
Similar conventions have been recommended for NEDSS. The CDC
data standards for automated data exchange, manual data entry for
event detection, public health information dissemination and alerting,
and information technology (IT) security and critical infrastructure
protection, and IT security and critical infrastructure protection technical specifications can be found at CDC's IT Functions and
Specifications web page.

EXAMPLES OF EMERGENCY INFORMATION SYSTEMS

The availability of pre–existing systems has expanded greatly as the need has been better understood across the country. A prototype surveillance system that measures morbidity and mortality is the American Red Cross–Centers for Disease Control and Prevention (CDC) Health Impact Surveillance System for Disasters. Through a joint agreement, the American Red Cross collects morbidity and mortality information from all disasters to which it responds in the United States and CDC conducts the analysis.

While in the U.S., multiple systems support the collection and reporting of information to public health labs, the clinical community, and state and local health departments, many of these systems operate in isolation, without a mechanism to exchange consistent response, health, and disease tracking data between systems. On the federal level, CDC and ATSDR have developed an ensemble of data collection systems that build on common technical standards and infrastructure. These initiatives include surveillance capacity, email and message centers, and communication networks. On the state and local level, systems have been built which function both in unique ways and in ways that interface with the federal architecture.

SYNDROMIC SURVEILLANCE

One surveillance tool that can be useful in identifying emerging infections and outbreaks is called syndromic surveillance. Syndromic surveillance systems collect both data describing actions that precede diagnosis such as laboratory test requests, emergency department chief complaint, ambulance run sheets, prescription and over–the–counter drug use, school or work absenteeism, as well as clusters of medical signs and symptoms that may signal a sufficient probability of an outbreak to warrant further public health response.

Syndromic surveillance data are usually collected at the point of medical care, and from existing data streams that can monitor disease patterns. Syndromic surveillance has five characteristics which make it ideal for identifying outbreaks. The data is routinely collected and does not rely on physician reporting. The data is immediately computerized, is population–based and categorized by syndrome. This emergency information system is further distinguished from surveillance of mandated notifiable disease in that standard case definitions may not have been established and detection thresholds are flexible.

Hospital–based syndromic surveillance systems often report data from emergency departments. Daily or twice daily transfer of electronic data about patients with fever, respiratory and gastro–intestinal illness allows for analysis and identification of increases seven days per week. Data can be analyzed by hospital and by zip code and should be analyzed as close to real time as possible.

When an alarm is sounded, it is necessary to distinguish between natural variability in the data, seasonal events, true outbreaks of an expected illness, and an event involving a biological agent. In evaluating the data, public health should be more concerned if there is a sustained or increasing visit rate, if multiple hospitals are involved, if there are dual syndromes in the same area, if other surveillance systems are alarming, and if there is a strong geographical clustering. Of less concern would be a one day increase, only a single hospital involved, no other evidence of an outbreak, and a diffuse increase across the city or region. Two possible methods of analyzing the data require baseline data. These include looking back for two weeks to see data trends, using a regression analysis on retrospective data to adjust each day's data for seasonality and using the Serfling method to establish an expected threshold for each day's statistic by using dual cyclical regression to account for seasonal variation. A third method would look back at the data for the two preceding weeks.

PUBLIC HEALTH INFORMATION NETWORK (PHIN)

In order to enhance early detection of public health emergencies and to facilitate information gathering, storage and dissemination, a framework called the Public Health Information Network (PHIN) was established by CDC/ATSDR. PHIN is a portal which provides for interoperable use of information technology by building on the technical standards of and coordinating existing and new public health information systems. PHIN initiatives include the Epidemic Information Exchange (EPI–X), the Health Alert Network (HAN), the National Electronic Disease Surveillance System (NEDSS), and Pulsenet. The PHIN supports the exchange of key health data by defining common data and vocabulary standards and by requiring collaborative partnerships working to collect data in a unified public health system. The key elements are:

- Detection and monitoring of disease and threat surveillance;

- Management of reference information, distance learning, and information for decision support;

- Transmission of emergency alerts, routine professional electronic collaboration;

- Real–time analysis of data feeds to inform public health response at local, state and federal levels; and

- Support for the response regarding recommendations, prophylaxis, vaccination, and adverse events through real–time exchange of critical health information among public health partners.

Epidemic Information Exchange (EPI–X)—EPI–X is CDC/ATSDR'S secure encrypted web–based communications network which connects designated public health professionals from each state during an emergency. EPI–X is discussed in Chapter 6 on Communications.

Health Alert Network (HAN)—HAN is an email messaging and distribution structure that ensures that local health departments have timely and rapid access to emerging health information during an emergency. HAN, an essential component of the PHIN, provides three primary capacities: 1) high–speed internet connectivity, 2) broadcast capacity for emergency communication, and 3) distance–learning infrastructure for real–time training. For detailed information about the HAN, please refer to Chapter 6, Disaster Communications.

Pulsenet, operating within the National Center For Infectious Diseases (NCID) foodborne and diarrheal branch, is an early warning system for identifying outbreaks of foodborne disease and providing linkages among sporadic cases which trace the illness back to its source. A national network of public health laboratories performs DNA "fingerprinting" on suspicious bacteria that may be foodborne. To identify related strains, the network identifies and labels each "fingerprint" pattern and permits rapid comparison of these patterns through an electronic database located at CDC/ATSDR. This technique allows public health laboratory staff to distinguish among strains or isolates of bacterial pathogens. Viruses and parasites may be added in the future. A contaminated food product shipped all over the country, and perhaps the world, would yield seemingly unrelated cases in different geographic areas; but as laboratories send specimens to state health departments for fingerprinting, the central Pulsenet facility at CDC/ ATSDR can function like an interpol system for microbes, identifying outbreaks and their sources. Pulsenet participants include all 50 state public health laboratories, five local public health laboratories, seven FDA laboratories, the USDA food safety and inspection laboratory, seven Canadian laboratories and participation from a variety of nations across Europe, the Middle East, Latin America and the Pacific Rim.

Biowatch—Biodetectors enable 24x7 monitoring of air quality through the collection and testing of air samples. Early detection of biological pathogens can generate early warnings of possible attacks. Biodetectors are best used in high risk, high traffic sites, as the lab analysis is very labor intensive and further work is needed to minimize the risk of false positives. Implementation of biodetector systems includes three components: field work (sampling devices, collection and transport), confirmatory–level laboratory analyses conducted by the Laboratory Response Network (LRN) (processing and polymerase chain reaction, PCR, analysis), and consequence management.

National Electronic Disease Surveillance System (NEDSS)—A primary goal of NEDSS is to be consistent with industry software standards and to facilitate the ongoing, automatic capture and analysis of data already available electronically. By integrating surveillance systems, NEDSS facilitates the efficient electronic entry, updating, and electronic transfer of demographic and notifiable disease data from clinical information systems located in health care settings to public health departments at local, state, and federal levels. To ensure uniformity, NEDSS recommends a minimum set of data elements to be collected as part of routine surveillance coupled with standards that facilitate data collection, management, transmission, analyses, access and dissemination.

In addition to being an effective tool for analysis, NEDSS reduces the provider burden and ensures the timeliness and quality of the information provided. When the data is entered locally, at hospitals or labs, the user only enters the data once. When the provider enters the data into the system, it automatically rolls into the NEDSS back–end, and the state receives the data automatically while the hospital or laboratory maintains their local database. States can do state level reporting. Further, data is shipped to CDC on a regular basis, providing a robust data set which enables CDC to more accurately and more quickly identify outbreaks.

NEDSS is compliant with the Health Insurance Portability and Accountability Act of 1996 (HIPAA) Privacy Rule which governs the use and disclosure of protected health information. HIPAA permits health care providers to share individually identifiable information with legally authorized public health entities for public health activities, including surveillance, investigation and intervention.

THE NEDSS BASE SYSTEM

The NEDSS Base System is a platform for states to use for entering, updating, and electronically transmitting demographic and notifiable disease data. The NEDSS Base System provides a platform upon which modules can be built to meet state and program area data needs as well as provides a secure, accurate and efficient way for collecting and processing data.

NEDSS AND GEOGRAPHIC INFORMATION SYSTEMS (GIS)

When combined with GIS (Geo–Information Systems), NEDSS can be a powerful tool for analysis. When data is loaded into the system, it goes through geocoding, which provides the latitude and longitude of data so that the user can see it visually as well as in a tabular report. Being able to visualize the data permits modeling of activity based on the parameters that have been set. The user can visually see the data like a series of transparencies overlaid on top of one another, each with a new set of information. Risk Map and Web Focus are two commercially available software programs that build a tunnel between the GIS and NEDSS databases providing interface.

To understand the advantages that this technology offers, it is worthwhile to describe how GIS operates and the opportunities for public health response and preparedness in emergencies.

Geographic Information Systems (GIS)—GIS can be a useful tool to support epidemiology and surveillance in preparation for, and in response to disasters. GIS technology allows the user to digitally link data, spatial information and geography and display the information in an easy–to–understand visual medium. GIS data combines information about where things are with information about what these things are so that we can identify which groups with different features are located together. Using spatial database management, visualization and mapping, and spatial analyses this technology allows us to see spatial and temporal relationships among data. These systems allow researchers, public health professionals, and policy makers to better understand geographic relationships that affect health outcomes, public health risks, disease transmission, access to health care and other public health concerns as they relate to all emergencies. GIS data is accurate to 15 centimeters and can show if buildings are shifting after a disaster. GIS maps allow departments to switch from an overview of sections of a city to the location of individual objects. For example, if a hospital needs to bring nurses from home following an emergency, using MapPoint software, GIS can provide information about transporting them to your hospital, department, etc. by identifying safe passageways. Further, a process available through GIS, Geographic Allocation Process (GAP) analysis, helps determine where gaps in service exist. GIS can be supported in a network environment. Table 18 identifies many of the public health uses of GIS in emergencies.

TABLE 18.   USES OF GIS IN EMERGENCY PREPAREDNESS

Community Preparedness Efforts

- Assess community risks
- Estimate populations in hazard zones
- Map demographic factors, (i.e., housing type, age, those needing special assistance) to target preventive activities for specific populations
- Develop treatment profiles of physicians so know how to target education (i.e., large number of physicians prescribed three pills of cipro as prophalaxis for anthrax).
- Predict location of disease transmitting vectors (i.e., mosquitoes)
- Predict, by model, demand for a service for known emergencies, (i.e., regions with frequent flooding, earthquake or hurricane prone, etc.) both before and after event.
- Identify capacity of the health care system:
  - Identify the market/treatment area for health care systems
  - Locate specialty physicians and specialized services in a community
  - Conduct small–area analysis to see how services are used by defined population

Response Capabilities

- Develop training scenarios
- Evaluate response
- Better distribute services in future disasters or reallocate preventive services in advance of emergency by analyzing both residence and treatment zip codes to identify where victims sought services
- Risk and vulnerability assessments
  - Estimate extent and location of potential damage
  - Monitor and track spread of infectious disease and predict path of disease by searching for spatial relationships.
  - Identify centers delivering services to identify gaps.
  - Map patterns of destruction, targeting recovery and reconstruction efforts
  - Inform establishment of medical care sites, or special needs shelters by locating injuries by zip code in relation to existing health care services
  - Monitor asset management
  - Manage field data in real time
  - Improve data sharing capabilities
  - Produce accurate maps for urban search and rescue
  - Locate resources
  - Track plumes of chemicals to see how they spread through air, soil or water and who and what will be effected
  - Automatically notify residents

HOW TO USE DATA IN GIS[1]

The purpose of a geo–spatial system is to combine data with the questions that are asked administratively. GIS provides spatial information in response to the query—what next should I look at? While analyses from relational databases present tabular data in tables and charts, GIS provides a more descriptive view of the information and expands what can be done beyond traditional aggregate reports. Built upon an underlying data model, GIS presents data about locations and attributes by looking spatially at layers of information.

The development of GIS as a management tool for public health as part of the larger community is best achieved through collaboration among several agencies. Establishing a team of GIS personnel often requires multi–disciplinary volunteers. A GIS volunteer list should include professionals or students who are vetted and credentialed in advance, just like the other public health and mental health personnel included in a response. The GIS volunteers need to be oriented in advance to the current GIS system being used in the community, the configuration of the files, etc., so they can quickly help in the event of disaster.

Traditionally, communities collect and use their data in stovepipes, where each agency creates and analyzes its own databases, often without sharing information with sister agencies. The National Spatial Data Infrastructure (NDSI)[1] Executive Order encouraged geospatial data acquisition and access throughout all levels of government, the private and non–profit sectors, and the academic community. Importantly, the order targeted data needed for emergency response efforts. An enterprise GIS solution, where all agencies have access to a centralized dataset of geographic data layers, reduces redundancies of data collection, of maintenance, and of processing. GIS applications such as ESRI® and ArcPad™ can be used in the field on personal digital assistants (PDAs) allowing field–level assessments in real time and the transmission of information back to the EOC. Interactive mapping applications, such as GEOMAC (geomac.usgs.gov) can be used to assess disaster conditions from anywhere in the U.S.

Through GIS, we can map case distributions, variability in disease agents, and analyze temporal and geographic trends in disease outbreaks, all of which can inform our decisions on targeting interventions

---

[1] Executive Order 12906 published April 13, 1994, Federal Register, Vol. 59, No. 71, pp. 17671–17674. Amended by Executive Order 13286, published March 5, 2003, Federal Register, Vol. 68, No. 43, pp. 10609 – 10633.

and preventive activities. Through address match geocoding, we can convert each address to a point on a map. For example, by creating a zip code map of high risk, areas of outbreaks, and areas with large numbers of non–English speaking residents, public health can identify where the development of educational materials in multiple languages is needed. By mapping areas with a lack of accessible services, with high density residential areas, and the location of injuries from a previous disaster, public health may be better able to plan the location of temporary treatment centers or of DMAT teams. By mapping data from our syndromic surveillance systems with GIS, we can predict where infections/outbreaks will spread. We can use a GIS–based application coupled with automated telephone dialing system to communicate an emergency message, such as warning citizens about impending or ongoing disasters. As example, NEDSS data is collected and entered at the hospital, is auto shipped to the state, and the state customizes it because it can set the parameters. If analyses are run and maps created that identify a community at risk, the system can trigger an automatic telephone notification where a series of phones ring automatically and tell people to do x, y or z depending on their address and its relationship to the emergency.

Using GIS, Departments of Health, working with OEM, have overlaid census data with information about power outages and maps of roads to see which major populations were being impacted. GIS has been used to map sites of dead crows and located pockets of breeding mosquitoes, helping identify where West Nile virus may be spreading. In the response to the World Trade Center bombing, officials used GIS to create a frame of reference for understanding where the buildings had been. They used GIS to see if buildings next to the site were shifting dangerously. Further, thermal maps were overlaid on ortho imagery to identify where fire suppression was necessary and where to avoid sending workers.

WHERE TO GET DATA

The potential sources for locating data is limitless and any data describing a characteristic of a community can better inform decision makers. See Table 19. Some data is available without cost while some must be purchased. For example, Geography Network has many links that permit download while state information technology/ GIS departments have parcel maps which can be bought.

When looking to create a database for your community, the local zoning and planning commission and local tax commission are the best source of data, since they make money from tracking activities of daily living. Property tax databases contain the names and phone numbers of homeowners (information that can be imported into an emergency telephone notification application). Information is available from the Department of Transportation, federal railways, census bureau, schools, the White Pages phone book, etc. To get additional data, search in "google," by entering the search term "GIS data." Locating a GIS user network in your area is an important place to get started as these groups will know where data sets are "buried." Further, research and nonprofit institutions will have datasets that will be valuable to your community. Rich datasets are possible in locales where land is owned by state or federal government, county, other public agencies or by public–interest organizations. To expand your data and improve resource and facility management, you can create electronic blueprints by zooming in on individual hospitals and getting a detailed map of which facilities are operational by tying hospital floor plans to the community's disaster plans. Two publicly available software packages, CATS and HAZUS, use GIS (ArcView® and ArcGIS®) and include extensive national data sets of assets necessary in disaster response. The assets include hospitals, pharmacies, and nuclear plants which can be mapped by GIS.

TABLE 19. TYPES OF DATA SETS USEFUL FOR GIS AND PUBLIC HEALTH

Airports
Community Based Organizations
Community centers
Demographics of the community
Doctors' offices where patients have signed HIPAA authorization
Fire and other Emergency Services
Government Buildings
Hospitals
Hospital surveillance
Law Enforcement Facilities
Long Term Care Facilities
Major Highways and railways
Pharmacies
Phone lines
Power generating plants
Schools and school surveillance
Sentinel reporting systems
Toxics Release Inventory
Veterinary clinics
Vital statistics

When planning a GIS–focused disaster management program, it is important to obtain complete and current data about both assets and hazards. It is also useful to collate and regularly update the contact names, current mobile telephone numbers, and email addresses of GIS personnel and current emergency management contacts.

Because it is difficult to know what data will be needed post–disaster, the goal should be to create as rich a data set as possible, including as many types of information as available. Once you find the data sets that you want to include, you will need to ensure their immediate availability following a disaster by negotiating data–sharing agreements beforehand. Sharing data facilitates a community's coordinated response activities through public–private response planning. The directory structure of your GIS dataset should be logical because potentially many people will use it. For naming conventions use simple, descriptive labels that will be easily recognizable.

PLANNING WITH GIS DATA

Once you have assembled your datasets, you could begin by identifying vulnerable assets, including critically important facilities. Examples include:

- Structures used for communication

- Fire and rescue

- Hospital and nursing facilities

- Pharmacies

- Police

- Schools and day care

- Shelter

- Transportation

- Utilities

You will also want to examine facilities whose destruction could result in severe public health problems for your community, such as hazardous material storage sites, food and water sources, sanitation centers, etc.

DEVELOPING YOUR DATA SET

Ideally, you would identify the historical events that have been hazardous to your community and prioritize those events as to frequency, magnitude, and area of impact. While specific datasets can be established as shapefiles for each hazard, other formats are ArcInfo export format (e.00) and Spatial Data Transfer Standard (SFTS) format. High risk areas get assigned a risk level based on probability and historic occurrence. Because critical decisions will be made based on the data, it is important to keep a log of the pedigree of the data you are using, such as summaries of origin, update schedules and contact numbers for data librarians. Some data, such as that collected through active short–term surveillance systems may be incomplete. While corrections to the reportable disease record can be made by using address data as geographical identifiers, the pedigree of the data may influence some decision making about public health interventions. Further, when you get data from a variety of data sources, it is often necessary to convert the data to make it usable.

USE OF GIS IN MITIGATION

GIS products and spatial analysis allow the user to map with precision where hazards exist and to visualize that information so that decisions can be made about possible preventive activities. GIS can be used to combine areas of high risk with areas where many high value assets or vulnerable populations are found. Examples include wildfire–prone areas where brush could be cut back. Once a community determines the areas and populations at risk, public health can work with emergency management and community leaders to target areas where preventive/mitigation activities would be beneficial.

Since many communities use GIS to create assessment maps of economic damage, the foundation has been set to create assessment maps for public health. Public health planners can focus mitigation efforts if calculations show a probability that a hazard common to the community would cause an unacceptable level of morbidity and mortality.

MAPS

Following an emergency, there will be a high demand for spatial information by many sectors. Where a disaster has destroyed a neighborhood or a community's landmarks, a geographic visualization of the area can help with reorientation and stabilization of the site. Maps provide a common platform for everyone to visualize needed information about the location of events, resources, transportation, emergency networks, etc, facilitating communication and decision–making. Further, through the Internet and inter–active mapping programs, public health can inform a community about interventions and recovery progress, enabling real time online changes.

GIS can create individualized maps, customized to the features needed in the user's tasks. As a start, it is necessary to create what are known as basemaps, basic generic maps used as a reference to the location of pre–existing community data. The attributes of basemaps will vary according to the risks of the community. Because disasters aren't confined to jurisdictional boundaries, basemaps often cross jurisdictional lines. Multiple basemaps, with differing attributes, may be needed. As example, for responders who traveled from out of the area to get oriented to the surroundings, the basemaps need to be very specific about landmarks that may still be standing. Basic operational field maps would be valuable for directing off–site support teams in the field, in identifying where supplies are needed, etc. You may also need a basemap of the location of pet shelters and others for the pre–existing location of hospitals and of schools.

Part of the implementation of GIS is the establishment of a system to create and distribute maps. OEM is often the agency responsible for the distribution of the maps. Three types of maps should be distinguished: standard, templates, and special needs. Maps can be created by using desktop mapping products such as ArcGIS and a relational database, such as SQL Server. By permitting online request for maps, you will be able to establish and track the parameters of map requests. This online site can also make readily available the complex array of ICS forms that are so often requested by responders and agencies.

You should also develop a log which tracks the history of maps and the data used to build them, especially as they are changed. It is important to keep a record of earlier maps and the data used because, such as was the case at Ground Zero, you may not know what hazardous substances were at the site until some time later. Public health will want to trace exposures over time, especially as new information is added or if decontamination stations are moved, etc.

Table 20 describes modeling programs which are free of charge.

TABLE 20. FREE MODELING PROGRAMS

ADIOS2 (Automated Data Inquiry for Oil Spills)

ADIOS2 integrates clean–up models with chemical data by incorporating a database of more than a thousand crude oils and refined products while providing quick estimates of the expected characteristics and behavior of oil spilled into the marine environment. ADIOS2 is designed to help answer questions that typically arise during spill response and cleanup. Available at [http://response.restoration.noaa.gov/software/software.html].

ALOHA (Aerial Locations of Hazardous Atmospheres)

Gas–dispersion modeling software that uses information the user provides, along with physical property data from its extensive chemical library, to predict how a hazardous gas cloud might disperse in the atmosphere after an accidental chemical release. Available at [http://response.restoration.noaa.gov/cameo/aloha.html].

CAMEO[R] (Computer Aided Management of Emergency Operations)

Developed by EPA's Chemical Emergency Preparedness and Prevention Office (CEPPO) and the National Oceanic and Atmospheric Administration Office of Response and Restoration (NOAA), to assist front–line chemical emergency planners and responders in planning for and responding to chemical emergencies. In addition, CAMEO supports regulatory compliance by helping users meet the chemical inventory reporting requirements of the Emergency Planning and Community Right–to–Know Act (EPCRA, also known as SARA Title III). The CAMEO system integrates a chemical database and a method to manage the data, an air dispersion model, and a mapping capability. Available at [http://www.epa.gov/ceppo/ cameo/].

CATS (Consequences Assessment Tool Set)

Estimates damage and probable casualty figures for broad range of natural and man–made disasters. Operates using ARcView and ARcGIS; Can be used in the field and can download real–time weather information from national weather centers, while modeling and predict outcome of disasters. Available through ESRI (originally Environmental Systems Research Institute) at [http://gis.esri.com/library/userconf/proc00/professional/papers/PAP722/p722.htm].

CVAT (Community Vulnerability Assessment Tool)

CD tool that consists of software, data, and tutorials; Can be used to identify a community's hazards; Can be ordered as a free CD from [csc.noaa.gov/products/nchaz/startup.htm].

HAZUS (Hazards U.S.)

Loss–estimation modeling program which allows users to forecast most probable physical and economic damage to a community. Initially developed as an earthquake modeling program, has been expanded to model floods and hurricanes. HAZUS package is bundled with federal data sets, but can be customized with local data. FEMA offers a training course on HAZUS. Available at [http://www.fema.gov/hazus/].

MARPLOT

Simple mapping application where you can download the maps of any area of the country. Available at [http://www.epa.gov/ceppo/cameo/marmaps/].

SLOSH (Sea, Lake and Overland Surges from Hurricanes)

Model which computes storm surge heights from tropical cyclones, available from National Hurricane Center at [http://www.nws.noaa.gov/mdl/].

EVALUATING DISASTER SURVEILLANCE

Finally, EIS must be evaluated in the disaster setting to know when the system is no longer needed. This endpoint is often determined by both the resources and personnel available to run the system and the ability to merge the emergency system into routine surveillance. In addition to describing the attributes, usefulness, and cost of EIS, evaluations can lead to recommendations on the initiation and conclusion of future surveillance related to disasters. See Chapter 13 for more information on such evaluation methods.

If concerned about risks in your area, check the assessment systems in Table 21:

TABLE 21   HAZARD SPECIFIC GIS TOOLS

HAZARD	DIGITAL MAPPING PROJECTS/TOOLS
Earthquakes	California Department of Conservation/Division of Mines and Geology (DOC/DMG) [http://www.consrv.ca.gov/cgs/DMG_redirect.htm]
	U.S. Geological Survey (USGS) National Seismic Hazard Maps [http://eqhazmaps.usgs.gov/]
Epidemics (Health–related)	Global Monitoring and Disease Prediction Program at Ames Research Center, National Aeronautics and Space Administration [http://geo.arc.nasa.gov/sge/health/links/links.html]
Fires	U.S. Wildland Fire Assessment System (WFAS), Fire Danger Rating Maps [http://forestry.about.com/library/weekly/aa071403a.htm]
	California Department of Forestry (CDF) maps of fire hazard severity zones [http://gis.ca.gov/catalog/BrowseRecord.epl?id=5290]
Floods	FEMA Flood insurance Rate Maps)(FIRMs) [http://www.fema.gov/fhm/]
	Sea, Lake, and Overland Surges (SLOSH), Hurricane Storm Surge Inundation Area Maps [http://www.csc.noaa.gov/products/sccoasts/html/hazards.htm]
Hurricanes	Consequences Assessment Tool Set (CATS) [http://gis.esri.com/library/userconf/proc00/professional/papers/PAP722/p722.htm]

	USGS Center for Integration of Natural Disaster Information (CINDI) [http://www.geo–guide.de/cgi–bin/ssgfi/anzeige.pl?db=geo&nr=002861&ew=SSGFI]
Landslides	USGS San Francisco Bay Landslide Team (SFBLT) CA DOC/DMG Landslide Hazard Identification Maps [http://www.mapmart.com/]
Social Unrest/War	National Geospatial–Intelligence Agency (NGA) (formerly National Imagery and Mapping Agency NIMA) [http://earth–info.nga.mil/gns/html/]
Toxic Spills, Explosions, and Fires	HAZUS (FEMA) [http://www.fema.gov/hazus/]
Tsunamis	National Oceanic and Atmospheric Administration (NOAA) Center for Tsunami Inundation Mapping Efforts (TIME) within the Pacific Marine Environmental Laboratory of NOAA (NOAA R/PMEL) [http://www.pmel.noaa.gov/]

Chapter 5

Hazard Assessment, Vulnerability Analysis, Risk Assessment, and Rapid Health Assessment

Needs assessment must be tailored to the timing, size, and impact of a specific disaster. This chapter reviews background information on vulnerability that can be assembled before a disaster, including acute needs assessment, longer term data collection, and surveillance, and examines methods and limitations of data collection.

PUBLIC HEALTH ROLE

- Identify disaster–related hazards and associated vulnerability in a community.

- Determine risk of public health needs likely to be created should such disasters occur.

- Prioritize health needs based on information from community needs assessment.

- Provide decision makers with objective information to guide prevention, mitigation, and response to disease.

RATIONALE FOR ASSESSING RISK

Different types of disasters are associated with distinct patterns of morbidity and mortality. To develop location–specific strategies for reducing negative health outcomes, public health officials and disaster managers must be aware of the types of hazards most likely to affect specific communities. Health planners in Florida, for example, should prepare primarily for hurricanes, while those in California should prepare for earthquakes and wildfires.

Six categories of disaster prevention measures can be implemented following the analysis of hazards, vulnerability, and risk:

- Prevention or removal of hazard (i.e., closing down an aging industrial facility that cannot implement safety regulations).

- Moving those at risk away from the hazard (i.e., evacuating populations prior to the impact of a hurricane, resettling communities away from flood–prone areas).

- Providing public information and education (i.e., providing information concerning measures that the public can take to protect themselves during a tornado).

- Establishing early warning systems (i.e., using satellite data about an approaching hurricane for public service announcements).

- Reducing the impact of the disaster (i.e., enforcing strict building regulations in an earthquake prone zone).

- Increasing local capacity to respond (i.e., coordinating a plan utilizing the resources of the entire health community, including health departments, hospitals, and home care agencies).

HAZARD IDENTIFICATION AND ANALYSIS

Hazard identification and analysis is used to determine which events are most likely to affect a community and to make decisions about who or what to protect as the basis of establishing measures for prevention, mitigation, and response. This community risk assessment has four steps:

- identifying hazardous sites and transport routes;

- identifying potential incident scenarios and their exposure pathways;

- identifying vulnerable populations, facilities and environments; and

- estimating the health impact of potential incidents and the requirements for health–care facilities and public health intervention.

The National Fire Protection Association 1600 Standard requires that a community's hazard identification include natural events, technological events, and human events (see Appendix H). Decisions about which mitigation steps to take frequently require a cost–benefit analysis and a prioritization of the assets being protected.

DATA COLLECTION

Information from several sources, including data from previous hazards, is needed to predict future events. This information can assist in the development of appropriate mitigation measures. Historical data include the nature of previous hazards, the direct causes or contributing factors of previous events (i.e., failure to observe industrial regulations led to chemical release), the frequency and intensity of past disasters, the magnitude or power (as measured with established standards, such as the Richter Scale for earthquakes or the Saffir–Simpson scale for hurricanes), and the reported effects of an event at a given location (i.e., number of homes destroyed by tornado, number of people displaced by flood).

Baseline data should be collected to assess current potential hazards in a community:

- Laboratories located in academic or other research institutions

- Agricultural facilities

- Chemical manufacturing and storage

- Dams, levies, and other flood control mechanisms

- Facilities for storage of infectious waste

- Firework factories

- Plants for food production or storage

- Military installations

- Munitions factories or depots

- Pesticide manufacturers or storage

- Petrochemical refineries or storage facilities

- Pharmaceutical companies

- Radiological power plants or fuel processing facilities

- Water treatment and distribution centers

- Ventilation systems for high occupancy buildings

Hazard Mapping

With these data, the location of both previous and potential hazards can be mapped. Aerial photography, satellite imagery, remote sensing, and geographic information system technology can all provide information through hazard mapping. Remote sensing can show changes to land–use maps over time. Geographic information system models enable managers to develop plans with information consolidated from numerous disciplines, including engineering, natural sciences, and public health. Various types of maps are available for different hazards, including inundation maps for floods and seismic zoning maps for earthquakes. Maps detailing the location of industrial sites and hazardous material storage facilities can also be used. Hazard maps may be macro or micro in scale. Multihazard maps are available from the scientific community, industry, the media, and governmental jurisdictions.

Scientific Resources

Use data from meteorology, seismology, volcanology, and hydrology to provide important predictive information concerning hazards. These data can be obtained from a variety of government agencies and private institutions, including the National Oceanic and Atmospheric Administration, the National Weather Service, the US Geological Survey, and the Natural Hazards Center at the University of Colorado. In addition, decision–support systems can analyze data from several core databases, such as data on building inventories, infrastructure, demographics, and risk. These systems can stimulate "what if" scenarios to aid in planning.

Hazardous Materials Documentation

In the United States, the Superfund Amendment and Reauthorization Act requires that all hazardous materials manufactured, stored, or transported by local industry that could affect the surrounding community be identified and reported to health officials. In most communities, gasoline and liquid petroleum gas are the most common hazardous materials, but other potential hazards include chlorine, ammonia, and explosives. Material Safety Data Sheets (MSDS) provide a standardized method of communicating relevant information about each material, including its toxicity, flammability, and known acute and chronic health effects. MSDSs are provided by the manufacturers of individual chemicals and can be searched via databases available on the Internet, such as CHEMTREC.

Hazard Assessment

Following compilation, the data are analyzed to determine which hazards are most likely to affect a given community. Data analysis attempts to predict the nature, frequency, and intensity of future hazards; the area(s) most likely to be affected; and the onset time and duration of future events. The hazard assessment and data analysis should be conducted at a level appropriate to both the perceived risk and the availability of resources.

Probability Estimate

The probability estimate attempts to determine the probability of an event of a given magnitude occurring in a certain area over a specified time interval. This estimate cannot predict the exact timing or the effects on the surrounding community. Several statistical formulations can be used to determine the probabilities. More complicated formulations take into account not only the hazard and vulnerability estimates, but also vulnerability mitigation efforts and disaster management issues.

Vulnerability Analysis

A vulnerability analysis is used to obtain information about the susceptibility of individuals, property, and the environment to the adverse effects of a given hazard to develop appropriate prevention strategies. The analysis of this information helps determine who is most likely to be affected, what is most likely to be destroyed or damaged, and what capacities exist to cope with the effects of the disaster. A separate vulnerability analysis should be conducted for each identified hazard. There are five categories of vulnerability described in Table 22.

TABLE 22. CATEGORIES OF VULNERABILITY

Category	Measures
Proximity and exposure	Identify population(s) vulnerable because they live or work near a given hazard
Physical	Assess vulnerability of buildings, infrastructure, agriculture and other aspects of the physical environment dur to factors such as site, materials used, construction technique, and maintenance
	Evaluate transportation systems, communications systems, public utilities (water, sewage, power), and critical facilities (i.e., hospitals) for weaknesses
	Estimate potential short- and long-term impact of hazard on crops, food, livestock, trees, and fisheries
	Identify people who require special planning because of demographics or physical condition
Social	Identify population most vulnerable to the effects of disaster (e.g., older adults, children, single-parent families, the economically disadvantaged, the disabled)
	Estimate the level of poverty, jobs that are at risk, and the availability of local institutions that may provide social support
Economic	Determine the community's potential for economic loss and recovery following a disaster
Capacity	Evaluate the availability of human resources, material resources, and the presence of mutual aid agreements with neighboring communities
	Review the existence and enforcement of government regulations that mitigate the effects of certain disasters (i.e., building codes)

A community's capacity to withstand disaster conditions is determined by collecting data on the several variables. Information on the size, density, location, and socioeconomic status of the at–risk community can be obtained from local governmental officials. Public utility companies, health departments, hospital associations, and school authorities can provide data on the location and structural integrity of lifeline structures (i.e., electricity, gas, water, sewer) as well as buildings with high occupancy. Information on the location and structural integrity of private dwellings is also useful. A structural engineer may be required to review these data. Additional community capacity elements to be assessed include the presence of early warning systems, the number of available emergency responders and medical personnel, the level of technical expertise among emergency responders, the availability of supplies, and the status of emergency transportation and communication systems.

Risk Assessment

Risk assessment is used during the prevention and preparedness phases as a diagnostic and planning tool to determine how many excess cases of outcome A will occur in a population of size B, due to a hazard event C of severity D. Key lessons learned from the risk assessment can be used in the development of local and regional disaster plans. Major objectives of risk assessment include:

- Determining a community's risk of adverse health effects due to a specified disaster (i.e., traumatic deaths and injuries following an earthquake).

- Identifying the major hazards facing the community and their sources (i.e., earthquakes, floods, industrial accidents).

- Identifying those sections of the community most likely to be affected by a particular hazard (i.e., individuals living in or near flood plains).

- Determining existing measures and resources that reduce the impact of a given hazard (i.e., building codes and regulations for earthquake mitigation).

- Determining areas that require strengthening to prevent or mitigate the effects of the hazard (i.e., constructing levees to protect the community from flood waters).

Modelling in Risk Assessment

Risk assessment uses the results of the hazard identification and vulnerability analysis to determine the probability of a specified outcome from a given hazard that affects a community with known vulnerabilities and coping mechanisms (risk = hazard x vulnerability). The probability may be presented as a numerical range (i.e., 30% to 40% probability) or in relative terms (i.e., low, moderate, or high risk). A good example of how such models are used is the environmental and climate prediction services provided by the National Weather Service. The results of this modelling are broadcast by the media to warn communities of the risks of thunderstorms, blizzards, tornadoes, and hurricanes.

Models can also be used to guide appropriate responses to disasters. For example, plume dispersion modelling has shown that the most appropriate response to a major chemical release is evacuation of the surrounding community. Other strategies, such as "sheltering in place" (i.e., remaining indoors with windows and doors closed), provide less protection to the population. Similar dispersion models are also used to determine the risks of other technological hazards, including releases from nuclear installations.

Rapid Health Assessment

Rapid health assessments are used in the early stages of disaster response, often simultaneously with emergency response, to characterize the health impact of the disaster on the affected community. The primary task of the assessment team is to collect, analyze, and disseminate timely, accurate health data. These data assist public health professionals in determining the health needs, in prioritizing response activities, initiating an appropriate emergency response, and evaluating the effectiveness of the response. Even if the rapid health assessment is only a basic estimate, it facilitates the rational allocation of available resources according to the true needs of the emergency.

Community plans for disaster response should include teams to provide medical care that are functionally separate from the rapid health assessment team(s). Appropriate medical responses can be planned in advance since specific disasters are associated with predictable patterns of morbidity and mortality. While rapid health assessments provide for the early collection of health data, emergency response activities to save life and limb and to rescue trapped or isolated individuals may be initiated before the results of the rapid health assessment are available. Subsequent detailed needs assessments are often conducted during the recovery and rehabilitation phases of the disaster cycle to provide information over time.

Objectives and Methods

The primary objectives of rapid health assessments are to assess:

- The presence of ongoing hazards (i.e., a persistent toxic plume following a major chemical release);

- The nature and magnitude of the disaster (i.e., number of people affected or geographic area involved);

- Major medical and public health problems of the community (including risk of further morbidity and mortality; observed patterns of injury, illness, and deaths; need for food, water, shelter, and sanitation);

- Availability of resources within the local community and the impact of the disaster on those resources;

- Community need for external assistance; and

- Augmentation of existing public health surveillance to monitor the ongoing health impact of the disaster.

Before field visits and preliminary data collection can begin, a team must be assembled. Members of this multidisciplinary team could include an epidemiologist, a clinician, an environmental engineer, and a logistician. If the area affected by the disaster is large and crosses jurisdictions, several assessment teams may be required, as might specialty teams to concentrate on transportation, communications, and infrastructure. It is important to coordinate with local agencies to ensure that your assessment will yield new information and that the information is shared with those who need it. If more than one assessment team is required, all teams should use the same standardized assessment form. Data forms can be developed in advance using existing protocols, such as the World Health Organization's Rapid Assessment Protocols.

Baseline data gathered prior to the field visit are essential. This information includes background on the population size and demographics, including the presence of vulnerable groups such as older adults, children, and disabled persons. Census data can provide an accurate estimate of the number of people affected by the disaster, though estimating the actual number of individuals present in the disaster area at the time of impact (i.e., after evacuation following hurricane warnings) can be difficult.

Advanced information on the health care infrastructure is also critical. The location, bed capacity, and capabilities of local and regional health facilities must be documented. The status of local Emergency Medical Services must be assessed as well, including search and rescue capabilities, which can serve as surrogate measure of likely response in case of disaster. Similar information on the location and status of public utilities (i.e., provision of water, sanitation, electricity) will likewise assist assessment efforts.

Detailed maps are absolutely essential for rapid health assessments. These maps should show high–risk areas (including vulnerable populations), major transport routes, main utility lines, locations of health facilities and water sources, and concentrations of residential, office, shopping, and industrial areas. These maps are often available from government departments, academic institutions, and utility companies.

All these data will be wasted if not supplied to decision makers with authority to shape the disaster plan. The rapid health assessment should be an integral component of emergency response planning.

Timeline

For acute onset disasters, such as transportation crashes and hazardous material incidents, conduct initial on–scene assessments within minutes to a few hours if possible. Where multiple casualties are suspected, such as following an earthquake or tornado, the initial assessment should be completed within several hours of impact. The assessment should be completed as soon as possible as the majority of deaths will occur within the first 24 to 48 hours. This early information will be critical in identifying the need for emergency medical services and urban search–and–rescue teams.

For slower–onset disasters, information can be collected in the first two to four days (i.e., floods, epidemics, population displacements). An even longer time frame may be used for assessments of droughts and famines. In these settings, it is often more appropriate for health officials and disaster managers to collect baseline data and then follow trends with ongoing public health surveillance.

Categories of Data and Priorities for Collection

Data collection priorities differ for sudden impact disasters (i.e., earthquake, tornado) and gradual onset disasters (i.e., famine, complex humanitarian emergency). Teams often have limited time in which to collect data for a rapid health assessment. In these situations, only the most relevant health–related information should be collected. The specific elements of data will vary according to the type of disaster and the stage of the response. A concise checklist, developed prior to the field visit, will ensure that the most critical health issues are assessed. Disaster assessment protocols have been developed by the World Health Organization for various events, including sudden impact natural disasters, chemical emergencies, and sudden population displacements.

Sudden Impact Disaster

Days 1–2. Baseline information should be gathered as discussed previously. The sole objective is to collect information needed for immediate relief. The priority at this stage is the emergency medical response to save life and limb. Since obtaining accurate data can be difficult directly after impact, initial relief efforts are frequently guided by rough estimates. Key data include:

- Ongoing hazards, since persistent hazards that pose a risk to rescue personnel must be eliminated or controlled prior to initiating relief efforts.

- Injuries, since the number, categories, and severity of injuries help characterize the impact of the disaster and prioritize relief activities.

- Deaths, since the number and causes of death help characterize the impact of the disaster (however, information about deaths is not as important in guiding relief efforts as injury data).

- Environmental health and the status of community lifelines (i.e., water, sewer, power), since an early estimate of the population's needs for shelter, food, water, and sanitation may prevent secondary disaster–related health problems.

- Health facilities, since the impact of the disaster on the physical integrity and functioning of the health infrastructure may indicate the need for temporary medical shelters and external medical assistance.

Days 3–6. At this stage, information will be needed to guide secondary relief. Emergency medical interventions and search and rescue activities are less important, as more than 96% of critically injured patients will already have received medical care. If disaster–related deaths are still occurring, any persistent hazards causing or contributing to these deaths must be identified. Injuries due to clean–up activities and secondary impact from the disaster (i.e., fire, electrocution, hazardous material release) must be monitored carefully to optimise recovery efforts. Ensuring the availability of and access to primary health care becomes more important at this point than emergency care since disaster–affected populations still require routine medical services. Assessment of environmental health and utilities must clarify the longer term needs related to food, water, sanitation, shelter, and energy.

Day 6+. During the recovery stage, disaster plans should be fully implemented, and resources made available for all sectors. Surveillance should concentrate on illness and injuries based on information available from all health facilities and infectious disease, since outbreaks are uncommon after sudden impact disasters unless major population displacement or disruptions of the public health system occur. The surveillance system should track diarrheal disease and acute respiratory infections if people are displaced into overcrowded shelters or if there is a disruption of environmental health services. The status of health facilities, the number of health personnel, and the availability of medical and pharmaceutical supplies should be accurately tracked. Environmental health (i.e., water quantity and quality, sanitation, shelter, and solid waste disposal) and vector populations must be monitored carefully. Floods are often associated with swells in mosquito populations, increasing the risk of arboviral infections, such as St. Louis encephalitis. Surveillance for arboviruses can assist in determining the need for vector control following flooding.

Gradual Onset Disaster

Baseline assessments are conducted, and a surveillance system established. Background information must include population size and demographics, major causes of morbidity and mortality, sources of health care, and the status of pre–existing public health programs, such as immunizations. Key health indicators address both morbidity and mortality. For mortality, the crude mortality rate (deaths/10,000/day) is the most sensitive indicator of the population's health. Age– and sex–specific rates should be collected. The under–6 mortality rate is used to assess the health status of one of the most vulnerable groups in the population. For morbidity, information must be collected on rates of disease with public health importance, including diarrheal disease, respiratory infection, measles, malaria, and hepatitis. Rate of malnutrition in children under 6 years of age is the second most important indicator of the population's health. Data on environmental health should be collected and compared with the standards of 16 to 20 liters of water per person per day and one pit latrine per family. The disaster impact on the health system can be assessed by measuring loss of staff, since major population displacements and complex humanitarian emergencies are frequently associated with health professionals not being available to communities; the status of health infrastructure, as populations may no longer have ready access to health facilities, and hospitals and clinics are frequently damaged or destroyed; and the status of public health programs, as immunization programs, maternal and child health services, and vector control programs may all have been disrupted.

Sources and Methods of Data Collection

Data collection methods may be classified as primary (direct observation or surveys) or secondary (interviews with key informants or review of existing records.)

Direct observation can be completed on the ground or from the air. Direct on–the–ground observations can provide team members with first–hand view of the impact and extent of the disaster. Major health problems in the observed area may be identified but may not be generalizable to other sites. Where possible, team members should conduct informal interviews with victims and responders. Aerial observation allows team members to confirm the geographic extent of the disaster and to view the impact in inaccessible areas. In addition, by viewing the entire geographic region, the most severely affected areas may be identified, so that relief efforts can be more appropriately targeted.

Four types of surveys can be conducted. Focused surveys may be used to collect health data. These are relatively resource–intensive and should therefore be reserved for data that are necessary but are not available through other sources. Surveys based on convenience samples may be conducted relatively rapidly and provide a gross estimate of the health care needs of the affected community. However, convenience samples do not provide population–based information, so are likely to be sources of bias. Telephone surveys using randomly selected telephone numbers may be useful in determining the impact of the disaster and the health care needs of the community. Phone surveys require an intact communications system and may not provide a representative sample. People who are at home during the time of calling (i.e., elderly) may be over–represented, introducing a potential source of bias. Surveys based on cluster–sampling methods are being used more frequently in disaster settings. Methods such as simple random sampling, stratified random sampling, and systematic random sampling are time– and resource–intensive, making them impractical for the purposes of a rapid health assessment. Cluster–sampling methods for natural disasters are based on the World Health Organization's Expanded Programme on Immunization method for estimating immunization coverage.

Cluster–sampling techniques provide population–based information both to guide and to evaluate relief operations. Modified cluster–sampling methods can be used to estimate the size of the population in the disaster–affected area, the number of people with specific health care needs, the number of damaged or destroyed buildings, and the availability of water, sanitation, food, and power in the community. Cluster surveys can usually be conducted rapidly, and the results made available within 24 hours. Follow–up surveys can be repeated in the same area over the following 3 to 14 days. Cluster surveys are particularly useful when the area of damage is generally uniform, such as after a hurricane. They have been less useful following earthquakes, where the distribution of damage may vary widely between locations. Among displaced and famine–affected populations, such as large refugee settlements, cluster surveys have been used to estimate the prevalence of acute malnutrition, disease rates, the major causes of mortality, and access to health care services.

For secondary data collection, interviews with key health and emergency personnel can be useful in obtaining qualitative data concerning the disaster. Gross estimates of the impact and population needs may also be available. Attempts should be made to corroborate these data with those collected through primary methods. Interviews may be conducted with hospital emergency room staff, medical personnel at temporary health facilities, community providers, public health officials, incident commanders, paramedics, police and fire department officials,

American Red Cross representatives, and coroners. To augment and confirm these interviews, an effort should be made to review documented medical records from health facilities. Health data may be available from hospital emergency rooms and inpatient units, temporary health facilities, community providers, public health officials, and coroners' offices.

Limitations of Data Assessment

Health officials and disaster managers should be aware of the limitations of data that are collected during the rapid health assessment. Assessment team members must balance their preferences for sound epidemiological methodology against the time constraints and other limitations of the data collection process. Inaccuracies may result from logistical, technical, and organizational problems. Potential limitations include incomplete data, poor internal or external validity, and reliance on secondary sources of information. Unless population–based methodologies are used, data collected may not be representative of the community being assessed, and data collected from one population may not be generalizable to those in other regions. Further, information may not be available from certain disaster–affected areas due to poor access and communications. Finally, under–reporting of health events by rescue and medical personnel may occur because accurate documentation ranks as a low priority during the initial disaster response, particularly during sudden impact disasters.

Chapter **6**

Disaster Communications

Communications before, during, and after disaster strikes dictate the success of prevention and relief efforts. This chapter reviews the strategies and methods of communicating during a disaster and the equipment and systems that public health will rely on or use. Specific chapter units include communicating risk, who is the audience, internal and external communications, communicating warnings and response needs, working with the media, communications systems, and public health communication systems.

PUBLIC HEALTH ROLE

- Communicate about health and public health matters with:
  - those providing medical care (hospitals and their emergency departments, community providers, and other public health and social service agencies),
  - first responders (fire, police, EMS) and other responders (national guard),
  - local and regional laboratories,
  - general public,
  - officials, mayors, governor(s), and
  - partners (American Red Cross, public works).

- Set up communication network with health–related agencies, the media, and the public by providing public health reports to the media on regular basis.

- Share information and conduct data analysis across agencies and organizations

COMMUNICATING ABOUT THREATS RELATED TO EMERGENCIES

While historically, communicating threats or risks has been part of the responsibility of professionals working in environmental areas, the evolution of practice is requiring all public health leaders to effectively communicate information about threats. Not only does our community look to us for information and guidance, but our colleagues, especially those in governmental agencies, seek our assistance in evaluating and informing them and the public about health risks.

In communicating in emergencies, strategies used in environmental practice can be applied, including principles which influence people's perception of risk. The principles established by Fischhoff, et al in 1981, are likely to have direct application to our communication practice in the threat of or following disasters. Individuals are less willing to accept risks which they perceive as imposed on them or controlled by others, risks having little or no benefit, risks that are unevenly distributed among different groups, risks created by humans, risks that are catastrophic or exotic in occurrence, risks generated by an untrusted source, and risks perceived to mostly affect children. In contrast, individuals are more willing to accept risks perceived as voluntary and under an individual's control, those having clear benefits, where the risk is perceived to be fairly distributed or of natural causation, whose occurrence is a statistical probability, generated by a trusted source and those mostly affecting adults.

WHO IS THE "AUDIENCE?"

The more you know about those with whom you are communicating, what their concerns are, how they perceive the emergent threat and whom they trust, the greater the likelihood that you will successfully communicate with what the media refers to as "your audience." The characteristics of these "audiences" will vary and this variance may impact how and what you communicate, such as the nature of their concerns, attitudes, level of involvement, level of knowledge, and experience. Depending on what the individuals experienced and what they were exposed to in the emergency, or their responsibility in responding to the emergency, the audience may be concerned about health and safety, impacts on the environment, economic implications, fairness as to exposure to the health risks, the process of responding, and/or the legalities of the process. In the response phase of an emergency, health and safety are likely to be the chief concerns.

INTERNAL AND EXTERNAL DISASTER COMMUNICATIONS

During the impact and post-impact phases of a disaster, communications occur both internally and externally. Public health communicates internally to provide information to other responders and to solve problems. Internal communications also occur among an organization's staff and includes call up and notification of the emergency, assignments to work, sharing of information, status reporting, monitoring and tracking of public health concerns, etc. Internally, a first step in preparing to communicate during an emergency is to compile a staff 24 hour contact directory so that you will be able to reach staff at any time. External communication occurs among health departments, hospitals, community providers, ambulatory care facilities, emergency management and first responders, laboratories, pharmacies, veterinarians, community decision-makers, community based organizations, other responders, volunteers, the media, area residents and the general public. External communication to the media and area residents must provide factual information that the public finds credible.

Initially, a spokesperson has 15-30 seconds to get your agency's message across to those responding to an emergency who have an "adrenaline high." Thus it is important to develop strategies in advance for communicating immediately after the event and during the response phase. You will have more time to plan your communications during recovery. Strategies may be different in each phase.

Three actions are critical to communicating during an emergency: advance planning, collaboration, and updating the message as needed. When planning for your agency's overall response, include communication as a section in the plan. This component should describe how you will communicate messages about the emergency and who will deliver the message. Identify what information could be needed for different emergencies and establish ways to gather that information as quickly as possible. Prepare communication messages to have on file or locate how you will access them through federal agencies.

Collaborate with other agencies responsible for communicating in an emergency. Arrangements for release of public information should be worked out in advance, including how you will communicate with community leaders and build on their views that public health is the "go to" source for health information.

It is important to build vertical connections from the local, state and federal levels and across response sectors. To create efficiencies in these networks, the channels of communication need to be interoperable. As neither natural nor technological disasters respect borders and boundaries, regions should try in advance to agree on best strategies for handling information about hazards and threats. The development of inter and intra-agency procedures may involve cross-state cooperative agreements. Web sites can be used for communication to both the press and the public. It is important to involve the stakeholders (public, responders, government officials, etc.) and incorporate their views into your message. Finally, during an event, you should track the publics' perceptions and alter the message if needed.

COMMUNICATING WARNINGS AND RESPONSE NEEDS

With improved forecast technology, such as the tracking of storms through satellite imagery from government and commercial sources, we can issue advance warnings to allow timely evacuation before hurricanes, taking shelter against tornadoes, and taking active steps toward vector control. Messages communicated to the public should be positive and reassuring yet factual. These bulletins must translate technical information into lay language that people can act upon. The messages must be accurate, timely, and congruent for both the internal and external audiences so consistency exists between the actions of the response agencies and the actions requested of the public. Messages should be clear, concise, and credible and include information about the nature of the expected hazards, specific step by step actions regarding safety precautions, where to go and what to bring if evacuating, and requirements for shelter-in-place, where necessary. Where possible, warnings should give sufficient time to enable everyone to take whatever preventive actions are required.

The stricken community is often inundated with requests for information and these requests interfere with the more urgent need to educate the public about injury prevention and food and water safety, to request supplies, and to share surveillance information with community officials. Knowing that this is likely to happen, part of the initial organizational response should be the establishment of and notification about a victim locator service. More information about victim locator services is found in Chapter 9.

Communication can be a weak aspect of a disaster response without safeguards to ensure both the transmission and reception of information. Senders of all messages must request and receivers supply verification that the transmission was both received and understood. Validation that the intent of the message was understood is evident by safety responses by citizens, use of shelters, and other appropriate actions.

Often residents do not want to evacuate areas threatened by impending disasters. In disasters for which adequate warning times are available, such as hurricanes, communities can prevent morbidity and mortality by making appropriate decisions, disseminating information, coordinating warnings, and writing messages that are easily understood and motivate evacuation. In disasters such as earthquakes and tornadoes, for which advanced warning is rare, the risk of injury and death increases. However, even with tornadoes, morbidity and mortality can be lessened by telephone or media warning as soon as conducive weather conditions are identified or the funnel cloud itself is spotted. Nocturnal tornadoes result in the most injuries because people do not hear the warnings.

Unfortunately, some officials withhold warnings until the last possible moment, sometimes until it is too late to take effective protective action. This has been attributed to the disaster myth that panic is a likely response and that panic following a call for evacuation might cause more deaths and injuries than the disaster itself.

Requests for aid following a disaster require the same clarity as warnings in advance. Otherwise, donations may be inappropriate (i.e., wool blankets shipped to hurricane victims in the Caribbean, shipment of outdated medications) and cause additional problems on the receiving end. The management of donations is one of the most time-consuming and difficult response activities in both large domestic and international disasters. The Pan American Health Organization has developed a supply management system called SUMA that facilitates the sorting, classifying, and inventorying of the supplies sent to a disaster–stricken area. However, monetary donations are much less disruptive to the disaster response and can be used more flexibly. Preventing the broadcast of broad appeals for help and volunteers often requires advance education of the media, local government officials, and even disaster relief organizations.

CHANNELS FOR COMMUNICATION

Effective communication depends on utilizing specific methods appropriate for both the message and the audience. Different messages are required for different audiences and media. Table 23 describes channels of communicating that are mapped for delivery to different audiences.

TABLE 23. AUDIENCE AND COMMUNICATION CHANNELS

AUDIENCE	COMMUNICATION CHANNELS
Colleagues	News releases and fact sheets Site tours Meetings to address questions and concerns Hotlines Unit newspaper articles
Area residents	Community meetings Newspaper articles and ads Radio and TV talk shows Fliers Films, videos, and other materials at libraries Direct mailings
Elected officials, agency leaders	Frequent telephone calls Fact sheets Personal visits Invitations to community meetings News releases Advance notices
Media	News releases that focus on your message Clear, informative fact sheets Site visits News conferences

Adapted from: ATSDR Health Risk Communication Primer

WORKING WITH THE MEDIA

A strategically planned campaign, worked out well in advance, will most likely lead to success in working with the media. Designate both a spokesperson or public information officer, who can guide the implementation of a comprehensive communications plan, and through whom all information is provided to the media. A designated spokesperson coordinates so that the organization speaks with a "single voice," and provides a consistent point of contact for media representatives. It is also important to assign an alternate or two, as the designated spokesperson may not always be available. The spokesperson will establish relationships with media professionals in advance and prepare advance protocols for the release of information, including situation specific messages. Part of your campaign will include media training for public health leaders.

The establishment of a Joint Information Center (JIC) as part of the community's response plan is critical to the success of communicating a uniform message. The JIC should provide information consistent with information provided by the state Joint Information Center in a statewide emergency. The local Joint Information Center must have multiple-line phone banks for answering calls from the public and redundant communication systems in case the phone lines are down.

PREPARING FOR AN INTERVIEW

The following provides some specific tips about interviewing with the media.

When the press calls, remember that reporters are usually working on a deadline. Call back right away. Since reporters' schedules may change if events create "breaking" news, interviews may get canceled or rescheduled for a more urgent story. However, in emergencies, your story is most likely the "urgent one."

Ask for the reporter's name and the media organization for which he or she is reporting. Ask the subject, format, and duration of the interview, some sample questions, and who else will be interviewed. If you need time to prepare and the deadline allows, offer to call back at a specific time and follow through. If a reporter shows up in your office or calls at a time when you are unprepared, try to schedule the interview for later in the day so you can prepare. If you are not the correct person to interview because you lack the knowledge, etc., let the reporter know that.

Prepare by thinking through the interview in advance. The media will be seeking information on who, what, when, where, why, and how. For broadcast media, prepare a 10- to 12-word "soundbite," and for print media prepare a 1- to 3-line quote for each of two or three main points about your subject. To support your ideas, gather facts and figures presented in printed material that can be given to the reporter to help minimize errors. If time allows, offer to fax or mail the reporter the printed information in advance of the interview. Anecdotes can also be useful in connecting your information to the experience of the reporter's audience. Prepare responses to other questions that the reporter might ask.

Choose a location where you can screen out extraneous noises, such as background hums from air conditioning or heating units, phones, computers, or printers. Find out in advance whether the interview is edited or "live." In a live interview, be prepared to "think on your feet" and respond "off the cuff." In edited interviews, pause briefly before answering a question to give yourself time to think out your answer and to give the reporter a "clean" sound bite. In a TV interview, look at the reporter and not the camera. The only exception is for a satellite interview, when the reporter or anchor may not be on location. If you are uncertain where to look, ask.

For television interviews, dress in a subtle manner. Wear solid-colored clothing and simple accessories. Stripes, plaids or other designs can cause problems with the picture on color televisions. Before you go on the air, practice how you will deliver your key points. If possible, look in a mirror before going on camera. Television magnifies images so be sensitive to nonverbal messages that you may communicate. Do not allow your body language, your position in the room, or your dress to be inconsistent with your message. Be aware of your nonverbal communication, particularly gestures or nervous habits. Assume you are on camera at all times, from all angles. Make an effort to appear to be a good listener when other people are speaking.

Sit or stand stationary in front of the radio or TV microphones and avoid moving from the microphone. Moving to and from the microphone can cause the recorded volume to rise and fall.

DURING THE INTERVIEW

If you are being interviewed by phone, the reporter is required by law to tell you when you are being recorded. Ask whether the interview is being taped if you are uncertain. Be brief in your responses. Television and radio stories may use only a 10–30 second sound-bite. The shorter your comments, the less likely they are to be edited.

State your conclusions first and then provide supporting data. Stick to your key message(s) and main points. Provide information on what your agency is doing to respond to the emergency or issue. Emphasize achievements made and ongoing efforts to respond. Don't talk too much and try not to raise other issues. Assume that everything you say and do is part of the public record. Repeat your points if necessary if you have wandered onto a tangential issue. Since you want your response to be understood on its own if the reporter's question is edited out, speak in complete thoughts.

Do not overestimate a reporter's knowledge of your subject and don't assume the facts speak for themselves. Offer background information where necessary. Explain the subject and content by beginning at a basic level using positive or neutral terms. Avoid academic or technical jargon and explain all terms and acronyms. Do not rely on words alone, visuals can be helpful to emphasize key points if the interview is in person. If you do not understand a question, ask for clarification rather than talking around it. Do not assume that you have been understood. Ask whether you have made yourself clear. It's OK to say, "This is an important issue and I want to be sure I convey our position precisely. Would you mind reading back what you just heard me say?" If you do not have the answer, say so. Offer to get the information or tell the reporter where to find the information.

Rather than say, "No comment," tell the reporter if you can not discuss a subject. For example, "I can't answer that because I haven't seen the research you are referring to." Be honest and accurate. Do not try to conceal negative information. Let the reporter know what you are doing to solve a problem. If you make a mistake, correct yourself by stating that you would like an opportunity to clarify.

Finally, do not assume the interview is over or the equipment is off until you are sure that it is.

AFTER THE INTERVIEW

Specify for the reporter how you would like to be identified. You will probably not be able to check the reporter's story before it appears. However, you can ask questions at the end of an interview. For example, you might inquire, "What do you think is the main story?"

Most reporters will be able to tell you when the story will appear. If you feel that you misspoke or gave incorrect information, call the reporter as soon as possible and let him or her know. Similarly, you can call with additional information if you forgot to make an important point. If an error appears, let the reporter know right away. Sometimes a correction can be printed or aired. You also will want to prevent the incorrect information from being used as background for future stories.

Watch for and read the resulting report. Thank the reporter if the story is even fairly good. If you are unhappy with a story, share your concerns with the reporter only if the story is factually wrong. For radio and TV stories, obtain a tape of the final broadcast if possible and critique your own performance, looking for ways you might improve in the future.

COMMUNICATION SYSTEMS

Emergency Alert System[1]

The first national emergency alert system was established in 1951 when President Harry Truman established CONELRAD (Control of Electromagnetic Radiation). CONELRAD later became the "Emergency Broadcast System" (EBS), which facilitated the sending of emergency messages to the public by providing access to thousands of broadcast stations. In 1994, the Federal Communications Commission (FCC) replaced the EBS with the current Emergency Alert System (EAS).

The EAS, the country's primary warning system, provides national, state, and local authorities with the ability to give emergency information to the general public via broadcast stations, cable, and wireless cable systems. The FCC designed the EAS in cooperation with the National Weather Service (NWS) and the Federal Emergency Management Agency (FEMA) so that if one link in the dissemination of alert information is broken, the entire system does not fail and it automatically converts to any language used by the broadcast station or cable system.

The NWS provides emergency information to the public about dangerous weather conditions, which represent about 80 percent of all EAS alerts. FEMA directs state and local emergency planning officials in the implementation of the EAS, under the management of the Department of Homeland Security. The EAS digital signal is the same signal that the NWS uses on the National Oceanic and Atmospheric Administration's Weather Radio (NWR). This allows NWR signals to be decoded by the EAS equipment at broadcast stations and cable systems. Broadcasters and cable operators can then send NWS weather warning messages almost immediately to their audiences. Interoperability (able to function together) is guaranteed because the FCC provides information to other participants in the EAS (i.e., broadcasters, cable system operators, etc.) regarding the technical and operational requirements and ensures that state and local EAS plans conform to the FCC's rules and regulations.

In 1997, EAS replaced the weekly (on-air) "only a test" broadcast notifications used by the EBS with weekly internal tests and monthly on-air tests. All AM, FM, TV broadcast stations, and cable systems, with 10,000 or more subscribers, use these procedures.

---

[1] Emergency Alert System: A Program Guide for State and Local Juristictions, FEMA Civil Preparedness Guide (CPG) 1-41, Interim Use, June 1996 B This document was developed for FEMA, in cooperation with the Federal Communications Commission aand the National Oceanic and Atmospheric Administration (NOOA), as an all-hazards aproach to assist state and local juristictions in implementing the EAS.

Communications Systems

As multiple agencies have to be able to share information and communicate without interruption during the impact and post-impact phases of a disaster, responding agencies should prepare to use interoperable information and communication systems. Communication lines must also be available between fixed and mobile locations. It is essential to build redundancy in communication systems due to technological limitations and the vulnerability of public networks.

Plans for communicating in emergencies needs to ensure interoperability in three conditions: when technology is totally intact; when some technology is intact (i.e., wind or snowstorm) and in spartan conditions when no or little technology is intact (i.e., electrical blackout). The building of compatible systems, not silo operations, requires careful interagency planning and the implementation of integrated systems and policies based on industry standards and partnering with the private sector. Public health officials must have alternative systems for communication and be able to establish a link to the community's emergency alert system. Radio systems and radio frequencies must be established, with staff trained on the use of these systems. Protocols should be developed between the 911 system, hospitals, and health departments so public health agencies are among the parties regularly notified as part of the community's emergency response. Users of cellular, analog, and radio communications must recognize that these networks are not secure and that anyone with a receiver can hear the conversations.

In April, 2004, the Department of Homeland Security's Science and Technology Directorate announced the release of the first comprehensive Statement of Requirements (SoR) document outlining future technology requirements for a system of public safety wireless communications with interoperability. The (SoR) provides information on base level requirements across all local, tribal, state, and federal "first responder" communications systems. The SoR can be found at [www.safecomprogram.gov].

Following both natural disasters (i.e., earthquakes, hurricanes, and tornadoes) and technological disasters (i.e., power blackouts), telephone landline services and data systems are likely to be nonfunctional. Arrangements must be made to receive calls through an emergency telecommunications system if the landline circuits are overloaded or not operational. A redundant, robust phone and data network would include landlines with phone—only units that plug directly into a wall jack, cell phones, wireless fidelity (wifi) or wireless Internet units, beepers, and "walkie talkies" (i.e., Nextel®). Cellular telephones, one solution for telecommunications during disaster response, depend on the existence of relay stations or cells. Each cell has a limited capacity for simultaneous communications and covers only a defined radius. If too many people are using their cellular telephones, these systems will crash. Further, it may not be possible to guarantee security or privacy on cell phones. More importantly, cells are usually located in urban areas and along major traffic routes. Rural areas, where disasters are as likely to occur, may not be covered by such systems. Table 24 lists options for wireless communication solutions.

TABLE 24. WIRELESS COMMUNICATION SYSTEMS

Radio paging (one–way, two–way)
800 MHz radio
Cellular (commercial, Nextel®, GSM)
Wireless extensions to PBX (Spectralink)
Free-space transmission (microwave, infrared)
Satellite phones (Globalstar, Motient)
OnStar (GPS)
Amateur (ham) radio

An alternative wireless model is available without a fixed infrastructure. Called MANETs (mobile ad hoc network), this technology establishes high–speed communications among mobile devices which double as a router. MANETS can carry all types of digital information, including text, voice, graphics and video. To send information from one device to another, low–powered radio signals relay the data in short "hops" from one node to the next until the data reaches its destination. MANETS can extend the range beyond that of traditional radios and can penetrate tall buildings. If a mobile computing device can accept the required communications card, it can serve as a node on a MANET. Other models include using a fixed communications station, such as a computer in a vehicle, linked to the internet via satellite.

In all cases, the system must have off–site data back–up. Some organizations will establish access to duplicate or triplicate networks. These might include separate access cables coming into a building with cable connections which are physically distant from each other. Further protection is provided by upgrading from basic straight–line links to more modern systems. Consider upgrading systems so they can route calls by firing signals through the air in light beams or radio signals. Such systems shoot invisible light beams capable of transmitting volumes of data between building rooftops. Some high speed internet providers can support voice service, thus enabling multiple functions.

While some cable television systems offer redundancy with cables run separately from phone lines, the downside is that transmission can slow down as the number of users increases because cable lines are shared. Fixed facilities (hospitals and health departments) should have standby sources of power to support communication equipment in addition to lighting, ventilation, heating, and air–conditioning.

Health departments and hospitals should have several unlisted phone numbers so that they can more easily make outgoing phone calls. Telephone lines coming into communication centers should be buried, clearly marked, and protected from damage. Records of the location of telephone lines must be maintained and updated so they can be located quickly post-impact.

For office–based communication about disaster–related activities, public health officials need basic computer equipment. Computers must have a CD ROM drive, continuous Internet email capacity, and sufficient security (i.e., firewall, password protection, virus scanning) to protect data and prevent against intrusion. Back–up power supplies are essential, as is off–site data back up and storage. A system for broadcasting health alerts 24 hours a day, 7 days a week, must also be maintained.

Radio Operations

The emergency management sector will have radio networks available, and public health should be part of a community's emergency communication network. Communities use a variety of radio frequencies to communicate during emergencies. These include Lo Band, Very High Frequency (VHF), Ultra High Frequencies (UHF), and 800 megahertz (digital). Both professional and amateur radio operators facilitate communication during emergencies.

Ideally, your community will establish a multi–channel, multi–site trunked 800 megahertz radio system to provide two–way radio communications. Such a system has dual use: it can provide day–to–day communications in support of public safety and intra/inter agency communications in the event of an emergency. Manufacturers recommend that the batteries of these radios be changed every two years.

To avoid overload on radio frequencies, protocols should be established to limit the length of conversations and to establish several radio transmitter–receivers operating on multiple frequencies. Radio transmissions should not last more than 30 seconds. If, while using a portable radio, the listener is unable to hear a transmission, the user should relocate his/her position. If poor reception is not corrected by relocating, portable users may need to spell out their message using the phonetic alphabet. (Table 25 lists the phonetic alphabet.) All times should be denoted as military time (i.e., 1 pm is 13:00). An institution should designate a person(s) responsible for carrying the radio and ensure that they are trained in its use.

It is important to follow the rules of etiquette established in your community when using the radios. Often these rules include identifying yourself and using the full name of your institution so that other users can be aware of who is on the system at all times. If one party is transmitting and another party attempts to transmit, the second party's communication will not be received and the second party will hear a tone.

In order to test that the system is transmitting, most communities conduct a daily roll call of radio users. The response to the daily roll call is a simple "10 – 4" or "5 by 5."

TABLE 25. PHONETIC ALPHABET

A= Adam	L = Lincoln	W = William
B = Boy	M = Michael	X = X–Ray
C = Charlie	N = Nora	Y = Young
D = David	O = Oscar	Z = Zebra
E = Eddie	P = Paul	
F = Frank	Q = Queen	
G = George	R = Robert	
H = Henry	S = Sam	
I = Ida	T = Thomas	
J = John	U = Union	
K = King	V = Victor	

NEXTEL®

Nextel® provides an integrated voice and data network with fully digital cellular voice communications, two–way radio communications (Direct Connect®), and both one and two–way messaging without roaming charges within the United States. With intrinsic security, Nextel® can run applications on the phone and has a wireless Java application that can be downloaded over the air to the phone. Nextel® now has Direct Connect® nationwide and from market to market. Furthermore, it allows the utilization of cellular assisted GPS for E911. Nextel's NOL Mobil Locater function is a web–based mapping application that allows the location of dispatchers or account administrators in the field.

SATELLITE COMMUNICATIONS

Although satellite communications may seem ideal when disaster disrupts all ground–based lines, if one link of a fixed satellite service goes down, the whole system goes down. In addition, mobile satellite receivers are expensive and may not work if weather interrupts the wavelength transmission. A relatively new category of service, which uses dozens of low–orbiting satellites, is called the Global Mobile Personal Communications Systems (GMPCS). This system uses hand–held satellite phones and helps address the problems of geographical coverage. However, network overload is also a possibility with this system, depending on the number of satellites used, or the size of the antenna footprint. The Inmarsat system, commonly used in international disaster relief operations, is based on only four main footprints, each covering up to one third of the earth's surface. This allows for a large number of simultaneous links over any one satellite. As a result, a sudden increase of traffic from a disaster–affected area would have little impact on the overall volume of traffic. All GMPCS systems are based on costly infrastructures. Like all communication systems, the GMPCS should be used as a redundant system.

RADIO AMATEUR CIVIL EMERGENCY SERVICE

The Radio Amateur Civil Emergency Service (RACES) was founded in 1952 as a public service to provide a reserve communications group within government agencies in times of extraordinary need. The Federal Communications Commission (FCC) regulates RACES operations; the amateur radio regulations (Part 97, Subpart E, §§97.407) were created by the FCC to describe RACES operations in detail.

Each RACES group of licensed amateurs is administrated by a local, county, or state agency responsible for disaster services, such as emergency management, police, or fire. In some parts of the United States, RACES may be part of an agency's Auxiliary Communications Service. Some RACES groups refer to themselves by other names such as Disaster Communications Service or Emergency Communications Service. The Federal Emergency Management Agency provides planning guidance, technical assistance, and funding for establishing RACES organizations at the state or local government level. Citizen band radio operators run the General Mobile Radio service, which requires repeaters and whose systems require battery back–up because it will go down if not hardened.

RACES provides a pool of emergency communications personnel prepared for immediate deployment in time of need. At the local level, hams may participate in local emergency organizations, or organize local "traffic nets" using VHF and UHF. At the state level, hams are often involved with state emergency management operations. Local,

TABLE 26.   COMMUNICATION SYSTEMS

PHONE SERVICE	RADIOS	INTERNAL COMMUNICATION METHODS	EXTERNAL INFORMATION SYSTEMS	CONTACT DIRECTORIES
Private Branch Exchange (PBX)	Radio link to local emergency management agency (800 MHz radio)	Walkie – Talkies	Stand Alone Computer and Internet Access: • Dial up modems • Cable modems	Updated directories for internal and external contacts
Analog phone lines	HAM radio (RACES)	Overhead speaker and paging systems	Staff have access rights to HAN, etc.	Alert facility operator when EOC activated
Long distance service provider trunks		Runner System		Vendor contact numbers
Cell phones				
Satellite phones				

county, or state government agencies activate their RACES group. Traditional RACES operations involve the handling of emergency messages on amateur radio frequencies. These operations typically involve messages between critical locations such as hospitals, emergency services, shelters, and other locations where communication is needed. RACES communicators may become involved in public safety or other government communications, emergency operations center staffing, and emergency equipment repair. RACES groups develop and maintain their communications ability by training throughout the year with special exercises and public service events. A comprehensive RACES manual, Guidance for Radio Amateur Civil Emergency Service, is available on the FEMA Web site: [http://www.fema.gov/library/civilpg.htm].

Hams also operate on the same radio wavelength through the Amateur Radio Emergency Service (ARES) which is coordinated through the American Radio Relay League and its field volunteers. In addition, in areas that are prone to tornadoes and hurricanes many hams are involved in Skywarn, operating under the National Weather Service. Many national organizations have other formal agreements with ARES and other Amateur Radio groups including: the National Communications System, the American Red Cross, the Salvation Army, and the Association of Public Safety Communications Officials.

PUBLIC HEALTH EMERGENCY COMMUNICATIONS SYSTEMS (ECS)

Emergency Communications Systems (ECS) are web–based systems that ensure rapid, effective and consistent communication to the news media, the public, and key stakeholders during public health emergencies, including terrorism. Federal ECS facilitate an ongoing two–way dialogue with state and local health officers, public health information officers, clinician associations, policy makers and other key stakeholders in all 50 states. Federal ECS have been used to respond to public inquiries, media telebriefings, press releases and interviews, and daily web–based updates.

There are two major components to an ECS, the portal and the content. The portal serves as a single gateway to an organization's web–based information. Portals create efficiencies, facilitate the categorization of groups of information, and integrate applications while ensuring security. Structured levels of access can be granted for employees, public health professionals and community providers, the emergency management community, and the general public as well. By establishing a portal and by setting individualized security levels, organizations are able to control access to their web–based systems with a single user ID and password. When a user logs onto a portal, the system looks at his/her credentials and allows the person to access those areas for which they have authorization. The PHIN (discussed in Chapter 4) is an example of a portal, as are many of the Health Information Networks established at the state Department of Health level.

EPIDEMIC INFORMATION EXCHANGE (EPI–X)

During an emergency, EPI–X links DHHS and CDC/ATSDR command centers with state surveillance and response programs, provides 24 hours a day, seven days a week (24x7) emergency alerts, and creates a secure forum to share important disease information nationwide. This secured list serve has been used to communicate with colleagues and experts about urgent public health events, to track information and create reports about outbreaks, to create online conferences, to alert health officials of urgent events by pager, phone, and e–mail, to post and discuss newly emerging information from CDC, and to communicate simultaneously with command centers at HHS, CDC, and all state and large metropolitan bioterrorism response programs. Available to its users in the field, in the laboratory, at the office, or at home, EPI–X was used to notify state epidemiologists by pager and phone of the first anthrax case in New York City and to track and notify new West Nile Virus activity throughout the United States.

Health Alert Network

The most prevalent content–based ECS is the Health Alert Network, commonly referred to as the HAN. The HAN, established to strengthen the public health infrastructure nationwide, is a subscription service for providers. The HAN is used to ensure communications capacity at all local and state health departments and to update on the presence of disease as often as needed. Locally, the Health Alert Network has daily practicality, including online dialogues where clinicians can confer with each other about syndromes presenting in their offices, emergency departments, and hospitals.

The 57 HANS—one in each state, the four largest cities, and others—provide an alerting mechanism to pass on alerts that CDC issues. CDC established three categories of alerts: alert (do something now), advisory (important, may not require immediate action), and update, no action, information only). The alerting function uses various communication modalities to notify its user base: e–mail, fax, cell phone, and pager. There are both general (routine) and specific (emergency) alerts.

There is variability among the 57 HANS as to their functionality. The most extensive web–based systems allow access to general and personalized information to the broadest community of users and access to more secure information to a more selected group. The HAN utilizes both a "pull" and a "push" method of disseminating information. These HANS are multi–functional. HANS send out emails to all subscribers to notify them that a new alert has been posted through a multi–channel broadcast. HANS also post health alerts, archive all alerts, have a document library, have a bulletin board for posting and threaded discussions, have multiple levels of security, and can conduct online conferences supplemented with visuals, such as powerpoint presentations.

Each HAN administrator determines the list of authorized users and their security level. Most users require a one–factor authentication, where the user name and password are linked with a professional license number or other identifier and a third part certifying authority. Key health care, public health and emergency response personnel undergo a two–factor authentication. Here they are issued a user name and password with a token or digital certificate that sits on the computer. Their access is controlled by the system administrator. Communication between the user's browser and the HAN application is encrypted.

DISASTER RECOVERY INFORMATION TECHNOLOGY CONTINUITY

It is critical that public health agencies and facilities develop an information technology (IT) component as part of their disaster plan to mitigate the risks that could effect their ability to deliver public health services. The disaster plan should include arrangements for both clinical and business applications and detail a plan for recovery in the event of a disaster. The plan should be tested every six (6) months to ensure that it is functional and viable. The test of the plan should be documented and the documentation retained.

The IT disaster plan should address the basic needs of the organization in maintaining a continuity of operations and at a minimum include:

- Prevention—a plan for protecting agency assets and identifying and managing the risks to the core activities of the organization;

- Response—protocols for managing the crisis and its short–term or long–term interruptions on agency operations;

- Recovery—recovery of all operations;

- Restoration—repair and restoration of facilities and organizational operations;

- Procedures to notify employees and partners and to escalate response activities;

- Inventory of critical forms, magnetic media, hardware, software, equipment and supplies;

- Development and maintenance of a vendor contact list;

- List of critical organization applications;

- Backup procedures and data recovery procedures;

- Written vendor agreements;

- Description of emergency recovery team roles and responsibilities; and

- Agreements with off–site data processing facilities in the event of an emergency.

Chapter 7

Essentials of Disaster Planning

While disasters are often unexpected, disaster planning can anticipate common problems raised and tasks required following large–scale emergencies. This chapter considers the principles of disaster planning, the common tasks of disaster response, and the components of a disaster preparedness plan.

PUBLIC HEALTH ROLE

- Use traditional planning principles in preparing for the delivery of public health and health care services during the impact and post–impact phases.

- Participate as full partners with the emergency management community in disaster response and recovery.

- Participate in the development of and serve as an integral part of a community's disaster preparedness plans.

PRINCIPLES OF DISASTER PLANNING

Along with their differences, disasters have similarities in that certain problems and tasks occur repetitively and predictably. On the other hand, disasters differ not only quantitatively but also qualitatively from common daily emergencies. Thus, effective disaster response involves much more than an extension of routine emergency response (i.e., the mobilization of more personnel, facilities, equipment, supplies). Understanding the planning process and the lexicon of emergency management increases the effectiveness of public health professionals.

Effective disaster plans are based on empirical knowledge of how people normally behave in disasters. Plans are easier to change than human behavior, so disaster plans should be based on what people are likely to do rather than on the expectation that the public will behave "according to the plan." Plans must be flexible and easy to change due to the number of laws, organizations, populations, technology, hazards, resources, and personnel involved in disaster response.

Disaster planning should focus on a local response with federal and state support. In any major natural disaster, the main rescue effort will most likely be executed by local authorities during the first 48–hour period to ensure a timely response for the severely injured (i.e., those trapped in a collapsed building). Thus, disaster plans must be acceptable to the elected officials, to the departments that will implement them, and to those whom the plan is intended to benefit. Plans should be widely disseminated among all those involved and should be exercised regularly as discussed later in this chapter.

Similarly, disaster plans should provide for some authority at the lowest levels of the organization since workers in the trenches must make many decisions during the impact and immediate post–impact phases. Disasters often present decision–making demands that exceed the bureaucratic capacities and information–processing abilities of the day–to–day management structure. Disaster plans that require all decisions to be made from the top–down do not optimize the resources of the organization.

INCREASED NEED FOR PLANNING

With the rising occurrence and greater damage associated with natural disasters, public health agencies should give priority to planning for disasters. No region of the United States is free from all disaster risk. In fact, the effects of disasters escalate each year due to increases in population and development in vulnerable areas (i.e., seismic fault lines, coastal areas, flood plains, wilderness areas). At the same time, immigration, imported goods, rapid international transportation, emerging and resident pathogens, and terrorism (chemical, nuclear, biological) increase the potential for technological disasters and epidemic spread of disease. Finally, the economic health of the United States affects the number of displaced persons following disaster (i.e., homeless, working poor) and recovery from disaster.

CONSTRAINTS ON ABILITY TO RESPOND

Trends in health care reimbursement and delivery interfere with efforts by health care facilities to prepare for disasters. First, decreasing reimbursement reduces the likelihood that facilities will allocate funds for disaster preparedness. Even if the budgetary allocations are adequate, fewer resources are available for the delivery of unusual services. Fewer supplies may be available for disaster response because hospitals and other health facilities have eliminated the local warehousing of supplies and instead reorder as needed. The trend to outsource services (i.e., laundry, kitchen, security) reduces the availability of important resources that would be needed post–impact. With shorter inpatient lengths of stay and greater use of ambulatory care, fewer hospital beds will be available or sufficiently staffed in a disaster. The availability of beds post–impact will be further complicated by the trend to hospitalize sicker patients who require more intensive care, so few patients will be ready for discharge to create room for victims seriously injured in the disaster. Finally, while the focus on delivering care in nonhospital settings has increased, a parallel effort to ensure disaster readiness in nonhospital health care settings has not been made.

PLANNING FOR VARIOUS DISASTERS

Two strategies for disaster planning include the agent–specific and the all–hazards approaches. In agent–specific planning, communities only plan for threats most likely to occur in their region (i.e., earthquakes, hurricanes, floods, tornadoes). For example, planning for earthquakes, floods, and wild fires will be more useful in California than planning for hurricanes and tornadoes. Further, officials and taxpayers are more likely to be motivated by what are perceived locally as the most viable threats.

With the all–hazards approach to disaster planning, the level of preparedness is maximized for the effort and expenditures involved. Since many disasters pose similar problems and similar tasks, an all–hazards approach involves planning for the common problems and tasks that arise in the majority of disasters.

COMMON TASKS OF DISASTER RESPONSE

Twelve tasks or problems are likely to occur in most disasters, as summarized below.

- *Interorganizational coordination* is critical and has been discussed in Chapters 2 and 3.

- *Sharing information* among organizations is complicated by the amount of equipment needed and the number of people involved. In the impact and post–impact phases, two–way radios are often the only reliable form of communications across distances. Even if ground and cellular telephone systems are not damaged, they are generally congested or overloaded. Communication via radio frequencies is difficult as no common frequency has been designated for mutual aid. The Federal Communications Commission has assigned public safety frequencies to several different bands, making it difficult for one agency to communicate with another on a common frequency. While newer radios can be programmed to operate on a different frequency or frequencies, they cannot be reprogrammed to a different band. A few radios can now operate on more than one band, but this is the exception.

- *Resource management*—the distribution of supplemental personnel, equipment, and supplies among multiple organizations—requires a process to identify which resources have arrived or are in transit and to determine where those resources are most needed. Once a security perimeter has been established at the disaster site, a check–in or staging area is usually established outside this boundary. Each staging area has a manager who has radio contact with the disaster command post or emergency operations center. Law enforcement or security personnel are usually notified to refer all responders or volunteers to the closest check–in area. There, personnel will be logged in, briefed on the situation, given an assignment, and provided with a radio, communications frequency, or hardware to link them to the broader response effort.

- When advance *warnings* are possible, *evacuation* from areas of danger can be the most effective life–saving strategy in a disaster. The warning process is complex and requires precise communication among numerous agencies. A threat must be detected and analyzed to assess the specific areas at risk as well as the nature of that risk. Warnings should be delivered in such a manner that the population at risk will take the threat seriously and take appropriate action based on the warning. Detection and assessment are usually the responsibility of one agency (i.e., the US Weather Bureau, flood districts, dam officials). The decision to order an evacuation is the responsibility of other organizations (i.e., the sheriff's office), and the dissemination of the warning is the responsibility of a third group (i.e., commercial television or radio stations).

- The public tends to underestimate risks and downplay *warnings* if messages are ambiguous or inconsistent. Factors that enhance the effectiveness of warnings include the credibility of the warning source, the number of repetitions (especially if emanating from multiple sources), the consistency of message content across different sources, the context of the warning (i.e., a visible gas cloud or odor accompanying warnings about a hazardous substance leak), the inclusion of information that allows recipients to determine if they are personally in danger (i.e., details on location or track), the inclusion of specific information on self–protective actions, and invitations from friends or relatives to take shelter.

- *Search and rescue* is an important aspect of post–disaster response. In many disasters, casualties are initially treated in the field, and this process influences their entry into the health care system. To the extent that search and rescue is uncoordinated, the flow of patients through the emergency medical services system and the health care system is also uncoordinated. Several characteristics of disaster search and rescue create problems amenable to improvement through organizational planning. Most disaster search and rescue, particularly in the immediate post–impact period, is not initiated by trained emergency personnel but by the spontaneous efforts of untrained bystanders who happen to be in the area. Care of patients also becomes complicated when the disaster occurs across jurisdictional boundaries or involves emergency responders from many agencies (i.e., private ambulance providers, municipal first responders, and county, state, and federal agencies).

- *Using the mass media* to deliver warnings to the public and to educate the public about the avoidance of health problems in the aftermath of a disaster—such as food and water safety, injury prevention through chain saw safety, avoidance of nail punctures, and monitoring carbon monoxide exposure from charcoal and unvented heaters—can be an effective public health tool.

- *Triage*, derived from the French verb trier or to sort, is a method of assigning priorities for treatment and transport for injured citizens. Untrained personnel and bystanders who may do the initial search and rescue often bypass established field triage and first aid stations because they do not know where these posts are located or because they want to get the victims to the closest hospital.

- In most domestic disasters, several medical resources can handle the *casualty distribution*. Often, the closest hospitals receive the majority of patients, while other hospitals await casualties that never arrive. Transport decisions made by untrained volunteers are difficult to control. Established protocols between emergency medical services and area hospitals will ensure the more even distribution of casualties.

- *Patient tracking* is complicated by the fact that most persons evacuating their homes do not seek lodging in public shelters where their presence will be registered by the American Red Cross. Tracking the location of victims is further obfuscated because no single agency serves as a central repository of information about the location of victims from area hospitals, morgues, shelters, jails, or other potential locations. Tracking of the injured is also confounded because most patients get to hospitals by nonambulance means, leaving emergency medical services with an incomplete record of injuries. When hospitals themselves are damaged, the evacuation of hospitalized patients further complicates tracking where victims might be located.

- *Caring for patients when the health care infrastructure has been damaged* requires careful advance planning. Following natural disasters, hospitals should plan to care for high numbers of minor injuries than for major trauma. Substantial numbers of patients seeking hospital care do so because of chronic medical conditions rather than trauma due, in part, to damage to or loss of access to usual sources of primary medical care. Persons often evacuate their homes without prescription medications or underestimate how long they will be prevented from returning home. In addition, many injuries are sustained not during the disaster impact but during rescue or clean–up activities. Hospitals, urgent care centers, home health care agencies, pharmacies, and dialysis centers must make appropriate plans to ensure that their facilities will not be damaged or disabled in a disaster and that they have backup arrangements for the care of their patients post–impact. This includes providing backup supplies of power and water; building structures resistant to wind, fire, flood, and seismic hazards; maintaining essential equipment and supplies that will be damaged by earthquakes or other disasters; supplying surge protection and data backup for computers with patient accounts, charts, or pharmacy information; making plans for alternative office, business, or clinical sites for displaced local health care resources (i.e., physicians, pharmacists, radiology); and developing plans to relocate the site of "home" health care to sites where the patients have temporarily relocated.

- The *management of volunteers and donations* is a common problem in disasters. Disaster planning often focuses on the mobilization of resources, when not infrequently more resources arrive than are actually needed, requested, or expected. Procedures should be established to manage large numbers of resources. First, expect large numbers of donations and unsolicited volunteers (spontaneous civilian bystanders, family members, neighbors, co–workers, other survivors). Second, channel public requests for aid to a locality outside the disaster area where resources can be collected, organized, and distributed without disrupting ongoing emergency operations.

- Plan for organized improvisation in response to the *disruption of shelter, utilities, communication systems, and transportation.* Regardless of the level of preplanning, disasters will require some unanticipated tasks. Public health officials must develop the capacity, mutually agreed upon procedures, and training to participate in the community's coordinated, multiorganizational response to unexpected problems.

COMPONENTS OF A PLAN

A regional plan will identify the potential jurisdictions that could be affected by a disaster and the corresponding agencies with assigned disaster response and recovery responsibilities. Such a plan will bring together the chief executives and operational leaders of these agencies, initiate a joint coordination and situation assessment process, identify likely types of disasters, establish communication channels for sharing information, and create a standard protocol to assess the scope of damage, injuries, deaths, and secondary threats.

BASELINE ASSESSMENT

To develop a regional plan, public health agencies must first work with the emergency management sector to assess the status of the health and health risks of the community, the status of health care facilities, the protection of vital records, the potential requirements for public shelters, available resources for alternative emergency and primary care, and the availability of and procedures for obtaining state and federal assistance.

Efforts to assess the health condition of the community must examine:

- Prevalent disease and persons with special needs who will need assistance related to evacuation and continuity of care.

- Ability of the affected population to obtain prescription medications.

- Building safety and ability to protect victims from injury, the elements, and hazardous material release.

- Ability to maintain air quality, food safety, sanitation, waste disposal, vector control, and water systems.

Hospitals, urgent care centers, physician offices, outpatient medical clinics, psychiatric clinics, dialysis centers, pharmacies, assisted living and residential facilities for aged or disabled, and home health care services must have the capacity to meet patient needs and to ensure continuity of power, communications, water, sewer, and waste disposal in disaster situations. Data processing and exchange of patient information will be particularly important in the post–impact and recovery phases.

Disaster plans must take into account the availability of alternate treatment facilities when any or all of these locations are closed. Public health departments should work with hospitals and community providers to develop a plan for providing both routine and continuity of care for victims experiencing acute exacerbations of chronic medical problems such as asthma, emphysema, diabetes, and hypertension. If their normal source of care is not available and no alternative plan is communicated to the public, patients could be expected to seek care from overburdened hospital emergency departments. Following Hurricane Andrew, for example, more than 1,000 physician offices were destroyed or significantly damaged, greatly adding to hospital patient loads.

In addition, plans should be developed for patients in both hospitals and residential care facilities (i.e., long–term care, assisted living, psychiatric treatment, rehabilitation) who may need to be evacuated and placed elsewhere. Plans should also be made to maintain poison control hotlines and to continue home health care services (i.e., dialysis, intravenous antibiotic, visiting nurses services, medical supply) at sites to which patients have been relocated.

Public health departments must collect background data on requirements for the medical needs, lodging, water, sanitation, and feeding arrangements for both victims and rescue and relief personnel. Plans for resource management—including directing incoming responders and volunteers to designated check–in or staging areas and determining what resources are present, available, or committed to the incident—should be established in advance. Assignments regarding which tasks will be coordinated or implemented by which agency or individual worker must be designated. This is particularly true for responsibilities that cross functional, geographic, or jurisdictional boundaries and for tasks for which no single person or agency has clear–cut statutory or contractual responsibility. Priorities for resource distribution, cost sharing, acquisition, training, and coordination must be set jointly and disseminated widely.

Finally, public health officials should ensure that the disaster preparedness plan identifies state and federal assistance programs (i.e., Stafford Act as explained in Chapter 3) for reimbursement and establishes procedures to verify that full reimbursement for disaster–related health care has been recovered.

SURGE CAPACITY

Surge capacity is the ability to treat a large increase in the number of persons, specimens, etc., requiring care or analysis following an emergency event. As a primary tenet, governments at all levels must first ensure that public health agencies have the manpower and resources to handle their core mission and responsibilities on a daily basis or they will not have the capacity to provide services when a surge is needed during emergencies.

The principles of "capacity planning management" are used in industry to determine how much production capacity is needed, under which conditions and where capacity has to be increased, and how that increase will be structured. In response to a disaster, health care systems often have to expand their configuration to care for those affected by the incident. Dr. Boaz Tadmor, former Chief Medical Officer for the Homefront Command in Israel, has said that in times of disaster, the organization of the response is more important than the delivery of patient care. Surge capacity requires regional systems which are resilient and flexible in order to respond effectively to an emergency.

The surge capacity for a community's public health system involves the connectedness of health departments, hospitals, and community agencies. As example, in an event involving infectious disease, the burden on the public health system is dependent on many factors, including the nature of the event, the demography and prevalence/incidence of disease in the local population, and the projected spread of the infection. The ability to care for patients will vary by the demand for services and the available staff, equipment, space and antibiotics etc. Community organizations and institutions may need to provide services such as housing for quarantine. With incidents involving WMD, communities are likely to experience "triage inversion" where the least injured patients present first and the most injured are extricated at the scene. In this type of scenario, the contaminated victims may appear for care before hospitals have received information from the scene. Thus preparations for surge capacity involve protecting hospitals from contamination and ensuring a mechanism for EMS to communicate quickly to hospitals so that they can set up the decontamination correctly.

SURGE CAPACITY PLANNING

To estimate the potential need for increased personnel, assets and other resources, a community has to inventory available sites of care and public health agencies, the volume, location and services delivered, and geographic area served. Once the capacity assessment is complete, coordination with community and regional resources is essential. As example, when space is needed for any service, alternatives are schools, gymnasiums, military facilities (i.e., National Guard) and conversion of existing space, such as hotels.

Projections for increasing capacity can be determined by estimating:

- potential types of casualties and care needed by the type of incident, (i.e., highly infectious biological event vs. single location blast event),

- volume, intensity and differing rates of morbidity and mortality among projected patients,

- impact of demographics,

- current services by location,

- knowledge and skill mix of current staffing,

- available treatment and triage onsite at the incident,

- how much care can be delivered by primary care physicians, such as caring for the "worried well,"

- alternative sources for capacity (i.e., mutual aid agreements, Medical Reserve Corp, etc.),

- the expected timeframe, length of the response, and work schedules, and

- types of public health and health care services to be added or increased based on these estimates.

Scheduling should allow for care/services to be provided over the entire projected length of a response (i.e., at 12, 24, 48, and 96 hours, etc.) so that staff is not "burnt out" in the first six hours. Capacity assessments might indicate that an agency needs to realign staffing assignments by shifting staff from one venue to another or from one location within an agency/facility to another. The same assessment is required for equipment and other resources. Once staffing projections are identified, plans should provide for training surge staff on:

- their role and responsibilities in the response,

- the chain of command within the organization in which they will report,

- reporting protocols and any legal responsibility to report, and

- clinical recognition of diseases (i.e., signs and symptoms) where indicated.

DRILLS AND TRAINING

The existence of a written emergency response plan does not ensure that it will be used or that the plan will be effective if needed. Ideally, local public health and health care facilities are integrated into a community–wide plan that is exercised and evaluated at least once every 12 months. When all of the agencies that will be called upon to respond to a disaster, including public health, have participated in the plan's development, they are more likely to ensure that the full needs of the community can be met and that individual organizations are not overburdened due to poor planning.

A disaster plan can be exercised in one of three ways. The first involves desktop simulation exercises, often called "Table Top Exercises," using paper, verbal, or computer–based scenarios designed to improve coordination, to share information, and to practice decision–making. Paper drills are often done to demonstrate how "response functions" work and communication together as part of the ICS plan. In table tops exercises, those involved include a facilitator and agency participants.

The second method, "functional exercises," relies on field exercises where the entire community response is evaluated. Functional exercises usually involve the activation and simulated activity of all sections of the ICS and are expensive because they test the disaster plan in simulated field conditions. In functional exercises, the participants include the players, simulators, controllers, and evaluators.

The third method, "field exercise drills," is effective because responders get to know each other and each other's roles, gain experience working with the community's plan, and understand what must be done—thus enhancing their ability to rely on each other's activities. Field exercises take place in real time as they test the mobilization, including the activation of the EOC, of all or as many as possible of the response components. In full–scale exercises, the participants include the responder, controller, evaluator, and victims.

The roles of the drill participants in drills are useful to understand. The controller ensures that the exercise is conducted per the pre–designed objectives and proceeds according to plan. He adds and discards messages to modify the pace and maintains order and professionalism in the control and simulation rooms. The simulator's role is to create an artificial reality by communicating events that might actually happen in a given emergency, assume the roles of outside agencies or people, and transmit pre–scripted or spontaneous messages to players. Players are representatives from agencies or organizations who would actually be called on in the event of an emergency. They assemble in the EOC and respond as realistically as possible to messages describing the events taking place. Evaluators observe the action, report on what went well and what did not, assess if the goals and objectives were met, and report on how the participants performed.

Because disasters often cross political, geographical, functional, and jurisdictional boundaries, drills and training are most effective when carried out on a multiorganizational, multidisciplinary, multijurisdictional basis. Coordination is also facilitated when participants are familiar with the skills, level of knowledge, and dependability of other responders on whom they may one day need to rely. The full–scale drill will often involve prehospital as well as hospital response.

Drills are used to improve planning. The "test–drill cycle" begins with an assumption about how agencies will function in a response. Following training, an objective for a drill is developed. The drill is organized and conducted. An evaluation occurs and the plan is revised based on the evaluation. Responders are then retrained for the new plan.

IDENTIFYING AVAILABLE RESOURCES

Disaster response may call for the use of resources (i.e., personnel, equipment, supplies, information) that do not commonly reside in one location or under the jurisdiction of one agency. Reducing morbidity and mortality in the early hours after disaster has struck may depend on locating resources that are not commonly used in routine emergency responses or are in short supply. A comprehensive plan should establish procedures for locating specialty physicians, search dogs, specialized devices for locating trapped victims in the rubble of collapsed buildings, tools for cutting through and lifting heavy reinforced concrete blocks, dialysis centers or equipment to treat crush injury, laboratories to rapidly analyze hazardous chemicals or biological agents, radiation detection instruments, confined–space rescue teams, and hazardous materials response teams with appropriate protective gear.

Chapter **8**

Environmental and Occupational Health Issues

Maintaining environmental health is essential to preventing disease following disasters. Because of the complexity of environmental issues, there is seldom a single environmental health specialist responsible for all of the environmental problems that follow a disaster. In urban areas and in complex large scale disasters, it is common for numerous governmental agencies and consultants at all levels to be pulled together to coordinate an environmental response. This chapter addresses public health interventions to ensure proper sanitation and waste disposal, to maintain safety of water and food supplies, to ensure adequate heating and shelter, to provide for worker safety, to protect against air contamination, handle human remains, and to control vector populations.

PUBLIC HEALTH ROLE

- Quantitative monitoring of environmental services, including environmental sampling, ensuring the replacement or repair of existing sanitary barriers.

- Contain or remove sources of environmental contamination, or evacuate people to ensure that they are no longer exposed to the hazard.

- Ensure that people have sufficient cooking utensils, equipment and fuel to cook and store food safely.

- Promote changes in the behavior of victims by providing guidance, education, and assurance of safe water, safe food, and safe shelter to compensate for disrupted sanitary environments.

- Protect worker safety by ensuring the use of protective measures, and by monitoring illness and injuries to inform modifications in the use of protective measures.

- Provide regular advisories to the public and the medical community.

REDUCING EXPOSURE TO ENVIRONMENTAL HAZARDS

Disrupted environments have variable effects on health depending on the presence of endemic disease, the susceptibility and habits of the population, and the availability of protective measures. The types of disease most often spread, such as respiratory infections and diarrhea, are those that have a short transmission cycle and incubation period and are widespread.

Public health can use three major approaches to reduce exposure to environmental hazards: measures of control, establishment of multiple barriers, and providing distance between the hazard and populations at risk.

Measures of Control. Certain hazards move through the environment and cause harm to humans. Public health professionals can control disease by preventing the hazard from being released or occurring, by preventing the transport of the hazard, or by preventing people from being exposed to the hazard. For example, malaria control involves a three–pronged approach of draining stagnant water to prevent mosquito breeding, spraying for mosquitoes to prevent the transport of pathogens, and diminishing exposure by encouraging the use of treated bed–netting and insect repellent.

Establishing Multiple Barriers. Since no single environmental measure is failsafe, redundant barriers must be set up between hazards and populations. Multiple sanitary barriers provide redundant protection where, for example, public health protects surface water used for drinking. If on a given day, any of the redundant measures is not functioning, the others will reduce the hazard. Most water–borne outbreaks in the United States occur when multiple barriers fail simultaneously. Protection from environmental hazards depends on awareness of the risk, diligence in surveillance, and investment in the multiple barriers needed to keep the population risk low.

Providing Distance Between Hazards and Populations. In general, the distance needed to protect a population from exposure to a hazardous substance varies according to the volume and nature of a hazardous substance. The greater the distance existing between a hazard and a population, the greater the amount of time before an inadvertent release of the hazardous material reaches the populated area. With a longer time delay, the release is more likely to be detected in time for the population to take protective measures. Since most pollutants degrade or disperse over distance, providing space between hazardous materials and populations may by itself reduce human exposure.

ENVIRONMENTAL SURVEILLANCE

Three conditions should be monitored to estimate the number of individuals whose environment is affected by a disaster: access to excreta disposal facilities, water consumption, and the percentage of people consuming safe water.

Access to Excreta Disposal Facilities. Public health officials must assess the number of people per latrine to determine the relative availability of latrines and the amount of sharing required. To estimate people per latrine, conduct a walk through survey or interview people. For those who indicate that they have a family latrine, ask how many people are in their family and if they share the latrine with anyone else. If families are using communal latrines, calculate sanitation coverage as the number of latrines divided by the number of people using them. Where people continue to live in dwellings in which not all toilets are functional, monitor the fraction of households with a functioning toilet or latrine as a proxy for sanitation coverage.

Water Consumption. Water consumption depends both on water availability and the population's ability to obtain the water. Bucket shortages, security concerns, and long lines can all prevent plentiful sources from being fully utilized. Public health officials must survey the population and estimate water consumption by asking for a 24–hour recall of water use or by monitoring how much water is collected at the various sources and dividing this by the number of people being served. Water consumption is defined in terms of gallons or liters per person per day.

Percentage of People Consuming Safe Water. In settings where ground-water supplies at wells or springs are determined to be safe, monitor the percent of people obtaining water from the safe sources versus unsafe sources. Public health workers should monitor the percentage of people who are getting "safe" water when it is being collected, remembering that collecting "safe" water from a source does not assure that the water is safe at the time of ingestion. With piped systems, workers must collect samples at household taps throughout the system, with a collection scheme such that each sample represents a similar number of people (i.e., 1 sample per 10,000 people). The percent of water samples that are safe to drink corresponds to the percent of people whose water arrives safely at the point where the water is collected.

SANITATION DURING DISASTER SITUATIONS

Sewage systems are a network of pipes that carry wastes away from a population. Sewers often become flooded or clogged during hurricanes, earthquakes, and floods. Hurricanes or other storms may cause untreated sewage to be washed into waterways. Clogged sewer lines may also cause waste to spill into the environment at locations where it is likely to expose large numbers of people to biological or chemical hazards. Typically, problems within sewage networks are mitigated by pumping or re–routing the sewage, which may not be possible following a disaster. Public health officials should document the location of by–pass valves, confirm that they are functional and that auxiliary pumping capacity exists, and have an operational plan for storm events as part of a disaster preparedness program.

Where sanitation systems are destroyed, one of the first activities should be the reestablishment of a system of latrines since containing human excreta is the most protective environmental measure that can be taken following disaster. Proper spaces for defecation fields must be set aside, and latrines should be built before the population arrives at a relocation site. When defecation fields are used, they must be planned in advance and located away from water sources and downhill from living quarters. The World Health Organization recommends the provision of one pit latrine per family. Where that is not possible, both the United Nations High Commission for Refugees and United Nations International Children's Education Fund have set a maximum target of 20 people per latrine. To the extent possible, households should not share latrines or toilets. Efforts should be made to build separate latrines for men and women or separate latrines for children. Privacy screens should be constructed. Establishing one latrine per household, rather than sharing latrines, will increase the likelihood that the facilities will be kept clean. With mortality and morbidity rates among displaced populations often higher in the first days and weeks following an event, it is essential to persuade everyone to use the latrines that have been set up.

To increase use of latrines by young children, two approaches may be useful. First, educate child–care providers about proper handling of children's feces and the importance of washing their hands after cleaning the child or handling the child's feces. Second, establish excreta disposal facilities that are child–friendly (i.e., well–lit, have an opening smaller than that used in adult latrines).

To ensure personal hygiene, paper, water, and soap must be readily available in or near the latrine, especially where diarrheal diseases and dysentery are likely to occur. Public health information officers should promote hand washing, particularly after defecating and before preparing food to protect against fecal–oral illnesses. The information campaign should promote measures known to prevent specific health threats. Educational messages should be short, relate to the route by which disease may be transmitted, and focus on behaviors that are not presently practiced by a significant portion of the population. Public health workers should likewise establish a simple monitoring component to assure that increased hand washing (or other preventive behavior) is actually occurring.

ENSURING WATER SAFETY

Providing people with more water is more protective against fecal–oral pathogens than providing people with cleaner water. Public health officials should work closely with the agencies that are monitoring the availability of water. Estimate water consumption at least weekly during the post–impact phase. Measure water consumption by what people receive, not by what the water operators produce. Water consumption can be measured through sampling, such as household interviews, or by the actual collection of water at watering points.

Attempts should be made to provide each family with their own water bucket to reduce the risk of illness. The average water consumption should be 3.9 gallons (15 liters) per day or more, with no one consuming less than 5 liters or 1 gallon per person per day. The World Health Organization recommends 4.2–5.2 gallons (16 to 20 liters) per day. A three to five day supply of water (five gallons per person) should be stored for food preparation, bathing, brushing teeth, and dish washing.

Where residents are preparing supplies in advance of a disaster, such as in earthquake–prone California, they should store water in sturdy plastic bottles with tight fitting lids. Stored water should be located away from the storage of toxic substances and should be changed every six months.

WATER FOR DRINKING AND COOKING

Safe drinking water includes bottled, boiled, or treated water. Residents should drink only bottled, boiled, or treated water until the supply is tested and found safe. They must be instructed not to use contaminated water to wash dishes, brush teeth, wash and prepare food, or make ice. All bottled water from an unknown source must be boiled or treated before use. To kill harmful bacteria and parasites, residents should bring water to a rolling boil for one minute. Water may also be treated with chlorine or iodine tablets or by mixing six drops (1/8 teaspoon) of unscented household chlorine bleach (5.25% sodium hypochlorite) per gallon of water. Mix the solution thoroughly, and let stand for about 30 minutes. This treatment, however, will not kill parasitic organisms.

The United Nations High Commission for Refugees considers water with less than 10 fecal coliforms per 100 ml to be reasonably safe, while water with more than 100 fecal coliforms is considered unsafe. Contaminated water sources should not be closed until equally convenient facilities become available.

It may be necessary to transport safe drinking water to the disaster site by truck. Trucks that normally carry gasoline, chemicals, or sewage should not be used to transport water. Trucks should be inspected and cleaned and disinfected before being used for water transportation because they may be contaminated with microbes or chemicals. Containers, such as bottles or cans, should be rinsed with a bleach solution before reusing them. Do not rely on untested devices for decontaminating water.

WATER SUPPLY

There are three sources of water: groundwater, surface water, and rainwater. Groundwater, while generally of higher quality microbiologically, is relatively difficult to access because it is located within the earth's crust. Surface waters, found in lakes, ponds, streams and rivers, have predictable reliability and volume and are relatively easy to gather but are generally microbiologically unsafe and require treatment. Rainwater is seldom used because collection is unreliable.

COLLECTING AND TREATING SURFACE WATER

Once collected, water quality deteriorates over time. The handling and storing of water is the main determinant in water safety. Where water is collected in buckets, it should be chlorinated either in the home or by health workers at the point of collection. Residents should be instructed to add an initial dose of 2.5 mg/l chlorine to the bucket so that after 30 minutes, at least 0.5 mg/l free chlorine remains in the water. People should be encouraged to wait for 30 minutes after chlorination before consuming water to allow for adequate disinfection to occur. The dipping of water from household storage buckets causes considerable contamination. To maintain clean stored water, residents should add a chlorine residual.

With a piped system, typically chlorine levels are adjusted to assure that 0.2 to 0.5 mg/l free chlorine is in the water at the tap level where it is collected. During times of outbreaks or in systems where there are broken distribution pipes, workers should aim to have 0.5 to 1.0 mg/l free chlorine.

To prevent cross–contamination, health officials should increase the pressure in the water pipes and increase the level of residual chlorine. Pressure can be augmented by increasing the rate of pumping into the system, by cutting down on water wastage, or by closing off sections of the distribution system. Because cross–contamination usually occurs in unknown locations in a distribution system, the chlorine residual must be kept high throughout the network. Monitoring of chlorine should be done throughout the system, and the dose put into the system should be set so that there is free chlorine in at least 95 percent of locations.

ACCESSING AND TREATING GROUNDWATER

To collect spring water without contamination, workers should build a collection basin that has an outflow pipe constructed at or just below the point where the water comes to the surface. To prevent contamination in wells, they can build a skirt around the opening of the well or a plate sealing off the surface at the top of the well.

Water should be disinfected when household water contamination is high, when there is a high risk of a waterborne outbreak, or when the groundwater is of poor quality. Chlorine can be used in buckets when the water is collected or stored at people's homes. To chlorinate wells, use a chlorine pot or the method of shock chlorination as described below.

A chlorination pot includes a small container, such as a one–liter soda bottle, with a few holes punched in it. This container is filled with a chlorine powder and gravel mixture and placed inside a larger vessel (such as a four–liter milk jug or a clay pot) that also has holes punched in it. The chlorine disperses from the double layered pot slowly. The number and size of holes in the vessels controls the disinfectant dose and must be tailored to match a specific well volume and withdrawal rate. Invariably, the first water drawn in the morning will have an offensively high level of chlorine, and if a well has hours of very high use, the dose may become too low. Thus, pot chlorination schemes are not widely used and should not be commenced during the acute phase of a crisis when a lack of time and attention will prevent proper monitoring and adjustment of the chlorine levels.

Shock chlorination is conducted by adding 5–10 mg/l to the water in a well and allowing it to sit unused for a period of hours. The first water drawn from the well after the disinfection period is discarded, and normal use is subsequently resumed. When a well is drawing from safe groundwater but has been contaminated by people or an unusual event (such as a major rainstorm), shock chlorination can eliminate a transient threat to water quality. Shock chlorination does not provide chlorinated water to the people in their homes because after the first few hours of use after treatment, little or no residual chlorine will remain in the drawn water.

DISINFECTING WELLS

Although recommendations and regulations vary from state to state, the same general principles apply to disinfecting wells. To disinfect bored or dug wells, use Table 27 to calculate how much bleach (liquid or granules) to use. To determine the exact amount required, multiply the amount of disinfectant needed (according to the diameter of the well) by the depth of the well. For example, a well 5.0 feet in diameter requires 4.5 cups of bleach per foot of water. If the well is 30 feet deep, multiply 4.5 by 30 to determine the total cups of bleach required (135 cups). Add this total amount of disinfectant (in this case, 135 cups ÷ 16 cups per gallon = 8 gallons and 7 cups of bleach) to about 10 gallons of water. Splash the mixture around the wall or lining of the well. Be certain the disinfectant solution contacts all parts of the well. Seal the well top. Open all faucets, and pump water until a strong odor of bleach is noticeable at each faucet. Then stop the pump and allow the solution to remain in the well overnight. The next day, operate the pump by turning on all faucets, continuing until the chlorine odor disappears. Adjust the flow of water faucets or fixtures that discharge to septic systems to a low flow to avoid overloading the disposal system.

TABLE 27. BLEACH REQUIRED TO DISINFECT A BORED OR DUG WELL

Well Diameter (feet)	Liquid bleach (5.25%) per foot of Water	Chlorine granules (70%) per foot of Water
3	1.5 cups	1.0 ounce
4	3.0 cups	2.0 ounces
5	4.5 cups	3.0 ounces
6	6.0 cups	4.0 ounces
7	9.0 cups	6.0 ounces
8	12.0 cups	8.0 ounces
10	18.0 cups	12.0 ounces

To disinfect drilled wells, determine the amount of water in the well by multiplying the gallons per foot (see table 28) by the depth of the well in feet. For example, a well with a 6-inch diameter contains 1.5 gallons of water per foot. If the well is 120 feet deep, multiply 1.5 by 120 to calculate the amount of water as 180 gallons.

TABLE 28. WATER VOLUME OF DRILLED WELLS

Well Diameter (inches)	Gallons per Foot of Water
3	0.37
4	0.65
5	1.00
6	1.50
8	2.60
10	4.10
12	6.00

SOURCE: ILLINOIS DEPARTMENT OF HEALTH. RECOMMENDATIONS MAY VARY FROM STATE TO STATE.

After calculating the total amount of water in the well (see Table 28), determine the amount of liquid or granular chlorine to add: use three cups of liquid laundry bleach (5.25 percent chlorine) or two ounces (four heaping tablespoons) of hypochloride granules (70 percent chlorine) per 100 gallons of well water. In the example above, the 180–gallon well would require 5.4 cups of liquid bleach or 3.6 ounces of granular chlorine.

Mix the total amount of liquid or granules with about 10 gallons of water. Pour the solution into the top of the well before the seal is installed. Connect a hose from a faucet on the discharge side of the pressure tank to the well casing top. Start the pump. Spray the water back into the well and wash the sides of the casing for at least 15 minutes. Open every faucet in the system and let the water run until the smell of chlorine can be detected. Then close all the faucets and seal the top of the well. Let stand for several hours, preferably overnight. Afterward, operate the pump by turning on all faucets continuing until all odor of chlorine disappears. Adjust the flow of water from faucets or fixtures that discharge into septic tank systems to a low flow to avoid overloading the disposal system.

EMERGENCY BASIC SERVICES

In catastrophic events, all basic services may need to be reestablished. Where the infrastructure to provide safe water and food is not intact, interim measures must be established to provide services until systems are fully operational. In catastrophic circumstances, public health officials may issue orders to boil water, warn about foods that may have spoiled during electrical outages, or announce where potable water will be provided.

Boil Water Order

Through the Safe Drinking Water Act, Congress requires the Environmental Protection Agency (EPA) to regulate contaminants that may be health risks and that may be present in public drinking water supplies. The EPA sets legal limits on the levels of certain contaminants in drinking water and establishes the water–testing schedules and methods that water systems must follow. The rules also list acceptable techniques for treating contaminated water. The Safe Drinking Water Act gives individual states the opportunity to set and enforce their own drinking water standards so long as the standards are at least as strong as EPA's national standards. Most states and territories directly oversee the water systems within their borders.

The Total Coliform Rule sets legal limits for total coliform levels in drinking water and specifies the type and frequency of testing to determine if legal limits are exceeded. Coliforms are a broad class of bacteria that live in the digestive tracts of humans and many animals. The presence of coliform bacteria in tap water suggests that the treatment system is not working properly or that a problem exists in the pipes. Exposure to coliform can cause gastroenteritis, which is characterized by diarrhea, cramps, nausea, and vomiting.

Coliforms cannot be found in more than five percent of the samples tested each month. If more than five percent of the samples contain coliforms, water system operators must report this violation to the state and the public. If a sample tests positive for coliforms, the system must collect a set of repeat samples within 24 hours. When a routine or repeat sample tests positive for total coliforms, it must also be analyzed for fecal coliforms and *Escherichia coli (E. coli)*, which are coliforms directly associated with fresh feces. A positive result to this last test signifies an acute Maximum Contaminant Level (MCL) violation, which necessitates rapid state and public notification due to its direct health risk.

Following a disaster that may compromise a community's water supply, those responsible for monitoring water safety may use the regular water–sampling plan or make modifications, depending on the severity and geographic location of concern. When a decision has been made that water sampled from one or more sites exceeds the maximum contaminant level and poses a threat to the public's health, a decision may be made to issue a boiled water order or advisory.

The EPA issued a revised set of Drinking Water Standards and Health Advisories in 2000. With few exceptions, the health advisory values have been rounded to one significant figure. Table 29 summarizes the section on microorganisms. The maximum contaminant level goal refers to the maximum level of a contaminant in drinking water at which no known or anticipated adverse effects occur and that allows for an adequate margin of safety. These are nonenforceable public health goals. The maximum contaminant level, which is an enforceable standard, identifies the maximum permissible level of a contaminant in water that is delivered to any user of a public water system. Treatment technique is an enforceable procedure or level of technical performance that public water systems must follow to ensure control of a contaminant.

The Surface Water Treatment Rule requires systems using surface water or ground water under the direct influence of surface water to disinfect their water and to filter their water or meet criteria for avoiding filtration so that the following contaminants are controlled at the following levels:

- *Giardia lamblia*: 99.9 percent killed/inactivated.

- Viruses: 99.99 percent killed/inactivated.

- *Legionella*: No limit, but EPA believes that if Giardia and viruses are inactivated, Legionella will also be controlled.

- Turbidity: At no time can turbidity (cloudiness of water) go above 5 nephelolometric turbidity units (NTU); systems that filter must ensure that the turbidity go no higher than 1 NTU (0.5 NTU for conventional or direct filtration) in at least 95 percent of the daily samples in any month.

TABLE 29. DRINKING WATER CONTAMINANTS

Microorganism	Maximum Contaminant Level Goal (mg/L)	Maximum Contaminant Level or Treatment Technique	Potential Health Effects from Ingestion of Water	Source of Contaminant in Drinking Water
Giardia lamblia	0	99.9% killed or inactivated	Giardiasis, a gastroenteric disease	Human and animal fecal waste
Heterotrophic plate count	n/a	≤500 bacterial colonies/ml	HPC has no health effects, but can indicate how effective treatment is at controlling microorganisms	n/a
Legionella	0	Use treatment technique for Giardia	Legionnaire's disease (pneumonia)	Found naturally in water; multiplies in heating systems
Total Coliforms (including fecal coliform and E. Coli)	0	≤5.0% samples total colirorm-positive in a mouth	Used as an indicator that other potentially harmful bacteria may be present*	Human and animal fecal waste
Turbidity	n/a	Systems that filter must ensure that the turbidity ≤I NTU (0.5 NTU for conventional or direct filtration) in at least 95% of the daily samples in any mouth	Turbidity has no health effects but can interfere with disinfection and provide a medium for microbial growth. It may indicate the presence of microbes.	Soil runoff

*Drinking Water Standards and Health Advisories, EPA, 2000

- Heterotrophic Plate Count: No more than 500 bacterial colonies per milliliter.

- Total Coliforms (including fecal coliform and *E. Coli*): No more than 5.0 percent samples total coliform–positive in a month. For water systems that collect fewer than 40 routine samples per month, no more that one sample can be total coliform–positive. Every sample that has total coliforms must be analyzed for fecal coliforms. There cannot be any fecal coliforms.

Public Notice Templates

The EPA has developed templates that can be used by water suppliers to ensure that the notice that they provide is complete. These templates can be downloaded from the EPA website: [http://www.epa.gov/safewater/pws/pn/templates.html].

Food Safety

Improper food storage is associated with *B. cereus, C. perfingens, Salmonella, S. aureus,* and group A *Streptococcus.* Lack of hand washing and personal hygiene are associated with shigellosis, hepatitis A, gastroenteritis, and giardiasis. Three food–handling techniques are a major source of food–borne illness following disaster: improper storage, inadequate cooking, and poor personal hygiene. In addition to careful hand washing, cooking utensils must be washed in boiled or treated water before being used. Table 30 provides tips for safe food handling.

Stored Food. When preparing for disasters, residents should store at least a three–day supply of food. Canned foods and dry mixes will remain fresh for about two years when stored in a cool, dry, dark place away from ranges or refrigerator exhausts at a temperature of 40 to 60°F. Residents should date all food items and use or replace food before it loses freshness. Food items should be heavily wrapped or stored in airtight containers above the ground to both prolong shelf life and to protect it from insects and rodents. Cans that bulge at the ends or that are leaking should be discarded.

Refrigerated Food. Refrigerators, without power, will keep foods cool for about four hours if left unopened. Block or dry ice can be added to refrigerators if the electricity is off longer than four hours. Perishable food in the refrigerator or freezer should be used before stored food. Unrefrigerated cooked foods should be discarded after two hours at room temperature regardless of appearance. Only foods that have a normal color, texture, and odor should be eaten.

Frozen Food. Twenty–five pounds of dry ice will keep a ten–cubic–foot freezer below freezing for three to four days. Dry ice freezes everything it touches and must be handled with dry, heavy gloves to avoid injury. Thawed food can usually be eaten or refrozen if it is still refrigerator cold or if it still contains ice crystals. Any food that has been at room temperature for two hours or more or that has an unusual odor, color, or texture should be discarded.

TABLE 30. MEASURES FOR ENSURING FOOD SAFETY

STEP	HAZARD	ACTION
Supply/purchase	Contamination of raw food-stuffs	• Obtain foods from reliable supplier
		• Specify conditions for production and transport
	Contamination of ready–to–eat foods	Purchase foods from reliable supplier
Receipt of food	Contamination of high–risk foods with pathogens	Control temperature and time of transport
Storage	Further contamination	Store foods in closed container or wrapped
		Control pests
	Growth of bacteria	Control temperature and duration of storage, rotate stock
Preparation	Further contamination, via hands or in other ways	Wash hands before handling food
		• Prevent cross–contamination via surfaces, cooking utensils
		• Separate cooked foods from raw foods
		• Use boiled water, especially if food won't be cooked again
	Growth of bacteria	Limit exposure of food to room temperature
Cooking	Survival of pathogens	Make sure that food is cooked thoroughly (i.e., all parts have reached at least 165 °F)
Cooling and cold holding	Growth of surviving bacteria or their spores, production of toxins	Cool food as quickly as possible to temperatures below 40 °F, e.g., place foods in shallow trays and cool to chill temperatures.
		Avoid overfilling the refrigerator or cold storage room.

TABLE 30. MEASURES FOR ENSURING FOOD SAFETY (CONTINUED)

STEP	HAZARD	ACTION
		During long periods of cold storage, monitor the temperature fluctuations by occasional measurement
	Contamination from various sources	Cover food properly, avoid all contact with raw foods and non–potable water
		Use clean utensils to handle cooked food
Hot holding	Growth of surviving bacteria or their spores, production of toxins	Ensure that food is kept hot (i.e., above 140°F)
Reheating	Survival of bacteria	Ensure that the food is thoroughly reheated
Serving	Growth of bacteria, spores, production of toxins	Ensure that leftovers, or foods prepared in advance, are thoroughly reheated
	Contamination	• Prevent contact with raw foods, unclean utensils and non–potable water
		• Do not touch food with hands
		• Serve food when it is still hot

Adapted from Table 9.1 Control measures for ensuring food safety from Wisner B and Adams J (eds.) (2002). Environmental health in emergencies and disasters. World Health Organization. Geneva. page 150

Flooded Food Supplies. Discard all food not stored in a waterproof container. Undamaged, commercially canned foods can be saved by removing the can labels, thoroughly washing the cans, and then disinfecting them with a solution consisting of one cup of bleach in five gallons of water. Cans should be relabeled, including expiration date, with a non–erasable marker. Food containers with screw caps, snap–lids, crimped caps (soda pop bottles), twist caps, flip tops, and home canned foods cannot be disinfected. Only pre–prepared canned baby formula that requires no added water should be used for infants.

Feeding Large Numbers of Displaced People

Food requirements can be estimated by assessing the effect of the disaster on food supplies and the number of people who are without food. Seasonal variations may affect the availability of food. Estimates of food requirements should be calculated for one week and one month: 35,274 pounds (16 metric tons) of food are needed for 1,000 people for one month, and 70.6 cubic feet (2 cubic meters) of space are needed to store 1 metric ton of food. Table 31 lists the elements needed to feed a large number of displaced person.

TABLE 31. ELEMENTS NEEDED AT MASS–FEEDING STATIONS

Water Supplies

Toilets for staff and others—at least 1 toilet for every 50 people

Hand—washing facilities —at food handler stations and near toilets

Facilities for liquid wastes from kitchens—grease trap or strainer is a must

Facilities for solid wastes from kitchens—dispose in rubbish bins which are tightly covered

Basins, tables, chopping blocks—thoroughly disinfect with strong chlorine solution after each meal

Facilities for dish washing—Separate basins for washing, eating and cooking

Adequate materials for cooking/refrigeration— Prepare food sufficient for one meal

Lay—out to prevent cross contamination—Adequate space and separation of raw food and animal products

Adequate serving pieces—Use disposables if no facilities to thoroughly wash and rinse

Control of rodents and other pests—Use traps for flies, screen kitchen areas, dispose of sullage and waste; Never place rodenticides on surfaces used for food preparation

Food safety information—Place posters in full view by those in the food preparation areas

Adapted from Table 9.2 Elements needed to at mass–feeding stations from Wisner B and Adams J (eds.) (2002). Environmental health in emergencies and disasters. World Health Organization. Geneva. page 155

FOOD SAFETY MONITORING

CDC has established a web–based network called FoodNet to respond to new and emerging foodborne diseases by monitoring the burden and by identifying the sources of specific foodborne diseases. FoodNet uses active surveillance (public health officials frequently contact laboratory directors to find new cases of foodborne diseases and report these cases electronically to CDC) to strengthen the ability of some state and local health departments to detect and respond to foodborne outbreaks. Because most foodborne infections cause diarrheal illness, FoodNet focuses on persons who have a diarrheal illness. FoodNet could be used to detect and monitor the emergence of foodborne disease secondary to disaster or related to intentional poisoning.

Control Strategies for Epidemic Diarrheal Diseases

Environmental measures and education campaigns should be specific to the fecal–oral disease public health officials seek to protect against.

Cholera. Public health bulletins must instruct residents to consume only chlorinated or boiled fluids and to eat only hot, cooked foods or peeled fruits and vegetables. Emphasize hand washing in food preparation and before eating. During a cholera outbreak, ensure that the water being consuming is chlorinated. Where chlorination is not possible, order the boiling of water or the addition of a lemon per liter. Acidic sauces added to foods, such as tomato sauce, can provide some protection against food–borne cholera.

Typhoid fever. As with cholera, residents must be told to consume only chlorinated or boiled fluids and to eat only hot, cooked foods or peeled fruits and vegetables. Public health officials must ensure that the water supply is chlorinated and emphasize hand washing in food preparation and before eating. Workers must also ensure that infected residents do not prepare food for others for three months after the onset of their symptoms.

Shigella. Public health campaigns must educate residents about a comprehensive personal hygiene program. Public health workers must provide soap and lots of water and promote hand washing, the chlorination of water, and the proper handling and heating of food. Educational efforts should be focused in households where cases have occurred because secondary cases within households are common.

Hepatitis A. Water is the main route of transmission during major outbreaks. The most common form of fecal–oral hepatitis, hepatitis A, is transmitted by food and other routes. Control measures should therefore concentrate on the chlorination of water. Since pregnant women are particularly vulnerable, special efforts should be made to educate them and help them carry out personal and food hygiene.

Heating and Shelter

Provision of sufficient shelter following disaster prevents, depending on weather conditions, hypothermia, frostbite, malaise, heatstroke, and dehydration.

In cold climates, higher caloric intake is required to maintain the same activity level. For each degree below 68° F, about 1 percent more calories is required. If a house is 50° F, residents will require 10 percent more food intake to sustain their activity level. Public health interventions following cold–weather disasters include making high energy foods available, providing blankets and sleeping bags, distributing plastic sheeting to cover windows and unused doorways, encouraging the sharing of a heated place by several people or households, and instructing residents of multistory buildings to heat the same room, allowing heat lost from one floor to augment heat in the room above. Educational messages should warn people about the signs of carbon monoxide poisoning and provide instructions to check for gas leaks.

In warmer climates, sheeting should be provided to keep people dry during rainstorms and to provide shade in the daylight.

WORKER SAFETY

The collapse of a building or the occurrence of a large fire are two environmental events where worker safety is of great concern. Workers can be exposed to hazards from the release of contaminants or from construction safety issues. In order to minimize worker injury in disaster response and recovery, planning is essential. The Occupational Safety and Health Administration (OSHA) issued a National Emergency Management Plan (NEMP), which details OSHA's policies and responsibilities during major incidents, (i.e., a presidential declaration, the activation of the Federal Response Plan, or a request for assistance from the Department of Homeland Security). The NEMP requires that each OSHA region develop a Regional Emergency Management Plan (REMP) coordinating federal and state plans. Further, it outlines logistical and operational procedures to ensure the health and safety of emergency responders and recovery workers.

Further direction for planning can be found within the Occupational Safety and Health Administration (OSHA) standard for protecting workers during a disaster response (OSHA 29 CFR 1910.120), commonly referred to as "HazWoper" and under OSHA's guidance for the development of emergency action plans (EAPs) for small businesses. Communities should review their contracts to ensure that full protection is provided by both the contractors and any sub–contractors who would be involved in search and rescue and/or recovery activities.

HazWoper is a useful framework for organizing the protection of those responding to a disaster. Among the requirements relevant to disaster response and recovery, HazWoper requires 1) extensive safety and health training, including instruction in decontamination for personnel, equipment and hardware, response required by levels A, B, and C and establishing appropriate decontamination lines, and donning and doffing of protective equipment; 2) the development of and implementation of a written safety and health program; 3) a medical surveillance program; 4) an effective site safety and health plan; 5) an emergency response plan and procedures; 6) provision of recommended sanitation equipment; 7) development of work practices to minimize employee risk from site hazards; 8) safe use of engineering controls, equipment, and relevant new safety technology or procedures; 9) establishing methods of communication including those used while wearing respiratory protection; and 10) provision of personal protective equipment (PPE).

Community disaster plans for small businesses should include emergency action plans (EAPs) that provide for worker safety. Some elements of EAPs required under OSHA's Employee Emergency Plans and Fire Protection Plans (29 CFR 1910.38) that are also applicable to the protection of rescue workers include providing for and training in 1) use of various types of fire extinguishers; 2) first aid, including cardiopulmonary resuscitation (CPR); 3) the requirements of the OSHA bloodborne pathogens standard; 4) chemical spill control procedures; 5) use of self–contained breathing apparatus (SCBA); 6) use of other personal protective equipment (PPE); 7) search and emergency rescue procedures; 8) emergency communication; and 9) hazardous materials emergency response in accordance with 29 CFR 1910.120. Further, it is important to ensure that subcontracts, where those are used, provide for the same protections.

Safety equipment, such as PPE, must meet the criteria contained in the OSHA standards or described by a nationally recognized standards producing organization. HazWoper (1910.120(c)(5)(i)) requires that PPE shall be "provided and used during initial site entry which will provide protection to a level of exposure below permissible exposure limits and published exposure levels for known or suspected hazardous substances and health hazards. If the preliminary site evaluation does not produce sufficient information to identify the hazards or suspected hazards of the site, an ensemble providing equivalent to Level B PPE shall be provided as minimum protection, and direct reading instruments shall be used as appropriate for identifying immediately dangerous to life or health (IDLH) conditions."

OSHA requires that employers are responsible for ensuring that their employees have adequate respiratory protection. However, depending on the size and location of the disaster, DOH may be responsible for assessing initial safety and health practices at the site of the disaster and for providing the initial distribution of PPE. An appropriate respirator program involves medical screening, fit–testing and training. Training includes instructing the workers on how to wear, clean and maintain the respirators. Employees exposed to accidental chemical splashes, falling objects, flying particles, unknown atmospheres with inadequate oxygen or toxic gases, fires, live electrical wiring, or similar emergencies need PPE, including:

• Safety glasses, goggles, or face shields for eye protection;

• Properly selected and fitted respirators;

- Hard hats and safety shoes for head and foot protection;

- Whole body coverings (chemical suits, gloves, hoods and boots for protection from chemicals); and

- Body protection for abnormal environmental conditions such as extreme temperatures.

Effective emergency communication is vital. A system should be established to account for personnel once workers have been deployed or evacuated, with a person in the control center responsible for notifying police or emergency response team members of persons believed missing. Management should provide emergency alarms and ensure that workers know how to report emergencies within the response activities. Handout materials need to be developed that are simple to read. Key ideas can be listed on a card, such as site safety rules or the use of PPE. The card can be laminated so that it can be posted on equipment used in the rescue and/or recovery.

Finally, a mechanism is needed to monitor environmental exposures of the community and of response workers. The establishment of a worker injury and illness surveillance system will permit the generation of daily injury reports which can guide the modification of prevention measures and the types of PPE needed. More specific information is available in the Occupational Safety and Health Standards (*Title 29, Code of Federal Regulations, Part 1910*, which are the OSHA General Industry Standards).

AIR CONTAMINANTS

Many disasters result in potential exposure to airborne substances, such as smoke, dust, or other contaminants. The Environmental Protection Agency (EPA) has established standards about particulate exposures which direct public health actions. Those at increased risk from exposures to contaminants include pregnant women and their unborn children, children, the elderly, those with chronic conditions, such as heart disease and asthma, and workers. Table 32 shows the EPA particulate standards.

TABLE 32. EPA PARTICULATE STANDARDS

	INHALABLE PARTICLES	RESPIRABLE PARTICLES
	10 microns or less (PM$_{10}$)	2.5 microns or less (PM$_{2.5}$)
LEVEL OF CONCERN		40 ug/m^3 for PM$_{2.5}$ over a 24 hour period

Adapted from Claudio L, Garg A., and Landrigan PJ, "Addressing Environmental Health Issues" in Terrorism and Public Health (Levy BS and Sidel VW, eds.). New York: Oxford University Press, Inc., 2003, page 75.

Departments of Health (DOH) are responsible for monitoring the air immediately after the event occurs when there is a public health concern. DOH reviews the numerous air quality, debris sample and personal air monitoring tests that other agencies may perform. Sometimes federal agencies, such as the Agency for Toxic Substances and Disease Registry (ATSDR) or the Environmental Protection Agency (EPA) or the local Department of Environmental Protection will be involved in the study of air and/or dust samples. These samples will be compared to standards, such as indoor air quality standards, to determine potential health effects. Exposures following disasters can also be measured by outdoor air monitors. One example, Biowatch, the system to monitor biological releases, is discussed in Chapter 11.

Depending on the disaster, the community may need instruments that provide instantaneous readings because of the length of time it takes to get a laboratory analysis. Data should inform use of PPE and actions the community can take regarding reentering homes and or businesses. HazWoper provides guidance by requiring an ongoing air monitoring program for workers that should guide public health actions on air monitoring. Public health response should include monitoring the air with test equipment that permits direct reading for IDLH and other conditions that may cause death or serious harm (combustible or explosive atmospheres, oxygen deficiency, toxic substances.) NIOSH and CDC have developed guidance on the installation of filtration and air cleaning systems that can protect building environments from airborne agents. A full description is beyond the scope of this book, but more information is available through the publications included in the reference section.

Careful thought should go into communicating information about potential air contaminants to the public. (Discussed more fully in Chapter 6.) DOH should develop advisories that can be communicated both to the public and to rescue personnel on air quality issues and on practical information about the particular hazards posed by the disaster. Examples include the advisories that the New York City Health

Departments posted about using wet methods, such as wet mopping or high efficiency particulate vacuum, after the World Trade Center collapse.

RECOVERY AND HANDLING OF HUMAN REMAINS

When establishing a temporary mortuary, look for a secure building which has the capacity for a reception room, a viewing room, a place for storing bodies at 39 °F, and a room for records and storing personal effects. Mortuary personnel should wear gloves and protective clothing and wash thoroughly with a disinfectant soap. Mortuary supplies include stretchers, leather gloves, rubber gloves, overalls, boots, caps, soap, cotton cloth and disinfectants, property bags, body bags and labels, wheeled trolleys to transport bodies, and plastic sheeting for the floor. Disasters in the U.S. have used ice skating rinks where available to store remains and refrigerator trucks to transport them. When setting up a facility for the identification of bodies, the World Health Organization recommends 2187 yards for 1000 unidentified bodies.

When a disaster involves the recovery of human body parts, there is no threat of a general outbreak of infectious disease. Workers are at risk of infection if they cut themselves with an object contaminated with blood, body fluids or tissue, or if these materials touch the rescuers eyes, nose, mouth or areas of broken skin. Bad odors coming from decomposing bodies are not harmful.

Rescue workers who expect that they might have direct contact with human remains should be advised to:

- Wear heavy–duty waterproof gloves to protect against injury from sharp objects;

- Use eye protection and respirators equipped with OVAG (organic vapor, chlorine, hydrogen chloride, and sulfur dioxide) cartridges to protect eyes, nose, and mouth from splash exposures and noxious odors;

- Wear protective garments to protect skin and clothes;

- Immediately wash hands with soap and water after removing gloves; and

- Use alcohol–based hand sanitizers only when hands are not visibly soiled.

INTEGRATED PEST MANAGEMENT

Vector control is always important for the prevention of communicable disease but becomes even more important when there is the potential for increased spread of disease due to the break down in environmental controls following disaster. The most effective way to control vector–borne disease is to establish sanitary disposal of waste as soon as possible. Where vector–borne disease is known to be endemic, control programs should be accelerated in the post–impact phase of a disaster. The principles of integrated pest management are to eliminate breeding sites, to eliminate food, and to control harborage (where pests can live). A community vector–control program includes several components:

- Collect and dispose of garbage as soon as possible.

- Educate the public about rat and mosquito control.

- Eliminate mosquito breeding sites by overturning receptacles, covering swimming pools, and draining or covering other stagnant water sources.

- Reduce rat population and spread by closing up cracks in walls and bring cats to chase the rats.

- Store food in enclosed, protected areas.

In flooded areas, rats will search for dry places to hide. Rats and other vectors can feed off dead animals and other organic waste. Therefore, animal carcasses should be sprinkled with kerosene to protect them from predatory animals.

Chapter **9**

Mental Health Strategies

Most victims and workers in disasters respond normally to an abnormal situation. This chapter reviews the psychosocial affects of natural and technological disasters, the interventions needed by special populations (i.e., children, older adults, emergency workers), and the considerations of post–traumatic stress disorder. Building upon that foundation, the chapter lays out a plan for organizing mental health services, including assistance centers and patient locator systems.

PUBLIC HEALTH ROLE

- Help restore the psychological and social functioning of individuals and the community.

- Reduce the occurrence and severity of adverse mental health outcomes due to exposure to natural and technological disasters through prevention, assessment, and response.

- Help speed recovery and prevent long–term problems by providing information about normal reactions to disaster–related stress and how to handle these reactions.

- Provide practical, concrete services that address shelter, food, and employment issues.

- Coordinate with medical providers to assist in the identification and referral of those in their practices who could benefit from further mental health intervention.

- In communities where mental health services are organized separately from public health, assure that coordination occurs as part of community planning.

PSYCHOSOCIAL IMPACTS OF DISASTER

The long–term psychosocial effects of disasters are mitigated by understanding what is likely to occur and preplanning the management strategy. Living through the experience of a disaster can have profound psychosocial effects and can alter social structure. When planning a response to or delivering services in the aftermath of a disaster, public health professionals must consider the wide range of responses among victims and responders.

Disasters are very stressful, disruptive experiences that can be life–changing. However, human behavior in emergency situations generally adapts to meet immediate needs, with people behaving within their usual patterns pre– and post–disaster. The challenge of dealing with a disaster can also result in positive responses by both individuals and communities. Residents typically work together and support one another as they rebuild their lives and their communities. Residents of disaster–stricken areas tend to exhibit prosocial behaviors, are proactive in remediating the effects of the event, and are willing to help one another in their recovery. People generally provide assistance to one another and support those managing the response to the emergency. Volunteer activity increases at the time of the impact and continues throughout the post–impact period. Many disaster tasks are carried out spontaneously by civilian bystanders (i.e., family, friends, co–workers, neighbors) rather than trained emergency or relief personnel.

In terms of morbidity, the social and psychosocial impacts of a disaster can greatly exceed physical injuries. The social and psychosocial effects of disasters can last months, years, or an entire lifetime. People who are involved in disasters, as either victim or responder, may experience a wide variety of stress symptoms. These symptoms can have the broadest range of emotional, physical, cognitive, and interpersonal effects. In some disaster situations, victims recover quickly without long–lasting effects. In others, victims and responders suffer major mental health problems both immediately and for years after the event. They may have lost loved ones, need to adjust to new role changes, need to clean and repair property, or need to move from their home and neighborhood.

Both victims and responders experience a disaster as a crisis. Unusual events exacerbate the trauma, as there may be deaths of family or friends, injuries, job difficulties, illness, loss of personal belongings, and disruption of the regular routine. Initially, people feel numbness rather panic. Those who experience a disaster want to talk about it with everyone who will listen. Victims may exhibit anger toward "the system," such as a perceived slow response by responding agencies. In time, everyone attempts to return to a normal routine, but delays in normalcy delay emotional recovery.

Normal Reaction to Abnormal Situations

In general, the transient reactions that people experience after a disaster, such as grief and stress reactions, represent a normal response to a highly abnormal situation. Victims of a disaster should be viewed as normal persons, capable of functioning effectively, who have been subjected to severe stress and may be showing signs of emotional strain. Mild to moderate stress reactions during the emergency and in the early post–impact phases of a disaster are highly prevalent among survivors, families, community members, and rescue workers. While some individuals may exhibit symptoms of extreme stress, these reactions generally do not lead to chronic problems. However, public health professionals should not ignore common stress reactions. Counselors can help speed recovery and prevent long–term problems by providing information about normal reactions and educating victims about ways to handle these reactions.

A portion of the population will suffer more serious, persistent symptoms. While most individuals exposed to traumatic events and disasters recover and do not suffer prolonged psychiatric illness, some exhibit behavioral change or develop physical or psychiatric illness. Troublesome reactions can result from exposure to both natural and technological disasters and can include depression, alcohol abuse, anxiety, somatization, domestic violence, difficulties in daily functioning, and post–traumatic stress disorder (PTSD). While less serious, insomnia and anxiety may also be experienced by disaster victims and workers.

Mental Health Morbidity and Mortality

Adults and children manifest symptoms of distress differently. Disasters can have emotional, cognitive, physical, and interpersonal effects. For adults, the initial emotional response is usually shock and disbelief. This lasts from a few minutes to a few hours. Behavior is dazed or stunned. For the next several days, victims are willing to follow directions and are grateful for assistance. They may fell guilty for surviving.

In the next several weeks, victims will likely seek out others who were affected and participate in group activities of recovery. This activity is often followed by despair and depression. Victims can experience flashbacks, anger, emotional numbing, or a dissociation, perceiving their experience as "dreamlike." Cognitive effects can include impaired memory, concentration, and decision–making ability. Interpersonal relationships can become strained. Some victims worry about their futures and blame themselves.

Long term, there is a risk of decreased self–esteem and self–sufficiency. Some victims experience intrusive thoughts and memories. Physical effects can include sleep disturbances leading to insomnia and fatigue. Some victims and responders experience hyperarousal or a startle response. There can be somatic complaints such as headaches, gastrointestinal problems, reduced appetite, and decreased libido. Finally, disasters can have profound and widespread interpersonal effects such as alienation, social withdrawal, increased conflict within relationships, and both vocational and school impairment.

Symptoms of Distress

Those most at risk for psychosocial impacts are children, older adults, people with serious mental illness, families of people who die in a disaster, and special needs groups. Different age groups are vulnerable to stress in different ways. Most people do not see themselves as needing mental health services following disaster and will not voluntarily seek out such services.

Children

Although a disaster affects everyone in the community, children are a particularly vulnerable group and require special attention and programs. Helping children will likely involve working closely with teachers and schools. The goal for those intervening with children is to help them integrate the experience and to reestablish a sense of security and mastery. Children who are most at risk are those who have lost family members or friends, who had a previous experience with a disaster, or who have preexisting family or individual crises. Children may not be able to describe their fears, which are a normal reaction stimulated by real events. Fear can outlast the event and can persist even if no physical injury occurred. Exposure to repeated media coverage can increase and prolong symptoms.

Preschool children needing extra help may appear withdrawn or depressed, or they may not respond to directed attention or to attempts to "draw them out." They may exhibit thumb–sucking, bedwetting, fears of darkness or animals, clinging to parents, night terrors, incontinence or constipation, speech difficulties, or changes in appetite. Preschoolers are vulnerable to disruptions in their environment, are affected by the reactions of their family, and are disoriented by changes to their regular schedule. Quickly re–establishing their regular schedule for eating, playing and going to bed is important. Other interventions to help preschoolers include reenactment of the events in play (i.e., with fire trucks, dump trucks, ambulances) non–verbal activities such as drawing, and games that involve touching (i.e., ring around the rosie, London bridge, duck–duck–goose). Verbal reassurance, physical comforting, frequent attention, expressions regarding loss of pets or toys, and sleeping in the same room as their parents may be helpful as well.

Children aged 5 to 11 years may exhibit irritability, whining, clinging, aggressive behavior, competition for parent's attention, night terrors or nightmares, fears of darkness, withdrawal from peers, and avoidance, disinterest, or poor concentration in school. Interventions for this age group include patience and tolerance, play sessions with adults and peers, discussions with adults and peers, relaxed expectations, structured free time with activities, and rehearsal of safety measures for the future.

Children aged 11 to 14 years can experience sleep disturbances, changes in appetite, rebellion at home, physical complaints, and problems with or less interest in school activities. At this age, children may benefit from encouraging the resumption of normal routines, organizing groups with peers, engaging in group discussions about the disaster, relaxing expectations temporarily, taking on structured responsibilities, and receiving additional attention as needed.

Children aged 14 to 18 years may exhibit psychosomatic symptoms, disturbances of sleep and appetite, hypochondriasis, changes in energy level, apathy, decline in interest in opposite sex, irresponsible or delinquent behavior, fewer struggles for emancipation from parents, and poor concentration. Junior and high school age children may become disoriented (i.e., to name, town or date), despondent, agitated, restless, severely depressed and withdrawn, unable to make simple decisions, and unable to carry out daily activities. These children may also pace, appear pressured, hallucinate, become preoccupied with one idea or thought, engage in self–mutilation, abuse drugs or alcohol, experience significant memory gaps, and become delusional or suicidal. Interventions include encouraging participation in community reclamation, resumption of social activities, discussion of experience with peers, reducing expectations temporarily, and discussion of experience with family. Adolescent activities should end on a positive note, such as talk of heroic acts, helping the community, and preparing for the next time. Small groups could develop a plan to help the community rehabilitate.

Older Adults

Older adults are in the highest risk group following a disaster. Generally, older adults have fewer support networks, limited mobility, or pre–existing illness. In addition, disasters can trigger memories of other traumas experienced earlier in life. Older persons worry about their deteriorating health and needing to be institutionalized and as a result may conceal the full extent of their physical problems. Research has shown that this population experiences a higher proportion of personal injury or loss because they often live in places more vulnerable to damage. Since they experience a greater loss of mobility, their independence and self–sufficiency are damaged because they are less able to rebuild their homes, businesses, and other losses due to disaster.

Responders

Those whose job is to respond to disasters have physically demanding work that is tiring, may interrupt sleep patterns, and may expose them to hazards which are life threatening or have potential long term health risks. Response tasks, such as search and rescue, expose them to mutilated bodies and mass destruction. Their role as a help provider is also very stressful. Some responders experience similar feelings to those experienced by the victims. They can be irritable, finding fault with things that never bothered them before. They can be suspicious and resent authority. They can be concerned for their own safety and the safety of their children. Responders can be stressed by their working environment, particularly in the presence of understaffing of their units, being overworked, and conflicts with other professionals. Responders may face anxiety about their competence, are more affected by the impact of the sights and smells, and can also struggle to balance family responsibilities and work demands in the face of an emergency.

Some responders may develop a condition known as critical incident stress. This syndrome must be recognized and treated because critical incident stress lowers group morale, increases absenteeism, interferes with mutual support, and adversely affects home life. The symptoms include deterioration in sense of well–being, exhaustion, depression, hostility, lost tolerance for victims, dread of new encounters, guilt, helplessness, or isolation. "Burn out" is often recognized by looking for detachment or overinvolvement.

POST–TRAUMATIC STRESS DISORDER

Post–traumatic stress disorder (PTSD) is a prolonged stress response associated with impairment and dysfunction. PTSD usually appears within three months of the trauma but may surface months or years later. The duration of the disorder varies. Sometimes the symptoms of PTSD disappear over time, and sometimes PTSD persists for many years. The seven factors which increase the likelihood of developing PTSD include being a young child, being a female, lacking social supports, having a history of psychiatric disorder, having previously experienced a traumatic event, experiencing a panic attack at the time of the event, and experiencing stressful events subsequent to the event.

While PTSD has been the subject of considerable research in recent years, other serious problems that can develop after a disaster include acute stress disorder, major depression, generalized anxiety disorder, and substance abuse. Acute stress disorder is characterized by post–traumatic stress symptoms lasting at least two days but not longer than one month following the trauma.

Criteria for PTSD[1]

A diagnosis of PTSD, as listed in the Diagnostic and Statistical Manual of Mental Disorders (DSM–IV), requires that several criteria be met. PTSD symptoms can be acute, chronic, or delayed in their onset.

The first criterion relates to the nature of the traumatic event and the response it evokes:

> The person has been exposed to a traumatic event in which both of the following were present: (1) the person experienced, witnessed, or [has] been confronted with an event or events that involved actual or threatened death or serious injury, or a threat to the physical integrity of self or others ... [and] (2) the person's response involved intense fear, helplessness or horror ... (p. 209)

The second criterion relates to the *reexperiencing* of the traumatic event:

> The traumatic event is persistently reexperienced in one (or more) of the following ways: (1) recurrent and intrusive distressing recollections of the event ... (2) recurrent distressing dreams of the event ... (3) acting or feeling as if the traumatic event were recurring ... (4) intense psychological distress at exposure to internal or external cues that symbolize or resemble an aspect of the traumatic event; (5) physiological reactivity on exposure to internal or external cures that symbolize or resemble an aspect of the traumatic event. (p. 209–210)

The third criterion relates to *avoidance,* that is, the person avoiding things that remind him or her of the traumatic event:

> Persistent avoidance of stimuli associated with the trauma and numbing of general responsiveness (not present before the trauma), as indicated by three (or more) of the following: (1) efforts to avoid thoughts, feelings or conversations associated with the trauma; (2) efforts to avoid activities, places or people that arouse recollections of the trauma; (3) inability to recall an important aspect of the trauma; (4) markedly diminished interest or participation in significant activities; (5) feeling of detachment or estrangement from others; (6) restricted range

---

[1]Diagnostic Criteria from DSM-IV. Washington, D.C. American Psychiatric Association, 1994:209-211

of affect (e.g. unable to have love feelings); (7) sense of a fore-shortened future ... (p. 211)

The fourth criterion relates to the person experiencing increased *arousal* after the traumatic event:

> Persistent symptoms of increased arousal (not present before the trauma), as indicated by two (or more) of the following: (1) difficulty falling asleep; (2) irritability or outbursts of anger; (3) difficulty concentrating; (4) hypervigilance; (5) exaggerated startle response. (p. 211)

The fifth criterion relates to the duration of the symptoms just described. In particular, for a diagnosis of PTSD to be made, the duration of the symptoms in the second, third, and fourth criteria must exceed one month.

Finally, the disturbance must cause "clinically significant distress or impairment in social, occupational or other important areas of functioning."

PTSD Risk Factors/Predictors

Several factors can help predict which individuals might be at risk for PTSD. The nature or severity of the trauma the person has experienced plays a major role. Higher risk scenarios potentially leading to long–term adjustment problems include exposure to life–threatening situations, having a loved one die, loss of home and belongings, exposure to toxic contamination, and exposure to terror, horror, or grotesque sights, such as multiple casualties. Additional risk factors relate to life events before the disaster. A history of prior exposure to trauma, concurrent stressful life events, and lack of social support all predispose to PTSD.

Family members of trauma victims and family members of disaster workers may also develop PTSD and related symptoms. Spouses and significant others should be included in debriefing, education programs, and treatment programs as indicated.

Ethnocultural Issues in PTSD

Rates of PTSD or other disaster–related impairment can differ among groups of different race or ethnicity due to culturally varying perceptions of what constitutes a traumatic experience as well as individual and social responses to trauma. PTSD has been detected in traumatized cohorts from very different ethnocultural backgrounds, and refugees from non–Western cultures who meet PTSD diagnostic criteria have shown a similar clinical course and response to treatment as have Euro–American individuals. Assessments of the stress reaction of non–Western individuals should be carried out in a culturally sensitive manner, accounting for factors that may be unknown. Major depression, generalized anxiety disorder, and substance abuse are well documented after exposure to trauma and disasters.

NATURAL DISASTERS AND TECHNOLOGICAL DISASTERS

The similarities and differences between human–made and natural disasters are the degree to which the events are felt to be preventable and controllable. The two types of disasters have in common the immediate threat and the potential for ongoing disruption. However, they differ with regard to whether someone can be "blamed" for the event and whether it could have been prevented. People understand that man has little control over nature and that some geographic locations are more prone to some natural disasters than others. In contrast, they believe people can control technology and thus feel a greater sense of a loss of control with technological events, since these events could have been prevented.

Residents who are victimized by technological disasters may have their stress exacerbated by knowing that their tragedy was caused by other human beings. Technological disasters of the same magnitude as natural disasters generally cause more severe mental health problems because it is harder in the former to achieve psychological resolution and to move on.

For several reasons, technological disasters present complex challenges for public health professionals. First, unlike the community cohesiveness that occurs after natural disasters, communities are often in conflict after an environmental disaster. Where the disaster involves contaminants, which are usually invisible, great uncertainty often exists as to exposure. Contaminants may not have dispersed evenly, resulting in very different perceptions of the events by people living in the same community. Victims of technological disasters often feel a great deal of uncertainty about the risks of exposure and the long–term risks. Because of this ambiguity and uncertainty, neighbors can become bitterly divided, and their support networks may be irreversibly damaged. Worse, residents of affected communities can be stigmatized by society due to the unknown risks of their exposure.

Technological disasters often cause chronic uncertainty and distress. Unlike natural disasters, which generally have a low point after which things can be expected to improve, in disasters involving chemicals and radiation, those affected often do not know when all of the recovery activities will resolve. Uncertainty continues about the chronic health effects of exposure to invisible contaminants. Furthermore, long–term consequences, such as cancer, may take years to develop. Events that have a beginning and an end, such as tornadoes or hurricanes, allow for a process of recovery. Technological disasters do not have this defined timeline, and as a result, the psychological threat can be continual and chronic.

Following a technological disaster, psycho–physiological symptoms are prevalent, along with chronic stress and demoralization. Exposure to chemicals often does not result in a large number of exposed seeking immediate medical treatment. Here concerns are long term. Psychological effects may result from either direct exposure or reaction to mitigation activities. Information about the level of exposure or contamination may not be available for some time. Loss of social support and status can cause stress, especially if evacuation is required. These symptoms can manifest as physical complaints, can lead to increased morbidity of chronic diseases, such as hypertension, and can lead to attributing medical problems acquired later in life to the earlier exposure. Groups at high risk for psychological health effects from environmental exposures include older persons living alone, mothers with young children, evacuees, responders, and persons with previous mental disorders. Table 33 describes causes of stress following major environmental exposures.

TABLE 33. CAUSES OF ENVIRONMENTAL EXPOSURE STRESS [2]

- acute stress reaction
- worry about long term health effects
- uncertainty about long term effects
- housing and job security
- media siege
- somatic complaints
- stigma and social rejection
- cultural pressures
- inadequate medical follow–up and compensation

[2]Adapted from Baxter, PJ "Public Health Aspects of Chemical Castastrophes" in Hevenaar JM et al (eds.) *Toxic Tumoil: Psychological and Societal Consequences of Ecological Disasters,* (2002) Kluwer Academic/Plenum Publishers, New York

ORGANIZING BEHAVIORAL DISASTER SERVICES

Section 416 of The Robert T. Stafford Disaster Relief and Emergency Assistance Act of 1988 (Public Law 100–707) establishes legislative authority for the President to provide training and services to alleviate mental health problems caused or exacerbated by major disasters. The Act reads as follows:

> "Crisis Counseling Assistance and Training. The President is authorized to provide professional counseling services, including financial assistance to State or local agencies or private mental health organizations to provide such services or training of disaster workers, to survivors/victims of major disaster in order to relieve mental health problems caused or aggravated by such major disaster or its aftermath."

Federally, the Crisis Counseling Assistance and Training Program (commonly referred to as the Crisis Counseling Program) is managed by the Federal Emergency Management Agency (FEMA) in cooperation with the Center for Mental Health Services (CMHS). Their "Training Manual for Mental Health and Human Service Workers in Major Disasters" is available at [http://www.mentalhealth.org/publications/allpubs/ADM90–538/tmpreface.asp] and should be used as a guide for establishing community programs and training personnel.

ORGANIZING MENTAL HEALTH DISASTER SERVICES

What Services are Needed

The organization for and delivery of mental health services should be part of a community's overall disaster plan to avoid the difficult task of recruiting and orienting masses of volunteers in the chaos immediately following a disaster. Before developing the community plan for behavioral services, it is useful to consider the range and types of services that might be required. Table 34 describes the types of behavioral services that are likely to be required in a major disaster. While the services needed may vary with the nature of the event, such as type of disaster, severity, and time of year, in previous events a pattern of social and counseling services have been required.

TABLE 34. COMMUNITY BEHAVIORAL SERVICES NEEDED FOLLOWING A DISASTER

Adult, adolescent and child services
Assessments, crisis interventions, evaluations and referrals
Bereavement counseling
Business counseling
Crisis counseling
Debriefing groups for healthcare and emergency workers
Drop-in crisis counseling
Emergency services in medical emergency departments
Family support center
Individual and group counseling
Mobile mental health crisis teams
Multi–disciplinary services to designated community sites (police precincts, fire departments, temporary business locations)
Multi–lingual services
Outpatient mental health services and counseling
On–going support groups
Outreach to schools for students, parents and teachers
Outpatient services
School presentations
Short–term treatment
Telephone triage
24 hour emergency psychiatric service
24 hour crisis hotline
Walk–in services
Weekly support groups

SURVEY OF EXISTING SERVICES

With the potential needs understood, a community can map those against the resources available to determine whether a community can handle these extra services or whether additional capacity is needed. The mental health community should gather a compendium of available resources, including experts in critical areas (i.e., post–traumatic stress disorder, children's mental health, death and dying, etc.), and identify where gaps exist. The list should include the credentials and emergency contact information for the available resources, the location of specialized treatment and outreach services in the community (i.e., employee assistance programs, housing, restoration of utilities, etc.), and be updated regularly.

STAFFING

With the increased interest and training that has been initiated in every mental health discipline since the 2001 attack on the World Trade Center, it is likely that larger communities can bring together a sufficient cadre of local mental health responders. It is advantageous, where possible, to establish a core of trained and credentialed professionals from the providers within a community. The advantage of using local providers is that they are knowledgeable about and work with local resources, local customs, existing organizations and support networks on a daily basis. In the initial stages, victims are interested in getting relief for practical, concrete problems, such as loss of shelter or business interruptions and volunteers from outside the community may not have information to match the local resources with the need. Further, in a major disaster, it will be an additional strain to divert staff to train out of town volunteers about the community.

However, where there are identified service gaps in a community and when the need exceeds the capacity, the mental health community may need to expand its capacity because of an anticipated surge in those needing both short term and long term services. The number of mental health professionals needed will vary by existing resources. Further, in the weeks and months during recovery, when volunteers have gone, programs need to be instituted for those individuals who need long term mental health intervention.

The needs assessment for determining the number of mental health providers required should look at the demographics of the community, the magnitude and scope of the disaster, the potential number of "communities" effected and the number of individuals within those "communities," the cultural issues of those communities, and the potential mental health resources available. Deployment of mental health staff will depend on the number of people affected and the circumstances of the event, but as a guide, communities have previously activated 40 mental health professionals per 250 victims.

When mental health resources from outside the community are likely to be required, advance planning should be done. Agency managers should establish memorandums of understanding (MOUs) with other organizations which address use of multi–agency providers and community providers, roles and boundaries of each agency, plans for deployment and delivery of service by type of service, and establishment of a chain of command for psychosocial and mental health services following a disaster. When developing these MOUs, coordination with the state or local office of emergency management is needed to ensure that your plan conforms with the community's broader emergency management plans. Finally, reimbursement for delivering mental health services will likely be funded through a federal contract with the state department of mental health, who in turn will contract with the local department who will contract with local agencies.

Immediately after a disaster impacts there is often an infusion of volunteer professionals from outside the community offering their help. The registration and orientation of the mental health volunteers who arrive from outside the impacted region is a time consuming task. A mechanism for incorporating and credentialing these volunteer providers should be worked out in advance with local mental health agencies and the various responding organizations.

Community emergency response plans provide for the American Red Cross (ARC) to deliver disaster services. If response to a significant disaster is projected to exceed resources, the local ARC chapter alerts the state ARC chapter, which alerts the national system. The national ARC determines if the response will be regional or national. When the ARC gets activated, it issues a call to respond to all chapters in that area. While the ARC views all disasters as local, with municipal or county governments initiating response, in large scale disasters, activation may start before any official call is made. When the ARC mental health unit is activated, the local Department of Mental Health is responsible for coordinating services delivered, though there will be close coordination with the ARC.

Mental health volunteers through the ARC are all credentialed/licensed professionals in the states in which they practice. Each chapter of the ARC is responsible for verifying the background of mental health volunteers, including receiving a copy of their professional license. These volunteers are trained in a 2 day, 16 hour course to provide three types of services: crisis intervention with clients, and modified defusing and debriefing for response workers. Another national non–profit organization which identifies psychiatrists and credentials them before they arrive is Disaster Psychiatry Outreach.

DEATH NOTIFICATION

In broad reaching disasters with many deaths, it is important to establish protocols in advance so that the coordination is smooth. Legally, notification of death is the task of the medical examiner who may extend that to the local law enforcement. The ARC prefers that mental health professionals from the community sit with law enforcement when they speak to families about the death of loved ones. Mental health coordination with local law enforcement should outline how the two disciplines will work together as loved ones file missing persons reports, review death lists and engage in DNA collection.

STAFF TRAINING

As part of the management plan for assessment, referral and treatment, social service agencies should provide general information (such as fact sheets, resource people, etc.) to all staff members. These documents can also be distributed to the public at the reception desk, waiting rooms, cafeteria, etc. They should provide behavioral health facts to the media spokespersons so that they can educate the community about issues related to grief and loss and explain the role of the behavioral response within the emergency. They should plan for the establishment of a toll–free hotline for the community including 24–hour 7 day coverage. Coordination with other behavioral health providers in the community (including hospitals, community mental health centers, youth services organizations, group homes, etc.) should be part of the plan. The mental health services plan must ensure that culturally competent providers will be available to meet the needs of their community both in the crisis period immediately after the disaster and in the months and years that follow. Finally, provisions should include a transition period for the staff and agencies involved in delivering services, as these individuals will personally need time to re–energize and recover from their experience before they can go back to "business as usual."

If your community does not have an advance plan for providing behavioral services, when determining whether to establish mental health and psychosocial services, seven criteria have been suggested[3] for determining the need to develop these services. These criteria include:

- The role of epidemiology and community concerns in determining the prevalence of health and mental health problems;

- Predictability, rapidity of onset, duration of the crisis, and severity of the problems;

- Adequacy of resources;

- Sustainability;

[3]Speckard A. "Voices from the Inside: Psychological Response from Toxic Disasters" in Hevenaar JM et al (eds.) *Toxic Turmoil: Psychological and Societal Consequences of Ecological Disasters*, (2002) Kluwer Academic/Plenum Publishers, New York.

- Political and ethical acceptability;

- Cultural sensitivity; and

- Effectiveness.

Table 35 summarizes the steps in establishing disaster mental health services.

TABLE 35. ESTABLISHING DISASTER MENTAL HEALTH SERVICES

- Establish a Disaster Mental Health Preparedness Committee whose membership represents administrative, environmental, allied mental health, and community agency interests.
- Establish an emergency management organization schematic.
- Establish objectives of disaster mental health services, including definition of roles and responsibilities.
- Establish procedures for emergency response.
- Incorporate procedures into community's disaster plan.
- Develop memorandums of understanding between your organization and other key agencies within the community (e.g., Red Cross, community agencies, medical examiner and law enforcement).
- Train mental health staff in disaster mental health plan, roles, and responsibilities.
- Prepare educational materials pre–assembled for distribution.
- Schedule regular mock exercises with outside review.
- Regularly review and update Emergency Plan, including evaluation of resources and potential impediments to implementation.

Adapted from Disaster Mental Health Services: A Guidebook for Clinicians and Administrators, Department of Veterans Affairs, June, 1997.

SETTING UP FAMILY ASSISTANCE CENTERS

In far–reaching disasters, one of the first activities is the establishment of a central place where victims, families, and loved ones can go for relief. Communities might consider establishing two distinct assistance centers: one for the victims, their families and friends, and one for the responders and caregivers. These centers are multi–purpose, established to meet the needs of a broad group of people, and are intended to bring all of the agencies or services, that a family needs to deal with, to one location. As part of a community's disaster plan, two elements should be identified in advance—location and adequate space and personnel.

The pre-identification of a location and adequate space is essential so that these centers do not have to be relocated once they are open. Sufficient space is needed for all of the functions and private space must be carefully thought out to minimize retraumatization in events where families have to identify the bodies of loved ones. Table 36 describes the type of services that might be provided at a victim assistance center.

TABLE 36. SERVICES PROVIDED AT FAMILY ASSISTANCE CENTERS

Child care
Crisis counseling
Death certificate processing
Disaster Medicaid
Distribution of gifts and donations received
Emergency financial assistance
Employment assistance
Food stamps
Follow–up phone calls to recipients of crisis counseling
Housing assistance
Immigration services
Legal assistance
Meals for victims, families, responders and caregivers
Medication assessments
Phone banks
Relief application assistance through FEMA
Small Business Association (SBA) loans
Stress management for relief workers
Training for FEMA interpreters
Workmen's compensation

The organization of the space must accommodate desks or areas where each of these activities can occur. Dedicated areas should be designated where private conversations can occur and where a drop in center, much like a surgical waiting room, can be an environment for social support. Locate the child care center away from places where there might be strong emotional reactions. The assistance centers can provide ample food and drink to the families and staff who use them, since families needing multiple services may spend many hours at the center. Decisions of staffing should consider how many shifts and how many people will simultaneously be served at each agency table. At the Family Assistance Center set up following the 2001 World Trade Center collapse, the assignment of mental health staff ranged from 8–30 per shift.

Following disasters where there has been a great loss of life, some family members may want to come to the center repeatedly while others may not. To help those who prefer less contact, when establishing the registration process, try to identify all of the things that families would need to bring to register a missing family member. This list for registration should include the legal documentation, such as birth certificate, driver's license, social security card, marriage license, and sources of scientific information used for DNA testing when such is necessary. Expect variability in family reactions, family behavior, and how much and what families "hear."

Especially following disasters where a prolonged search and rescue operation is necessary, the assistance center for responders and caregivers will provide food and drink, showers, sleeping cots, changing rooms and debriefing areas. These should be located in close proximity to where the disaster occurred while the victim/family assistance center should be located in a different, more distant part of the community.

The second component is the designation of personnel (by title and organization) who will serve as the administrators of this center, once it is opened. An advance agreement on leadership is essential to avoid spending time establishing the management scheme while you are trying to set up the assistance centers.

In planning for the establishment of assistance centers, it is useful to consider who the users will be. In planning for the delivery of services, it is important to have pre–established protocols for the delivery of basic crisis intervention, for medical intervention (i.e., prescriptions), for making referrals to psychiatry for prescriptions, and for providing services to those waiting in line needing immediate attention. Table 37 lists the types of individuals who may use these centers.

TABLE 37. TYPES OF INDIVIDUALS USING ASSISTANCE CENTERS

Family members of the deceased
Those displaced from or lost housing
Workers who lost jobs
Those whose business was interrupted
People who experienced prior trauma, have pre–existing mental health or have substance
   abuse conditions
Those who lost financial and social supports
Responders and other caregivers

PATIENT LOCATOR SYSTEM

After a disaster resulting in many injuries and deaths, the most pressing mental health needs are family and friends knowing what happened to their loved ones and employers wanting to track their employees. When phones do not work, the ability to contact hospitals is impeded. Even if loved ones can connect, hospital operators only have the names of those admitted to their facility. In incidents such as these, the need for a patient locator system is paramount. While people want to know the information immediately, it may take several days to get the system running if it is not in place in advance. If no pre–existing system is in place, hospitals will likely fax their emergency department (ED) logs to a central collection point and someone, such as volunteers, will need to sort through the logs and organize a database. Importantly, there will be numerous legal hurdles to overcome, because of privacy concerns.

To establish a patient locator system in advance, several steps are necessary. Create a website or placeholder on a website of a central authority, such as the State Department of Health. Every hospital should be able to log in and using the PHIN messaging standards securely upload patient information to create a database searchable by match. Reportable information should include the patients who present at each emergency department (ED), including unidentified patients and those who come into a burn unit and cannot speak. The data from the ED may not be precise, so it is better to include the name of every one of the hospital's patients and their age, and sort though the list later. Each list should identify the hospital and provide contact information. In time, the list will get "cleaned" as names of patients whose visits were unrelated to the disaster will be removed. To ensure patient privacy, those using the list should be permitted to search by typing in a name and look for a match, rather than scrolling through names. The plan for the patient locator system should include daily printing and posting of the identified list at the family assistance center(s). Part of the system should include training of hospital switchboards on how the system is set up and how to provide information about patients who were treated and released, within the guidelines of HIPAA.

PUBLIC HEALTH INTERVENTION

Natural

Psychosocial services strongly emphasize the principle of prevention using a multifaceted, multilevel approach aimed at helping individuals, groups, and the community as a whole. Most of the early work will be the provision of concrete services to normal people under stress, such as information about available services, how to get insurance benefits or loans, assistance with applications at government agencies, health care, child care, transportation, and other routine needs. Public health workers should initiate counseling as a preventive measure and encourage open communication. Some of the most important ways of helping may be in simply listening, providing a ready ear, and indicating interest or concern.

If evacuation is required, responders should keep families together and try to keep support systems intact. Workers can also help in the rebuilding of support networks as quickly as possible. During the short– and long–term recovery phases, public health and human service professionals must go to community sites where survivors are involved in the activities of their daily lives. Such places include neighborhoods, schools, shelters, disaster application centers, meal sites, hospitals, churches, community centers, and other central locations. Among the services typically provided after disaster are telephone helplines, information and referral services, literature on the emotional effects of disaster, facilitation of self–help, support groups, crisis counseling, public education through the media, information sessions for community groups, grief support services, and advocacy services. Mental health workers are important members of the teams who help workers cope with the recovery and identification of dead bodies and who communicates positive identification to families and significant others.

Encouraging parents to reduce their children's exposure to the media is important as is encouraging them to talk. In addition, it is important to reach out not only to those directly involved, but those with indirect exposure (having a friend who knew someone killed or injured). Further, it is important to ensure that trauma and grief counseling interventions are included in a community's disaster plan.

Technological

There is evidence to suggest that the most advantageous intervention with communities exposed to a technological disaster is to establish open communication with the community. Because of the potential spread in environmental disasters, planning should be regional. It is important to establish cooperation among public health, medical community, media, and advocacy groups as part of everyday practice around environmental issues so that if a technological disaster strikes your community, good working relationships are already in place. Part of the plan should include the training of service workers so they have a basic understanding of the technical aspects of environmental contamination, and the needs of the community in these complex situations.

Interdisciplinary cooperation is needed among psychologists, social workers, and educators. Just as in natural disaster, initial programs should offer practical assistance with concrete services— advice, shelter, clothing, referral to medical care/evaluation, etc. The community will need a broad range of social needs—family counseling, support groups, day care, play therapy, information services, and health education. Immediately after the incident or release, provide accurate health information, assure the availability of physical exams, provide supportive counseling, and prepare specialized materials to help the entire community understand and deal with the situation.

Throughout the disaster relief effort, several general management strategies should be followed:

- Show clear decision–making in actions so victims feel that the designated leaders are active in the response.

- Issue warnings with instructions of specific actions to take.

- Plan ahead for necessary resources, with call–up procedures in place.

- Tailor activities and services provided in the aftermath of disaster to the community being served and involve them in the development and delivery of services.

- Target psychosocial services toward "normal" people responding normally to an abnormal situation.

- Identify persons at risk for severe psychological or social impairment due to their experience of the disaster.

Chapter 10

Disasters and People with Disabilities

The elderly and persons with disabilities require dedicated attention to assure that their needs are met during community emergencies. This chapter defines the members of the community needing special assistance, recommends the establishment of a disaster planning council, and describes training of response personnel and community preparedness, personal preparedness for these individuals, shelter preparedness, communications, building preparedness, and emergency health information.

PUBLIC HEALTH ROLE

- Assure that community preparedness plans accommodate the needs of the disabled and elderly.

- Educate the community about actions that can be taken to protect the disabled and elderly in times of emergency.

- Coordinate disability–specific preparedness efforts in health care delivery sites, shelters and distribution centers.

WHO IS THE DISABLED COMMUNITY?

The National Organization on Disability defines individuals with disabilities as persons who have a physical and/or mental impairment that limits their major life activities, or who have an ongoing or chronic physical or mental condition, or are regarded by the community as disabled even without such a condition. Further, the group who may require special assistance is even larger if we include the growing number of elderly in the U.S.

According to the 2000 U.S. Census, 54 million Americans (about 20 percent of the total population) have a disability, including 4 million people who require assistance with dressing, eating or bathing, 8 million with limited vision of which 130,000 are totally blind, 28 million Americans with hearing loss of which 500,000 are completely deaf, 4 million who require the use of canes or walkers, and 1.5 million who use a wheelchair. Further, there are over 4,000 adult day care centers in the U.S. and about 800,000 people live in assisted living facilities. These statistics may not account for the segment of the population with chronic illnesses that would inhibit the ability to function in a disaster situation and are aggravated by the loss of medications, loss of access to care, and the secondary impacts resulting from loss of power, (i.e., non–functioning nebulizers, oxygen therapy, suction devices, etc), increasing the potential number of those needing special assistance.

Preparedness for disasters should include specific safeguards to ensure the safety of this segment of the population both in the workplace and in the community. The Americans with Disabilities Act of 1990 (ADA, Public Law 101–336 enacted on July 26th, 1990) mandates "reasonable accommodation" or assuring the same level of safety and utility for people with disabilities and other limitations as that provided to the entire population. The ADA provides a process to determine if individuals with disabilities have been discriminated against or denied services because of their disability, including the emergency preparedness activities of a community. The process involves a complaint filed with the U.S. Department of Justice, followed by an investigation, mediation, litigation and/or suit.

The ADA Accessibility Guidelines (ADAAG), which primarily cover new construction and alterations, include specifications for accessible means of egress (ADAAG 41.3(9), 4.3.10), emergency alarms (ADAAG 4.1.3(14), (4.28), and signage (ADAAG 4.1.3(16), 4.30). State and local governments have additional ADA requirements, including the provision of auxiliary aids and services, the acquisition or modification of equipment or devices, appropriate adjustment or modification of training materials or policies, the provision of qualified readers or interpreters, and other similar accommodations. In addition, 47 C.F.R. Section 79.2 obliges distributors of video programming to make emergency information accessible to people with hearing disabilities or vision loss.

DISASTER PLANNING COUNCILS FOR INDIVIDUALS WITH DISABILITIES

Ideally, planning for individuals with disabilities occurs at both the mega–community and the micro–building level. As part of community planning, one strategy is to organize a disaster planning council for the disabled. In coordination with emergency management, public health can reach out to the organizations which represent the breadth of individuals with disabilities. The planning group should identify what is needed during a disaster, what strategies can be used to address those needs, and which agency, or group will be responsible for providing which services to those with disabilities. Planning groups for the disabled should always include persons for whom the equipment and procedures are intended to ensure both that the solutions will work and to provide confidence to those who need them that they will be protected. Effective planning requires the utilization of multiple methods as the needs of those with disabilities are both broad and varied. Further, an important part of the task is to inform the groups of individuals with disabilities about the community's specific disaster plans to assist them.

Disaster planning councils should include governmental agencies, community providers, community based organizations (CBOs), advocacy groups, and the local affiliate of national disability organizations, where available. Disaster planning councils should be an essential part of a community's emergency response network, ensuring that the segment of the disability population that the CBOs serve is prepared. When forming the council, locate disability leaders in the community who will know the issues and the agencies that should be included. These leaders, often known as advocates, can help identify both the groups that represent their community and the organizations which represent the interests of more than one disability area. Table 38 lists examples of the groups which vary by locale and by region of the country. Because different organizations may have different names in each community, public health can work with an umbrella organization such as the United Way to identify which disability related groups are present and active in your locale.

TABLE 38: POTENTIAL MEMBERS OF A PLANNING COUNCIL FOR INDIVIDIALS WITH DISABILITIES

Government Agencies	Mayor's office or County Executive; Committee on People with Disabilities	Department of Health and/or Mental Health	Departments of Rehabilitation and Aging	Department of Social Services and Regional Centers
Community Providers	Visiting Nurse Service; Meals on Wheels	Residential and assisted living; Home Health Agencies	Ambulette and paratransit businesses	Easter Seals; United Cerebral Palsy
Advocacy Groups	National Association of the Deaf Self Help for Hard of Hearing (SHHH) Telecommunications for the Deaf, Inc. (TDI); National Organization on Disabilities	Local chapters of the American Foundation for the Blind (AFB) and Council for the Blind	Alliance for Technology Access (ATA)	Center for Independent Living Center (ILC).

This council can determine the specific plans, equipment, resources, and response activities required to ensure the safety of individuals with disabilities during and in response to a disaster. Disaster plans for the disabled should specify the assignment of personnel, identify specialized equipment needed, and inform on the location of and availability of necessary assets. As part of preparedness activities, disaster planning councils can submit proposals to foundations to establish pre–event agreements so that in times of emergency, replacement equipment, medications, assistive devices, and the numerous other needs of those with disabilities can be quickly met.

Communities should consider the designation of a coordinator for disability services who can work as part of the council and serve as liaison with CBOs. The council can identify specific responsibilities that would be carried out by community and institutional providers in cooperation with advocacy specific groups as part of a community's emergency response. Most importantly, the members of the disability planning council have to be trained how to develop a disaster plan for their organizations, their role and responsibilities as part of the overall community plan, and how to communicate and serve their clients during an emergency.

TRAINING

Training is necessary for the response personnel so that they are equipped and skilled in using assistive equipment to aid individuals with disabilities during emergencies. In addition, the disabled communities need to know what to do in a disaster. Building from the materials developed by the American Red Cross on sheltering and evacuation and emergency planning for people with disabilities and other needs, the council can establish educational tools and work with the community to conduct train the trainer sessions about the creation of accessible facilities and services; transportation, lifting or carrying; accessible communications and assistance, developing personal support networks, home preparation, preparation of "Go Packs," and assistance animals.

COMMUNITY PLANS FOR THOSE WITH DISABILITIES

A community's plan should provide for guidance to its constituent organizations on improving preparedness for the disabled in their homes, where they work, attend school, conduct activities of daily living, and receive services. Because the abilities and needs vary from one disabled group to another, it is important to develop emergency procedures which are specific to each group. The range of disabilities that would impact the ability to respond in a disaster is broad and while some disabilities are permanent, others are temporary. Both permanent conditions, such as arthritis, and temporary conditions, such as a sprained ankle or a broken le.g., can limit one's ability to respond in a disaster. Planning is complicated because an otherwise able–bodied person may have a "situational disability" because of the environment in which an emergency occurs. As example, how many people would be able to walk down hundreds of stairs in a high rise building?

At a minimum, disabled–specific planning should account for those with learning and developmental disabilities, those with medical impairments (asthma, emphysema, and other respiratory disorders, cardiac conditions, cerebral palsy, communication disorders, pregnancy, psychiatric disorders, seizure disorders, and strokes) those with mobility impairments (arthritis, broken legs, paraplegia, sprained ankles, and wheelchair users), and those with sensory disabilities (visually impaired or blind, hard of hearing or deaf). Even if some with these disabilities perform well in a drill, they may experience problems in an actual emergency.

As part of community planning, public health can work with CBOs to help them create internal organizational registries of the elderly and people with disabilities. A broad range of organizations provide service to these groups, including group homes and other licensed residential facilities. While some communities may want to distribute these registries to appropriate government departments and local emergency management teams, it is difficult to keep the lists current and failure to provide information due to concerns of privacy may result in a list distributed to external agencies that is incomplete. Because of privacy concerns, communities should assess the balance between what is needed to be prepared and what should be kept private and base their actions on the community.

Because individuals with disabilities are connected through CBOs, home health care organizations, and health care providers, an effective alternative is to train these organizations to communicate and provide direct services to their clients in times of emergency. The CBOs, community centers, and programs where individuals with disabilities spend time or receive services can distribute information about preparedness in their newsletters. Liaison relationships should be established with local social service departments to work out procedures for contacting clients in an affected disaster area. CBOs should encourage those with disabilities to assess their own needs during a disaster, and to develop contingency plans. Disease registries, particularly those that actively collect longitudinal case information, are another source for communicating with the disabled.

Community disaster plans should include a specific section on the resources and response needed by individuals with disabilities. Experience in previous disasters has demonstrated the need for pre–established procedures which facilitate the approval of and payment for medication and the replacement of durable medical equipment, such as wheelchairs, respirators, hearing aids, and other adaptive devices. This includes pre–established arrangements with designated pharmacies for the provision of pharmaceuticals on an emergency basis. Where communities set up a registry of individuals who are dependent on power for life–saving equipment, these persons can be registered with utilities companies and utilize lifeline service. The planning council discussed above could arrange for the utility companies to provide immediate notification to persons who are dependent on life–sustaining electrical equipment if they are aware that power is going to be reduced. Further, arrangements could be made for the priority restoration of power to those persons dependent on adaptive equipment.

PERSONAL SUPPORT NETWORKS

Community plans should encourage those who are elderly or who have disabilities to develop a network of relatives, friends or co–workers who can check on and assist in an emergency. These are often referred to as personal support networks or PSNs. PSNs help the disabled evaluate their home, prepare for a disaster by identifying and gathering the resources they'll need, and provide emergency assistance through a redundant set of people who know the individual's needs. Disabled individuals may need to organize more than one PSN, (home, school, workplace, etc.) depending on where they spend their time. If there are a minimum of three people at each location in which the disabled individual regularly spends time, the disabled person can be assured that there are several persons who will check on them immediately after a disaster to see if they need assistance, as one person may be not available for any one of a number of reasons. The members of the PSN should have a written list of what the individual needs, as well as copies of their medical information, disability–related supplies and special equipment list, evacuation plans, relevant emergency documents, and personal disaster plan. Pre–arranged plans detailing the circumstances for when and how the members of the network will contact the disabled individual are essential. Members of the PSN should be provided with written instructions and trained in the location of the person's keys, the operation and movement of any adaptive or durable equipment used, locating their medical supplies, and familiarity with any service animal and needed personal care. Table 39 identifies basic elements of a personal assessment that will guide the plans worked out with the PSN. The personal assessment is best based on the environment after the disaster, on individual capabilities, on the individual's limitations; and on the lowest anticipated level of functioning.

TABLE 39: ELEMENTS OF A PERSONAL ASSESSMENT

- List personal needs and resources
- Evaluate activities of daily living
  - — Assistance needed with personal care
  - — Use of adaptive equipment to get dressed
- Assess needs if water service or hot water cut off for several days
- Identify equipment needed for personal care (i.e. shower chair, tub–transfer bench)
- Identify adaptive feeding devices and need for special utensils to prepare or eat food independently
- Arrange for continuation of electricity–dependent equipment (dialysis, electrical lifts, etc.)
- Plan for getting around if the disaster causes debris in home
- Plan for specially–equipped vehicle or accessible transportation
- Practice evacuating a building in the community or at home
- Locate and plan for finding mobility aids and equipment necessary for service animal
- Evaluate ramp access
- Plan for care of service animal (provide food, shelter, veterinary attention, etc.) during and after a disaster
- Arrange for another caregiver for the service animal if unable to care for it

GO–PACKS

Those with disabilities should prepare a "Go Pack;" know where to go if they need shelter, transportation, and support services; keep needed assistive devices and equipment nearby; know their evacuation options; and repeatedly practice their plan. A "Go Pack" is an individualized portable kit (preferably housed in a waterproof plastic box) that is prepared in advance. For those on medications, it should include at least 7 days of medication stored at the recommended temperature, which is rotated every week to ensure that it hasn't exceeded its expiration date. For others, the "Go Pack" may include an extra cane, hearing aid batteries, a walker, a ventilator, light-weight emergency evacuation chair, augmentative communication equipment, insulin supplies, food and water for guide dog, etc. This procedure was very effective in New York after September 11, 2001, because it ensured that life-saving medication was available when pharmacies were not. Since some states will not permit patients on Medicaid to receive more than a 30 day supply of medication, it is important to check state rules and determine what is allowable to ensure enough medication to include in a "Go Pack." Finally, if the individual receives Social Security benefits (SSI or SSD), the "Go Pack" should include a copy of the most recent award letter.

SHELTERS AND DISTRIBUTION CENTERS

In working with the community, public health can do a great deal to help those who are elderly and disabled prepare for evacuating from home during emergencies. In the event of an emergency, individuals who are elderly or disabled should be encouraged to plan how to get out of their home, work, or any building where they receive services. Since some roads may be closed or blocked in a disaster, plans are needed for two evacuation routes. Plans should include the assembly of a "Go Pack," as discussed above and the storage of extra food, water and supplies for any service animals.

Working with the American Red Cross, public health can develop a list of all ADA suitable shelters that can accommodate wheelchair access, larger restroom facilities and service animals. Once identified, these locations should be communicated to the advocacy groups and providers who deliver services to the elderly and disabled. Plans for shelters and distribution centers should include accessible and adequate electrical outlets so that adaptive equipment, such as battery powered wheelchairs, light talkers, computers, and respirators, can be operated. Emergency running lights should be installed along floors.

Pre–established procedures for shelters should include pre–established arrangements with providers of durable medical equipment who can loan, repair, or replace adaptive equipment (e.g. battery charger, wheel-chair) following a disaster. Hotlines should include TTY/EDD numbers.

Distribution centers for forms, food stamps, and hotel vouchers must meet the ADA standard of accessibility. Educational and informational materials prepared for distribution in these shelters should be prepared in Braille, large print, languages other than English, and audio cassette tape formats because the ADA requires that written materials used in disaster response be available in multiple formats upon request. Phone communication following a disaster must include TTY access for those who are deaf or hard of hearing, as required by the ADA. Physical access must be assured at the facility, in waiting lines, restrooms and telephones. Materials for home use should include formats with an assistive computer device like text to speech.

Community plans can incorporate alternative procedures such as the delivery of food and water directly to those who cannot access a shelter. Another solution is to establish a process where community residents can access information and complete applications over the internet, by phone, by TTY, or by e–mail.

COMMUNICATION: COMPLIANCE WITH THE EMERGENCY CAPTIONING RULES

Federal Communications Commission (FCC) rules require broadcasters and cable operators to make local emergency information accessible to persons who are deaf or hard of hearing, and to persons who are blind or have visual disabilities as part of a community's emergency plan. For public health, this means that emergency information must be provided both aurally and in a visual format. All information being communicated through video programming distributors (broadcasters, cable operators, satellite television services, and other multi–channel video programming distributors) must meet this standard. TV stations can be helpful in broadcasting both text and audible emergency information to all their viewers.

ACCESSIBILITY OF EMERGENCY INFORMATION REQUIRED

For persons who are deaf or hard of hearing, emergency information provided in the audio portion of programming must include either closed captioning or other methods of visual presentation, such as open captioning, crawls, or scrolls that appear on the screen. Emergency information provided by means other than closed captioning should not block any closed captioning, and closed captioning should not block any emergency information provided by means other than closed captioning. In the case of persons with vision disabilities, emergency information that is provided in the video portion of a regularly scheduled newscast or a newscast that interrupts regular programming must be made accessible. This requires the oral description of emergency information to be included in the main audio portion of the broadcast. If the emergency information is provided in the video portion of a regularly scheduled newscast or interrupts regular programming (e.g., the programmer provides the emergency information through "crawling" or "scrolling" during regular programming), this information must be accompanied by an aural tone. This tone alerts persons with vision disabilities that the broadcaster is providing emergency information, and alerts the viewer to tune to another source such as a radio, for more information.

Situations in which emergency information must meet this standard include warnings and watches of impending changes in weather, community emergencies such as a discharge of toxic gases, widespread power failures, industrial explosions, civil disorders, school closings, and changes in school bus schedules resulting from any of these conditions. The information provided must include details regarding the emergency and how to respond, evacuation and shelter information, and how to shelter in place. Educational announcements made during and right after disasters such as earthquakes or tornadoes should encourage those with disabilities to check for hazards at home, since items that have moved can cause injury or block an escape path for someone with limited mobility. Finally, announcements should inform those with chronic medical conditions to bring their medication with them when they evacuate.

Some local news stations provide captions when broadcasting information on weather emergencies, such as tornados. An alternative source of notification is a NOAA weather radio which displays a short text message describing the nature of any emergency declared in the area. Weather radios can be left on in stand–by mode indefinitely. These radios are silent until an emergency is declared, at which time they sound an alarm and then broadcast a spoken message concerning the emergency. Strobe lights and bed vibrators are available as attachments for people who cannot hear the alarm, and most models display text messages.

BUILDING PREPAREDNESS FOR INDIVIDUALS WITH DISABILITIES

To develop an evacuation plan that accounts for both staff and visitors with disabilities, organizations/buildings should develop an emergency committee whose first task is to understand general evacuation issues. The evacuation committee might meet with the building management, local fire department, police, and HazMat personnel, a manufacturer of evacuation equipment, and other agencies and groups with evacuation interests involving persons with disabilities. In addition to identifying the individuals who regularly work in a building, preparations should be made for visitors who may require assistance. Further, the committee should identify and train personnel who can properly lead individuals who need assistance to safety. Conducting regular drills and assessing the effectiveness of the drills are as essential to the evacuation plan as they are to the larger community preparedness plan.

It is useful to assess the number of employees and their types of disabilities and to meet with disabled individuals to discuss their preferences for evacuation as part of the planning process. The U.S. Equal Employment Opportunity Commission has stated that federal disability discrimination laws do not prevent employers from obtaining and appropriately using information necessary for a comprehensive emergency evacuation plan. Employers may ask employees to self–identify if they will require assistance in the event of an evacuation because of a disability or medical condition. This list, which will be essential if emergency evacuation is necessary, should be updated at least annually. There are three times when employers can obtain this information: after making a job offer, but before employment begins, during periodic surveys of all employees when the employer indicates that self–identification is voluntary, and by asking employees with known disabilities if they will require assistance in the event of an emergency. An employer should inform individuals and ensure that the information is confidential and shared only with those who have responsibilities under the emergency evacuation plan. An employer may ask individuals who indicate a need for assistance because of a medical condition to describe the type of assistance needed. Employers can give all employees a memo with an attached form requesting information. The employer also may have individual follow–up conversations when necessary to obtain more detailed information. The ADA has provisions requiring employers to maintain confidentiality about employee medical information. However, in the event of an evacuation, employers can share medical information, including the type of assistance an individual needs, with safety personnel, medical professionals, emergency coordinators, floor captains, colleagues who are part of the disabled person's personal support network, building security officers who need to confirm that everyone has been evacuated, and other non–medical personnel who are responsible for ensuring safe evacuation under the employer's emergency evacuation plan.

DETECTION

The detection of some hazards, such as fires, often occurs through systems which function automatically. Automatic systems, such as strobes and horns, must be compliant with the ADA updated regulations and the Underwriters Laboratories Standard for Emergency Signaling Devices for the Hearing Impaired (UL Standard 1971). This standard requires that signaling devices alert those with hearing loss through the use of light, vibrations, and air movement. Where facilities use manual devices that pull, codes require that these pull stations be mounted at a height of 48" to 54" so that someone in a wheelchair could reach the alarm.

NOTIFICATION

Plans should include a process to inform all building occupants that emergency action is needed. Because emergencies often disrupt technology, it is important to have low–tech solutions with built in redundancy. While special considerations might be needed for those with disabilities, plans should consider the community in general, because everyone will benefit from improved notification systems.

The ADAAG provides specifications for emergency alarms so that they are accessible to persons with disabilities, including those with sensory impairments (ADAAG 4.1.3(14), (4.28). Where emergency alarm systems are provided, they must meet criteria that address audible and visual features. It is important to install multiple systems because events may cause one or another system to fail. As example, audible signs may not be distinguishable above the sound of alarms, the signs may not be heard or distinguishable from siren alarms, or without electricity, the systems may not be operable. Further, interpreters must be provided where indicated.

Since audible instructions through emergency paging systems are not effective for the hard of hearing or deaf, visual strobes with high intensity flashing lights should be used to notify these individuals that the alarm has sounded. ADAAG specifications for visual appliances address intensity, flash rate, mounting location, and other characteristics. Audible alarms installed in corridors and lobbies can be heard in adjacent rooms but a visual signal can be observed only within the space it is located. Audible directional instructions are described below. Alternative devices include a two–part battery operated smoke detector and receiver which are attached to a wall and a companion vibrator device which is placed on a desk or held by the person. The vibrator is activated when a smoke detector transmits a signal to the receiver. Visual alarms are required in hallways, lobbies, restrooms, and any other general usage and common use areas, such as meeting and conference rooms, classrooms, cafeterias, employee break rooms, dressing rooms, examination rooms and similar spaces. Alternatively, visual instructions can be provided through television monitors, scrolling text, or pagers that vibrate. Closed Circuit TV Magnifiers (CCTV) consist of a television camera which takes the picture of a printed page and displays the enlarged image on a television monitor. In addition, low level signage needs to be placed 6" to 8" above the floor as a supplement to required exit signs placed higher on the wall because exit signs are usually located over exits or near the ceiling and can become obscured by smoke.

Currently, telephone communication with those who are deaf is also possible using the Ultratec 4425, a portable, 20–character display Telecommunications Device for the Deaf (TTY) which provides printed records of conversations and optional auto–answer.

TACTILE AND AUDIBLE SIGNAGE

The ADAAG (ADAAG 4.1.3(16), 4.30) requires that certain types of building signs be tactile using raised and Braille characters. This is intended to cover signs typically placed at doorways, such as room and exit labels, because doorways provide a tactile cue in locating signs. Tactile specifications also apply to signs which identify rooms whose function, and thus designation, is not likely to change over time and includes floor level designations provided in stairwells. Examples include signs which designate restrooms, exits, and rooms and floors by numbers or letters. ADAAG also addresses informational and directional signs. These types of signs are not required to be tactile but must meet criteria for legibility, such as character size and proportion, contrast, and sign finish.

Braille signs, commonly found as raised patterns of dots on elevator control panels, have been installed in many buildings to assist people who are visually impaired. The usefulness of these panels is limited because the person must be at the location of the Braille signs in order to feel them. Plans should include an alternative way to provide directional guidance to find exits, such as audible directional signage. Audible directional, or remote signage, is a device used to inform those with visual impairments about their environment. Audible instructions are transmitted by low power radio waves or infrared beams. Small receivers, carried by the individuals, pick up these signals and are equipped with a voice which announces directions "the exit is 10 steps from the front desk," or a word identifying where they are, ("stairway," "elevator"). Another example of audible signs are Talking Signs™ which provide those who are blind with the information that helps them navigate in the environment. These signs "speak" by sending information from installed infrared transmitters. Hand held sensors pick up information from the transmitters and give verbal directions to those carrying them.

When assisting persons with vision impairments, announce the person's presence when entering the area, grasp that person's elbow for guidance, and describe what they will be doing, including the mention of stairs, doorways, narrow passages, ramps, etc. Someone should remain with these individuals until they are safe.

PREPAREDNESS AT THE BUILDING LEVEL: EVACUATION

Moving people to safe areas is an important part of any disaster response, especially in tall buildings. While contingency plans should be developed for providing evacuation assistance for all building occupants, there will always be someone who will need special assistance in an emergency requiring evacuation. Further, unique evacuation problems are created where the elderly or disabled live or work on higher floors in high rise buildings.

The methods of accommodation and the choice of assistive devices should be discussed with those needing them. There may be different procedures or preferences among local fire departments regarding evacuation procedures for persons with disabilities but many evacuation plans will include the use of evacuation chairs. These devices are designed with rollers, treads, and braking mechanisms that enable a person to be transported down stairs with the assistance of another individual. For additional information, planners should check with the local fire, police, or hazmat department.

Following an inventory of the number of employees requiring assistance and estimating the number of visitors to the building, it will be possible to determine how many evacuation chairs are needed. Decisions may be made to also stock heavy gloves to protect individuals' hands from debris when pushing their manual wheelchairs, a patch kit to repair flat tires, and extra batteries for those who use motorized wheelchairs or scooters. Staff should be trained on the use of evacuation chairs, through viewing the training videotape provided by the manufacturer and receiving on–site training from the manufacturer. When buildings conduct mandated "fire drills," part of their exercise should test the ability to evacuate those with disabilities. Drills should focus on the use of evacuation and other assistive devices, and occur on all shifts so that evening and night staff are familiar with the procedures and their responsibilities. Drills also provide an opportunity for individuals requiring assistance to practice transferring into and out of the evacuation chairs. It is important to practice evacuation procedures with blocked exists and service animals, such as guide dogs, who accompany their owners during the evacuation. Drills can include the use of protective gear, such as booties made of Velcro which service animals wear when evacuating from fire or walking over glass.

In planning for those with limited mobility, such as in residential institutions, there may be scenarios where "sheltering in place" is the best plan, even temporarily. Disaster plans should include the designation of several offices as "waiting areas" where individuals using wheelchairs or mobility devices and others can report and await assistance from the fire department, as required in new construction (ADAAG 4.1.3(9), 4.3.11). Known as "areas of rescue assistance" or "areas of refuge," in new construction these spaces must meet specifications for fire resistance and ventilation and are often incorporated into the design of fire stair landings. These areas can also be provided in other recognized locations meeting the design specifications, including those for fire and smoke protection. An exception is provided for buildings equipped with sprinkler systems that have built–in signals used to monitor the system's features. In older buildings, designated offices can be located at different parts of the building, i.e., front and back. Each designated waiting area should have a pre–printed sign requesting rescue assistance, a window, supplies that enable individuals to block smoke from entering the room from under the door, respirator masks, and a telephone and a two–way radio as areas of rescue assistance must include two–way communication devices so that users can communicate about evacuation assistance. Employees should be instructed to post rescue signs in the window to alert the fire department of their location. The location of these "waiting areas" should be communicated to the local fire department.

EVACUATION EQUIPMENT

The ability to evacuate during an emergency is highly dependent on one's mobility. The types of equipment discussed here are not meant to be all inclusive, as experimental equipment is continuously being developed and improved. Wheelchair users are one group with mobility limitations. Because wheelchairs are frequently fitted to the specific physical needs of the user, those evacuated will need to have their own chairs returned to them if they are separated during the evacuation.

Several types of evacuation or fold–up chairs allow for people to be moved up or down stairs and can be permanently installed within stairways to accommodate wheelchair users or stored near emergency exits. In one type, the person transfers or is transferred from the wheelchair to a portable chair. These chairs are designed to move down stairs on special tracks equipped with friction braking systems, rollers, or other devices which control the speed of descent. With another device, the wheelchair user rolls onto the transporter and the wheelchair is secured to the device as it descends. In addition, there are chairs that can be rolled down stairs. Examples are the Garaventa Evacu–Trac CD–7™ , the EVAC+CHAIR™ or the Scalamobil™ · Evac–u–Straps are an assisted wheel–chair carrying device which consists of padded leather wrist bands with velcro closures. The wrist bands have large metal hooks which attach to the sides of the wheelchair. This system requires three people to bring a person down stairs in a wheelchair.

TABLE 40 ASSISTIVE DEVICES FOR EVACUATION

- EVAC+CHAIR   Weighs 18 pounds and has a 300–lb. carrying capacity.
- EVACU–TRAC   Designed so passenger's weight propels it down the stairs and has a 360–lb. carrying capacity.
- Scalamobil   Battery operated portable stair climber, attaches to most manual folding wheelchairs and has a 264–lb. carrying capacity
- Ferno   Adjustable and portable devices enable easy maneuvering through confined spaces with 350–lb. carrying capacity.
- LifeSlider   Flat–bottomed, toboggan–like device that slides down stairs, around landings, through small doorways, around inside corners, and across pavement.

CARRYING TECHNIQUES

Wheelchair users are trained in special techniques to transfer from one chair to another. There are two techniques for carrying people in an emergency, the cradle lift and the swing or chair carry. The cradle lift is preferred when the person to be carried has little or no arm strength. It is also safer if the person being carried weighs less than the carrier. In the cradle carry, the person needing assistance is sitting and the carrier bends his knees and places one arm under the person's legs and the other arm around the person's back. The person being carried puts an arm over the shoulder of the carrier. The carrier lifts up with the person in front of him.

For the swing or chair carry, a two–person technique, the carriers stand on opposite sides of the individual. They take the arm of the person and wrap it around each of their shoulders. Each carrier grasps their partner's forearm at the small of the back of the person being carried. They reach under the person's knees and grasp the wrist of the carry partner's other hand. Both partners lean in, close to the person, and lift on the count of three. The carriers should continue pressing into the person being carried for additional support.

SERVICE ANIMALS

In preparation for any emergency, those who have service animals should ensure that the animal's identification tags, licenses, and vaccinations are current, and that the tags display the owner's contact information and an out of town contact. Public health should work with the community to identify and list the shelters that are set up for service animals. A supply kit for the animal is needed which includes bowls for water and food, food, plastic bags, a toy, a collar, and an extra leash or harness.

EMERGENCY HEALTH INFORMATION

Everyone who has a diagnosis that may impact emergency treatment should always carry information about their health needs and emergency contacts, update it twice a year, and give a copy to a family member and a friend or neighbor. This emergency health information lets others know about their medical condition or disability if the person is unable to provide information. For those with disabilities, this information should detail special equipment and supplies that they use, such as hearing aid batteries, detailed information about the specifications of their medication regime, include current prescription names and dosages, shelf life and temperature at which it should be stored, and list the names, addresses, and telephone numbers of doctors and pharmacists.

Emergency health information should be kept in emergency supply kits, wallets (behind driver's license or official identification card), wheelchair packs, etc. A Medic Alert tag or bracelet identifies the type of disability or medical condition, and an 800 number with the wearers' current medication, diagnosis, etc., on file. Medic alert bracelets are available through pharmacies. Table 41 provides a template for emergency health information and Table 42 provides a general planning checklist for those with disabilities.

TABLE 41: EMERGENCY HEALTH INFORMATION

Emergency Health Information	Date:		Updated:	
Name				
Address	City		State	Zip
CONTACT METHOD	HOME		WORK	
Phone:	Cell:	Fax:	E–mail:	
Birth Date	Blood Type		Social Security No.	
Health Plan	Individual #:		Group #:	
Emergency Contact:				
Address	City		State	Zip
CONTACT METHOD	HOME		WORK	
Phone:	Cell:	Fax:	E–mail:	
Primary Care Provider:				
Address	City		State	Zip
Phone:	Cell:	Fax:	E–mail:	
Disability / Conditions:				
Medication:				
Allergies:				
Immunizations		Dates		
Communication / Devices / Equipment / Other:				

Reprinted with permission from Be a Savvy Health Care Consumer, Your Life May Depend on It! by June Isaacson Kailes, [http://www.jik.com/resource.html].

TABLE 42: DISABILITY–RELATED ISSUES FOR EMERGENCY PLAN COORDINATORS

(Give a copy of this checklist to personnel who are responsible for creating, reviewing, maintaining, practicing and revising emergency plans.)

Date Completed	Activity
	Make sure a relationship is established with your local fire department that includes: • Fire Department reviewing the plan at least once a year; • Fire Department receiving a copy of a current log containing names and location of all people needing assistance, • The plan being coordinated and practiced with fire department.
	Practice plans through regular drills.
	Know how to get to all the exits and practice this as part of regular drills.
	Practice using evacuation devices.
	Practice dealing with different circumstances and unforeseen situations, such as blocked paths or exits.
	Ensure that shift workers and others who are at the site after typical hours, (cleaning crews, evening meeting coordinators, etc.) are included in drills.
	Plans should include: • people who are at the site on a regular basis; • people who are at the site outside of the typical working hours; • how visitors, guests and customers with small children who require extra time to evacuate will be assisted; • specific dates for revisions and updates.
	Orient all people to the plan.
	Plan Dissemination • Have people read the plan? • Have people been oriented to the plan? Placing plans in a drawer or even a prominent place on a bookshelf is as good as burying them. • Is the plan distributed and reviewed with all people at the site? • Do people get a copy of the plan in a usable format (Braille, large print, text file, and cassette tape, or in appropriate formats for non–English speakers and people who have poor reading skills)? • Are these formats always updated when the plan is revised?
	Make sure that people know how to report safety hazards (i.e. fire extinguishers that need servicing, exits which are not kept clear, furniture and other items that block barrier–free passages).

Reprinted with permission from Kailes, Jl. Emergency Evacuation Preparedness: Taking Responsibility for Your Own Safety and Other Activity Limitations, 2002. Published and distributed by Center for Disability Issues and the Health Profession, Western University of Health Sciences, 309 E. Second Street, Pomona, CA 91766–1854, Phone (909) 469–5380, TTY ((09) 469–5520, Fax: (909) 469–5407, Email: [evac@westernu.edu.]

PLAN IMPLEMENTATION AND MAINTENANCE

After the final evacuation plan is written, a copy should be distributed to all company employees and key personnel. In addition, evacuation drills should be regularly performed to make sure all employees are familiar with the plan. To insure that accommodations continue to be effective, the plan should be integrated into the standard operating procedures, practiced and accommodations updated periodically. In addition, a system for reporting new hazards and accommodation needs should be developed; a relationship with local fire, police, and HazMat departments should be maintained; and new employees should be made aware of the plan. Finally, all accommodation equipment used in emergency evacuation should be inspected and maintained in proper working order.

Chapter 11

Public Health Response to Emerging Infections and Bioterrorism

As invisible disaster threats, epidemics of infectious disease and bioterrorism agents pose special concerns and response requirements for public health departments. This chapter reviews response to unknown disease, covert and overt threats, categories of bioterrorism agents, and the public health and medical response required at the federal, regional, and community levels.

PUBLIC HEALTH ROLE

- Develop and use multidisciplinary protocols for collaboration among state and local public health agencies, community hospitals, academic health centers, community health care providers, laboratories, professional societies, medical examiners, emergency response units, safety and medical equipment manufacturers, the media, government officials, and federal agencies such as the US Office of the Assistant Secretary for Public Health Emergency Preparedness, the Centers for Disease Control and Prevention, and the Agency for Toxic Substances and Disease Registry.

- Establish specific criteria for monitoring emerging infections and activate surveillance systems that can quickly identify emerging or re–emerging diseases, closely monitor unexplained morbidity and mortality due to infectious disease, and improve surveillance for flu–like illness.

- Increase lab capacity, educate microbiologists about reporting, and establish communication linkages with a laboratory response network for the rapid evaluation and identification of bioterrorism agents.

- Develop and activate diagnostic clinical and treatment protocols that are communicated to the medical community which improve rapid reporting of suspect cases, unusual clusters of disease, and unusual manifestations of disease.

- Plan for and respond, where necessary, to reduce the morbidity and mortality from a bioterrorism event by stockpiling antibiotics, preparing multilingual patient information, developing contingency plans for quarantine, and developing community plans for the delivery of medical care to large numbers of patients and to the "worried well."

- Utilize and expand access to the Health Alert Network.

- Develop contingency plans, with the local medical examiner, for mass mortuary services, including plans for the utilization of Federal Disaster Medical Assistance Teams (DMAT) and Mortuary Teams (DMORT).

- Train all health organizations required to deliver care.

- Communicate emergency instructions, prevention, control and treatment information.

- Resolve legal issues related to public health authority in emergencies.

RESPONSE TO UNKNOWN DISEASE

With global climate change, globalization of commerce, inadvertent transport of vectors, and zoonotic disease, it is inevitable that the U.S. public health system will continue to confront serious diseases that are not common today. Further, while incidents involving weapons of mass destruction[1] may involve many victims and damage to buildings and other property, these incidents and emerging infections are dissimilar to typical disasters in several ways. A major difference between natural disasters and an event involving an infectious disease is the widespread health impact. Officials may not recognize that an incident has occurred until there are several casualties and multiple releases have occurred. The scope of the incident may expand geometrically and affect multiple jurisdictions as victims unknowingly carry the agent to health care facilities and across geographic areas. The fear of the unknown may generate concern from the public, resulting in larger numbers of "worried well" than of actual victims. The workings of the typical response team could be disrupted as the scope of the events requires expansion of the emergency response personnel who normally work together.

Depending on the emerging infection or type of agent used, there may be a shortage of any of a number of medical resources including: ICU beds, ventilators and other critical–care needs, and antibiotics and/or antiviral agents. If a release of a contagious disease occurred, such as smallpox, several patients will likely appear in emergency rooms with rash illness that hopefully will be reported to authorities as "suspect smallpox." "Non–traditional" treatment centers may need to be established on short notice. There is potentially a high demand for mortuary or funeral services and social and counseling services. Unlike morbidity and mortality associated with natural disasters, demands on medical care in each community are likely to be prolonged as the illness spreads among the population. The need for home care may increase if the elderly and other high–risk and special–needs populations can't or won't leave their homes to receive care for chronic medical conditions because of the threat of exposure to infectious disease. In addition to surveillance and activating the participation of other agencies, public health officials may initiate actions to protect the community, including quarantine and immunization. Further, the fire and safety workforce may be reduced in number and overwhelmed if first responders, who normally are the main core of personnel on the scene of an event, become ill from early or repeated exposure to communicable disease. Finally, communities will need to be self–sufficient, if resources cannot be diverted from other geographic areas because of regional spread.

Unlike the response to an overt chemical event where fire, police, or hazardous material units are the first responders, the public health

[1] Weapons of Mass Destruction include biological (bacteria, virus, toxins), nuclear (detonation or "dirty" explosives), incendiary (intentional fire–starting), chemical (nerve, blister, blood, choking), and explosive (rapid release of gas and heat) agents. This chapter focuses primarily on the public health preparedness and response to biological agents, although many of the principles discussed in this book will apply to preparedness for the other agents.

department is charged with identifying infectious disease in a community. This response to bioterrorism requires an interdependent working relationship among local, state, and federal agencies and among community clinicians, emergency responders, and local public health personnel. Once a plan is in place, the public health response to unknown disease outbreaks has five components: detection of usual events, investigation and containment of potential threats, organization of care, laboratory capacity, and coordination and communication.

OVERT AND COVERT RELEASES

Overt releases are those where an assessment of the threat is made before the response is initiated, perhaps because the threat is announced. Public health officials should assume that potential hoaxes are in fact real when accompanied by increased morbidity or mortality even if the microorganisms have not been confirmed. Communities may choose a limited response to hoaxes based on a sophisticated analysis of the situation and a relatively easy resolution of the incident.

Covert releases are those without prior warning in which a biologic agent presents as illness in the community and where traditional surveillance methods are needed to detect the agent. With covert releases, patients fall ill or die from unknown causes or unusual origins. Covert dissemination of a biological agent in a public place will probably not have an immediate impact due to the incubation period of the disease, resulting in a delay between exposure and onset.

The covert release of a contagious agent or the appearance of a highly infectious illness has the potential for multi–national spread prior to detection. Release in a transportation hub or in a highly mobile population could disseminate a highly contagious agent such as smallpox across boarders before the epidemic is recognized. As person–to–person contact continues, successive waves of transmission could carry infection to other localities around the globe. In a very short time, public health authorities would be asked to determine that an attack has occurred, identify the organism, and prevent more casualties through prevention strategies (i.e.,mass vaccination, prophylactic treatment, or universal precautions and quarantine). The ability to detect covert releases depends on enhancing public health infrastructure and increasing the skills of front line medical practitioners so they recognize and report suspicious syndromes.

CRITICAL BIOLOGICAL AGENTS

The Centers for Disease Control and Prevention (CDC) identify three major categories of agents.

Category A

Category A is a list of the nine highest priority agents. While the frequency of these diseases is relatively low, their impact is high because of the speed with which they spread. The agents on the Category A list pose a risk to national security because they can be easily disseminated or transmitted person–to–person; cause high mortality, with potential for major public health impact; could cause public panic and social disruption; and require special action for public health preparedness.

Bacillus anthracis. Anthrax, an acute bacterial disease affecting the skin, chest, or intestinal tract is considered to be a highly efficacious biological warfare agent because it forms spores (providing stability in aerosol form), is relatively easy to disseminate using off–the–shelf technology, and is frequently fatal if inhaled. Its incubation period is 1 – 7 days, but disease is possible up to 60 days. Transmission from person to person is very rare.

Clostridium botulinum. Botulism is poisoning by a toxin produced by a common environmental organism that can be easily cultured from soil. Victims of the toxin often require intensive supportive medical care. Foodborne botulism results from ingesting contaminated food. Botulism in wounds occurs when the organism grows in a deep wound and forms toxin carried to bloodstream. Intestinal botulism occurs mostly in infants, less than one year old, from the ingestion of spores which grow in their intestines. The case fatality rate for infants is less than 1 percent.

The public health response to botulism is complicated. If paralysis occurs in a large number of individuals, the short supply of respiratory intensive care beds and ventilators will not be enough. The immune globulin used in the routine treatment of both wound and foodborne botulism can be lifesaving if given early but is limited in both supply and availability. Public health preparedness requires a major stockpiling effort to cover possible bioterrorism needs resulting from botulism.

Variola major. Smallpox, for which dissemination requires person–to–person transmission, is highly contagious in unimmunized populations and has a mortality rate as high as 35 percent. Smallpox has a cycle time of 10 to 14 days, an attack rate of up to 90 percent and a secondary attack rate among the non–vaccinated of 50 percent.

Yersinia pestis. Pneumonic plague is a respiratory–acquired illness that is spread from person–to–person through sneezing or coughing. It is diagnosed by culturing bacteria from sputum, blood, spinal fluid or infected glands. Pneumonic plague is almost 100 percent fatal if not treated quickly. Bubonic plague is the form characterized by severely swollen and infected lymph nodes in the groin or axilla, called buboes. Plague occurs as an enzootic disease of rodents in the United States, making it relatively easy to attain an isolate for use as a terrorist agent. Infected rats and their fleas transfer bacterial infection to animals and humans through bites or from cat scratches. Symptoms occur 2 – 7 days after exposure. If untreated, bubonic plague has 50–60 percent mortality.

Francisella tularensis. Tularemia is a zoonotic bacterial disease with varying clinical manifestations related to the route of transmission. It can be transmitted from rabbit, tick or fly bites, or handling infected animal carcasses. Tularemia can also be disseminated in water. Tularemia is not transmissable person to person. In aerosol form, the organism produces a severely debilitating pneumonia but with a lower mortality rate than anthrax. The incubation period, related to strain, can range from 1–14 days, but is commonly 3 – 5 days.

Two filoviruses, Ebola hemorrhagic fever and Marburg hemorrhagic fever, and two arenaviruses, Lassa fever and Argentine hemorrhagic fever (Junin), complete the Category A agents.

Category B

Category B agents are considered the second highest priority because they are moderately easy to disseminate, cause moderate morbidity and low mortality, and require specific enhancements of CDC's diagnostic capacity as well as enhanced disease surveillance. Category B agents include:

- *Coxiella burnetii* (Q fever),

- *Brucella species* (brucellosis),

- *Burkholderia mallei* (glanders),

- alphaviruses (Venezuelan encephalomyelitis, eastern and western equine encephalomyelitis), and ricin toxin from *Ricinus communis* (castor beans),

- *epsilon toxin* of Clostridium perfringens, and

- *Staphylococcus enterotoxin* B.

A subset of List B agents includes pathogens that are food– or water-borne. These pathogens include but are not limited to:

- *Salmonella* species,

- *Shigella dysenteriae,*

- *Escherichia coli* O157:H7,

- *Vibrio cholerae,* and

- *Cryptosporidium parvum.*

Category C

Category C, the third highest priority agents, include emerging pathogens that could be engineered for mass dissemination in the future due to availability, ease of production and dispersion, and potential for high morbidity, mortality, and major public health impact. Preparedness for List C agents requires ongoing research to improve disease detection, diagnosis, treatment, and prevention. Category C agents include:

- Nipah virus,

- Hantaviruses,

- Tickborne hemorrhagic fever viruses,

- Tickborne encephalitis viruses,

- Yellow fever, and

- Multidrug–resistant tuberculosis.

BIOTERRORISM RESPONSE PLAN

Chapter 7 describes general principles that apply to disaster planning for natural hazards or technological events. Tasks related to bioterrorism that require similar preparation include interorganizational

TABLE 43 BIOTERRORISM AGENT SUMMARY

ADAPTED FROM HTTP://WWW.BT.CDC.GOV/DOCUMENTS/PPTRESPONSE/TABLE/AGENTS/SUMMARY.PDF

	Inhalation Anthrax	Brucellosis	Botulism	Tularemia	Pneumonic Plague	Smallpox	Viral Hemorrhagic Fever
Infective Dose	8000-50,000 spores	10-100 organisms	0.001 g/kg (type A)	10-50 organisms	<100 organisms	10-100 particles	1-10 particles
Incubation	1-6 d	5-60 d	6 h to 10 d	1-21 d	2-3 d	7-17 d	4-21 d
Duration	3-5 d	Weeks to months	24-72 h	~2 wk	1-6 d	~4wk	7-16 d
Mortality Untreated	~100%	~5%*	1st case: 25% Subsequent cases: 4% Overall: 5-10%	33%	40%-70%	Variola minor: <1% Variola major: 20%-50%	53%-88%
Mortality Treated	~99%	<1%	1st case: 25% Subsequent cases: 4% Overall: 5-10%	<4%	5%	Variola minor: <1% Variola major: 20%-50%	53%-88%
Person to Person Transmission†	No	No	No	No	Yes (high)	Yes (high)	Yes (moderate)
Isolation Precautions‡	Standard	Standard	Standard	Standard	Droplets§	Airborne§	Airborne and Contact§
Persistence	40 y in soil	10 wk in water/soil	Weeks in food/water	Months in moist soil	1 y in soil	Very stable	Unstable

*Endocarditis accounts for the majority of brucellosis-related deaths.

†For inhalation antrax, brucellosis, botulism, or tularemia, no evidence of person to person transmission exists; for pneumonic plague, for 72 h following initiation of appropriate antimicrobial therapy or until sputum culture is negative; for smaallpox, approximately 3 weeks, which usually corresponds with the initial appearance of skin lesions through their final disappearance, though most infections during the first week of rash via inhalation of virus released from oropharyngeal-lesion secretions of the index case; for viral hemorrhagic fever, varies with virus but at minimum, all for the duration of illness and for Ebola/Marburg, transmission via semen may occur up to 7 weeks after clinical recovery.

‡Graner JS, Hospital Infection Control Practices Advisory Committee. Guideline for isolation precautions in hospitals. Infect Control Hosp Epidemiol 1996; 17:53-80, and Am J Infect Control 1996; 24:24-52. (http://www.cdc.gov/ncidod/hip/isolat/isolat.htm)

§In addition to standard precautions that apply to all patients.

coordination, sharing information, resource management, triage, casualty distribution, using the media to communicate to the public, and patient tracking. Because of the potential for the rapid spread of disease, however, planning to mitigate the impacts of emerging infections or bioterrorism relies heavily on skills that are uniquely those of public health and health care systems and include additional functions that are not normally included in a community's comprehensive emergency plan.

FEDERAL STRUCTURE

Following the events of the fall, 2001, the U.S. Congress passed the Public Health Security and Bioterrorism Preparedness and Response Act of 2002 (Public Law 107–188) to improve the ability of the United

States to prevent, prepare for, and respond to bioterrorism and other public health emergencies, to enhance controls on dangerous biological agents and toxins, and to protect the food, drug, and water supply.

The Bioterrorism Act of 2002 amends the Public Health Service Act (42 U.S.C. 201 et Seq) and creates a position of Assistant Secretary for Public Health Emergency Preparedness to develop and implement a coordinated interagency interface between the Department of Health and Human Services and other federal, state and local departments, agencies, and offices responsible for emergency preparedness, including NDMS and the Veterans Affairs in the maintenance of the Strategic National Stockpile. The Act requires plans be developed and implemented which prepare for and respond to bioterrorism and other public health emergencies by including: 1) federal assistance to State and local governments, 2) public health surveillance and reporting mechanisms at the State and local levels, 3) laboratory readiness, 4) properly trained and equipped personnel, 5) protection of health and safety of workers, 6) coordination by public health, health, and mental health services, with minimal duplication of Federal, State, and local planning, preparedness, and response, 7) secure communications networks for the dissemination of relevant information, 8) development and maintenance of medical countermeasures against biological agents and toxins (i.e., stockpiling of drugs, vaccines, other biological products, medical devices, and other supplies), and 9) enhancing the readiness of hospitals and other health care facilities to respond effectively to such emergencies. The Bioterrorism Act of 2002 gives the President the power, in consultation with the Surgeon General and the Secretary of Health and Human Services, to issue quarantine rules.

Further, the Centers for Disease Control and Prevention is assured "an essential role in defending against and combating public health threats and requires secure and modern facilities, and expanded and improved capabilities related to bioterrorism and other public health emergencies."

As in all disaster plans, federal activities are initiated to support local activities not supplant them, when federal health and medical assistance is required to augment local and state health care delivery systems. Local officials are expected to establish control at the scene of the incident, initiate appropriate protective and response measures, establish distribution systems, organize mass immunization or prophylactic centers, maintain records, refer to treatment centers, and inform the public.

Presidential Decision Directive 39 (PDD 39, Clinton: 21 June 1995: Counterterrorism) establishes the framework for two broad responsibilities of planning and response to a biological incident – crisis management and consequence management. Crisis management is a law enforcement function, led by the Federal Bureau of Investigation. Consequence management is an emergency management function, led by FEMA. In May 1998, PDD 62 was issued, reaffirming the policy in PDD 39 and detailing a systematic approach to fighting terrorism. The Public Health Service is designated the lead agency for planning and preparing for medical issues related to weapons of mass destruction. The federal response plan assigns agency specific responsibilities under the unified plans. In addition to the federal plan, states and localities have their own plans.

Since the issuance of PDD 39 and PDD 62, a Concept of Operations Plan (CON PLAN) was developed and agreed to by the various federal agencies involved in the response of incidents to terrorism. The CONPLAN provides overall guidance to federal, state, and local agencies for a coordinated federal response to potential threats or incidents involving WMD. The CONPLAN establishes procedures for assessing and monitoring an emerging threat; notifying appropriate federal, state, and local agencies of the nature of the threat; and deploying advisory and technical resources to assist the Lead Federal Agency (LFA) in facilitating interagency/interdepartmental coordination.

REGIONAL PLANNING

Regional planning can improve a community's response in preventing the spread of disease. Regional agreements should specify how coordination will work, including roles, chain of command, reimbursement, distribution of scarce resources, information management strategies, and the maintenance, inventory, and supply of response equipment.

Following a bioterrorist attack, a community needs:

- An emergency management program—Comprehensive plan, coordination with emergency management and health sectors, training and drills;

- Personnel—Clinicians, public health officials, logisticians and pharmacists;

- Material— Pharmaceuticals, isolation facilities, sites for mass vaccination, PPE and decontamination showers, and supplies with back–up for mass care;

- Monitoring and providing information—Prevention guide-lines, home–care instructions for patients, and information regarding characteristics of the infectious agent to aid deci-sionmaking about quarantine, isolation, and evacuation;

- Communication system—Redundant equipment tested regularly;

- Security— identification badges, restricted vendor access, security patrol, access control for entire facility, mail handling procedures, etc., and

- Financial support for each of the above.

At the local or regional level, public health planning for a bioter-rorism event can be modeled after planning models for pandemic influenza because many bioterrorism agents present as flu–like illness. A planning committee should be established with key representatives from the health, emergency management, and public safety sectors. This committee is responsible for establishing an overall command and control structure (see Chapter 3 on incident command); for overseeing the prevention, planning, response, and recovery activities; and for ensuring that a jurisdiction's plan is developed, reviewed, and revised when needed. Because bioterrorism response will require cooperation from a broad variety of community groups, it is important to identify who the stakeholders are and to solicit their support. Participation from the community should involve personnel knowledgeable about com-municable disease and immunization, hospitals, laboratories, specialists in information systems, the media, citizen band radio groups, social service agencies, the American Red Cross, law enforcement, fire and emergency medical services, the medical community, the medical examiner and coroner, funeral directors, local utilities, local veterinary facilities capable of handling affected animals, and local government officials, among others. The planning committee will ask that stake-holders develop the components of the plan for which they have expertise. Local public health departments interested in obtaining "Public Health Ready" certification need to develop comprehensive emergency preparedness and response plans and train personnel. Planning guidance for local public health agencies is available from the

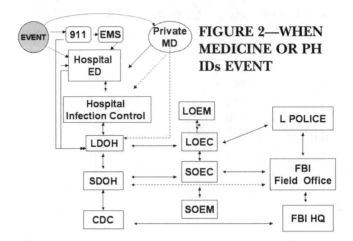

FIGURE 2—WHEN
MEDICINE OR PH
IDs EVENT

National Association of City and County and Health Officials (NAC-CHO). Figure 2 shows the chain of communication if public health is the first to recognize an event.

Communities or regions should plan for three levels of response to a bioterrorism event. Examples of this three–tiered approach include separate plans for incidents with up to 100 victims, for incidents with 100 to 10,000 victims, and for incidents with more than 10,000 victims. An important part of each plan will be the logistics of obtaining and dispensing vaccines and antibiotics. Plans should identify the location of local or federal depositories, designate dispensing sites, and establish priorities for dispensing. Stockpiles will most likely be flown into commercial airports or trucked from private vendors. A protocol must be established for off loading antibiotics and supplies, and a site located for re–packaging the materials into smaller units. In addition, a system must be established for ensuring that the antibiotics are used before their expired shelf life. If a push pack is pre–deployed in anticipation of an event, permission is required to open it.

Planning for surge capacity[2] should consider higher estimates for the morbidity and mortality resulting from a release of highly contagious agents such as smallpox or pneumonic plague. (Surge capacity planning is discussed in Chapter 7.) Attempts should be made to direct patients to alternative sites, away from hospitals which could become

---

2 The CDC has developed software to assist local planners in estimating the potential impact of large flu outbreaks that can be adapted to planning for bioterrorist events. The software can be downloaded from [http://www2.cdc.gov/od/fluaid/default.htm].

quickly overwhelmed. To assure adequate staffing, prepare contingency plans for replacements of essential personnel, such as reassignment of personnel from non–essential programs within the local agencies, or calling up retired personnel and /or private–sector personnel with relevant expertise. Establish a protocol for the protection of public safety personnel early in the outbreak through inoculation or the distribution of PPE, etc. Further, to ensure the maintenance of a healthy workforce, those wearing PPE to decontaminate victims can only stay in the PPE for about 15 minutes. Multiple teams need to be trained and these responders should be required to pre–hydrate themselves.

While estimates vary widely for those who might seek care because they think they are sick, a comprehensive plan should arrange to triage a large number of unaffected patients who are the "worried well." In major metropolitan regions, a conservative estimated ratio of "worried well" to affected patients has been as high as 30 to 1, yet we saw over 30,000 people nationwide receive prophylaxis for anthrax in 2001, far exceeding this ratio. Large numbers of potential patients would require the rapid establishment of alternative care facilities. Because patients have been found to seek health care from locations where they regularly receive care, alternative care facilities should be set up as close in proximity to healthcare facilities as possible.

PUBLIC HEALTH COMMUNITY PLAN FOR BIOTERRORISM RESPONSE

In addition to a description of a unified command and control, a management structure, and responsibilities (including protocols for coordinating activities of the health sector with those of the emergency management sector), a public health community plan for bioterrorism includes the following:

- Protocols for large–scale outbreak investigation and infection control which detail what personnel are supposed to do;

- Notification and response protocols for suspected and confirmed cases;

- Protocols for field decontamination and transfer to hospitals;

- Assessment of staffing and maintenance of health care and essential community functions during periods of high absenteeism, including outreach criteria, guidelines for worker safety, and training needs;

- Protocols on the handling of laboratory specimens to ensure rapid diagnostic testing including collection, transfer and laboratory confirmation of samples, safe disposal, labeling, and appropriate chain–of custody of samples related to suspected terrorism and referrals to reference or national laboratories as well as whether laboratory reports require the attention of the local public health department;

- Assessment of facility needs/type/availability/location of drugs, vaccines, beds and equipment;

- Stockpiling and monitoring expiration dates of pharmaceutical inventories for a range of potential agents;

- Plans for mass medical care;

- Resolution of legal issues;

- Protocols for both external communication to the public and internal communication among those coordinating the response;

- Measures to assure environmental decontamination, biosafety, arrangements for mass burials, and mortuary management;

- Protocols for management of mental health issues;

- Coordination with civic organizations and other volunteers to provide food, medical and other essential support for persons confined to their homes;

- Baseline data with scheduled updates on:

  - hospital admissions

  - acute bed occupancy

  - intensive care unit bed occupancy

  - emergency room visits for infection

  - ambulatory department utilization

- influenza–like illness

- flu cases in patient billing and emergency department visit data

- unexplained deaths

- unusual syndromes in ambulatory patients

- 911 calls

- diarrheal disease

- weekly sales of antidiarrheal medicine from a regional distributor

- daily number of stool samples submitted to labs

- daily incidence of gastrointestinal illness in nursing home populations

- calls to poison control centers

- antibiotic and other pharmaceutical supplies

- total number of respirators

- workforce and school absenteeism

INITIAL TASKS DURING AN INFECTIOUS DISEASE EMERGENCY:

- Activate response plan, public health OEC and ICS.
- Interface with appropriate state and federal counterparts.
- Activate communications plan: disseminate information on the infectious disease emergency, prevention and control, etc.
- Increase surveillance at hospitals and clinics.
- Initiate vaccine/pharmaceutical distribution if appropriate.
- Coordinate activities with neighboring juristictions.
- Notify key government officials and legistators of the need for additional resources where needed.

DEFINING, DETECTING, AND RESPONDING TO BIOTERRORIST EVENTS

A possible bioterrorist event includes one of the following:

- A single, definitively diagnosed or strongly suspected case of an illness due to a recognized bioterrorist agent occurring in a patient without a plausible explanation for his/her illness.

- A cluster of patients presenting with a similar clinical syndrome with either unusual characteristics (age distribution) or unusually high morbidity or mortality, without an obvious etiology or explanation.

- An unexplained increase in the incidence of a common syndrome above seasonally expected levels.

A biologic event or emerging disease would most likely present as one of the above, with the initial detection likely to take place at the local level. Because most agents that could be used for bioterrorism have incubation periods, an attack may not be apparent until days or even weeks after the attack has occurred. During the early stages of illness, many related diseases have vague, nonspecific symptoms making them difficult to differentiate from numerous naturally occurring diseases. Primary health care providers in the local medical community may be the first to recognize unusual disease due to a covert attack, with state and local health departments most likely to initiate a community–wide response. A potential bioterrorism event might be a group of patients with a similar clinical syndrome with unusual characteristics, such as age distribution, unusually high morbidity or mortality without obvious explanation for the illness, unusual concurrence of geographic exposure, unusual disease not previously found in the region, a case of inhalation anthrax or smallpox, or unexplained increase in a common syndrome above seasonally expected levels (i.e., cluster flu epidemic in summer with negative virology, food poisoning without a single source).

TABLE 44: SUPPLIES AND ANTIDOTES FOR POTENTIAL BIOTERRORISM AGENTS

Agent Supplies	Needed
Bacterial Agents	Ciprofloxacin, doxycycline, penincillin, chloramphenicol, and azithromycin
Botulinum toxin	Mechanical respiratory ventilators and associated supplies
Burn/Vesicants	Sterile bandages, intravenous fluids, and broad spectrum antibiotics
Cyanide	Cyanide antidote kits containing amyl nitrite, sodium nitrite, and sodium thiosulfate
Lewisite	British anti-Lewisite
	Nerve Agents Atroine, pralidoxime chloride, and diazepam
Radiologic Exposure	Potassium iodide
All	Resuscitation equipment and supplies, vasopressors

Veterinarians should be encouraged to report suspicious illness in their patients. The beginning of the West Nile epidemic in the U.S was marked by the avian veterinarian at the Bronx, New York zoo reporting birds dying around the time that a community physician called the New York City Department of Health and Mental Hygiene about an unusual cluster of meningitis cases.

Since accurate diagnosis of diseases caused by the most likely bioterrorist agents may be delayed due to the initial flu–like presentation and the several days needed for a positive laboratory identification, public health officials cannot depend on passive surveillance systems. Labor–intensive active surveillance requires outreach and can be costly but will be essential in identifying when "the flu" is not "the flu." "Flu–like symptoms" usually come on suddenly and may include:

- High fever

- Headache

- Tiredness/weakness (can be extreme)

- Dry cough

- Sore throat

- Runny nose

- Body or muscle aches

- Diarrhea and vomiting also can occur, but are more common in children.

A full mobilization of public health efforts includes sending suspected samples to reference laboratories for rapid confirmation of bioterrorist agents, the galvanizing of active surveillance and epidemiological teams to identify source of initial exposure (i.e., review charts of suspected patients), ensuring appropriate isolation and universal precautions where indicated, initiating treatment and prophylaxis to reduce morbidity and mortality, assessing geographic spread, identifying unexpected features of the outbreak, and the launching of pre–established communication protocols among many medical community and emergency management agencies and between government and the public. The public health team should be organized to respond to potential biological, chemical, or radiological events and include professionals from multiple disciplines, such as laboratory scientists, emergency management, emergency medical technicians and paramedics, environmental health scientists, epidemiologists, hazardous material response teams, health physicists, industrial hygienists, infectious disease specialists, medical examiners, occupational health physicians, public health laboratory designees, toxicologists, and veterinarians.

An effective surveillance system will be able to rapidly track changes in disease trends, be based on clinical syndromes, and be generated by data that are collected continually, reviewed daily, and remain geographically representative. An "alert" in these systems prompts an epidemiological investigation to determine if there is an outbreak and to identify the potential microbial etiology and the source of transmission. Sources of data for bioterrorism and emerging disease include:

- Biosurveillance

- Hospital reports (admissions to intensive care units of previously healthy persons with unexplained febrile illnesses)

- Infectious disease and laboratory reports

- Diagnostic categories with trends and unusual patterns from emergency departments

- Outbreaks in institutional settings (i.e.,nursing homes)

- Workforce and school absenteeism

- Prescription and over–the–counter medication sales

- Animal outbreaks and deaths

- Police and emergency medical services reports

- Geographic analyses of 911 calls categorized by disease
  syndrome (i.e.,codes for difficulty breathing, respiratory
  distress, and other markers for influenza–like disease)

While medical examiner reports are useful, a two to three day delay often occurs between the time of death and the filing of the death certificate. In addition, it is difficult to identify clusters using death certificates. Optimally, electronic death reporting can be instituted so that this information is more timely. In addition, epidemiologists will want to look at environmental factors, such as food, the presence of vectors (i.e., ticks, fleas, flies, rodents, cats, mosquitoes, bats), and trends in animal populations and food crops.

Early detection of a covert release is designed to occur through autonomous detection systems (ADS), which include focused active surveillance and diagnostic laboratory testing. In the system known as Biowatch, "vacuum cleaner" like machines, operating both indoors and outdoors, continuously collect air samples which are tested in public health laboratories seven days a week. The U.S. Postal Service is installing machines designed to detect *Bacillus anthracis* nationwide and plans to conduct hourly Polymerase Chain Reaction (PCR) testing on air samples. When the ADS indicates that there is a possible exposure, the machine will sound an automatic alarm and the building will be evacuated and hospitals notified, per protocol. Those who have been potentially exposed will be triaged into those needing personal hygiene, clothing change, and/or prophylaxis. Responding to an ADS detection of *B. anthracis* involves coordinating with community partners, including hospitals. Preparations should include regular drills and exercises with partners on sample collection, chain of custody, forensic investigation, decontamination and patient care. Because of the number of tests that will be run, hospitals should be prepared to respond to patients with false positive test results.

Active Surveillance and Epidemiological Investigations

To activate a rapid surveillance, materials must be prepared in advance. Essential tools include preplanned instruments of generic questions designed to determine case and risk exposure, a sampling strategy, a centralized database with fields defined, and a mechanism to call–up and deploy 24–hour/7–day–a–week teams to conduct the surveillance. The instrument might ask questions about location of residence and work, usual commuter routes, and a detailed diary of the patient's activities during the incubation period of the suspected agent.

If there is a confirmed bioterrorist event, health departments will be responsible for tracking the cases and performing epidemiological investigations to determine the source and sites of exposure. Public health will implement active hospital based and enhanced passive surveillance, including hard to reach populations (i.e., homeless), contact tracing similar to that used for measles or syphilis, and coordination with local poison control centers. This information will be essential in determining who else might have been exposed and will require prophylaxis. Epidemiological investigations will help identify the determinants, the distribution, and the frequency of disease in both human and animal populations. Epidemiology will detect possible vector–control requirements and the likelihood of secondary spread. These investigations will be coordinated with neighboring health departments as well as interstate and international agencies.

Mass Medical and Mortuary Care

In addition to baseline surveys that provide information about a community's capacity to care for patients exposed to bioterrorist agents, guidelines are needed for the care of exposed patients. Community care guidelines should include distributing protocols and disease–specific information to the health care community on identifying cases, medical management of exposed, initiating mass medical care including triage and surge capacity with trained personnel, turning shelters or schools into hospitals, establishing patient isolation in many locations including the home, drug distribution to large numbers of the population (i.e.,vaccinations or medication management), transportation of patients, and mortuary care.

Managing the media and keeping the general public accurately informed is a crucial component of a mass care plan. Communication is accomplished with providers through the HAN, through broadcast alerts, and through communication hotlines. Consider establishing three separate hotlines, one for physicians, one for persons requiring the services at a Point of Dispensing (POD) center,[3] and one for the general public with staff being given prepared scripts to answer questions. Use the media to issue warnings to the public and for public service announcements about preventing exposures and/or distinguish symptoms, control measures, who may need antibiotics, and local effects of disease etc.[4]

While hospitals are required to have a disaster plan to be accredited by the Joint Commission on Accreditation of Healthcare Organizations, a sequence of stand–alone facility plans do not prepare a community to respond to bioterrorism. The hospitals in a community or region must coordinate their efforts, including the transport of patients, the ordering and stockpiling of supplies and pharmaceuticals, communications during the event, the handling of bodies, and other major tasks. The coordination of resources is all the more important as more hospitals practice "just in time" delivery of supplies and pharmaceuticals. Designating the delivery of services to certain hospitals in advance of a bioterrorist event, (i.e., limiting high–cost specialty care to hospitals with most experience in treating severely injured patients) and formalized protocols for pre–hospital and hospital trauma care (i.e., establishing protocols for first responders to rapidly transport exposed patients) has been shown to contribute to improved patient outcomes. The regional plan should ensure that all hospitals participate in multihospital drills.

Hospitals plans for responding to a large infectious disease outbreak include provisions for triaging large numbers of patients in the emergency department, patient decontamination and patient overflow, increasing bed capacity, calling in additional staff, and establishing isolation units on short notice including airborne, contact, and universal precautions. Staff should be educated about any specific roles they have in HEICS and instructed to continue with their regular duties if they are not involved in the hospital's incident command structure. Hospital staff should know who to notify if they are the first to learn about the event, what questions to ask (where is it and what is happening), and how to use universal precautions. Multilingual information sheets and consent forms should be prepared. In addition, instructional sheets on the methodology for administering vaccines (i.e., smallpox) should be ready for use.

3Dispensing refers to the activities of getting prophylatic medications/vaccines to affected populations. Distribution refers to the logistics of breaking up and transporting materials from stockpile locations.

4CDC has established notification procedures for state and local public health officials, available on their website.

Hospital plans establish the medical protocols that will be followed, the stockpiling and distribution of medications or vaccines, and whether to set up community–based mass prophylaxis clinics. At a minimum, the emergency department protocol when a patient presents and the providers suspect an infectious disease, should include:

- Contacting DOH with the specifics of the case;

- Rapid screening of individuals in waiting room;

- Check for supply of isolation equipment, particulate respirators, isolation rooms for negative pressure;

- Triage and isolation in negative—pressure rooms for those with known contact with the index case or with fever/suspicious rash;

- Contacting hospital infection control/disease experts;

- Standard precautions including fit–tested N95 or N100 masks; and

- Rapid screening and gathering of contact information for all in waiting area.

A plan for mass antibiotic prophylaxis or immunization of the population should include:

- Description of the decision–making process that would be used to initiate a mass immunization campaign;

- Method of identifying the affected population;

- Adjustable distribution plans to provide vaccine or antibiotics to high–priority target groups and the general population where there is a severe vaccine shortage, a moderate vaccine shortage, or an adequate vaccine supply;

- Plans for moving a pharmaceutical stockpile to dispensing points;

- Designated personnel who will manage the arrival, distribution, and local dissemination of vaccines and antibiotics, ensure the smooth flow of clients into the POD, and translate where needed, including sign language;

- Plans for the storage, transportation, and handling of pharmaceuticals. One refrigerated tractor–trailer would be adequate to handle the storage of 12 million doses of vaccine;

- Clinical algorithm and preprinted instruction sheets for different prophylactic regimens, including procedures for immunization of differing age groups, etc.;

- Procedures for record keeping and strict accountability, including a log for recording the manufacturer, lot number, expiration date and quantity of vaccine received and distributed in compliance with federal vaccine administration guidelines;

- Plans for the availability of protective clothing for personnel;

- Plans for ensuring community participation;

- Development of Information Sheets in all relevant languages. Templates are available at [http://www.immunize.org/] or at CDC's [http://www.governmentguide.com/govsite.adp? bread=*Main&url=http%3A//www.governmentguide.com/ams /clickThruRedirect.adp%3F55076483%2C16920155%2Chttp% 3A//www.cdc.gov/.];

- Regional coordination of proposed pharmaceutical distribution plan; and

- Procedures for monitoring compliance with medication protocols, symptom or illness attributable to the vaccine, illness following immunization attributable to vaccine failure, and adverse events.

POINT OF DISPENSING (POD)

When large numbers of persons require prophylaxis by medication or vaccine, it is necessary to establish a Point of Dispensing (POD). POD activities include registration, triage, taking swab samples, medical evaluation or screening, dispensing antibiotics/vaccine, reassuring the worried well, briefing clients about anthrax and POD operations, collecting information for investigative purposes, transferring persons to a medical facility (when needed), counseling, managing client flow, and maintaining security. Preplanning is essential because once an event occurs necessitating mass distribution of medication, there is not a lot of time between the decision to open a POD and the initiation of operations. Prior arrangements should be made with other community agencies and medical volunteers so that issues of credentialing, medical–legal responsibility, and reimbursement are worked out in advance.

Experience, such as that of the New York City Department of Health and Mental Hygiene, suggests that depending on the type and scope of event, the services within the PODs may be organized or function differently. Allocate sufficient time to ensure that supplies have arrived and trained staff are ready before opening a POD for operations. Adequate staffing is essential, including a dedicated physician–in–charge, liaison, supplies coordinator, and clinic manager. To provide antibiotic prophylaxis to up to 10,000 persons in 72 hours, you'll need approximately 50–55 persons per shift for round–the–clock coverage in 12–hour shifts. In selecting a site for the POD, it should be located in a place convenient to those who have to use it and be large enough to distribute antibiotics or vaccine to the necessary population. To dispense antibiotics to 500 to 10,000 persons over a 72–hour period, a space of at least 2,500 square feet is needed. Establishing good communication is critical from the incident command center to the POD, from the health department to the public, and from the health department to community medical providers. When events do not indicate immunizing or prophylaxing large segments of the population, it will be necessary to establish a plan for triaging the "worried well." Figures 3 and 4 show a schemata of a model POD layout.

Where an event involves bioterrorism (a criminal act) law enforcement agencies require separate space for investigation away from the POD to minimize concerns about confidentiality. The FBI and CDC developed a guide which describes the role of public health and law enforcement in these investigations, and is included in the reference section.

FIGURE 3: POD FLOOR PLAN

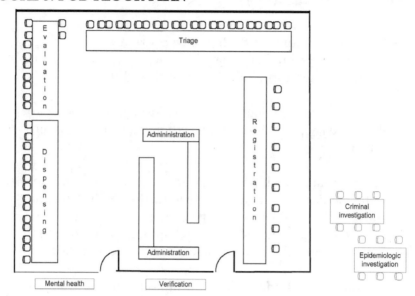

FIGURE 4: POD FLOOR PLAN

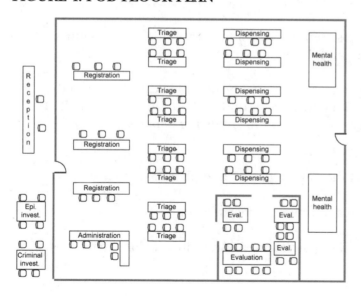

REPRINTED WITH PERMISSION FROM BLANK S., MOSKIN LC., AND ZUCKER JR., (2003) "AN OUNCE OF PREVENTION IS A TON OF WORK: MASS ANTIBIOTIC PROPHYLAXIS FOR ANTHRAX: NEW YORK CITY, 2001" EMERGING INFECTIOUS DISEASES, VOL.9 (6) JUNE 2003.

POD FUNCTIONAL AREAS

- Screening station: verify eligibility; provide writing tools, information sheets, epidemiologic interview forms, law enforcement interview forms, and medical record forms;

- Client registration: logbook or spreadsheet on a laptop, or data–entry screens and wireless connections to an on–site server;

- Triage area: assess if persons go to the dispensing station, need to be medically evaluated, or need further evaluation and transfer to a healthcare facility; Provision of printed material (i.e., medication fact sheets, epidemiological interviews); Staff at triage: physicians, nurses, and physician assistants;

- Briefings on risks of exposure, symptoms, and side effects of antibiotics;

- Specimens collection, as needed (i.e., nasal swabs);

- Dispensing station for antibiotic distribution. Staff—nurses, physicians, and/or pharmacists;

- Counseling: Staff — mental health, medical advisors, and public health educators at the POD entrance, near the POD exit, and as consultation for referring persons to hotlines and web sites;

- Security at the entrance, exit, and pharmaceutical supplies;

- Clerical area for medical charting; and

- Space for filling out forms and conducting interviews.

POD MEDICAL CHART

Use a two-sided, one-sheet, self-administered questionnaire as a medical chart, limited to information relevant to the rapid distribution of antibiotics (similar medical record for pediatrics) which includes:

Contract information:
address, telephone numbers, and emergency contacts.

Signed consent form for testing and treatment,

Brief medical history:
presence or absence of current symptoms, relevant drug allergies, use of specific medications known to interact with drugs of choice (i.e. doxycycline or ciprofloxacin for anthrax) and pregnancy status

Place to document:
Specimen collection, dispensing and receipt (or refusal) of antibiotics/vaccine, and antibiotic/vaccine lot numbers.

Adapted from Blank S., Moskin LC., and Zucker JR., (2003) "An Ounce of Prevention Is a Ton of Work: Mass Antibiotic Prophylaxis for Anthrax: New York City, 2001" Emerging Infectious Diseases, Vol. 9(6) June 2003.

LABORATORY RESPONSE NETWORK

The Laboratory Response Network (LRN) was established in 1999 by the Association of Public Health Laboratories and the Centers for Disease Control and Prevention (CDC) to assist in the U.S. response to biological and chemical terrorism. The LRN is now an integrated national network of about 120 biological and chemical labs with the capacity to respond to bioterrorism, emerging infectious diseases and other public health threats and emergencies. The LRN includes the following types of labs:

- Federal—CDC, NIH, and other federally run facilities.

- State and local Departments of Health.

- Military—Department of Defense, including the U.S. Army Medical Research Institute for Infectious Diseases (USAMRIID).

- Food testing—Food and Drug Administration (FDA) and the U.S. Department of Agriculture.

- Environmental—Testing water and other environmental samples.

- Clinical—Local hospitals

- Veterinary—USDA (animal testing).

- International—Labs in Canada, the United Kingdom and Australia.

The LRN supports surveillance and epidemiological investigations by identifying disease, providing direct and reference services, and conducting environmental, rapid, and specialized testing. Five of the major threats (i.e., botulism, plague, anthrax, tularemia, poxvirus illnesses) occur naturally in the United States, and specimens for these diseases are routinely evaluated by public health laboratories. In addition, the standard techniques for detecting bacterial agents (i.e., gram stain, culture on selective media, visual colony morphology, growth after heat shock and confirmatory methods using phage and direct immunofluorescence) are well recognized for establishing definitive diagnosis. Methods such as isolation in cell culture, inoculation of animals, direct fluorescence methods, and electron microscopy are considered definitive methods in virology.

The personnel who work in public health laboratories are highly skilled and familiar with following complex identification algorithms. The procedures used can be readily adapted to environmental samples that might be collected after an overt threat or in the attribution of the source of a sample. Further, the laboratories are all certified under the Clinical Laboratory Improvement Act as employing appropriate quality assurance and quality control procedures. Although definitive identification requires a day or two, preliminary results can be available in minutes or hours. In particular, the minimum response time for a definitive negative result with a rapidly growing organism such as anthrax may be 16 hours. More slowly growing organisms or complex procedures may take 48 hours or more. Further, many methods require a fixed facility with traditional lab techniques not readily adaptable to a field situation.

The laboratory response network has three levels of performance designated as sentinel, reference, or national. Designation depends on the types of tests a laboratory can perform and how it handles infectious agents to protect workers and the public. Membership in the LRN is not automatic. State lab directors determine the criteria and whether public health labs in their states should be included in the network. Prospective reference labs must have the equipment, trained personnel, properly designed facilities, and demonstrate testing accuracy.

Sentinel labs (formerly Level A) represent the thousands of hospital-based clinical labs that are on the front lines. In an unannounced or covert terrorist attack, sentinel labs could be the first to identify a suspicious specimen and screen out a presumptive case during routine patient care. A sentinel laboratory's responsibility is to recognize, rule out and refer a suspicious sample to the right reference lab. They may assess risks for aerosol agents. They use Bio Safety Level 2 (BSL) techniques.

Reference labs, (formerly Levels B and C) can perform tests to detect and confirm the presence of a threat agent. These labs, also called "confirmatory reference labs," ensure a timely local response in the event of a terrorist incident or other emergency. Rather than having to rely on confirmation from labs at CDC, reference labs are capable of producing conclusive results. Reference labs can be county, state, or major state public health laboratories that perform direct fluorescence or phage testing such as molecular diagnostics. Using BSL–3 techniques, reference labs have the safety and proficiency to confirm and characterize susceptibility and to probe, type, and perform toxigenicity testing.

National laboratories (formerly Level D) are the network of federal and private partners in the U.S. Public Health Service, Department of Defense, national laboratories, and industry that can perform research on and develop new techniques that are disseminated to the other levels of the network. National labs have unique resources to handle highly infectious agents and are responsible for definitive high level characterization (seeking evidence of molecular chimeras) or identifying specific agent strains. The CDC and US Army Medical Research Institute of Infectious Diseases USAMRIID national labs, operating at BSL 4, handle the most dangerous agents.

If a covert event occurs that is not recognized immediately, the incidence of disease in the community would trigger public health to submit samples to the laboratory and to report to the surveillance network. With an announced threat or an overt event, the situation would be reported to the Federal Bureau of Investigation, which would in turn determine which level of laboratory is required and transport samples to the nearest appropriate laboratory in the network. Figure 5 shows the chain of events when law enforcement is the first to recognize an event.

LEGAL ISSUES

As legal authority varies from state to state, it is necessary for public health to investigate specific state laws regarding emergency preparedness. Legal questions that may arise regarding the powers of the health commissioner upon a declaration of emergency must be clarified and include:

FIGURE 5—WHEN LAW ENFORCEMENT IDENTIFIES EVENT

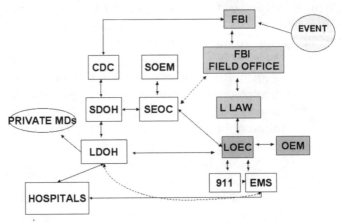

- The ability to remove legal barriers relative to dispensing of medicines,

- Licensing of out of state physicians and nurses,

- Transfer of patients between hospitals during the emergency,

- Emergency credentialing of providers who are not credentialed through the federal response,

- Isolation, quarantine, blockade, zone perimeters, requisitions, curfews, governance, restricted access, and due process under different scenarios,

- The power to define diseases deemed dangerous to public health,

- Control and prevention,

- Reportable disease,

- The liability of hospitals in the reporting of information, and

- The process of declaring a state of emergency in your locale.

Public health authorities should identify who has the authority, what criteria must be met, what legal mechanism must be followed, and who is responsible for enforcement. Once the legal mechanism is defined, contingency plans to quarantine patients and protocols for implementation and enforcement should be established. Finally, while the HIPAA Privacy Rule regulates how "Covered Entities" use and disclose "Protected Health Information (PHI)," PHI disclosures without patient authorization may occur if the disclosure was required by law, authorized by the individual, is for treatment purposes, or is released to legally authorized public health entities for public health activities. Public health activities include surveillance, investigation, and intervention.

Chapter 12

Public Health Considerations in Recovery and Reconstruction

Disaster preparedness plans must also consider the long–term process of recovery and reconstruction. This chapter examines the three post–impact phases of disaster and the priorities in planning for each. Particular attention is paid to transitional services, such as special needs shelters.

PUBLIC HEALTH ROLE

- Organize community–wide programs for delivery of health care and public health services, including special needs shelters.

- Provide community education to enhance public awareness (i.e., injury control), to aid community adjustment, to form the basis for future disaster mitigation, and to educate the community about likely health risks and how to deal with them.

- Assess health needs in the community.

PRINCIPLES OF DISASTER RECOVERY AND RECONSTRUCTION

Factors that influence recovery planning and policy include the accuracy of needs assessments, intense pressure by citizens to rebuild as soon as possible, the amount of time and resources allocated to problem solving and to recovery, and the many and often conflicting preferences of affected groups. Community participation is essential for planning the rehabilitation phase because local people better understand their own needs and the problems that create these needs. Residents should be the direct beneficiaries of rehabilitation projects since they will be responsible for monitoring development projects that continue after relief workers have left.

In planning each activity, aid agencies and the community must consider the positive and negative impacts, both short term and long term. For example, aid should be provided in such a way that people can stay at home (i.e., not building relocation camps) and continue with what more closely approaches normal life and promotes resumption of other normal activities when possible. Integrated recovery programs may include work schemes to repair community facilities that pay residents cash to replace lost possessions. This injection of money will stimulate local markets and help speed recovery. To aid recovery further, loans or grants can be made available to small business.

PHASES OF RECOVERY AND RECONSTRUCTION

Three phases describe what happens post–impact in the affected community: emergency, transition or recovery, and reconstruction. The timing of each phase varies with the nature of the disaster, its location, and the capacity of the community to recover.

In the *emergency phase*, activity focuses on saving lives through search and rescue, first aid, emergency medical assistance, and overall disaster assessment. Efforts immediately begin to repair critical facilities, to restore communications and transportation networks, and, in some cases, to evacuate residents from areas still vulnerable to further disaster.

During the *transition or recovery phase*, people return to work, repair damaged buildings and infrastructure, and initiate other actions that allow the community to return to normal as soon as possible. Victims begin their emotional recovery and may experience depression and post–traumatic stress disorder (see Chapter 9). External assistance is provided in the form of cash and credit. Construction projects and other types of job creation are the most appropriate types of aid.

Traditionally, four stages of recovery have been categorized. These stages are not necessarily sequential, and different parts of a community can be at different stages, depending on the extent of devastation and resources available. These include emergency response, including debris removal, provision of temporary housing; restoration of public services, including electricity, water, and telephone; replacement and reconstruction of capital stock; and initiation of improvements and developmental reconstruction that stimulate economic growth and local development.

The *reconstruction phase* is characterized by physical reordering of communications, utilities, roads, and general physical environment. Residents repair or rebuild their housing, and agricultural activities resume. The timeframe for reconstruction may span years, especially for the restoration of housing and other buildings.

Factors affecting recovery time include the risk of secondary disasters, motivation, communications, technical assistance, conflicts in technical advice, cash flow, reuse of salvaged materials, cost and supply of materials, general economy, public rejection of recovery plans, irrelevant aid, bureaucracy in government and other responding agencies, and efforts by interest groups to channel aid to rebuild their areas first.

POST–DISASTER ASSESSMENTS

Post–impact needs assessments provide information necessary to begin recovery. The first step is to assess community capacities and vulnerabilities, including physical environment (i.e., intact infrastructure, resources), social conditions (i.e., existing organizations, support networks), and population attitude toward and motivation to recover. Communication must be established between the people affected by the disaster and responding jurisdictions and organizations. Needs are determined by visiting representative areas, by talking to selected groups in affected communities, and by conducting rapid health assessment surveys (see Chapter 5). Emergency needs are more easily apparent than long–term needs, and long–term needs vary over time. When possible, needs should be quantified, (i.e., percentage of families without running water, number of patients served by pharmacies that were destroyed), even if the number is determined by extrapolation. Public health workers should highlight gaps in the community's emergency response, where identified. Once the baseline capacities and vulnerabilities have been assessed, this information must be gathered again over time.

POST–DISASTER PRIORITIES

Local people must set the priorities and direct the use of resources. In the recovery phase, priorities include the assurance of adequate shelter, medical services, infrastructure, utilities, business, economic activity, and social networks. Recovery is a federal obligation as written in the Stafford Act. While Congress restricted the reimbursement, it is very important for all to account for everything that was lost and everything that was spent in recovery, regardless how miniscule because Congress could make an exception and without documentation, opportunities for reimbursement may be lost.

Post–impact, shelter may be provided as emergency or temporary housing and permanent structures. Securing permanent shelter is a top priority. When establishing an emergency shelter, the American Red Cross allocates 40 to 60 square feet per person. Emergency or temporary shelters require a facility that can withstand a disaster and that has communication capabilities, power, and running water. The ideal shelter would have separate areas for registering residents, conducting physical examinations, offering mental health treatment, sleeping, eating, and recreation. American Red Cross shelters do not permit pets but do allow service animals (i.e., seeing eye or hearing dogs).

SPECIAL NEEDS SHELTERS

Disaster victims who cannot be evacuated to a regular American Red Cross shelter include those with certain health or medical conditions, such as an infectious disease requiring isolation, serious injury or disease requiring regular medication or monitoring, or a chronic illness requiring assistance with activities of daily living. Those who need special medical equipment, such as Foley catheters or intravenous therapy, can not be housed in a routine shelter either.

For these patients, communities must establish plans for alternative care facilities referred to as special needs shelters (SNS). These facilities can be associated with a hospital such that persons requiring medical management but not hospital–level care can be safely housed. These SNS are generally intended to operate for a limited period of time (i.e., one to four days).

SNS Facilities

Special needs shelters are usually refuges of last resort intended to maintain the current health, safety, and well–being of the individuals who are medically dependent yet are not acutely ill or injured. SNS must be set up to meet a range of physical and psychological human needs under adverse conditions. Most SNS operate out of school buildings, churches, or other community buildings. Facilities that must accommodate expanded medical needs should provide 100 square feet per person. These shelters are usually not equipped as a medical care facility. Some have bedding, while others require residents using the shelter to bring their own. Staffing often relies on volunteers. Planning for SNS should include discussions with local hospitals and home care agencies regarding possible assistance if higher–level skilled staff are needed.

The SNS may not have the supplies needed by those who must take shelter there. Home care agencies should prepare a cardex (indicating all of their treatment information) that can accompany the patient during relocation. In addition, patients must prepare a portable kit (preferably housed in a waterproof plastic box) that includes sufficient medical supplies and medication for one week.

As part of their plan for SNS facilities, communities should include a unit that coordinates emergency replacement of medical supplies, prescriptions, glasses, teeth, hearing aids, prosthetic devices, mobility aids, and other medical necessities often lost in disaster situations. Plans should detail how bed–ridden patients will be moved if additional evacuation is necessary (i.e., flat–bed trucks). Planning can be facilitated by identifying in advance those who will need the services of a SNS and by matching that population with the appropriate shelters, supplies, and resources.

Triage

Public health should establish a system to triage the patients who require SNS. Advance identification of the medical needs of community's residents will facilitate this triage. The following example, derived from the Training Guide prepared by the Florida Department of Health as part of the Public Health Nursing Disaster Resource Guide (August 2000), suggests criteria that can be used to determine appropriate shelter assignment.

Category I: Special Needs Shelter

Patients should be ambulatory, though they can have a medical problem and be accompanied by a care giver. These patients can be divided according to whether they need assistance in activities of daily living or whether they need monitoring by a nurse or require the use of medical equipment and assistance with medication. Patients directed to a SNS may have the following medical needs: Foley catheter, diabetes care, maintenance of medication, blood pressure monitoring, nasogastric tube feeding, ostomy care, or oxygen or nebulizer therapy. Patients with severe arthritis, stable stroke, heart disease, cancer, and Alzheimer's disease can also be accepted at SNS, as can those with disabilities (i.e., blind, hearing impaired, amputee, wheelchair–bound). Bedridden and total care patients must bring a responsible caregiver and not require a hospital bed.

Category 2: Inpatient Hospital Care

For category 2 patients, public health officials are advised to make arrangements with providers and hospitals as part of global community planning. In the event of natural disasters such as hurricanes, earthquakes, and tornados, hospitals themselves may be damaged or may receive large numbers of severely injured patients, necessitating the discharge of stable medical patients and the inability to handle medical patients whose conditions have become acute.

Category 2 patients include those who require infusion therapy, complex sterile dressing changes, hyperalimentation, oxygen (including ventilator care), dialysis, intensive care, or life–support equipment. Medically complex, unstable, and terminally ill patients with do not resuscitate orders must also be hospitalized.

Supportive Care in SNS

Communities should establish protocols for staff assistance and procedures for triage, supportive care, and universal precautions (i.e., no smoking, proper handling of body fluids and medical waste, continuous monitoring of patients by caregivers). Nurses and other staff at SNS can offer supportive care while patients and their caregivers manage routine needs. Caregivers focus on helping with activities of daily living, administering medications, and providing oxygen and other medical support. SNS nurses offer supervision and assistance, if needed, when patients or caregivers assume responsibility for their own procedures.

The community plan must anticipate SNS staffing requirements, including the types of personnel (i.e., medical director, nurses, emergency medical technicians, social workers, support staff), credentialing process, scheduling, and onsite recruitment, registration, and supervision of volunteers. Plans for SNS must ensure cultural and linguistic competence among staff members. Protocols must be established for admitting and registering patients and caregivers and for acquiring and storing supplies. Staff members must be capable of handling a range of medical and nursing requirements, including labor in pregnant women, violent situations, and deaths. Procedures for closing down the SNS and relocating patients as needed must be established as part of the overall plan.

REESTABLISHING LOCAL BUSINESS AND ECONOMIC ACTIVITY

When reestablishing lost infrastructure, communities should take the opportunity to make improvements and to reduce future vulnerability to disaster. Local efforts can influence the pace, location, type, density, design, and cost of redevelopment. In addition to providing guidance on disaster–resistant building techniques, community leaders can aid reconstruction by ensuring optimal urban planning, letting families rebuild housing according to their tastes and incomes, and financing the delivery of electricity, water, and sewer lines.

A major disaster usually causes a decline in income and employment, thus reducing the resources of the population at their time of greatest need. This reduction in income cuts the tax base when increased government resources are needed. Jobs and economic activity give people a sense of return to normalcy (reestablishing schools also serves this function). Jobs, economic growth, and housing repair influence long–term recovery more than disaster relief efforts.

SOCIAL ENVIRONMENT

To aid in social recovery, local leaders must be familiar with basic family structure, economic patterns, governmental structure, religious affiliations, customs and practices, and power relationships within their community before disaster strikes. Effective intervention after a disaster requires an understanding of coping mechanisms. Each community has a variety of internal social structures that help individuals and families through difficult periods. Coping mechanisms exist at the level of the individual, family, community, and regional levels.

Strengthening horizontal community ties provides a means of redevelopment and of preparing for future disasters. In some cases, the disaster may provide an opportunity for the community to work together in ways it never has before, resulting in a stronger community and a stronger sense of community than existed before the crisis.

Emphasis on reestablishing community means that, where options exist, leaders should choose the option that strengthens or maintains the community. For example, disaster recovery plans should avoid building camps or large shelters wherever possible and instead provide aid in such a way that people can stay at home or in their neighborhood, which will allow residents to rely on preexisting social connections and to promote resumption of other normal activities.

INCORPORATING DISASTER PREPAREDNESS INTO RECOVERY

Vulnerability assessments require a review of land use based on post–disaster needs. Vulnerability assessments can also be used to predict the effects (both positive and negative) of redevelopment by projecting the impact of anticipated changes. The assessment of vulnerabilities should be used to avoid or reduce negative outcomes from future disasters. Encouraging communities to rebuild and commit to their communities long term requires attracting investment and demonstrating that the community has worked to reduce the negative impact if disaster repeats. For example, if housing is needed following a flood, a vulnerability assessment can tell officials where to build new houses to reduce the risk of damage from future flooding. Reconstruction should use improved designs and standards that reduce the vulnerability of structures. Reconstruction may also involve the erection of structures to reduce future mortality, such as cyclone shelters, and to detect possible events, such as early warning systems.

Chapter 13

Evaluation Methods for Assessing Medical and Public Health Response to Disasters

Evaluating disaster response is essential for preparedness planning. This chapter addresses the principles involved in comprehensive and objective disaster plan assessment and provides details on how to develop effective evaluation tools.

PUBLIC HEALTH ROLE

- Conduct systematic reviews of health and public health aspects of disaster response to improve efforts to reduce morbidity and mortality.

- Use professionally recognized measures of process and outcome to monitor health and public health programs and to direct resources in all phases of disaster response and recovery.

EVALUATION METHODS

Evaluation has several purposes, the most fundamental of which is to determine the extent to which an organization, program, or unit achieves its clearly stated and measurable objectives in responding to a disaster. Evaluations are used to adjust disaster plans, to focus practice drills and preparedness, to improve planning for rapid assessment and management of daily response operations, to provide input for the refinement of measures of effectiveness, and to collect data for hypothesis–driven research. Evaluations provide objective information for managers to formulate and revise policy through a retrospective and descriptive design for capturing information. While disaster response evaluation cannot always use traditional experimental design for data collection or analysis, administrators can improve their management of health systems affected by disasters from retrospective studies that draw information systematically from a variety of sources. For example, collecting information from broad categories of personnel and lay informants could be used in lieu of probability sampling.

Disaster evaluation research seeks to obtain information that can be used in preparation for future disasters by:

- Developing profiles of victims and types of injuries to inform the revision of existing or preparation of enhanced disaster plans.

- Assessing whether program adjustments can reduce disability and save lives.

- Determining if better methods to organize and manage a response exist, including the use of resources in a relief effort.

- Identifying measures that can be implemented to reduce damage to communities.

- Assessing the long–term physical and emotional effects of a disaster on individuals and communities.

Evaluations should examine the structure of the health system's response to the disaster, the allocation of health and public health resources, the sequence of events, the impact of the program at each stage, issues that arose during the health system's response to the disaster, the limitations of the response, and policy lessons.

DATA COLLECTION

During the impact and post–impact phases of a disaster, a record of important medical, environmental, and social events is usually created in journalistic features, photographs, videos, official records, recollections of participants, and other trained reporters. To study these events, information must be obtained from a variety of informants, documents, and records. Thorough preplanning of the evaluation is essential to ensure that the evaluation will yield valid findings. Multidisciplinary teams must design studies, collect data, and interpret the findings. A typical team consists of a physician, Emergency Medical Services specialist, social or behavioral scientist, epidemiologist, and disaster management specialist. This research team should hold daily debriefings to discuss issues and problems related to the implementation of the evaluation protocol.

While record keeping during a disaster is difficult and gaps often occur, some written record on a case–by–case basis is usually available. Public health officials can look for data in the hospital patient record, hospital E–codes, emergency department records, field station logs, and autopsy reports. Impressions of patient treatment can be made by reviewing available patient records, supplemented by interview data. Other sources of evaluation data include journalistic accounts and interviews with injured survivors, public health and health care professionals, search and rescue personnel, relief workers, lay bystanders, and disaster managers.

For interviews, a series of questions designed to probe the effectiveness of the disaster relief operation can be incorporated into the administered questionnaire. The questions should be structured, calling for a fixed response, although a small number of open–ended questions can provide useful information. Use medical record abstract forms to collect hospital and autopsy data. The data should be validated by cross–checking multiple sources.

DESIGNING EVALUATION STUDIES

Evaluations begin by reviewing the disaster response plan and its measurable objectives. Without measurable objectives, a disaster response plan cannot be evaluated. A structured evaluation must begin before the disaster with preparedness activities and participants and plans for rapid surveillance. Equipment needs, strategies for medical and public health intervention, and the chain of command among participating response organizations must all be assessed. Internal and external communication methods and participants must be examined. All personnel who participate in disaster response must be evaluated for the timing and execution of duties in relation to their planned assignments and actual implementation in the field.

In the process of conducting an evaluation, assessments are directed for five domains of activity: structure, process, outcomes, response adequacy, and costs. The following sections describe each domain and provide sample questions that might be asked to evaluate the response to a disaster involving a large number of casualties.

Structure

Evaluation of structure examines how the medical and public health response was organized, what resources were needed, and what resources were available. Questions used to evaluate structure for the response to mass casualty incidents include:

- Were ambulances, hospital emergency departments, and critical care units sufficiently equipped and supplied to meet the demands of the disaster?

- Were sufficient numbers of properly trained staff available, especially volunteers, first responders, ambulance personnel, emergency department nurses, critical care physicians, and communications staff?

- Did staff receive prior training in methods specific to the provision of public health and medical care during a disaster?

- Did the communications system have sufficient capacity, flexibility, and back–up capabilities during the disaster for both internal and external communications?

- How were patients transported to the hospital? To what extent was the ambulance system overloaded? What equipment shortages were experienced?

- How well did the following functions operate during the impact and post–impact phases: resource management (i.e., dispatch, coordination with Emergency Medical Services and public services), medical supervision, and communication among hospitals, mobile units, and other services?

Process

Process assesses how the system (both medical and public health components) functioned during the impact and post–impact, how well individuals were prepared, and what problems occurred. The process questions should be sorted into those that probe the operation of the disaster response system and those that assess the process of treating patients. Process questions to ask in a mass casualty incident include:

- Were medical staff available during the search and rescue of patients? How soon after the response as initiated did they arrive?

- Did medical staff trained in detection and extrication have the skills and knowledge required to perform their functions during the disaster?

- Were medical staff trained in detection and extrication able to apply their medical knowledge under disaster conditions? What factors, if any, prevented optimum performance?

- How effectively was the triage function performed? What, if any, factors interfered?

- Was there adequate control over the management and deployment of resources during the post–impact response? Was responsibility for decision making clear? Were appropriate decisions made concerning the process of patient triage, transfer, and treatment?

- What first aid was provided to victims, by whom, and when? Was this appropriate and effective?

- How were patients transferred from the scene of the disaster to treatment sites?

- Did effective coordination and communication among agencies occur?

- How did the hospital respond to the volume of patients?

- How did volunteers function? Was their participation supportive, or did it interfere with the treatment of patients? What controls, if any, were exercised?

- Did any compromises in standard medical care occur? Were these compromises necessary and acceptable?

- Was the public prepared to act appropriately when the disaster occurred? Should the plan to provide public education and information be modified to facilitate a future public health or medical response?

Outcomes

Outcomes assessments identify what was and was not achieved as a result of the medical and public health response. This assessment focuses on the impact of care provided to patients during the disaster. Outcome assessment can be achieved using either implicit or explicit criteria through a review of patient records. If implicit standards and criteria are used, a panel of critical care and emergency care specialists can review a sample of patient records and make judgments about the appropriateness of treatment related to patient outcomes. If explicit standards and criteria are employed, the reviewer uses written guidelines to determine the adequacy of treatment. Forms for summarizing patient treatment and outcome data should be developed well in advance of their use and evaluated for completeness after use to assess a disaster response. Data to be collected should include at a minimum:

- Personal characteristics of patient (i.e., age, sex, residence),

- Medical condition/status prior to injury,

- Principal diagnosis, secondary diagnosis, type of injury,

- Body location of injury (i.e., extremities, back, chest, head, neck, abdomen),

- Prehospital care provided and by whom,

- Method of transportation to hospital,

- Hospital treatment provided,

- Patient status on discharge,

- Cause of death, if applicable.

Response Adequacy

Assessing the adequacy of the disaster response examines the extent to which the response systems were able to meet the needs of the community during the disaster. The analysis of the adequacy of the response is valuable for planning for future disasters. The main concern is, overall, how much death and disability occurred that could have been prevented? To assess this dimension of the response for a mass casualty incident, obtain information about the following:

- To what extent was the prehospital system able to function as designed?

- What types of victims were cared for and what types were the hospital and prehospital systems unable to treat? For what reasons?

- How many victims were transported to more than one hospital due to limitations in hospital beds, intensive care beds, supplies, or staff?

- How effectively did hospitals cooperate to distribute patients to share the burden of treatment and to refer patients in need to specialty care?

Costs

Disaster response costs can be measured in several ways: the total cost of the relief effort, the cost per every life saved, the cost for various subsystems that operated during the response phase, and the costs of preparedness. Questions to ask include:

- What were each of the previously defined costs?

- Did the cost of the program correlate with the benefits to the community?

Appendix **A**

Common Terms Used
in Disaster Preparedness and
Response

Adaptive equipment—Equipment that helps a person move, groom, or eat independently, such as mobility aids, grooming aids, feeding aids, and similar devices used to offset functional limits.

Advanced life support—A medical procedure provided by paramedics that includes sophisticated diagnosis of patient conditions, followed by protocol-driven on-site initial medical treatment for conditions that will receive definitive treatment in hospitals.

Aftershocks—A sequence of smaller earthquakes that follow a larger-magnitude earthquake for months to years and that can exacerbate the damage. Also, a type of ground failure.

Alarm procedure—A means of alerting concerned parties to a disaster. Various optical and acoustical means of alarm are possible, including flags, lights, sirens, radio and telephone.

Analysis–epidemiologic measures—Includes indicators such as descriptive statistics, specific diseases and/or death rates, secular trends, and tests for sensitivity and validity.

Assessments—The evaluation and interpetation of short term and long term measurements to provide a basis for decision-making and to enhance public health officials' ability to monitor disaster situations. The goal of conducting assessments is to convey information quickly in order to recalibrate a system's response.

Augmentative communication device—A device used to help a person communicate by voice.

Avalanche—The sudden slide of a huge mass of snow and ice, usually carrying with it earth, rocks, trees and other debris.

Average throughput time—Time from a client's entry into a Point of Dispensing site until exit.

Basic life support—Noninvasive measures (such as elimination of airway obstruction, cardio-pulmonary resuscitation, hemorrhage control, woundcare, and immobilization of fractures) used to preserve life of ABC—unstable patients.

Becquerel (Bq)—A unit of nuclear activity. 1 Bq represents the amount of radioactive substance that disintegrates in one second. This unit has replaced the curie.

Blast Wave (primary)—The intense over-pressurization impulse created by a detonated high-energy explosive (HE). Blast injuries are characterized by anatomical and physiological changes from the direct or reflective over-pressurization force impacting the body's surface. The HE "blast wave" (over-pressure component) should be distinguished from "blast wind" (forced super-heated air flow). The latter may be encountered with both HE and low-energy explosive.

Blindness/Visual disability—A visual condition that interferes with a person's ability to see or results in the absence of all sight.

Bioterrorism—The unlawful release of biologic agents or toxins targeted at humans, animals, or plants with the intent to intimidate or coerce the government or civilian population to further political or social objectives.

Branch—See page 289.

Case—A unit of observation.

Case definition—Standardized criteria for deciding whether a person has a particular disease or health-related condition, used for investigations and for comparing potential cases. Case definitions provide the basis for deciding which disaster-specific health conditions are be monitored through an emergency information surveillance system.

Casualty—Any person suffering physical and/or psychological damage by outside violence leading to either death, injuries, or material loss.

Casualty clearing station—A collecting point for victims located in the immediate vicinity of the disaster site where triage and medical treatment can be provided.

Central holding area—A location where ambulances assemble and from where they either leave to pick—up patients from the casualty clearing station or leave for one of the neighboring hospitals according to a victim distribution plan.

Closed captions—Visual text displays used to display information for those who are deaf or hearing impaired that are hidden in the video signal. Closed captions can be accessed through a TV remote control, an on—screen menu or through a special decoder. All TVs with a 13" or larger diameter screen manufactured after 1993 have caption decoder circuitry. Open captions are an integral part of the television picture, like subtitles in a movie, and cannot be turned off. Text that advances very slowly across the bottom of the screen is referred to as a crawl; displayed text or graphics that move up and down the screen are said to scroll.

Cognitive impairment—A medical condition or injury that affects a person's ability to understand spoken or written information.

Communication disability—A medical condition or injury that interferes with a person's ability to communicate by using one's voice.

Community profile—The characteristics of the local environment that are prone to a chemical or nuclear accident. These characteristics can include population density, age distribution, roads, railways, waterways, types of dwellings and buildings, and local relief agencies.

Comprehensive Emergency Management—An integrated approach to organizing multiple emergency programs and activities. These activities are organized into the four phases comprising the "life cycle" of emergency management: *mitigation, preparedness, response, and recovery.*

Contamination—An accidental release of hazardous chemicals or nuclear materials that pollute the environment and place humans at risk of contamination.

Contingency plan—An emergency plan developed in expectation of a disaster. Contingency plans are often based on risk assessments, the availability of human and material resources, community preparedness, and local and international response capabilities.

Coordinate—A systematic exchange of information among principal participants in order to carry out a unified response in the event of an emergency.

Covert releases (of a biologic agent)—An unannounced release of a biological agent that causes illness in the community. Detection of the agent is dependent on traditional surveillance methods. If undetected, the covert release of a contagious agent has the potential for large scale spread.

Cracker—An individual who uses computer programming to gain unauthorized or illegal access to a computer network or file.

Data collection—Gathering, assembling, and delivering data to a centralized collection point.

Deafness/hearing disability—A medical condition or injury that interferes with a person's ability to hear sounds.

Decontamination—The removal of hazardous chemical or nuclear substances from the skin and/or mucous membranes by showering or washing the affected area with water, or by rinsing with sterile a solution.

Disaster—Any event, typically occurring suddenly, that causes damage, ecological disruption, loss of human life, deterioration of health and health services, **AND** which exceeds the adjustment capacity of the affected community on a scale sufficient to require outside assistance. These events can be caused by nature, equipment failure, human error, or biological hazards and diseases (e.g., earthquakes, floods, fires, hurricanes, cyclones, major storms, volcanic eruptions, spills, air crashes, droughts, epidemics, food shortages, and disasters of civil strife).

Disaster continuum, or emergency management cycle—The life cycle of a disaster or emergency.

Disaster epidemiology—The study of disaster-related deaths, illnesses, or injuries in humans. Also includes the study of factors that affect death, illness, and injury following a disaster. Methodology involves identifying and comparing risk factors among disaster victims to those who were left unharmed. Epidemiologic investigations provide public health professionals with information on the probable public health consequences of disasters.

Disaster informatics—The theoretical and practical aspects of information processing and communication, based on knowledge and experience derived from processes in medicine and health care in disaster settings.

Disaster–prone—The level of risk that is related to the disaster agent, the hazard or the immediate cause of a disaster. Disaster-proneness is determined by a history of past events and the risks of new events.

Disaster Severity Scale—By 1) classifying disasters by the following parameters: the radius of the disaster site, the number of dead, the number of wounded, the average severity of the injuries sustained, the impact time, and the rescue time, and 2) By attributing 0, 1 or 2 to each of variables, with 0 being the least severe and 2 the most, (for intensity, number or time) a scale with a range of 0 and 18 can be created.

Disaster vulnerability—The ability to absorb the effects of an extreme event or situation, and the ability to recover. Vulnerability varies from one society to another or from one place to the other, because the same type of disaster may have differing impacts on different populations or groups.

Dispatch communications system—A system used to assign ambulance personnel and other first responders.

Drills—Supervised activities designed to test a procedure which is a component of the overall emergency management plan. A drill may be a step leading towards an exercise, or may be an actual field response. A drill provides the ability to closely examine a limited portion of the overall plan, such as the patient tracking system or the transmission of surveillance data

Emergencies—Any occurrence which requires an immediate response that may be due to epidemics, technological catastrophes, strife or to natural or man-made cause.

Emergency Medical Technicians (EMTs) or **Paramedics (EMT–Ps)**—Trained emergency medical responders; EMTs and paramedics (higher level) are trained to identify and field-treat the most common medical emergencies and injuries, and to provide medical support to victims while enroute to the hospital.

Emergency Support Function (ESF)—A functional area of response activity established to coordinate the delivery of federal assistance during the response phase of an emergency. Each ESF represents the type of federal assistance most needed by states overwhelmed by the impact of a catastrophic event on local and state resources.

Epidemic—The occurrence, in excess of normal expectancy, of a disease, known or suspected to be of infectious or parasitic origin. A **threatened epidemic** occurs when the circumstances are such that a specific disease may reasonably be anticipated to occur in excess of normal expectancy.

ESF 6 Mass Care—Mass Care includes the tasks of sheltering, feeding, emergency first aid, family reunification, and distribution of emergency relief supplies to disaster victims. The Federal Response Plan designates the American Red Cross (ARC) as the primary agency responsible for this function.

ESF 8 Health and Medical—Basis of federal response to the health needs of disaster victims; lead agency is the US Public Health Service's Department of Health and Human Services.

Evacuation assistive equipment—Equipment or devices used to help people leave a building in an emergency.

Evaluation—A detailed review of a program, designed to determine whether program objectives were met, to assess its impact on the community, and to generate 'lessons learned' for the design of future projects; conducted during, and at the completion of important milestones, or at the end of a specific period.

Evaluation research—The application of scientific methods to assess the effectiveness of programs, services or organizations designed to improve health or prevent illness.

Exposure surveillance—To look for exposure or risk. Also known as a risk factor variable, predictor variable, independent variable, or putative causal factor. In disaster settings, exposure may be based on physical or environmental properties of the disaster event.

Exposure variable—A characteristic of interest. Also known as risk factor or predictor variable.

Famine Early Warning System—Established by the United States Agency for International Development to monitor climate and meteorology, availability of food in the market, and morbidity related to nutrition to predict the occurrence of famine.

Far–field—Following a nuclear accident at a nuclear plant, the immediate vicinity is called near-field with a diameter varying between 2 and 20 kilometers, depending on the source strength. The area outside the near-field is called the far-field, where effects are still noticeable after an accident.

Federal Coordinating Officer (FCO)—The person appointed by FEMA following a presidential declaration of a severe disaster or of an emergency to coordinate federal assistance. The FCO initiates immediate action to assure that federal assistance is provided in accordance with the disaster declaration, any applicable laws or regulations, and the FEMA–state agreement.

Federal On-Scene Commander (OSC)—The official designated upon the activation of the Joint Operations Center that ensures appropriate coordination of the United States government's overall response with federal, state, and local authorities.

Federal Response Plan (FRP)—The plan that coordinates federal resources in disaster situations. The FRP is designed to address the consequences of any disaster or emergency situation in which there is need for federal assistance under the authorities of the Robert T. Stafford Disaster Relief and Emergency Assistance Act, 42 U.S.C. 5121 et seq. The FRP is also the federal government's plan of action when assisting affected states and local jurisdictions in the event of a severe disaster or emergency. The plan consists of 12 Emergency Support Functions (ESFs).

Firewall—A computer or peripheral running a software that is a barrier between a LAN (local area network) and the internet.

First Responder—Local police, fire, and emergency medical personnel who arrive first on the scene of an incident and take action to save lives, protect property, and meet basic human needs.

Functional Model of Public Health Response in Disasters—Paradigm for identifying disaster related activities for which each core area of public health has responsibility; interface between the core components of professional public health training and the matrix of emergency management functions; relation between the framework of activities defined by the emergency management community and public health practice.

Fujita scale—A scale used to measure the strength of tornadoes.

Geographic Information System (GIS)[1]—A collection of computer hardware, software, and geographic data for capturing, storing, updating, manipulating, analyzing, and displaying all forms of geographically related information.

Access rights (computing)—The privileges given to a user for reading, writing, deleting, and updating files on a disk or tables in a database. Access rights are stated as "no access," "read only," and "read/ write."

Address—A point stored as an x,y location in a geographic data layer, referenced with a unique identifier.

Address geocoding—Assigning x,y coordinates to tabular data such as street addresses or Zip codes so they can be displayed as points on a map.

Altitude—1) The elevation above a reference datum, usually sea level, of any point on the earth's surface or in the atmosphere. 2) The z-value in a three dimensional coordinate system.

Area chart—A chart that emphasizes the difference between two or more groups of data; for example the changes in a population from one year to the next. The area of interest is usually shaded in a different color.

Attribute—Information about a geographic feature in a GIS, generally stored in a table and linked to the feature by a unique identifier.

Base data—Map data over which other information is placed.

---

[1]   Reprinted with permission from Kennedy, Heather (2001) Dictionary of GIS Terminology, ESRI Press, Redlands, California

Basemap—A map depicting geographic features used for locational reference and often including a geodetic control network as part of its structure.

Cell—The smallest square in a grid. Each cell usually has an attribute value associated with it.

Clean data—Data that is free from error

Connectivity—How geographic features in a network of lines are attached to one another functionally or spatially.

Database—A GIS database includes data about the spatial locations and shapes of geographic features recorded as points, lines, areas, pixels, grid cells, as well as their attributes.

Data dictionary (Metadata)—A set of tables containing information about the data stored in a GIS database, such as the full names of the attributes, meanings of codes, scale of source data, accuracy of locations, and map projections used.

Geocode—Code representing the location of an object, such as an address, census tract, postal code or x,y coordinates.

Global Positioning System (GPS)—A constellation of 24 satellites, developed by the U. S. Department of Defense, that orbit the earth at an altitude of 20, 200 kilometers. These satellites transmit signals that allow a GPS receiver anywhere on earth to calculate its own location. GPS is used for navigation, mapping, surveying, and other application where precise position is necessary.

Hierarchical database—A database that stores related information in a structure very like a tree, where records can be traced to parent records which in turn can be traced to a root record.

Lookup table—A tabular data file that contains additional attributes for records stored in an attribute table.

Overlay—Superimposing two or more maps registered to a common coordinate system, either digitally or on a transparent material, in order to show the relationships between features that occupy the same geographic space.

Raster—A spatial data model of rows and columns of cells. Groups of cells that share the same value representing geographic features.

Relational database—Data stored in tables that are associated with shared attributes, which can be arranged in different combinations.

Shapefile—A vector file format for storing location, shape, and attributes of geographic features. It is stored in a set of related files and contains one feature class.

Spatial analysis—Studying the locations and shapes of geographic features and the relationships between them. Traditionally includes overlay and contiguity analysis, surface analysis, linear analysis and raster analysis.

Vector—A data structure used to represent linear geographic features. Features are made of ordered lists of x,y coordinates and represented by points, lines, or polygons; Points connect to become lines, and lines connect to become polygons. Attributes are associated with each feature (as opposed to a raster data structure, which associates attributes with grid cells).

Golden hour—The principle that ABC-unstable victims must be stabilized as soon as possible, at least within one hour following injury, or they will die.

Hazard—The probability that a disaster will occur. Hazards can be caused by a natural phenomenon (e.g., earthquake, tropical cyclone), or by failure of manmade sources of energy (e.g., nuclear reactor, industrial explosion) or by uncontrolled human activity (e.g., conflicts, overgrazing).

Hazard identification/analysis—The process of determining what events are likely to occur in a specified region or environment (e.g., earthquakes, floods, industrial accidents).

Hazard surveillance—An assessment of the occurrence, distribution, and secular trends relating to different levels of hazards (e.g., toxic chemical agents, physical agents, biomechanical stressors, as well as biologic agents) that are responsible for disease and injury.

Impact phase—A phase during a disaster event where emergency management activities focus on warning and preparedness.

Incident Action Plan (IAP)—A written document, developed by the Incident Commander or the planning section of the ICS, that details the actions that will be conducted through the ICS in response to an incident. IAPs are developed for specific time periods, referred to as operational periods, and are based on the needs of the incident. The Incident Commander is responsible for overseeing and implementing the IAP.

Incident Command System (ICS)—ICS is the model for command, control, and coordination of a response and provides a means to coordinate the efforts of individual agencies.

Branch—An organizational level having functional or geographic responsibility for major parts or incident operations. The Incident Commander may establish *geographic Branches* to resolve span-of-control issues—or may establish *functional Branches* to manage specific functions (e.g., law enforcement, fire, emergency medical etc.). A Branch is managed by a *Branch Director)*.

Division—The organizational level having responsibility for operations within a defined geographic area. The Division level is the organizational level between Single Resources, Task Forces or Strike Teams, and the Branch level.

Emergency Operations Center (EOC)—Location where department heads, government officials, and volunteer agencies coordinate the response to an emergency event.

Group—The organizational level having responsibility for a specified *functional* assignment at an incident (e.g., perimeter control, evacuation, fire suppression, etc.). A Group is managed by a *Group Supervisor.*

Integrated Communications—System using a common communications plan, standard operating procedures, clear text, common frequencies, and common terminology.

Resource management—Maximizes use, consolidates control, reduces communication, provides accountability, and ensures safety for personnel.

Section—The organizational level with responsibility for a major functional area of the incident. The Section is located organizationally between Branches and the Incident Commander.

Sizeup—Problem identification and an assessment of the possible consequences. Initially, sizeup is the responsibility of the first officer to arrive at the scene. Sizeup continues throughout the response to update continually 1) the nature of the incident; 2) hazards that are present; 3) the size of the affected area; 4) whether the area can be isolated; 5) if a Staging Area is needed and the best location; 6) where to establish entrance and exit routes for the flow of personnel and equipment.

Span of control—Number of individuals that one supervisor manages. The manageable span on control for one supervisor ranges between three to seven resources, with five being optimum.

Staging Area—Where resources are kept awaiting assignment.

Strike Team—A group of resources of the same size and type, (e.g., five patrol units, three drug K-9 teams).

Task Force—A combination of single resources assembled for a particular operational need, with common communications and a leader.

Top–down—The Command function is established by the first arriving officer who becomes the Incident Commander.

Unity of command—Each person within an organization reports to only one designated person.

Integrated Recovery Programs (IRPs)—Balanced recovery programs that respond to a variety of community needs. IRPs often coordinate activities that repair community facilities and enable people to get cash to replace lost possessions. IRPs are characterized by stimulation of activity in various sectors, sequencing of activities at appropriate times, and the use of both indirect and direct methods.

Intensity—A Roman numerical index from I to XII that describes the physical effects of an earthquake to a specific location, to man, or to structures built by man. These values are subjective. The most commonly used scale is the Modified Mercalli Intensity (MMI), developed in the 1930s. Intensity VI denotes the threshold for potential ground failure such as liquefaction. Intensity VII denotes the threshold for architectural damage. Intensity VIII denotes the threshold for structural damage. Intensity IX denotes intense structural damage. Intensities X to XII denote various levels of destruction up to total destruction. An earthquake has many intensities, but only one magnitude.

International assistance—Assistance provided by one or more countries or international and voluntary organizations to a country in need, usually for development or for an emergency. The four main elements of assistance within the international community are: (a) The intergovernmental agencies—United Nations, Common Market, (b) nongovernmental organizations, (c) the Red Cross, and (d) bilateral agreements.

Interoperable Communications—Ability to talk, with whom you want, when you want, when authorized, but not all at the same time.

Joint Information Center (JIC)—A center located at the scene of an emergency established to coordinate federal public information. It is also the central point of contact for all news media. Public information officials from participating state and local agencies often collocate at the JIC.

Joint Operations Center (JOC)—The JOC acts as the focal point for the management and direction of onsite activities, coordination, and establishment of state requirements and priorities, as well as the coordination of the federal response.

Landslide—A massive and more or less rapid sliding down of soil and rock, causing damage in its path; the most common and wide spread type of ground failure; consists of falls, topples, slides, spreads, and flows of soil and/or rock on unstable slopes.

Liquefaction—Occurs mainly in young, shallow, loosely compacted, water saturated sand and gravel deposits when subjected to ground shaking; results in a temporary loss of bearing strength.

Logistician—Individual who is skilled at calculating and arranging for various needs of moving and providing personnel, supplies, etc. required within a response

Loss—A range of adverse consequences impacting communities and individuals (e.g., damage, loss of economic value, loss of function, loss of natural resources, loss of ecological systems, environmental impact, health deterioration, mortality, morbidity).

Latrines—A pit designed to capture and contain excreta. Usually there is a platform covering the hole, and some type of wall to provide privacy. The pit may be dug as a trench with multiple platforms across it, or it can be a solitary pit with a self-standing structure.

Magnitude—A numerical quantity, invented by Charles F. Richter, that characterizes the size and scope of an earthquake in terms of the total energy released after adjusting for difference in epicentral distance and focal depth. Magnitude differs from intensity in that magnitude is determined on the basis of instrumental records; whereas, intensity is determined on the basis of subjective observations of the damage. Moderate-magnitude earthquakes have magnitudes of 5.5 to 6.9; large-magnitude earthquakes have magnitudes of 7.0 to 7.9; and great-magnitude earthquakes have magnitudes of 8.0 and greater. The energy increases exponentially with magnitude e.g. a magnitude 6.0 earthquake releases 31.5 times more energy than a magnitude 5.0 earthquake or approximately 1,000 times more energy than a magnitude 4.0 earthquake.

Manmade or technological disasters; complex emergencies—Technological events that are not caused by natural hazards but that occur in human settlements, such as fire, chemical spills and explosions, and armed conflict.

Medical coordination—In the chain of medical care, the coordination between the pre-hospital and hospital phases between doctors, nurses and paramedics. Simplification and standardization of materials and methods utilized is a prerequisite.

Measuring environmental hazards—Assessing the occurrence of, distribution of, and the secular trends in levels of hazards (toxic chemical agents, physical agents, biomechanical stressors, as well as biologic agents) responsible for disease and injury.

Measures of biological effects—A gauge of health in humans that indicates the impact of a disaster. Examples include 1) age-specific injury and death rates associated with earthquakes; 2) laboratory typing of organisms events event where infectious disease outbreaks occur; 3) biochemical testing of exposures to toxic chemicals to assess exposure levels; 4) anthropometric measurements, such as height to weight ratios, to indicate the type and degree of malnutrition in famine situations.

Measures of physical effects to indicate magnitude—An assessment of environmental conditions whose levels are negatively impacted due to a disaster. Examples include 1) height of river above flood stage; 2) level of pollutants in air after forest fire; and 3) level of toxic chemicals in drinking water or sediment.

Mitigation—Measures taken to reduce the harmful effects of a disaster by attempting to limit impacts on human health and economic infrastructure.

Mobility disability—A medical condition or injury that impedes a person's ability to walk or move.

Modified Mercalli scale—A scale that indicates the intensity of an earthquake by measuring the degree of damage at a particular location.

Monitoring—A process of evaluating the performance of response and recovery programs by measuring their outcomes against stated objectives. Monitoring is used to identify bottlenecks and obstacles that cause delays or programmatic shortfalls that require reassessment.

Mortality data—Information about the number of deaths used to assess the magnitude of the disaster event, evaluate the effectiveness of disaster preparedness, evaluate the adequacy of warning systems, and identify high risk groups for contingency planning.

Natural disasters—Natural phenomena with acute onset and profound effects, such as earthquakes, floods, tropical cyclones, tornadoes.

Na–tech (natural–technological) disasters—Natural disasters that create technological emergencies, such as urban fires resulting from seismic motion or chemical spills resulting from floods.

Outcome surveillance—To look for a health outcome or health event of interest, usually illness, injury, or death. Also known as the response variable, dependent variable, or effect variable; for example, the American Red Cross (ARC)–Centers for Disease Control and Prevention's Health Impact Surveillance System which records mortality and morbidity in disaster events where ARC has served.

Outcome variable—A health event, usually encompassing illness, injury, or death. Also known as response variable.

Overt release—An announced release of a biological agent, by terrorists or others; a release of a biological agent that is recognized at the time of release. This type of release allows for treatment before the onset of disease.

Personal Support Network (PSN)—A group of people who will help those with disabilities at their home, school, workplace, volunteer site, or any other location in which they spend a lot of time. Members of a support network can include roommates, relatives, neighbors, friends, and co-workers. A PSN must be able to check if an individual needs assistance, knows their capabilities and needs, and be available to help within minutes.

Phases of the functional model—The functional model is composed of seven phases which correspond to the type of activities involved in preparing for and responding to a disaster. The phases include planning, prevention, assessment, response, surveillance, recovery, and evaluation.

PHIN messaging system—Message transport system that allows secure data transmission over internet.

Planning—To work cooperatively with other disciplines, in advance of a disaster event, in order to initiate prevention and preparedness.

Point of Dispensing (POD)—A space established when mass distribution of antibiotics or vaccine is needed and where patients are registered, triaged, have swab samples taken, medically evaluated, and provided with antibiotics or vaccine.

Post–disaster surveillance—Observations conducted by health authorities after a disaster to monitor health events, to 1) detect sudden changes in disease occurrence, 2) follow long term trends of specific diseases, 3) identify changes in agents and host factors for the diseases of interest, and 4) detect changes in health practices for treating relevant diseases.

Postimpact phase—The period of time after a disaster event. Often associated with activities of response and recovery.

Power–dependent equipment—Equipment that requires electricity to operate.

Preimpact phase—The period of time before a disaster strikes where activities of mitigation or prevention occur.

Preparedness—All measures and policies taken before an event occurs that allow for prevention, mitigation, and readiness. Preparedness includes designing warning systems, planning for evacuation, relocation of dwellings (eg, for floods), storing food and water, building temporary shelter, devising management strategies, and holding disaster drills and exercises. Contingency plans and responses is also included in preparedness as well as planning for post-impact response and recovery.

Presidential Decision Directives (PDDs)—U.S. government policy decisions on foreign policy and national security which follow the National Security Council; gathering facts, conducting analyses, determining alternatives, and presenting policy choices to the President for decision.

Prevention—Primary, secondary, and tertiary efforts that help avert an emergency. These activities are commonly referred to as "mitigation" in the emergency management model. For example, preventing a disaster from occurring, such as cloud seeding to stimulate rain in a fire. In public health terms, prevention refers to actions that may prevent further loss of life, disease, disability, or injury.

Primary prevention—Preventing the occurrence of deaths, injuries, or illnesses related to the disaster event (e.g., evacuation of a community in a flood—prone area, sensitizing warning systems for tornadoes and severe storms).

Public access system—An emergency telephone system by which the public notifies the authorities that a medical emergency exists. Accessed by dialing 911.

Public health surveillance—The systematic collection, analysis, and interpretation of health data used for planning, implementing, and evaluating public health interventions and programs. Also used to determine the need for public health action and to assess the effectiveness of programs.

Radiation

Acute radiation exposure—A single large dose or a series of lesser but substantial doses over a short period of time.

Acute radiation syndrome—Radiation illness that is associated with an acute radiation exposure.

ALARA—A concept and administrative program that is meant to keep workers'exposures to ionizing radiation "as low as reasonably achievable." This specific action program, which takes economic and social factors into account, is expected to reduce collective medical and/or occupational doses (person–rems) while maintaining an individual worker's dose at 10 percent or less of the dose limits contained in 10 CFR 20.

Alpha particle—A positively-charged subatomic particle consisting of two protons and two neutrons, identical with the nucleus of the helium atom. The most energetic alpha particle is incapable of penetrating the skin.

Background radiation, natural—Ionizing radiation that is a natural part of a person's environment; primarily, cosmic rays and natural radioactivity.

Beta particle—A charged particle that is ejected from the nucleus of an atom; it has a mass and charge equal in magnitude to that of the electron.

Buffer zone—An intermediate area between the radioactively contaminated zone and the rest of the "clean" hospital.

Cytogenetic dosimetry—Estimation of radiation dose based on typical radiation—induced chromosomal aberrations as calibrated against standard exposures

Film bandage—A type of personal radiation monitor, or dosimeter, that records the extent of one's radiation exposure by means of sensitized photographic film.

Gamma ray—High energy radiation of short wavelength emitted during radioactive decay of many radioactive elements. Similar in properties to x-rays, gamma rays are of nuclear origin, while x-rays are formed by the excitation of orbital electrons.

ICRP—International Commission on Radiological Protection, a group formed in 1928, whose function is to recommend international standards for radiation protection.

Ionizing radiation—That form of radiation which is able to cause a neutral atom or molecule to gain or lose orbital electrons and thereby acquire a net electrical charge.

Isotope—One of two or more atoms with the same atomic number (thus, of the same chemical element) but with different atomic weights. Isotopes usually have similar chemical properties but somewhat different physical properties.

Low–level radiation—Generally considered for occupational purposes to be less than 5 rem/yr, or 20 rem of a single dose, of uniform wholebody radiation. A high-level dose, on the other hand, is arbitrarily defined as being from 150-350 rem (NCRP 64).

NCRP—National Council on Radiation Protection and Measurements, a nonprofit corporation chartered by Congress in 1964, to develop information and recommendations regarding radiation protection and measurements.

Personal monitor—A device for measuring a person's exposure to a physical or chemical agent in the environment, such as radiation. Information on the dose-equivalent of ionizing radiation to biological tissue is derived from film badges, ionization chambers and thermoluminescent devices; from determinations based on wholebody counting and analysis of biological specimens; and from area monitoring and special surveys. Also referred to as a personnel dosimeter or monitor.

Rad—A special unit for an "absorbed dose" of ionizing radiation. Cf. "rem" and "Roentgen."

Radionuclide—A radioactive nuclide.

Rem—"Radiation equivalent man;" a special unit of dose equivalent based on biological effect. The dose equivalent in rem units is numerically equal to the absorbed dose in rad units multiplied by a modifying factor; however, for simplicity and for the types of radiation most often encountered environmentally, the rem is numerically equivalent to both the rad and Roentgen. Cf. "rad" and "Roentgen."

Roentgen (R)—A special unit of radiation exposure based on measurement in air, or before the radiation strikes the body. Cf. "rad" and "rem."

Sealed source—A radioactive source that is contained within an impervious and durable package so as to prevent contact with or release and dispersal of the source.

Thermoluminescent dosimeter (TLD)—A personnel monitor in which orbital electrons are displaced or trapped within a crystal such as manganese activated calcium or lithium fluoride as a result of the crystal's exposure to ionizing radiation; when the crystal is later heated to a certain point, the stored energy of the electron displacement is released as light, which is then measured and related to radiation dose.

Transuranic elements—Those elements with an atomic number greater than 92, or heavier than uranium. All are radioactive and not naturally occurring; e.g., americium and plutonium.

Radio bands—A collection of neighboring radio frequencies. Frequencies are allocated on different bands. Each two-way radio is designed for a specific band, and a radio designed to work on one band, will not work on another.

Rapid needs assessment—A collection of techniques (epidemiologic, statistical, anthropological) designed to provide information about an affected community needs after a disaster.

Readiness—Links preparedness to relief. An assessment of readiness reflects the current capacity and capability of organizations involved in relief activities.

Recovery—Actions of responders, government, and the victims that help return the community to normal by stimulating community and government cohesion and involvement. One type of recovery involves repair of infrastructure, damaged buildings, and critical facilities. This phase occurs between the onset of the emergency and reconstruction period.

Red Cross—(also known as American Red Cross, or International Red Cross) general terms used for one or all the components of the worldwide organization active in humanitarian work. The official overall name is the International Red Cross and Red Crescent Movement, which has 3 components: 1) International Committee of the Red Cross (ICRC): acts mainly in conflict disasters as neutral intermediary in hostilities and for the protection of war victims. Guardian of the Geneva Conventions; 2) League of the Red Cross and Red Crescent Societies (LRCS): international federation of the National Societies, active in nonconflict disasters and natural calamities; and 3) The individual National Red Cross or Red Crescent Society of every country.

Rehabilitation or reconstruction—Efforts to reconstruct a system or infrastructure to the level which existed pre-emergency, through long term development. Reconstruction is often an opportunity for change rather than to simply "reconstruct" the pre-existing system.

Relief—Action focused on saving lives. Relief activities include search and rescue, first aid, and restoration of emergency communications and transportation systems, and attention to immediate care and basic needs of survivors, such as food, clothing, and medical or emotional care.

Report format—The instrument on which surveillance data are reported.

Reporting unit for surveillance—The data source that provides information for the surveillance system, such as a hospital, clinic, health post, mobile health unit, etc. determined after a case is defined.

Representativeness—The accuracy of the data when measuring the occurrence of a health event over time and its distribution by person and place.

Response—The phase of a disaster which encompasses relief, recovery, and rehabilitation. Also includes both the delivery of services and the management of activities.

Richter scale—A scale that indicates the magnitude of an earthquake; by providing a measure of the total energy released from source of the earthquake.

Risk assessment—A systematic process that determines the likelihood of adverse health effects in a population following exposure to a specified hazard. Health consequences may depend on the type of hazard and damage to infrastructure, loss of economic value, loss of function, loss of natural resources, loss of ecological systems, environmental impact, deterioration of health, mortality, and morbidity. The major components of a risk assessment include: hazard identification/analysis and vulnerability analysis that answers the following questions: What can happen? How likely are each of the possible outcomes? When the possible outcomes happen, what are the likely consequences and losses? Risk is frequently presented as a probability estimate. Risk assessment is a key planning tool for overall disaster management, especially prevention and mitigation activities.

Risk as a function of hazard and vulnerability—A relationship that is frequently depicted by the following useful formula, although the association is not strictly arithmetic: Risk = Hazard × Vulnerability.

Risk indicator—Descriptor that briefly denotes a risk that may cause a disaster.

Risk Management—The process of deciding what action to take when a risk assessment indicates that risk, or a danger of loss, exists. Risk management includes a range of actions (e.g., prevention, mitigation, preparedness, and recovery) that are designed to mitigate an increasing risk of natural and technological hazards; decrease risk to existing levels; and plan ways to respond to natural and technological hazards including catastrophic events.

Saffir–Simpson scale—A scale used to measure strength of hurricanes.

Secondary prevention—Mitigates the health consequences of disasters (e.g., use of carbon monoxide detectors when operating gasoline-powered generators after loss of electric power after ice storms, employing appropriate occupant behavior in multistory structures during earthquakes, building a "safe room" in dwellings located in tornado-prone areas); may be instituted when disasters are imminent.

Service Animal—A specially-trained animal used by a person with a disability to help with daily living. These animals are allowed by law to accompany their owners anywhere.

Span of Control—The number of resources for which any one supervisor is responsible.

Stockpile—A place or storehouse where material, medicines, and other supplies are kept in the event of an emergency.

Stress—Physical, mental, or emotional strain or tension.

SUMA (*Supply management* program)—Developed by the Pan American Health Organization, a computer-based system provides a mechanism for sorting, classifying, and preparing an inventory of relief supplies sent to a disaster-stricken country.

Surge capacity—The health care system's ability to rapidly expand and deliver services beyond what is required during normal care.

Surveillance—The ongoing and systematic collection, analysis, and interpretation of health data essential to the planning, implementation, and evaluation of public health practice. Surveillance systems are designed to disseminate data in a timely manner and often include both data collection and disease monitoring.

Technological hazard—A potential threat to humans and their welfare caused by technological factors (e.g., chemical release, nuclear accident, dam failure). Earthquakes and other natural hazards can trigger technological hazards.

Tertiary prevention—The minimization of the effects of disease and disability among those with pre-existing conditions. Tertiary prevention shields persons with health conditions from negative health effects relating to a disaster. Examples include appropriate sheltering of persons with respiratory illnesses and those prone to such conditions, particularly the elderly and young children, from haze and smoke originating from forest fires, and sheltering elderly who are prone to heat illnesses during episodes of extreme ambient temperatures.

The EMS system—The prehospital system (public access, dispatch, EMTs/medics, and ambulance services) and the in-hospital system (Emergency Departments, hospitals and other definitive care facilities and personnel).

Tiger Team—Military term for a group that probes security to find weaknesses that can be remedied.

Timeliness—How quickly information (surveillance data) can be made available.

Toxicological disaster—A serious environmental pollutant that causes illness by the massive, accidental escape of toxic substances into the air, soil or water, and to man, animals, or plants.

Toxin—A substance capable of causing a harmful effect.

Treatment technique (TT)—An enforceable procedure or level of technological performance that public water systems must follow to ensure control of water contamination. When there is no reliable method that is economically and technically feasible to measure contaminants at particularly low concentrations, a treatment technique (TT) is set rather than a maximum contaminant level (MCL). An example of a treatment technique rule is the surface water treatment rule, which includes disinfection and filtration.

Triage—Selection and categorization, of the victims of a disaster, for appropriate treatment according to the degree of severity of illness or injury, and the availability of medical and transport facilities.

Transportation to definitive medical care—Ground ambulances are the vehicle of choice for most transports, but helicopters, boats, and snow cats may be utilized under specific circumstances. Medical transports allow for the continued medical support of patients while in transport, usually to a hospital.

Traumatic stress—While not a clearly defined area, traumatic stress has tended to include events and circumstances that are both extreme and outside of the realm of everyday experiences (e.g., events that are dangerous, overwhelming, and sudden marked by their extreme or sudden force, typically causing fear, anxiety, withdrawal, and avoidance). Traumatic events also have high intensity, are unexpected, infrequent, and vary in duration from acute to chronic.

Tsunami—An oceanic tidal wave generated by an underwater upheaval such as earthquake or volcanic eruption. Tsunami waves move out in all directions and can travel over 100 miles and cause massive destruction.

Tsunami run up—A type of ground failure that affects low lying areas along coastlines and results from long periods of high ocean waves generated by the sudden, impulsive, vertical displacement of a submarine earthquake.

Victim—Persons who have been affected by a disaster. There are three classes of victims:

• **Primary victims**—Those who are affected by the physical impact of the disaster.

• **Secondary victims**—Those who reside within an affected community or on the border of an affected area and suffer economic loss due to the disaster or actions taken by relief operations.

• **Tertiary victims**—Those who are indirectly affected; who may live in the same country but not necessarily in the disaster affected area; for example, people receiving development aid who suddenly lose it due to diversion of aid.

Victim distribution—A victim distribution plan established in advance to define the transport and distribution of victims among neighboring hospitals according to their hospital treatment capacity. Victim distribution plans often avoid taking victims to the nearest hospital since walking victims will overcrowd the hospital closest to the disaster site.

Voluntary agency (VOLAG)—A nonprofit, nongovernmental, private association maintained and supported by voluntary contributions, which provides assistance in emergencies and disasters.

Vulnerability—The susceptibility of the population to a specific type of event; the degree of possible/potential loss to a given element at risk resulting from a given hazard at a given intensity. The factors that influence vulnerability include: demographics, the age and resilience of the built environment, technology, social differentiation and diversity, regional and global economies, and political arrangements.

Vulnerability analysis—The assessment of an exposed population's susceptibility to the adverse health effects of a given hazard.

Warning and forecasting—Monitoring events to determine the time, location, and severity of a disaster.

Watch—A "watch" means that severe weather is threatening and may occur in your area. Hearing of a watch indicates that citizens should listen to the radio or watch television for information and advice.

Weapons of Mass Destruction (WMD)—A WMD is any device, material, or substance used in a manner, in a quantity or type, or under circumstances evidencing an intent to cause death or serious injury to persons or significant damage of property.

White hat tools—Security tools used to protect systems. Crackers use black-hat tools.

List of Acronyms Commonly Used in Public Health Disaster Preparedness, Response and Recovery

ACIP	Advisory Committee on Immunization Practices
ACPHP	Academic Center for Public Health Preparedness
ADS	Automatic Detection System
ALS	Advanced Life Support
AMA	American Medical Association
APHL	Association of Public Health Laboratories
AVA	Anthrax Vaccine Adsorbed
AVRP	Anthrax Vaccine Research Program
ARC	American Red Cross
ASPHEP	Assistant Secretary for Public Health Emergency Preparedness
ASTHO	Association of State and Territorial Health Officials
ATSDR	Agency for Toxic Substances and Disease Registry
BLS	Basic Life Support
BSL	Bio Safety Level
CAT	Crisis Action Team
CBRN	Chemical, biological, radiological/nuclear
CCP	Casualty Collection Point
CCRF	Commissioned Core Readiness Force
CDC	Centers for Disease Control and Prevention

CDRG	Catastrophic Disaster Response Group
CEPPO	Chemical Emergency Preparedness and Prevention Office
CERCLA	Comprehensive Environmental Response, Compensation, and Liability Act
CFR	Code of Federal Regulations
CHI	Consolidated Health Informatics
CMHS	Center for Mental Health Services
CINC	Commander-In-Chief
CIO	Centers, Institutes and Offices
CLIA	Clinical Laboratory Improvements Act
CMT	Crisis Management Team
CPHP	Center for Public Health Preparedness
CRP	Cardio Pulmonary Resuscitation
COOP	Continuity of Operations Plan
CRC	Crisis Response Cell
CRM	Crisis Resource Manager
CSTE	Council of State and Territorial Epidemiologists
CWA	Clean Water Act
DAE	Disaster Assistance Employee
DFO	Disaster Field Office
DFSG	Disaster Financial Services Group
DHHS	Department of Health and Human Services
DHS	Department of Homeland Security
DMAT	Disaster Medical Assistance Team
DMORT	Disaster Mortuary Response Team, National Disaster Medical System
DPO	Disaster Psychiatry Outreach
DRM	Disaster Recovery Manager
DWI	Disaster Welfare Inquiry
EAP	Emergency Action Plan
EAS	Emergency Alert System
EBS	Emergency Broadcast System
EC	Emergency Coordinator
ECS	Emergency Communications Staff/System
EEI	Essential Elements of Information
EICC	Emergency Information and Coordination Center
EIS	Epidemic Intelligence Service
EISO	Epidemic Intelligence Service Officer
ELR	Electronic Laboratory-based Reporting
EMS	Emergency Medical Services

EMT	Emergency Medical Technician
EOC	Emergency Operations Center
EPI-x	Epidemic Information Exchange
EPA	Environmental Protection Agency
EPO	Epidemiology Program Office
ERC	Emergency Response Coordinator
ERCG	Emergency Response Coordination Group
ERT	Emergency Response Team
ERT-A	Advance Element of the Emergency Response Team
ESF	Emergency Support Function
EST	Emergency Support Team
FAA	Federal Aviation Administration
FAX	Facsimile
FBI	Federal Bureau of Investigation
FCC	Federal Communications Commission
FCC	Federal Coordinating Center
FCO	Federal Coordinating Officer
FECC	Federal Emergency Communications Coordinator
FEMA	Federal Emergency Management Agency
FERC	FEMA Emergency Response Capability
FESC	Federal Emergency Support Coordinator
FHWA	Federal Highway Administration
FMO	Financial Management Office
FNS	Food and Nutrition Services
FRCM	FEMA Regional Communications Manager
FRERP	Federal Radiological Emergency Response Plan
FRP	Federal Response Plan
GAR	Governor's Authorized Representative
GIS	Geographic Information System
GPMPS	Global Mobile Personal Communication System
GPMRC	Global Patient Movement Requirements Center
GSA	General Services Administration
HAN	Health Alert Network
HAZMAT	Hazardous Material
HAZWOPER	OSHA Standard for Protecting Workers during a disaster
HEICS	Hospital Emergency Incident Command System
HET-ESF	Headquarters Emergency Transportation–Emergency Support Function
HIFI	High Frequency
HHS	Department of Health and Human Services

HICPAC	Healthcare Infection Control Practices Advisory Committee
HQUSACE	Headquarters, United States Army Corps of Engineers
HRSA	Health Resources and Services Administration
HSPD	Homeland Security Presidential Directive
HUD	Department of Housing and Urban Development
HWC	Health and Welfare Canada
IAEA	International Atomic Energy Agency
ICC	Interstate Commerce Commission
ICPAE	Interagency Committee on Public Affairs in Emergencies
ICRC	International Committee of the Red Cross
ICS	Incident Command System
IMS	Incident Management System
IRAT	Immediate Response Assessment Team
IT	Information Technology
JCAHO	Joint Commission on Accreditation of Healthcare Organizations
JIC	Joint Information Center
JIS	Joint Information System
LRN	Laboratory Response Network
MANETS	Mobile Ad Hoc Network
MARS	U.S. Army Military Affiliate Radio System
MASF	Mobile Aeromedical Staging Facility
MC	Mobilization Center
MMWR	*Morbidity and Mortality Weekly Report*, published by CDC
MOA	Memorandum of Agreement
MOU	Memorandum of Understanding
MRC	Medical Reserve Corps
MRE	Meals Ready to Eat
MSEHPA	Model State Emergency Health Powers Act
NACCHO	National Association for County and City Health Officials
NBC	Nuclear, Biological, Chemical
NCBDDD	National Center for Birth Defects and Developmental Disease
NCCDPH	National Center for Chronic Disease Prevention and Health Promotion
NCEH	National Center for Environmental Health
NCHS	National Center for Health Statistics
NCHSTP	National Center for HIV, STD and TB Prevention
NCID	National Center for Infectious Disease

NCIPC	National Center for Injury Prevention and Control
NCC	National Coordinating Center
NCP	National Oil and Hazardous Substances Pollution Contingency Plan
NCS	National Communications System
NCS/DCA-OC	National Communications System/Defense Communication Agency–Operations Center
NDMOC	National Disaster Medical Operations Center
NDMS	National Disaster Medical System
NDMSOSC	National Disaster Medical System Operations Support Center
NECC	National Emergency Coordination Center
NEDSS	National Electronic Disease Surveillance System
NEIS	National Earthquake Information Service
NEMP	National Emergency Management Plan
NFDA	National Funeral Directors Association
NGO	Non–Governmental Organization
NHSN	National Healthcare Safety Network
NIC	NIMS Integration Center
NICC	National Interagency Coordination Center
NIFCC	National Interagency Fire Coordination Center, U.S. Forest Service
NIMH	National Institutes of Mental Health
NIMS	National Incident Management System
NIP	National Immunization Program
NIOSH	National Institute for Occupational Safety and Health
NIH	National Institutes of Health
NLTN	National Laboratory Training Network
NOAA	National Oceanic and Atmospheric Administration
NNRT	National Nurse Response Team
NPPTL	National Personal Protective Technology Laboratory
NPRT	National Pharmacy Response Team
NP	National Preparedness
NRC	Nuclear Regulatory Commission
NRP	National Response Plan
NRT	National Response Team
NSEP	National Security Emergency Preparedness
NSF	National Strike Force
NTIA	National Telecommunications and Information Administration
NTSP	National Telecommunications Support Plan
NVOAD	National Voluntary Organizations Active in Disaster

NWR	National Oceanic and Atmospheric Weather Radio
NWS	National Weather Service
OC	Office of Communication
OCHAMPUS	Office of Civilian Health and Medical Program of the Uniformed Services, Department of Defense
OD	Office of the Director
OEP	Office of Emergency Preparedness, U.S. Public Health Service
OET	Office of Emergency Transportation
OFDA	Office of U.S. Foreign Disaster Assistance
OIG	Office of Inspector General
OHS	Office of Health and Safety
OSC	On–Scene Coordinator
OSG	Office of Surgeon General
OSHA	Occupational Safety and Health Administration
OSEP	Office of Security and Emergency Preparedness
OTPER	Office of Terrorism Preparedness and Emergency Response
OVAG	Organic vapor, chlorine, hydrogen chloride and sulfur dioxide
PAHO	Pan-American Health Organization
PHA	Public Health Advisor
PHI	Protected Health Information
PHICS	Public Health Incident Command System
PHIN	Public Health Information Network
PHS	U.S. Public Health Service, Department of Health and Human Services
PIO	Public Information Officer
POD	Point of Distribution
POD	Point of Dispensing
PPE	Personal Protective Equipment
PTSD	Post Traumatic Stress Disorder
PVO	Private Voluntary Organization
PVS	Pre-event Vaccination System
RACES	Radio Amateur Civil Emergency Services
RCP	Regional Oil and Hazardous Substances Pollution Contingency Plan
RD	Regional Director
RDC	Office of Research and Development Coordination
REACT	Radio Emergency Associated Communication Team
REC	Regional Emergency Coordinator

RECC	Regional Emergency Communications Coordinator
RECP	Regional Emergency Communications Plan
REP	Regional Evacuation Point
RET	Regional Emergency Transportation
RETCO	Regional Emergency Transportation Coordinator
RHA	Regional Health Administrator (HHS)
RISC	Regional Inter-Agency Steering Committee
SAMHSA	Substance Abuse and Mental Health Services Administration
SA	Staging Area
SAP	Select Agent Program
SAR	Search and Rescue
SARA	Superfund Amendments and Reauthorization Act
SCBA	Self Contained Breathing Apparatus
SCC	Secretary's Command Center
SCO	State Coordinating Officer
SEMO	State Emergency Management Office
SLPP	State and Local Preparedness Program
SLPS	State and Local Programs and Support Directorate (FEMA)
SNS	Strategic National Stockpile
SOP	Standard Operating Procedure
SUMA	SUpply MAnagement
SVP	Smallpox Vaccination Program
TARU	Technical Advisory Response Unit
TED	Training, Education and Demonstration
TOPOFF	Top Officials
TRPLT	Terrorism Response and Preparation Leadership Team
24x7	Twenty four hours a day, seven days a week
UN	United Nations
UNDRO	United Nations Disaster Relief Organization
UNHCR	United Nations High Commission for Refugees
UNICEF	United Nations International Children's Education Fund
U.S.	United States
USACE	United States Army Corps of Engineers
USAID	U.S. Agency for International Development
USCG	United States Coast Guard
USDA	United States Department of Agriculture
USGS	United States Geological Survey
USPHS	United States Public Health Service

USAR	Urban Search And Rescue
VA	Department of Veterans Affairs
VAERS	Vaccine Adverse Effects Reporting System
VHA	Veterans Health Administration, Department of Veterans Affairs
VIG	Vaccinia Immune Globulin
VMAT	Veterinary Medical Assistance Team
VPA	Voluntary Protection Act
VMI	Vendor Managed Inventory
VOAD	Voluntary Organizations Active in Disaster
WHO	World Health Organization
WMD	Weapons of Mass Destruction
XML	Extensible Markup Language

Useful Internet Sites

Agency for Toxic Substances and Disease Registry:
www.atsdr.cdc.gov/

Agency for Healthcare Research and Quality, Bioterrorism Planning and Response:
www.ahrq.gov/browse/bioterbr.htm

All Hazards:
www.colorado.edu/hazards/library
www.riskinstitute.org
visibleearth.nasa.gov/

American Academy of Child and Adolescent Psychiatry:
www.aacap.org/

American Academy of Experts in Traumatic Stress:
www.aaets.org

American College of Physicians:
www.acponline.org/bioterr/

American Medical Association:
www.ama-assn.org/

American Public Health Association:
www.apha.org

American Psychiatric Association:
www.psych.org/disasterpsych/

American Red Cross:
www.redcross.org

American Veterinary Medical Association Disaster Preparedness and Response Program:
www.avma.org/pubhlth/biosecurity/resources.asp
www.avma.org/disaster/default.asp
www.avma.org/disaster/vmat/default.asp

Armed Forces Institute of Pathology:
www.afip.org

Armed Forces Radiobiology Research Institute:
www.afrri.usuhs.mil/

Association for Infection Control Practitioners:
www.apic.org/

Association of State and Territorial Health Professionals:
www.statepublichealth.org

Agency for Toxic Substances and Disease Registry:
www.atsdr.cdc.gov/HEC/primer.html

Australian Trauma Web:
psy.uq.edu.au/PTSD/trauma/ogcross.html

Bioterrorism Resources:
www.usuhs.mil/med/milmedgoalsbio.htm
www.moxietraining.com/oshalinks/bioterrorism.htm
www.bioterrorism.uab.edu

Canada Center for Emergency Preparedness:
www.ccep.ca/

California Office of Emergency Services:
www.oes.ca.gov/

Centers for Disease Control and Prevention (CDC):
www.cdc.gov/
www.bt.cdc.gov/masstrauma/index.asp

CDC Bioterrorism Preparedness & Response:
www.bt.cdc.gov/
www.bt.cdc.gov/Documents/Planning/PlanningGuidance.PDF

CDC Health Alert Network homepage:
www.phppo.cdc.gov/han/

CDC Public Health Law Program:
www.phppo.cdc/gov/phlawnet

**Center for Earthquake Research and Information
at University of Memphis:**
www.ceri.memphis.edu/

**Center for Food Safety and Applied Nutrition, US Food and
Drug Administration:**
vm.cfsan.fda.gov/list.html

**Center for Nonproliferation Studies, Monterey Institute for
International Studies:**
cns.miis.edu/

Center for Research on the Epidemiology of Disasters (CRED):
www.cred.be/

Center for State Homeland Security:
www.cshs-us.org

Computer Emergency Response Team (CERT):
www.cert.org/security-improvement/

Counterterrorism Tools:
www.counterterrorismtraining.gov

Defense Threat Reduction Agency:
www.dtra.mil/

Department of Defense/Dept of the Army, Director of Military Support:
www.dtic.mil/

Department of Defense, Nuclear, Biological, Chemical Medical reference site:
www.nbc-med.org

Department of Defense, Office of Counterproliferation and Chemical/Biological Defense:
www.acq.osd.mil/cp/

Department of Homeland Security (DHS) FEMA:
www.fema.gov

DHS FEMA Disaster Curriculum:
www.fema.gov/tab_education.shtm

DHS FEMA Disaster Help:
disasterhelp.gov/portal/jhtml/index.jhtml

DHS FEMA's Higher Education Project:
www.training.fema.gov/emiweb/cgi-shl/college/User.cfm

DHS FEMA Kids:
www.fema.gov/kids/

DHS FEMA State and Local Guide to All-Hazards Emergency Operations Planning:
www.fema.gov/preparedness/state_local_prepare_guide.shtm

DHS FEMA State Offices and Agencies:
www.fema.gov/fema/statedr.shtm

Department of Homeland Security (DHS):
www.dhs.gov
www.ready.gov

DHS Grants:
www.dhs.gov/dhspublic/interapp/editorial/editorial_0355.xml

DHS National Disaster Medical System:
www.ndms.dhhs.gov/

DHS Office of Domestic Preparedness (ODP):
www.ojp.usdoj.gov/odp/

The Disaster Center Website:
www.disastercenter.com/

Disaster Recovery Yellow Pages:
www.disasterrecoveryyp.com/listing.html

Disaster Research Center, University of Delaware:
www.udel.edu/DRC

Earthquakes:
www.geohaz.org/radius
www.earthquake.usgs.gov
www.eqnet.org
www.colorado.edu/hazards/resources/sites.html

Earthquake Engineering Research Library California Institute of Technology:
(National Information Service for Earthquake Engineering:
www.eerl.caltech.edu/library/library.html

Effective Disaster Warnings:
www.noaa.gov/

The Emergency Information Infrastructure Partnership:
www.emforum.org/

The Emergency Net, Emergency Response and Research Institute:
http://www.emergency.com/

Emerging Infectious Disease Journal:
www.cdc.gov/ncidod/EID/index.htm

Environmental Protection Agency, Chemical Emergency Preparedness and Prevention Office:
www.epa.gov/swercepp/
www.epa.gov/ceppo

Emergency Response Guidebook:
www.envectra.com/env/erg/erg.htm

Fire:
www.osha.gov/dep/fire-expmatrix/index.html

First Responders.com (Private Web site for first responders)
wmdfirstresponders.com/

Floods:
www.nws.noaa.gov/os/water/tadd/
www.earthsat.com/wx/flooding/index.html
www.floodsmart.gov/

Flood Insurance Manual, FEMA:
www.fema.gov/nfip/manual.htm

Gateway to Food Safety Information:
www.foodsafety.gov/~fsg/bioterr.html

Gender and Disasters Network:
online.northumbria.ac.uk/geography_research/gdn/resources/
  bibliographies.html

Global Emerging Infections Surveillance and Response System, Department of Defense:
www.geis.fhp.osd.mil/

Government Emergency Telecommunications Service (GETS):
gets.ncs.gov

Health Information Network for Advanced Planning (HINAP):
ennonline.net/fex/04/ne19-2.html

Health Library for Disasters:
www.disaster-info.net/newsletter/92/helid.htm

Henry L. Stimson Center, Chemical and Biological Weapons Non-proliferation Project:

www.stimson.org/index.html

Hospital Emergency Incident Command System:

www.emsa.ca.gov/dms2/history.htm

Health Resources and Services Administration (HRSA), National Bioterrorism Hospital Preparedness Program:

www.hrsa.gov/bioterrorism.htm

Humanitarian Supply Management:

www.disaster-info.net/SUMA/

Hurricane Watch Net:

www.hwn.org

Infectious Disease Society of America:

www.idsociety.org

International Association of Emergency Managers:

www.iaem.com/

International Critical Incident Stress Foundation (ICISF):

www.icisf.org

International Federation of the Red Cross:

www.ifrc.org

International Rescue Committee:

www.intrescom.org

International Society for Traumatic Stress Studies (ISTSS):

www.istss.org

Johns Hopkins Office of Critical Event Preparedness and Response:

www.hopkins-cepar.org/sites/index.html

Lawrence Livermore National Laboratory Counterterrorism and Incident Response:

www.llnl.gov/nai/rdiv/rdiv.html

Medical Reserve Corps:

www.medicalreservecorps.gov

Mental Health Field Manual:

www.mentalhealth.org/publications/allpubs/ADM90-537/
  default.asp

National Academies of Science, Institute of Medicine Disasters Roundtable:

dels.nas.edu/dr/

National Association of Amateur Radio:

www.arrl.org/

National Association of County and City Health Officials (NACCHO), BT site:

www.naccho.org/project63.htm

National Association of Social Workers (NASW):

www.socialworkers.org/pressroom/events/911/disasters.asp

National Association of School Psychologists:

www.nasponline.org

National Environmental Health Association:

www.neha.org/

National Fire Protection Association (NFPA 1600):

www.nfpa.org/catalog/home/index.asp
www.nfpa.org/Research/FireInvestigation/Homeland/
  homeland.asp

National Center for Post-Traumatic Stress Disorder:

www.ncptsd.org

National Disaster Medical System:

ndms.dhhs.gov/

National Institute on Mental Health:

www.nimh.nih.gov/

National Institute for Occupational Safety and Health (NIOSH):
www.cdc.gov/niosh/homepage.html

National Weather Warning:
iwin.nws.noaa.gov/iwin/nationalwarnings.html

NIOSH Disaster Site Management:
www.cdc.gov/niosh/topics/emres/sitemgt.html

The National Emergency Management Association:
www.nemaweb.org/index.cfm

The National Emergency Rescue and Response Training Center, Texas A&M University:
teexweb.tamu.edu/nerrtc/

National Institutes of Health:
health.nih.gov/result.asp/201

National Institute for Occupational Safety and Health:
www.cdc.gov/niosh/homepage.html

National League of Cities, Local Officials Guide: "Homeland Security: Political Tools for Local Government":
www.nlc.org/nlc_org/site/files/reports/terrorism.pdf

National Oceanic and Atmospheric Administration:
www.noaa.org

National Organization for Victim Assistance (NOVA):
www.try-nova.org

The National Response Center, US Coast Guard:
www.nrc.uscg.mil/

The National Response Team, HAZMAT & Chemical Spills:
www.nrt.org/

National Safety Council:
www.nsc.org/

National Voluntary Organizations Active in Disaster (NVOAD):
www.nvoad.org

NOAA weather radio:
www.nws.noaa.gov/nwr/

National Weather Service:
www.nws/

Natural Hazards Center, University of Colorado:
www.colorado.edu/hazards
www.colorado.edu/hazards/library/

Occupational Safety and Health Administration:
www.osha.gov/
www.osha-slc.gov/pls/publications/pubindex.list

The Office for Domestic Preparedness Office:
www.ojp.usdoj.gov/odp/training.htm

Office of Foreign Disaster Assistance:
www.usaid.gov/our_work/humanitarian_assistance/
    disaster_assistance/

Pan-American Health Organization (PAHO):
www.paho.org
www.paho.org/english/dd/ped/newsletter.htm

PREEMT, Medical Counterterrorism, Inc., Nonprofit organiza-tion for Emergency Medical Tng for WMD issues:
home.eznet/%20Kenberry/

Presidential Decision Directives:
www.fas.org/irp/offdocs/direct.htm

U.S. Army Soldier and Biological Chemical Command Links:
www.apgea.army.mil/

ReliefWeb:
www.notes.reliefweb.int/

Regional Disaster Information Center (CRID, San Jose, Costa Rica):

www.disaster-info.net/crid/eng/990924_index.htm

Rural EMS and Trauma Assistance:

www.ruralhealth.hrsa.gov/ruralems/

State Emergency Management Web Sites (links):

www.osp.state.or.us/oem/Related%20Web%20Sites/states.htm

State Health Department Web Sites:

www.phppo.cdc.gov/phtn/sites.asp#state

Southern California Earthquake Center:

www.scec.org/

Substance Abuse and Mental Health Services Administration:

www.mentalhealth.samhsa.gov/cmhs/

Surge Capacity:

www.dtic.mil/ndia/2003terrorism/barb.pdf
www.ahrq.gov/news/ulp/btbriefs/btbrief3.htm.html
www.hospitalconnect.com/aha/key_issues/disaster_readiness/
   resources/vaccination

Terrorism training:

www.fema.gov/compendium

United Nations High Commissioner for Refugees (UNHCR):

www.unhcr.ch

U.S. Army Chemical School:

www.wood.army.mil/usacmls/

U.S. Army Medical Command:

www.armymedicine.army.mil/armymed/default2.htm

US Army Medical Research Institute of Chemical Defense:

chemdef.apgea.army.mil/

US Office of Foreign Disaster Assistance (OFDA):

www.info.usaid.gov/hum_response/ofda/

US Army Center for Health Promotion & Preventive Medicine:
chppm-www.apgea.army.mil/

US Army Medical Research Institute of Infectious Diseases:
www.usamriid.army.mil/index.htm

US Fire Administration:
www.usfa.fema.gov/

US Army Soldier and Biological Chemical Command (SBCCOM):
www.sbccom.apgea.army.mil/

US Census Bureau:
www.census.gov

US Coast Guard, Command Center:
www.uscg.mil/hq/commandcenter/oc.htm

US Coast Guard, National Response Center:
www.nrc.uscg.mil/

US Food and Drug Administration, Investigations Operations Manual 2003; Chapter 9 Investigations Subchapter 940 - Disaster Procedures:
www.fda.gov/ora/inspect_ref/iom/ChapterText/940.html

US Geological Survey:
www.usgs.gov

University of Wisconsin Disaster Management Center:
epdwww.engr.wisc.edu/dmc

World Health Organization (WHO):
www.who.int/

DISABILITY REFERENCES AND RESOURCES

Access Board:
www.access-board.gov

Americans with Disabilities Act (ADA):
www.usdoj.gov/crt/ada/pubs/ada.txt

ADA Design Requirements for Accessible Egress (Summary):
www.access-board.gov/evac.htm

Braille and/or "ADA" Signage:
www.jan.wvu.edu/cgi-win/OrgQuery.exe?Sol231

Center for an Accessible Society:
www.accessiblesociety.org

Communication Aides:
www.jan.wvu.edu/cgi-win/OrgQuery.exe?Sol267
www.jan.wvu.edu/cgi-win/OrgQuery.exe?Sol419

Cross-Agency Government Website Devoted to Disaster Preparedness:
www.disasterhelp.gov

Disability Preparedness Center:
www.disabilitypreparedness.org/Resources.htm
www.disabilitypreparedness.org/additional%20resources.htm

Disaster Preparedness for Persons with Disabilities: Improving California's Response:
www.oes.ca.gov
www.oes.ca.gov/Operational/OESHome.nsf/a0f8bd0ee918bc35
    88256bd400532608/66952778a6d2fa7c88256cef006a8967?
    OpenDocument&Highlight=0,disabled

"Disaster Preparedness: Reasoning Why":
www.helpusafety.org/3PREPSDI.pdf

Disability Resources Monthly:
disabilityresources.org/DISASTER.html

Eastern Paralyzed Veterans Association:
www.epva.org

Easter Seals S.a.f.e.t.y. First Evacuation Program:

www.easter-seals.org
www.easterseals.com/site/PageServer?pagename=ntl_safety_first
  _evacuation

Emergency Access Rules, Federal Communications Commission (FCC):

hraunfoss.fcc.gov/edocs_public/attachmatch/DA-02-1852A1.pdf

National Business and Disability Council, Emergency Evacuation Checklist for People with Disabilities in the Workplace:

www.nbdc.com

Emergency Warnings: Notification of Deaf or Hard of Hearing People:

www.nad.org
www.nad.org/infocenter/infotogo/emergency/Emergency
  Notification.html

Emergency Procedures for Employees with Disabilities:

www.usfa.fema.gov/applications/publications/display.cfm?id=&
  mc=&sc=&ol=&it=&st=Emergency%20Procedures%20for%20
  Employees%20with%20Disabilities&sp=&sr=1&rp=5&sp=
www.jan.wvu.edu/media/emergency.html

eSight Careers Network:

www.esight.org

Equal Employment Opportunity Commission (EEOC), Fact Sheet on Obtaining and Using Employee Medical Information as Part of Emergency Evacuation Procedures:

www.eeoc.gov/facts/evacuation.html

Evacuation Devices:

www.jan.wvu.edu/cgi-win/OrgQuery.exe?Sol193

Federal Communications Commission:

www.fcc.gov

Federal Emergency Management Agency: Assisting People with Disabilities in a Disaster:

www.fema.gov/rrr/assistf.shtm
www.fema.gov/library/disprepf.shtm
www.usfa.fema.gov/downloads/txt/publications/fa-154.txt

Job Accommodation Network (JAN):

www.jvu.edu/media/emergency.html
www.jan.wvu.edu/cgi-win/DisQuery.exe?Em001
www.jan.wvu.edu/media/emergency.html

June Kailes websites:

www.jik.com/disaster.html
www.cdihp.org/evacuationpdf.htm
www.ilrc-trico.org/sbanews/eeppub.html
www.ilrcsf.org/Publications/prepared/pdf/Health_Card.pdf

Lifts and Carries: California Emergency Response Team:

www.cert-la.com/liftcarry/Liftcarry.htm

Lighthouse International:

www.lighthouse.org

Missouri State Emergency Management Agency (SEMA): Evacuation Considerations for the Elderly, Disabled and Special Medical Care Issues:

www.sema.state.mo.us/elderly1.htm

National Association of the Deaf:

www.nad.org

National Center on Emergency Preparedness for People with Disabilities:

www.disabilitypreparedness.com/

National Organization on Disability:

www.nod.org

Prepare Now:

www.preparenow.org

Project Cope: Coping with Disaster: A Guide for Families and Others who Support Adults with Cognitive Disabilities:

www.nymc.edu/wihd/projectcope/pc/adultguide1.html

Tactile Graphics and Maps:

www.jan.wvu.edu/cgi-win/OrgQuery.exe?Sol401

Visual and Tactile Alerting Devices:

www.jan.wvu.edu/cgi-win/OrgQuery.exe?Sol231

U.S. Department of Health and Human Services Administration on Aging:

www.aoa.dhhs.gov

Website Design Accessibility Standards:

Bobby Web Accessibility Software Tool
bobby.watchfire.com

W3C Web Accessibility Initiative Resources:

www.w3.org/WAI/Resources/#gl

The Federal Government's Section 508 Resource:

www.section508.gov/

Web Accessibility in Mind:

www.webaim.org/

GIS WEBSITES:

www.geographynetwork.com/
data.geocomm.com/
www.esri.com/
www.geocomm.com/
www.cast.uark.edu/local/hunt/
water.usgs.gov/maps.html
www-sul.stanford.edu/depts/gis/web.html
www.fws.gov/data/gishome.html
www.cast.uark.edu/local/catalog/national/
esri.com/hazards/index.html
geoplace.com/gw/2003/0311/0311gngis.asp

www.csc.noaa.gov/hfloyd
www.ngdc.noaa.gov/ngdc.html
ciesin.org/index.html (international data)
csc.noaa.gov/products/nchaz/startup.htm (Community
    Vulnerability Assessment Tool)
cindi.usgs.gov
Geospace.com

PERIODICALS & PUBLICATIONS:

Air University Index to Military Periodicals:
www.dtic.mil/search97doc/aulimp/main.htm

The Chemical and Biological Information Analysis Center Newsletter:
ss-cbiac.apgea.army.mil/awareness/newsletter/intro.html

CHPPM News Bulletins, US Army Center For Health Promotion and Preventive Medicine:
chppm-www.apgea.army.mil/imo/ddb/dmd/DMD/
    NEWS.HTML

CML, Army Chemical Review, U.S. Army Chemical School Periodical:
www.wood.army.mil/CHBULLETIN/Default.htm

Contingency Planning and Management:
 www.contingencyplanning.com/

Disaster Recovery Journal:
www.drj.com/

Dispatch, The Chemical and Biological Arms Control Institute:
www.cbaci.org/dispatch.htm

Emerging Infectious Diseases, CDC, National Center for Infectious Diseases:
www.cdc.gov/ncidod/eid/index.htm

Emergency Information Infrastructure Partnership Newsletter:
www.emforum.org/eiip/news.htm

Emergency Medical Services Magazine:
www.emsmagazine.com/home.html

Emergency Preparedness Information Exchange (EPIX):
css.sfu.ca/groups/group.cgi?GroupID=55

FEMA IMPACT newsletter:
www.fema.gov/regions/v/newsletter/

FEMA News Listing:
www.fema.gov/library/newz.shtm

Floods:
www.dh.sa.gov.au/pehs/publications/monograph-floods.pdf

Hazardous Technical Information Service Newsletter, Dept. of the Army:
www.dscr.dla.mil/htis/

The Homeland Defense Journal:
www.homelanddefensejournal.com/#

Humanitarian Times:
www.humanitariantimes.org/

The Journal of Homeland Defense:
www.homelanddefense.org/

The Journal of Homeland Security:
www.homelandsecurity.org/journal/index.cfm

Medicine and Global Survival Magazine:
www.healthnet.org

Morbidity and Mortality Weekly Report, CDC:
www.cdc.gov/mmwr/

National Fire and Rescue Magazine:

www.nfrmag.com/

Natural Hazards Observer:

www.colorado.edu/hazards/o/

The Nonproliferation Review, Center for Nonproliferation Studies, Monterey Institute of International Studies:

cns.miis.edu/pubs/npr/index.htm

OSHA Job Safety and Health Quarterly Magazine:

www.osha-slc.gov/html/jshq-index.html

PROCEDURES/PROTOCOLS/INCIDENT COMMAND INFORMATION/RESPONSE RESOURCES:

Air Force Hazardous Materials Information Resource System:

www.hazmat48.wpafb.af.mil/

Bioterrorism Readiness Plan: A Template for Healthcare Facilities, CDC:

www.cdc.gov/ncidod/hip/BIO/bio.htm

CDC Emergency Preparedness and Response:

www.bt.cdc.gov/protocols.asp

Decontamination, Commercial Resources:

www.nbcindustrygroup.com/index03.htm
www.nbcindustrygroup.com/handbook/index08.htm

EPA, Reconciling Federal Emergency Response Plans:

http://www.nrt.org/production/nrt/home.nsf/resources/
    Publications1/$File/Final_NRT_Plan_Reconciliation_Analysis
    _Report.pdf

EPA, National Response System:

www.epa.gov/superfund/programs/er/nrs/nrsrrt.htm

FEMA, Federal Response Plan:

www.fema.gov/rrr/frp/

FEMA Library of Reference Documents:
www.fema.gov/library/

FEMA, State and Local Guide (SLG) 101: Guide for All-Hazard Emergency Operations Planning:
www.fema.gov/rrr/gaheop.shtm

Homeland Security Preparedness Technical Assistance:
www.ojp.usdoj.gov/osldps/ta.htm

Incident Command System, NY State Site:
www.nysemo.state.ny.us

Incident Command System Forms:
www.wildlandfire.net/

Incident Command System, US Coast Guard Site:
www.uscg.mil/hq/g-m/mor/Articles/ICS.htm

Joint Information Center Guide, 21 Jan 2000, The National Response Team:
www.nrt.org/production/nrt/home.nsf

Medline Plus: Emergency Preparedness and Response:
www.nlm.nih.gov/medlineplus/disastersandemergency
   preparedness.html

NACCHO Planning Primer:
www.naccho.org/files/documents/Final_Effective_
   Bioterrism.pdf

The National Response Center, Chemical/HAZMAT Spills:
www.nrc.uscg.mil/index.html

Outbreak Investigation Toolbox:
bt.naccho.org/Bt-Toolbox/
www.vetmed.wsu.edu/courses-jmgay/OutBResources.htm
mmrs.fema.gov/PublicDocs/NDPO_2000_05.pdf

Public Health Imaging Library:
phil.cdc.gov/Phil/default.asp

PROMED:

www.promedmail.org

Rapid Response Information System (RRIS), FEMA:

www.nvfc.org/news/hn_rapidresponse.html

Virology BT website:

www.virology.net/garryfavwebbw.html

REFERENCE WEBSITES:

Anthrax, Department of Defense Information Web Site:

www.anthrax.osd.mil/

Army Medical Department Publications:

www.armymedicine.army.mil/default2.htm

ATSDR TOXFAQs, Medical Summary Sheets for Hazardous Material:

www.atsdr.cdc.gov/toxfaq.html

Bibliography of Terrorism, The Disaster Center:

www.disastercenter.com/terror.htm

Biological Agent Information, Centers for Disease Control:

www.bt.cdc.gov/bioagents.asp

Biosafety in Microbiological and Biomedical Laboratories, 4th Edition:

www.cdc.gov/od/ohs/biosfty/bmbl4/bmbl4toc.htm

CANUTEC's Home Page (HAZMAT Transport, Canadian Government):

www.tc.gc.ca/cauntec/english/main-e.htm

CDC, Bioterrorism Planning:

www.bt.cdc.gov/planning/index.asp

Chemical, Biological, Nuclear Terrorism/Warfare Bibliography:

library.nps.navy.mil/home/bibs/chemweb.htm

The Chemical and Biological Defense Information Analysis Center:

www.cbiac.apgea.army.mil/

Chemical Contamination Treatment Guidelines. Medical Management Guidelines for Acute Chemical Exposures. Agency for Toxic Substances and Disease Registry:

www.atsdr.cdc.gov/MHMI/mmga.html

CNS-Chemical and Biological Weapons Resource Page:

cns.miis.edu/research/cbw/index.htm

Department of Defense Dictionary of Military and Associated Terms:

www.dtic.mil/doctrine

Department of Defense, Technical Information Center (Search engine for Federal Laws, Regulations and documents, relating to emergency management):

www.dtic.mil

Department of Transportation, Emergency Response Guidebook (First Responder's Guide for HAZMAT operations):

hazmat.dot.gov/gydebook.htm

Developing a Hazardous Materials Exercise Programs: A Handbook for State and Local Officals, US Department of Transportation:

www.bts.gov/smart/cat/254.html

FEMA Bibliography Listing for Emergency Management:

www.fema.gov/rrr/talkdiz/biblio.shtm

Federal Response Plan, Emergency Support Function #8 Health and Medical Services Annex:

www.fema.gov/about/esf.shtm

Field Operations Guide, Office of Foreign Disaster Assistance, USAID:

www.usaid.gov/policy/ads/200/fog_v3.pdf

Field Operating Guide, US Coast Guard:

www.uscg.mil/hq/g-m/mor/Articles/ICS.htm

First Responder HAZMAT guide, US Fire Administration, FEMA:

usfa.fema.gov/fire-service/hazmat/hazmatguide/hmgfr2b.shtm

Foodborne Pathogenic Microorganisms and Natural Toxins Handbook, US Food & Drug Administration, Center for Food Safety & Applied Nutrition:

vm.cfsan.fda.gov

Global Emerging Infections Surveillance and Response System:

www.geis.fhp.osd.mil/

Medical Management of Biological Casualties Handbook, US Army Medical Research Institute of Infectious Diseases:

www.nbc-med.org/SiteContent/MedRef/OnlineRef/FieldManuals/medman/Handbook.htm

Medical Management of Chemical Casualties Handbook, US Army Medical Research Institute of Chemical Defense:

ccc.apgea.army.mil/site_info/site_guide/site_map.htm

Medical Management of Radiology Casualties Handbook, US Army:

www.afrri.usuhs.mil/www/outreach/pdf/radiologicalhandbooksp99-2.pdf

Misc. Terrorism Articles, Emergency Response and Research Institute:

www.emergency.com/cntrterr.htm

Mitigation Practitioner's Handbook, Office of Foreign Disaster Assistance, USAID:

www.usaid.gov/policy/ads/200/hbkoct18.pdf

National Center for Infectious Diseases Electronic Publications/Documents:

www.cdc.gov/ncidod/publicat.htm

National Institutes of Health Periodical Listing and Browser:
health.nih.gov/search_results.asp

National Institute of Occupational Safety and Health (NIOSH) Publications:
www.cdc.gov/niosh/publistd.html

National Library of Medicine:
www.nlm.nih.gov/

National Library of Medicine Search Service, PUBMED:
www.ncbi.nlm.nih.gov/PubMed/

National Technical Information Service Health and Safety Home Page, Links to Government Health Pubs:
www.ntis.gov/index.asp

NIOSH Pocket Guide to Chemical Hazards:
www.cdc.gov/niosh/npg/npg.html

Rare Diseases, National Institutes of Health:
rarediseases.info.nih.gov/

Strategic Plan, CDC, National Center for Infectious Diseases:
www.cdc.gov/ncidod/emergplan/1toc.htm

Terrorism Legislation and Executive Orders:
nsi.org/terrorism.html

TOXNET, Toxicology Data Network, National Library of Medicine:
toxnet.nlm.nih.gov/

University of Michigan, Tips on Working with the Media:
www.umich.edu/news/tips.html

USA Today Health Information/Archive Article Index:
asp.usatoday.com/search/search.aspx

Websites accessed August 9, 2004.

First Aid
and Survival Kits

First aid supplies should be stored in a tool box or fishing tackle box so they will be easy to carry and protected from water. The kit should be inspected regularly and kept freshly stocked. Important medical information and most prescriptions can be stored in the refrigerator, which also provides excellent protection from fires. In addition, copies of important papers (i.e., contact information, copies of most recent social security award letter, if applicable, drivers' license, insurance policies, medical plan cards, name and phone number of physician, social security card, and personal phone book) should be secured.

FIRST AID KIT

Ace bandages

Adhesive tape roll

Alcohol swabs (individually wrapped)

Antacid

Antibiotic ointment

Antidiarrhea medicine

Antiseptic

Aspirin and nonaspirin tablets

Assorted sizes of safety pins

Bandage strips

Cleansing agent/soap

Cotton–tipped swabs

Dressings

Drugs and Medications

Eye drops

Hydrogen peroxide to wash and disinfect wounds

Latex gloves

Moistened towelettes

Needle

Prescriptions and any long–term medications (keep prescriptions current)

Rolled gauze

Rubbing alcohol

Thermometer

OTHER FIRST AID SUPPLIES

Bar soap

First aid book

Instant cold packs for sprains

Needle and thread

Paper cups

Pocket knife

Safety pins

Sanitary napkins

Scissors

Small plastic bags

Splinting materials

Sunscreen

Thermometer

Tissues

Tweezers

SURVIVAL KIT OR YOUR HOME

Assemble a survival kit for your home with the following items:

Tools and supplies

Ax, shovel, broom

Screwdriver, pliers, hammer, adjustable wrench

Rope for towing or rescue

Plastic sheeting and tape

Nonelectric can opener

Water

ITEMS TO ENSURE SAFETY AND COMFORT

Sturdy shoes that can provide protection from broken glass, nails, and other debris

Gloves (heavy and durable for cleaning up debris)

Candles

Waterproof matches

Change of clothing

Knife

Garden hose (for siphoning and firefighting)

Tent

Recreational supplies for children and adults

Blankets or sleeping bags

Portable battery operated radio, flashlight, and extra batteries

Essential medications and eyeglasses

Fire extinguisher—multipurpose, dry chemical type

Food and water for pets

Toilet tissue

Cash

SURVIVAL KIT FOR THE CAR

Assemble a survival kit for your automobile with the following items. Storing some of these supplies in a small bag or backpack will make them more convenient to carry if you need to walk.

Blankets

Bottled water

Change of clothes

Coins for telephone calls or extra charged battery for cell phone

Fire extinguisher—multipurpose, dry chemical type

First aid kit and manual

Emergency signal device (light sticks, battery–type flasher, reflector, etc.)

Flashlight with fresh batteries

Food (nonperishable—nutrition bars, trail mix, etc.)

Gloves (heavy duty and waterproof)

Local map and compass

Rope for towing, rescue, etc.

Paper and pencils

Premoistened towelettes

Prescription medicines

Battery-operated radio with fresh batteries

Sturdy shoes

Small mirror for signaling

Toilet tissue

Tools (pliers, adjustable wrench, screwdriver, etc.)

Whistle for signaling

Jumper cables

Duct tape

SURVIVAL KIT FOR THE WORKPLACE

Assemble a survival kit for the workplace with the following supplies:

Food (nonperishable—nutrition bars, trail mix, etc.)

Bottled water

Jacket or sweatshirt

Pair of sturdy shoes

Flashlight with fresh batteries

Battery–operated radio with fresh batteries

Essential medications

Blanket

Small first aid kit

Extra pair of eyeglasses and/or contact lens solution

Whistle or other signaling device

Sanitation

Toilet paper, towelettes

Soap, liquid detergent

Feminine hygiene supplies

Personal hygiene items

Plastic garbage bags, ties (for personal sanitation uses)

Plastic bucket with tight lid

Disinfectant

Household chlorine bleach

Facial tissues

Tools and Supplies

Mess kits or paper cups; plates and plastic utensils

Cash or traveler's checks, coins.

Nonelectric can opener, utility knife

Pliers, screwdriver, hammer, crowbar, assorted nails, wood screws

Shutoff wrench, to turn off gas and water

Tape, such as duct tape

Compass

Matches in a waterproof container

Aluminum foil

Plastic storage containers

Signal flare

Paper, pencil

Needles, thread

Medicine dropper

Adhesive labels

Safety goggles

Heavy work gloves

Whistle

Heavy cotton of hemp rope

Patch kit and can of seal-in-air

Videocassettes

Disposable dust masks

Plastic sheeting

Map of the area (for locating shelters)

DISABILITY–RELATED SUPPLIES AND SPECIAL EQUIPMENT LIST

Glasses

Eating utensils

Grooming utensils

Dressing devices

Writing devices

Hearing device and extra batteries

Oxygen

Suction equipment

Dialysis equipment

Sanitary supplies

Urinary supplies

Ostomy supplies

Wheelchair

Wheelchair repair kit

Motorized or manual walker

Crutches

Cane(s)

Dentures

Monitors

Key Elements of a Public Health Preparedness Program

- Must be in place in advance of emergency (Emergency pre-paredness)

- Identify the type of events that might occur in your community (Hazard analysis)

- Plan emergency activities in advance to ensure a coordinated response to the consequences of a credible event (Emergency response planning)

- Build capabilities necessary to respond effectively to the conse-quences of those events (Emergency preparedness)

- Identify the types or nature of an event when it happens (Health surveillance, epidemiological investigation, laboratory, diagnosis)

- Implement the planned response quickly and efficiently (Consequence management)

- Recovery

Derived from The Public Health Response to Biological and Chemical Terrorism: Interim Planning Guidance for State Public Health Officials , CDC, July, 2001 (www.bt.cdc.gov/Documents/Planning/Planning Guidance.PDF)

Also see April 2000 MMWR Supplement and National Association of County and City Health Officers website

Incident Commander's Considerations for Managing Nuclear, Biological, and Chemical Incidents

ELEMENT OF COMMAND	OPERATIONAL CONSIDERATIONS	RESPONSE
Scene safety	Responder protection Secondary devices Shelter-in-place versus evacuation	Crew rotation
Command, control, and communication	Initial warning Incident Command Post location Evidence preservation and collection Airspace restriction	Apparatus approach Communication capabilities Management Transition to unified command
Medical support	Control patient's fear and modesty Casualty transport	Control patient's movement On-scene treatment
Decontamination	Casualty decontamination Water source for decontamination	Decontaminate the site Decontaminate site's run-off
Media and public information	Overwhelming response	Information control
Resource management	Available resources	Additional resources

Emergency Management Standards of the Joint Commission on Accreditation of Health Care Organizations (JCAHO)

CLARIFIED EMERGENCY MANAGEMENT STANDARDS

Standard

EC.1.4 The organization has an emergency management plan.

Intent of EC.1.4

The emergency management plan comprehensively describes the organization's approach to responding to emergencies <u>(1)</u> within the organization or in its community that would suddenly and significantly affect the need for the organization's services, or its ability to provide those

---

1. **emergency** *A natural or man–made event that significantly disrupts the environment of care (for example, damage to the organization's building(s) and grounds due to severe winds, storms, or earthquakes); that significantly disrupts care and treatment (for example, loss of utilities, such as power, water, or telephones, due to floods, civil disturbances, accidents, or emergencies within the organization or in its community); or that results in sudden, significantly changed or increased demands for the organization's services (for example, bioterrorist attack, building collapse, or plane crash in the organization's community). Some emergencies are called "disasters" or "potential injury creating events" (PICEs).*

services. The plan addresses four phases of emergency management: mitigation, (2) preparedness, (3) response, and recovery. At a minimum, the emergency management plan is developed with the involvement of the organization leaders, including those of the medical staff. The planning process provides for:

a. The conduct of a hazard vulnerability analysis (4) to identify potential emergencies that could affect the need for the organization's services, or its ability to provide those services.

b. The establishment, in coordination with community emergency management planning (where available), of priorities among the potential emergencies identified in the hazard vulnerability analysis for which mitigation, preparation, response and recovery activities will need to be undertaken.

c. Identification of specific procedures to mitigate, prepare for, respond to, and recover from the priority emergencies.

d. Definition of and, where appropriate, integration of the organization's role in relation to community–wide emergency response agencies, including identification of the command structure in the community.

e. Definition of a common (that is, "all–hazards") command structure within the organization for responding to and recovery from emergencies, that links with the command structure in the community.

f. * Cooperative planning among health care organizations that, together, provide services to a contiguous geographic area (for example, among hospitals serving a town or borough) to facilitate the timely sharing of information about:

---

2. **mitigation activities** *Those activities an organization undertakes in attempting to lessen the severity and impact of a potential emergency.*
3. **preparedness activities** *Those activities an organization undertakes to build capacity and identify resources that may be used should an emergency occur.*
4. **hazard vulnerability analysis** *The identification of potential emergencies and the direct and indirect effects these emergencies may have on the health care organization's operations and the demand for its services.*
* *This new requirement became effective January 1, 2002, for hospitals but will not be scored for accreditation purposes until January 1, 2003.*

- Essential elements of their command structures and control centers for emergency response.

- Names, roles, and telephone numbers of individuals in their command structures.

- Resources and assets that could potentially be shared or pooled in an emergency response.

- Names of patients and deceased individuals brought to their organizations to facilitate identification and location of victims of the emergency.

g. Initiation of the procedures in the response and recovery phases of the plan, including a description of how, when, and by who the phases are to be activated.

h. Notification of emergencies to external authorities, including possible community emergencies identified by the organization (for example, evidence of a possible bioterrorist attack).

i. Notification of personnel when emergency response measures are initiated.

j. Identification of care providers and other personnel during emergencies.

k. Identification and assignment of personnel to cover all necessary staff positions under emergency conditions.

l. Management of the following under emergency conditions:

- Individual care–related activities (for example, scheduling, modifying, or discontinuing services; control of individual information; individual transportation).

- Staff support activities (for example, housing, transportation, incident stress debriefing).

- Family support activities.

- Logistics relating to critical supplies (for example, pharmaceuticals, medical supplies, food, linen, water).

- Security (for example, access, crowd control, traffic control).

- Communication with the news media.

m. Evacuation of the entire facility (both horizontally and, when applicable, vertically) when the environment cannot support adequate individual care and treatment.

n. Establishment of an alternate care site(s) that has the capabilities to meet the clinical needs of individuals when the environment cannot support adequate individual care, and procedures that address, where applicable,

- Transportation of individuals, staff, and equipment to the alternate care site.

- The transfer of individual necessities (for example, medications, medical records) to and from the alternate care site.

- Individual tracking to and from the alternate care site.

- Interfacility communication between the organization and the alternate care site.

o. Re–establishment of usual operations following an emergency.

The plan identifies:

a. An alternative means of meeting essential building utility needs (for example, electricity, water, ventilation, fuel sources, medical gas/vacuum systems) when the organization is designated by its emergency management plan to provide continuous service during an emergency.

b. Backup internal and external communication systems in the event of failure during emergencies.

c. Facilities for radioactive, biological, and chemical isolation and decontamination.

d. Alternate roles and responsibilities of personnel during emergencies, including who they report to within the organization's command structure, and, when activated, within the command structure of the local community.

The plan further provides for:

a. An orientation and education program for all personnel, including licensed independent practitioners, who participate in implementing the emergency management plan. Education addresses, as appropriate to the individual:

- specific roles and responsibilities during emergencies.

- how to recognize specific types of emergencies (for example, the symptoms caused by agents that may be used in chemical or bioterrorist attacks).

- the information and skills required to perform assigned duties during emergencies.

- the backup communication system used during emergencies.

- how supplies and equipment are obtained during emergencies.

b. Procedures for an annual evaluation of the organization's hazard vulnerability analysis and of the emergency management plan, including its objectives, scope, functionality, and effectiveness.

Standard

EC.2.9.1 Drills are conducted regularly to test emergency management.

Intent of EC.2.9.1

The response phase of the emergency management plan is tested twice a year, either in response to an actual emergency or in planned drills. Drills are conducted at least four months apart and no more than eight months apart.

Testing includes:

a. For organizations that offer emergency services or are designated as disaster receiving stations, at least one drill yearly that includes an influx of volunteer or simulated individuals.

b. Participation in at least one community–wide practice drill yearly (where applicable) relevant to the priority emergencies identified by the organization's hazard vulnerability analysis, that assesses communication, coordination, and the effectiveness of the organization's and community's command structures.

Notes:

1. *Tests of a and b may be separate, simultaneous, or combined.*

2. *Drills that involve packages of information that simulate individuals, their families, and visitors are acceptable.*

3. *Tabletop exercises, though useful in planning or training, are **not** acceptable substitutes for test a.*

4. *Staff in each freestanding building classified as a business occupancy, as defined by the* Life Safety Code®, *that do not offer emergency services nor are designated as disaster receiving stations need only participate in one emergency preparedness drill annually. Staff in areas of the building that the organization occupies must participate in such drills.*

5. *In test b, "community–wide" may range from a contiguous geographic area served by the same health care providers, to a large borough, town, city, or region.*

Standard EC.4.10

The hospital addresses emergency management.

Rationale for EC.4.1 0

An emergency in the hospital or its community could suddenly and significantly affect the need for the hospital's services or its ability to provide those services. Therefore, a hospital needs to have an emergency management plan that comprehensively describes its approach to emergencies in the hospital or in its community.

Elements of Performance for Ec.4.1 0

1. The hospital conducts a hazard vulnerability analysis to identify potential emergencies that could affect the need for its services or its ability to provide those services.

2. The hospital establishes the following with the community:

- Priorities among the potential emergencies identified in the hazard vulnerability analysis.

- The hospital's role in relation to a communitywide emergency management program. An "all-hazards" command structure within the hospital that links with the community's command structure

3. The hospital develops and maintains a written emergency management plan describing the process for disaster readiness and emergency management, and implements it when appropriate.

4. At a minimum, an emergency management plan is developed with the involvement of the hospital's leaders including those of the medical staff.

5. The plan identifies specific procedures that describe mitigation, preparedness, response, and recovery strategies, actions, and responsibilities for each priority emergency.

6. The plan provides processes for initiating the response and recovery phases of the plan, including a description of how, when, and by whom the phases are to be activated.

   The plan provides processes for notifying staff when emergency response measures are initiated.

7. The plan provides processes for notifying external authorities of emergencies, including possible community emergencies identified by the hospital (for example, evidence of a possible bioterrorist attack).

8. The plan provides processes for identifying and assigning staff to cover all essential staff functions under emergency conditions.

9. The plan provides processes for managing the following under emergency conditions:

   - Activities related to care, treatment, and services (for example, scheduling, modifying, or discontinuing services; controlling information about patients; referrals; transporting patients)

- Staff support activities (for example, housing, transportation, incident stress debriefing)

- Staff family support activities

- Logistics relating to critical supplies (for example, pharmaceuticals, supplies, food, linen, water)

- Security (for example, access, crowd control, traffic control)

- Communication with the news media.

11. Not applicable

12. The plan provides processes for evacuating the entire facility (both horizontally and, when applicable, vertically) when the environment cannot support adequate care, treatment, and services.

13. The plan provides processes for establishing an alternative care site(s) that has the capabilities to meet the needs of patients when the environment cannot support adequate care, treatment, and services including processes for the following:

- Transporting patients, staff, and equipment to the alternative care site(s)

- Transferring to and from the alternative care site(s), the necessities of patients (for example, medications, medical records)

- Tracking of patients

- Interfacility communication between the hospital and the alternative care site(s)

14. The plan provides processes for identifying care providers and other personnel during emergencies.

15. The plan provides processes for cooperative planning among hospitals that together provide services to a contiguous geographic area (for example, among hospitals serving a town or borough) to facilitate the timely sharing of information about the following:

- Essential elements of their command structures and control centers for emergency response.

- Names and roles of individuals in their command structures and command center telephone numbers.

- Resources and assets that could potentially be shared in an emergency response.

- Names of patients and deceased individuals brought to their hospitals to facilitate identifying and locating victims of the emergency.

16. Not applicable

17. Not applicable

18. The plan identifies backup internal and external communication systems in the event of failure during emergencies.

19. The plan identifies alternate roles and responsibilities of staff during emergencies, including to whom they report in the hospital's command structure and, when activated, in the community's command structure.

20. The plan identifies an alternative means of meeting essential building utility needs when the hospital is designated by its emergency management plan to provide continuous service during an emergency (for example, electricity, water, ventilation, fuel sources, medical gas/vacuum systems).

21. The plan identifies means for radioactive, biological, and chemical isolation and econtamination.

DISASTER PRIVILEGES

Standard MS.4.11 0

Disaster privileges may be granted when the emergency management plan has been activated and the hospital is unable to handle the immediate patient needs (*see* standard EC.4.l0).

Rationale for MS.4.11 0

During disaster(s) in which the emergency management plan has been activated, the CEO or medical staff president or their designee(s) has the option to grant disaster privileges.

Elements of Performance for MS.4.11 0

1. The medical staff identifies in writing the individual(s) responsible for granting disaster privileges.

2. The medical staff describes in writing the responsibilities of the individual(s) granting disaster privileges. (The responsible individual is not required to grant privileges to any individual and is expected to make such decisions on a case–by case basis at his or her discretion.)

3. The medical staff describes in writing a mechanism to manage individuals who receive disaster privileges.

4. The medical staff includes a mechanism to allow staff to readily identify these individuals.

5. The medical staff addresses the verification process as a high priority.

6. The medical staff begins the verification process of the credentials and privileges of individuals who receive disaster privileges as soon as the immediate situation is under control.

7. This verification process is identical to the process established under the medical staff bylaws or other documents for granting temporary privileges to meet an important patient care need (*see* standard MS.4.100).

8. The CEO or president of the medical staff or their designee(s) may grant disaster privileges upon presentation of any of the following:

   - A current picture hospital ID card.

   - A current license to practice and a valid picture ID issued by a state, federal, or regulatory agency.

- Identification indicating that the individual is a member of a Disaster Medical Assitance Team (DMAT).

- Identification indicating that the individual has been granted authority to render patient care, treatment, and services in disaster circumstances (such authority having been granted by a federal, state, or municipal entity)

- Presentation by current hospital or medical staff member(s) with personal knowledge regarding practitioner's identity.

Reprinted with permission, Joint Commission on Accreditation of Health Care Organizations (JCAHO).

Required Elements of Hazard Analysis

The National Fire Protection Association, Inc. NFPA 1600 Standard on Disaster/Emergency Management and Business Continuity Programs 2004 Edition defines the required elements of a hazard analysis. This standard states that the hazard identification and risk assessment determine *what* can occur, *when* how often it is likely to occur, and *how bad* the effects could be. Hazard identification should include, but is not limited to, the following types of potential hazards:

NATURAL EVENTS	TECHNOLOGICAL EVENTS	HUMANS EVENTS
Drought	Hazardous materials release	Economic failures
Fire (eg. forest, range, urban)	Explosion or fire	General strikes
Avalanche	Transportation accident	Terrorism (eg eco, cyber, nuclear, biological, chemical)
Snow, ice, hail		
Tsunami	Building or structure collapse	Sabotage
Windstorm/typhoon/cyclone	Power or utility failure	Hostage situation
Hurricane/typhoon/cyclone	Extreme air pollution	Civil unrest
Biological event	Radiological accident	Enemy attack
Extreme heat or cold	Dam or levee failure	Arson
Flood or wind-driven water	Fuel or resource shortage	Mass hysteria
Earthquake or land shift	Strike	Special crowd producing events
Volcanic eruption	Business interruption	
Tornado	Financial collapse	
Landslide or mudslide	Communication disruption	
Dust or sand storm		
Lightening storm		

The methodologies and techniques for risk assessment and the resources for program administration include, but are not limited to, the following:

METHODS FOR RISK ASSESSMENT	**RESOURCES FOR ADMINISTRATION**
What if?	Inventory of equipment (e.g., location, quantities, accessibility, operability, maintenance)
Check list	Supplies (e.g., medical, personal hygiene, consumable, administrative)
Hazard operability studies	Sources of energy
Failure modes and effect analysis	Communication systems
Fault tree	Food, water, and ice
Failure logic diagrams	Technical information
Dow and bond indices	Clothing
Event tree analysis	Shelter
Human reliability analysis	Specialized personnel (e.g., medical, religious, emergency, utility, morticians, private contractors)
Capacity readiness for state and local governments	Volunteer groups (e.g., Red Cross, RACES, religious relief and charitable agencies)
	External government resources (e.g., Federal Response Plan, Federal Radiological Emergency Plan, National Guard)

Common Foodborne Diseases Caused by Bacteria

The table on the next page will be helpful when public health professionals require a quick reference to comparative information about foodborne diseases caused by bacteria. Professionals can consult this table to review the clinical symptoms for common foodborne diseases and the typical foods associated with each disease. Finally, specific prevention and control measures are provided.

REPRINTED FROM OWEN AL, SPLETT PL, AND OWEN GM, NUTRITION IN THE COMMUNITY: THE ART AND SCIENCE OF DELIVERY SERVICES, *4TH ED., BOSTON, MA: WCB MCGRAW HILL: 1999.*

Disease (causative agent)	Principal symptoms	Typical foods	Prevention and control measures
Food poisoning, diarrhea (*Bacillus cereus*)	Diarrhea, cramps, occasional vomiting	Meat products, soups, sauces, vegetables	Cook all potential food sources thoroughly, serve at correct temperature, cool rapidly.
Food poisoning, emetic (*B. cereus*)	Nausea, vomiting, sometimes diarrhea and cramps	Cooked rice and pasta	Minimize hot holding times.
Botulism; food poisoning (heat-labile toxin of *Clostridium botulinum*)	Fatigue, weakness, double vision, slurred speed, respiratory failure, sometimes death	Type A&B: Vegetables, fruits; meat, fish, and poultry products; condiments; Type E: fish and fish products	Purchase commercially processed foods, serve foods sauteed or infused in oils, promptly discard leftovers.
Botulism; food poisoning infant infection (heat-labile toxin of *C. botulinum*)	Constipation, weakness respiratory failure, sometimes death	Honey, soil	Do not feed honey to infants
Campylobacteriosis (*Campylobacter jejuni*)	Diarrhea, abdominal pain, fever, nausea, vomiting	Infected food-source animals	Cook animal foods thoroughly, cool rapidly, avoid cross-contamination, use pasteurized milk.
Food poisoning (*Clostridium perfringens*)	Diarrhea, cramps, rarely nausea and vomiting	Cooked meat and poultry	Cook animal foods thoroughly, cool rapidly, avoid cross-contaminations.
Foodborne infections, enterohemorrhagic (*Escherichia coli*)	Watery, bloody diarrhea	Raw or uncooked beef, raw milk	Cook animal foods thoroughly, cool rapidly, avoid cross-contaminations.
Foodborne infections, entroinvasive (*E. coli*)	Cramps, diarrhea, fever, dysentery	Raw foods	Teach food handlers good hygiene practice, have food handlers wear gloves, minimize holding time.

Disease (organism)	Symptoms	Foods involved	Prevention
Foodborne infections, enterotoxigenic (E. coli)	Profuse watery diarrhea; sometimes cramps, vomiting	Raw foods	Teach food handlers good hygiene practice, have food handlers wear gloves, minimize holding time.
Listeriosis (Listeria monocytogenes)	Meninfoencephalitis; stillbirths; septicemia or meningitis in newborns	Raw milk, cheese, and vegetables	Use pasteurized milk, cook foods thoroughly.
Salmonellosis (Salmonella species)	Diarrhea, abdominal pain, chills, fever, vomiting, dehydration	Raw, undercooked eggs; raw milk, meat and poultry	Cook animal foods thoroughly, minimize hot holding time, chill food rapidly, avoid cross-contamination.
Shigellosis (Shigella species)	Diarrhea, fever, nausea; sometimes vomiting, cramps	Raw foods	Cook animal food thoroughly, minimize hot holding time, chill food rapidly, avoid cross-contamination.
Staphylococcal food poisoning (heat-stable enterotoxin of Staphylococcus aureus)	Nausea, vomiting, diarrhea, cramps	Ham, meat, poultry products, cream-filled pastries, whipped butter, cheese	Restrict food handlers with skin lesions or respiratory infections from handling foods.
Streptococcal foodborne infection (Streptococcus pyogenes)	Various, including sore throat, erysipelas, scarlet fever	Raw milk, deviled eggs	Use pasteurized milk, teach foods handlers good hygiene practices, chill foods rapidly
Foodborne infections, (Vibrio parahaemolyticus)	Diarrhea, cramps; sometimes nausea vomiting, fever, headache	Fish and seafood	Cook fish and seafood thoroughly, minimize hot holding time.

Diseases Affecting Displaced Persons in Disasters

Disease	Symptoms	Environmental Risk Factors	Health Hazards
Acute upper respiratory tract infections	Symptoms of common cold; In pneumonia—chest pain and pain between shoulder blades	Crowding, poor hygiene	Influenza and pneumonia can result in severe complications in groups at risk
Cholera	Fever; severe liquid diarrhea; abdominal spasms; vomiting; rapid weight loss and dehydration	Same as diarrhea	Same as diarrhea
Diarrhea	Watery stools at least 3xday; may have fever, nausea, or vomiting	Contaminated drinking-water or food or poor sanitation	Dehydration, especially in children; dark color of urine, dry tongue, leathery skin
Diptheria	Inflamed and painful throat, coughing	Crowding, poor hygiene	A secretion is deposited in the respiratory tract which can lead to asphyxiation
Heat Stress	Elevated body temperatures, nausea, vomiting, headache	Excessive temperatures	Risk of coma

continued

Disease	Symptoms	Environmental Risk Factors	Health Hazards
(Viral) hepatitis A	Nausea, slight fever, pale-colored stools, dark-colored urine, jaundiced eyes and skin	Poor hygiene	Long-term disabling effects
Malaria	Painful muscles and joints, high fever with chills, headache, possible diarrhea and vomiting	Breeding of *Anopheles* mosquitoes in stagnant water bodies	Disease may rapidly become fatal unless medical care provided first 48 hours
Measles	Fever, and catarrhal symptoms, followed by maculopapular rash	Crowding, poor hygiene	High case fatality rate
Meningococcal meningitis	Infected persons may show no symptoms for a considerable time. When an epidemic is in progress, headache, fever and general malaise suggest diagnosis	Crowding	Only fatal if untreated in early stage; neurological problems in survivors
Rabies	Fatigue, headache, disorientation, paralysis, hyperactivity	Bite from infected animal host	Fatal if untreated
Shigella dysentery	Diarrhea with blood in stool, fever vomiting and abdominal cramps	Contaminated drinking water or food, or poor sanitation, poor hygiene	Case fatality rate may be high
Tetanus	Muscle spasms, starting in the jaws and extending to rest of body over several days	Poor hygiene, injury	Fatal
Typhoid fever	Starts off like malaria, sometimes with diarrhea, prolonged fever, occasionally with delirium	Same as diarrhea	Without appropriate medical care, can lead to fatal complication in a few weeks
Louse-borne typhus	Prolonged fever, headache, body pains	Unhygienic conditions leading to lice infestations	May be fatal without treatment

Adapted from Table 11.1. Control measures for ensuring food safety. In: Wisner B, Adams J, eds. (2002). Environmental health in emergencies and disasters. Geneva: World Health Organization. page 170.

Maintaining and Managing the Vaccine Cold Chain

Vaccine storage temperature requirements

	Instructions	Vaccine
35°F-46°F (2°C-8°C)	Do not freeze or expose to freezing temperatures. Set temperature at mid–range (40°F). Use a continuous temperature monitor that gives a visual record of the temperature fluctuations in the refrigerator. Contact state or local health department or manufacturer for guidance on vaccines exposed to temperatures above or below the recommended range.	Diphtheria, tetanus, or pertussis–containing vaccines (DT, DTaP, Td) Haemophilus conjugate vaccine (Hib) Hepatitis A (HepA) and hepatitis B (HepB) vaccines[1] Inactivated polio vaccine (IPV) Measles, mumps, and rubella vaccine (MMR) in the lyophilized (freeze–dried) state[2] Meningococcal polysaccharide vaccine Pneumococcal conjugate vaccine (PCV) Pneumococcal polysaccharide vaccine (PPV) Trivalent inactivated influenza vaccine (TIV) Smallpox vaccine Anthrax Vaccine Absorbed[3]

continued

continued	Instructions	Vaccine
<5°F (-15°C)	Maintain in continuously frozen state with no freeze–thaw cycles. Contact state or local health department or manufacturer for guidance on vaccines exposed to temperatures above the recommended range.	Live attenuated influenza vaccine (LAIV) Varicella vaccine

1   ActHIB® (Aventis Pasteur, Lyon, France) in the lyophilized state is not expected to be affected detrimentally by freezing temperatures, although no data is available.
2   MMR in the lyophilized state is not affected detrimentally by freezing temperatures
3   Biothrax™ Not to be used after expiration date given on the package.

Adapted from 1) Centers for Disease Control and Prevention. (2003). "Notice to Readers: Guideline for Maintaining and Managing the Vaccine Cold Chain, Table 1. Vaccine storage temperature requirements." MMWR 52(42): 1023–1025; and 2) Centers for Disease Control and Prevention (2003) Guidelines for Smallpox Vaccine Packing & Shipping; and 3) Bioport Corporation (January 31, 2002) Biothrax Product Insert.

Comparison of thermometers used to monitor vaccine temperatures

Thermometer type	Advantages	Disadvantages
Standard fluid–filled	Inexpensive and simple to use. Thermometers encased in biosafe liquids can reflect vaccine temperatures more accurately.	Less accurate (+/– 1°C). No information on duration of out of specification exposure. No information on min/max temperatures. Cannot be recalibrated. Inexpensive models might perform poorly.
Min–max	Inexpensive. Monitors temperature range.	Less accurate (+/-1°C). No information on duration of out of specification exposure. Cannot be recalibrated.
Continuous chart recorder	Most accurate. Continuous 24–hour readings of temperature range and duration. Can be recalibrated at regular intervals.	Most expensive. Requires most training and maintenance.

Adapted from Centers for Disease Control and Prevention. (2003). "Notice to Readers: Guideline for Maintaining and Managing the Vaccine Cold Chain, Table 2. Vaccine storage temperature requirements." MMWR 52(42): 1023–1025.

Manufacturers of Emergency Evacuation Devices

AOK Global Products, Ltd.
90 Jefryn Blvd.
Deer Park, NY 11729
Toll Free: (800) 649-4265
Direct: (631) 242-1642
www.rescuechair.com/
    index.html

Concept Development Associates, Inc.
1375 Central Ave.
Santa Rosa, CA 95401
Toll Free: (877) 379-2638
info@cda-designs.com
www.safetychairs.net

Evac+Chair
P.O. Box 2396
New York, NY 10021
Direct: (212) 369-4094
sales@evac-chair.com
http://www.evac-chair.com

Ferno-Washington, Inc.
70 Weil Way
Wilmington, OH 45177
Toll Free: (800) 733-3766
emergency.ferno.com

Frank Mobility Systems, Inc.
1003 International Drive
Oakdale, PA 15071
Toll Free: (888) 426-8581
Direct: (724) 695-7822
Fax: (724) 695-3710
info@frankmobility.com
www.frankmobility.com/

Garaventa Accessibility
P.O. Box 1769
Blaine, WA 98231
Toll Free: (800) 663-6556
www.garaventa.ca

LifeSlider, Inc.

25553 61st Road
Arkansas City, KS 67005
Toll Free: (888) 442-4543
Fax: (620) 442-2320
www.lifeslider.com

MAX–Ability, Inc.

1275 Fourth Street, Suite 304
Santa Rosa, CA 95404
Toll Free: (800) 577-1555
Direct: (707) 575-5558
www.max-ability.com/evac.html

Stryker EMS

6300 S. Sprinkle Rd.
Kalamazoo, MI 49001
Toll Free: (800) Rugged6
Direct: (269) 324-6566
www.ruggedcots.com

Information Technology Security Checklist

I. POLICY AND ORGANIZATION

❑ Set up overall information security policy with executive oversight and support.

❑ Develop an enterprise-wide approach to planning to include all stakeholders.

❑ Appoint an enterprise information security officer with authority, independence and budget.

❑ Appoint or establish external security auditors to ensure compliance with established information security policies and program objectives.

❑ Appoint information security managers at the agency or departmental level that report to the enterprise information security officer.

❑ Create an information security handbook covering information that everyone needs to know.

❑ Develop staff training and awareness procedures and ensure these are implemented.

❑ Set policy for handling sensitive and/or confidential data by appropriate information classification and retention schemes.

II. PREVENTION AND DETECTION

Physical Security Procedures:

❑ Make computer rooms secure with appropriate locks, password controls, user and visitor log-in systems.

❑ Deploy dropped ceilings and raised floors to protect hardware and network wiring with appropriate environmental monitoring systems or mechanisms.

❑ Install fire detection and containment equipment and establish safety and evaluation procedures. Adopt a no-smoking policy.

❑ Ensure networking equipment is secure in a separate room (not in the janitorial closet).

❑ Install restraints, if appropriate, on equipment for earthquake protection.

❑ Protect equipment from flooding, storms or area-specific weather threats.

Staff Security Procedures:

❑ Check new staff references and perform background checks.

❑ Keep staff informed of new security regulations and their role in enforcement.

❑ Set agreements with vendors to check the backgrounds of their employees.

❑ Train staff to watch for suspicious activity and provide appropriate reporting procedures.

❑ Train supervisors to watch for possible employee problems and ensure that corrective action plans are in place.

Overall Information Security Controls:

❑ Provide a framework for ensuring that risk assessments are understood and that mitigating controls are implemented.

- ❑ Inventory all equipment, and network access points—including employees and contractors that have remote access to network infrastructure—to ensure that security protocols are known and enforced.

- ❑ Ensure that only authorized individuals can read, alter or delete data and that audits are being performed

- ❑ Make sure that only authorized software programs are implemented and that a consistent change control process is in place.

- ❑ Restrict the ability of one individual to independently perform a task without detection. Ensure separation of duties.

- ❑ Protect sensitive programs from tampering and misuse—especially if they support multiple applications—and have alarms in place for violation notification.

- ❑ Ensure that computer-dependent operations experience no significant disruptions and, as necessary, disaster recovery procedures are in place and are frequently tested.

Software Controls:

- ❑ Adopt information security policies for new software development, testing and production implementation.

- ❑ Set information security guidelines for developing new systems. Use system development life cycle, include information security and auditing standards.

- ❑ Adopt standard procedures for obtaining security patches from software developers and post in a centralized area to ensure access and validity.

- ❑ Restrict the use of system tools on both test and production environments.

Overall Administrative and Operations Information Security Controls:

- ❑ Keep an up-to-date inventory of hardware and software for disaster recovery and business continuity planning.

❑ Information owners should review user privileges on a regular basis.

❑ Account for all dial-in accounts to ensure they are authorized

❑ Establish and maintain comprehensive disaster recovery and business continuity plans with every stakeholder.

❑ Conduct random information security checks using white-hat tools.

❑ Establish procedures for dealing with computer crime to include handling of information for forensic and evidence value.

Intrusion and Detection Planning:

❑ Perform penetration audits using Tiger Teams who are trained on how to locate and exploit system and network vulnerabilities.

❑ Conduct a business impact analysis to ensure resources are recoverable as the business needs require.

❑ Deploy an intrusion detection system that both detects and notifies appropriate staff.

❑ Install appropriate virus detection software.

❑ Deploy appropriate firewall technology.

❑ Ensure passwords are strong; use one-time passwords, deploy tokens or biometric authentication when required.

❑ Turn off unneeded network services.

III. RECOVERY AND CONTINUITY

❑ Develop and test a robust business continuity plan.

❑ Ensure that contingency planning and incident response teams are enabled in the event of unplanned outages or breached systems.

❑ Make sure staff involved in recovery efforts are well trained and that secondary personnel are available.

❑ Enable hot and cold recovery sites where the business case justifies the return on investment.

❑ Practice recovery and continuity plans frequently.

❑ Keep the plans up to date as the risks change.

Originally printed in February, 02 Government Technology
Reprinted with permission from Center for Digital Government (http://www.centerdigitalgov.com/)

Emergency Support Function (ESF) #8— Health and Medical Services

A. Purpose

Emergency Support Function (ESF) #8—Health and Medical Services provides coordinated Federal assistance to supplement State and local resources in response to public health and medical care needs following a major disaster or emergency, or during a developing potential medical situation. Assistance provided under ESF #8 is directed by the Department of Health and Human Services (HHS) through its executive agent, the Assistant Secretary of Health. Resources will be furnished when State and local resources are overwhelmed and public health and/or medical assistance is requested from the Federal Government.

B. Scope

1. ESF #8 involves supplemental assistance to State and local governments in identifying and meeting the health and medical needs of victims of a major disaster, emergency, or terrorist attack. This support is categorized in the following functional areas:

   a. Assessment of health/medical needs;

   b. Health surveillance;

c. Medical care personnel;

d. Health/medical equipment and supplies;

e. Patient evacuation;

f. In-hospital care;

g. Food/drug/medical device safety;

h. Worker health/safety;

i. Radiological/chemical/biological hazards consultation;

j. Mental health care;

k. Public health information;

l. Vector control;

m. Potable water/wastewater and solid waste disposal;

n. Victim identification/mortuary services; and

o. Veterinary services.

Federal Communications Commission Rules: RACES

SUBPART A—GENERAL PROVISIONS

§§97.3 Definitions.

(a) The definitions of terms used in Part 97 are:
(37) RACES (radio amateur civil emergency service). A radio service using amateur stations for civil defense communications during periods of local, regional, or national civil emergencies.

§§97.17 Application for new license grant.

(a) Any qualified person is eligible to apply for a new operator/ primary station, club station or military recreation station license grant. No new license grant will be issued for a RACES station.

SUBPART E—PROVIDING EMERGENCY COMMUNICATIONS

§§97.401 Operation during a disaster.

(a) When normal communication systems are overloaded, damaged, or disrupted because a disaster has occurred, or is likely to occur, in an area where the amateur service is regulated by the FCC, an amateur station may make transmissions necessary to meet essential communication needs and facilitate relief actions.

(b) When normal communication systems are overloaded, damaged, or disrupted because a natural disaster has occurred, or is likely to occur, in an area where the amateur service is not regulated by the FCC, a station assisting in meeting essential communication needs and facilitating relief actions may do so only in accord with ITU Resolution No. 640 (Geneva, 1979). The 80 m, 75 m, 40 m, 30 m, 20 m, 17 m, 15 m, 12 m, and 2 m bands may be used for these purposes.

(c) When a disaster disrupts normal communication systems in a particular area, the FCC may declare a temporary state of communication emergency. The declaration will set forth any special conditions and special rules to be observed by stations during the communication emergency. A request for a declaration of a temporary state of emergency should be directed to the EIC in the area concerned.

(d) A station in, or within 92.6 km of, Alaska may transmit emissions J3E and R3E on the channel at 5.1675 MHz for emergency communications. The channel must be shared with stations licensed in the Alaska-private fixed service. The transmitter power must not exceed 150 W.

§§97.403 Safety of life and protection of property.

No provision of these rules prevents the use by an amateur station of any means of radio communication at its disposal to provide essential communication needs in connection with the immediate safety of human life and immediate protection of property when normal communication systems are not available.

§§97.405 Station in distress.

(a) No provision of these rules prevents the use by an amateur station in distress of any means at its disposal to attract attention, make known its condition and location, and obtain assistance.

(b) No provision of these rules prevents the use by a station, in the exceptional circumstances described in paragraph (a), of any means of radio communications at its disposal to assist a station in distress.

§§97.407 Radio amateur civil emergency service.

(a) No station may transmit in RACES unless it is an FCC-licensed primary, club, or military recreation station and it is certified by a civil defense organization as registered with that organization, or it is an FCC-licensed RACES station. No person may be the control operator of a RACES station, or may be the control operator of an amateur station transmitting in RACES unless that person holds a FCC-issued amateur operator license and is certified by a civil defense organization as enrolled in that organization.

(b) The frequency bands and segments and emissions authorized to the control operator are available to stations transmitting communications in RACES on a shared basis with the amateur service. In the event of an emergency which necessitates the invoking of the President's War Emergency Powers under the provisions of Section 706 of the Communications Act of 1934, as amended, 47 U.S.C. §§606, RACES stations and amateur stations participating in RACES may only transmit on the following frequencies:

(1) The 1800-1825 kHz, 1975-2000 kHz, 3.50-3.55 MHz, 3.93-3.98 MHz, 3.984-4.000 MHz, 7.079-7.125 MHz, 7.245-7.255 MHz, 10.10-10.15 MHz, 14.047-14.053 MHz, 14.22-14.23 MHz, 14.331-14.350 MHz, 21.047-21.053 MHz, 21.228-21.267 MHz, 28.55-28.75 MHz,29.237-29.273 MHz, 29.45-29.65 MHz, 50.35-50.75 MHz, 52-54 MHz, 144.50-145.71 MHz, 146-148 MHz, 2390-2450 MHz segments;

(2) The 1.25 m, 70 cm, and 23 cm bands; and

(3) The channels at 3.997 and 53.30 MHz may be used in emergency areas when required to make initial contact with a military unit and for communications with military stations on matters requiring coordination.

(c) A RACES station may only communicate with:

(1) Another RACES station;

(2) An amateur station registered with a civil defense organization;

(3) A United States Government station authorized by the responsible agency to communicate with RACES stations;

(4) A station in a service regulated by the FCC whenever such communication is authorized by the FCC.

(d) An amateur station registered with a civil defense organization may only communicate with:

(1) A RACES station licensed to the civil defense organization with which the amateur station is registered;

(2) The following stations upon authorization of the responsible civil defense official for the organization with which the amateur station is registered:

(i) A RACES station licensed to another civil defense organization;

(ii) An amateur station registered with the same or another civil defense organization;

(iii) A United States Government station authorized by the responsible agency to communicate with RACES stations; and

(iv) A station in a service regulated by the FCC whenever such communication is authorized by the FCC.

(e) All communications transmitted in RACES must be specifically authorized by the civil defense organization for the area served. Only civil defense communications of the following types may be transmitted:

(1) Messages concerning impending or actual conditions jeopardizing the public safety, or affecting the national defense or security during periods of local, regional, or national civil emergencies;

(2) Messages directly concerning the immediate safety of life of individuals, the immediate protection of property, maintenance of law and order, alleviation of human suffering and need, and the combating of armed attack or sabotage;

(3) Messages directly concerning the accumulation and dissemination of public information or instructions to the civilian population essential to the activities of the civil defense organization or other authorized governmental or relief agencies; and

(4) Communications for RACES training drills and tests necessary to ensure the establishment and maintenance of orderly

and efficient operation of the RACES as ordered by the responsible civil defense organization served. Such drills and tests may not exceed a total time of 1 hour per week. With the approval of the chief officer for emergency planning in the applicable State, Commonwealth, District, or territory, however, such tests and drills may be conducted for a period not to exceed 72 hours no more than twice in any calendar year.

From: Code of Federal Regulations, Title 47: Telecommunications, Chapter I — Federal Communications Commission, Subchapter D- Safety and Special Radio Services, Part 97 — Amatuer Radio Service

Federal Communication Commission Rules: Accessibility

47 C.F.R. § 79.2

§ 79.2 Accessibility of Programming Providing Emergency Information.

(a) Definitions.

(1) For purposes of this section, the definitions in Sections 79.1 and 79.3 apply.

(2) Emergency information. Information, about a current emergency, that is intended to further the protection of life, health, safety, and property, i.e., critical details regarding the emergency and how to respond to the emergency. Examples of the types of emergencies covered include tornadoes, hurricanes, floods, tidal waves, earthquakes, icing conditions, heavy snows, widespread fires, discharge of toxic gases, widespread power failures, industrial explosions, civil disorders, school closings and changes in school bus schedules resulting from such conditions, and warnings and watches of impending changes in weather.

Note to paragraph (a)(2): Critical details include, but are not limited to, specific details regarding the areas that will be affected by the emergency, evacuation orders, detailed descriptions of areas to be evacuated, specific evacuation routes, approved shelters or the way to take shelter in one's home, instructions on how to secure personal property, road closures, and how to obtain relief assistance.

(b) Requirements for Accessibility of Programming Providing Emergency Information.

(1) Video programming distributors must make emergency information, as defined in paragraph (a) of this section, accessible as follows:

(i) Emergency information that is provided in the audio portion of the programming must be made accessible to persons with hearing disabilities by using a method of closed captioning or by using a method of visual presentation, as described in Section 79.1 of this part.

(ii) Emergency information that is provided in the video portion of a regularly scheduled newscast, or newscast that interrupts regular programming, must be made accessible to persons with visual disabilities; and

(iii) Emergency Information that is provided in the video portion of programming that is not a regularly scheduled newscast, or a newscast that interrupts regular programming, must be accompanied with an aural tone.

(2) This rule applies to emergency information primarily intended for distribution to an audience in the geographic area in which the emergency is occurring.

(3) Video programming distributors must ensure that:

(i) Emergency information should not block any closed captioning and any closed captioning should not block any emergency information provided by means other than closed captioning; and

(ii) Emergency information should not block any video description and any video description provided should not block any emergency information provided by means other than video description.

(c) Complaint Procedures. A complaint alleging a violation of this section may be transmitted to the Commission by any reasonable means, such as letter, facsimile transmission, telephone (voice/

TRS/TTY), Internet e-mail, audio–cassette recording, and Braille, or some other method that would best accommodate the complainant's disability. The complaint should include the name of the video programming distributor against whom the complaint is alleged, the date and time of the omission of emergency information, and the type of emergency. The Commission will notify the video programming distributor of the complaint, and the distributor will reply to the complaint within 30 days.

International Nuclear Event Scale (INES), used to inform the public about the severity of events at nuclear facilities

LEVEL	Description of event
level 0 (deviation)	No safety significance
level 1 (anomaly)	Does not involve significant safety failures, spread of contamination, or overexposure of workers.
level 2 (incident)	Significant failure of safety provisions, but with sufficient defense to cope with additional failures; and/or resulting in a dose to a worker exceeding a statutory dose limit; and/or leading to the presence of activity in on-site areas not expected by design and which require corrective action.
level 3 (serious incident)	Near–accident, (only the last layer of in–depth defense remained operational); and/or involving severe spread of contamination on–site or to a worker; and/or a very small release of radioactive material off-site.
level 4 (accident without significant off-site risk)	Accident involving significant damage to the installation (e.g., partial core melt); and/or overexposure of one or more workers that results in a high probability of death; and/or an off–site release with a critical group dose of a few mSv.
level 5 (accident with off-site risk)	Accident resulting in severe damage to the installation, likely to result in partial implementation of countermeasures covered by emergency plans. (i.e., 1979 accident at Three Mile Island)

continued

continued

LEVEL	**Description of event**
level 6 (serious accident)	Accident involving significant release of radioactive material, and likely to require full implementation of planned countermeasures, but less severe than a major accident. (i.e., 1957 accident at Kyshtym, USSR)
level 7 (major accident)	Accident involving major release of radioactive material with wide spread health and environmental effects. (i.e., 1986 accident at Chernobyl, USSR)

Adapted from Table 13.1 International Nuclear Event Scale (INES), used to inform the public about the severity of events at nuclear facilities from Wisner B and Adams J (eds.) (2002). Environmental health in emergencies and disasters. World Health Organization. Geneva. page 192

List of the Regional Offices of the Federal Emergency Management Agency (FEMA)

Region 1
Connecticut, Maine, Massachusetts, New Hampshire, Rhode Island, Vermont
Federal Emergency Management Agency
99 High Street, 6th Floor
Boston, MA 02110
(617) 223-9540

Region 2
New Jersey, New York, Puerto Rico, Virgin Islands
Federal Emergency Management Agency
26 Federal Plaza, Room 1337
New York, NY 10278-0002
(212) 225-7209

Region 3
Delaware, District of Columbia, Maryland, Pennsylvania, Virginia, West Virginia
Federal Emergency Management Agency
One Independence Mall, 6th Floor
615 Chestnut Street
Philadelphia, PA 19106-4404
(215) 931-5608

Region 4

Alabama, Florida, Georgia, Kentucky, Mississippi, North Carolina, South Carolina, Tennessee
Federal Emergency Management Agency
3003 Chamblee-Tucker Road
Atlanta, GA 30341
(770) 220-5200

Region 5

Illinois, Indiana, Michigan, Minnesota, Ohio, Wisconsin
Federal Emergency Management Agency
536 South Clark Street, 6th Floor
Chicago, IL 60605
(312) 408-5501

Region 6

Arkansas, Louisiana, New Mexico, Oklahoma, Texas
Federal Emergency Management Agency
Federal Regional Center
800 N. Loop 288
Denton, TX 76201-3698
(817) 898-5104

Region 7

Iowa, Kansas, Missouri, Nebraska
Federal Emergency Management Agency
2322 Grand Blvd, Suite 900
Kansas City, MO 64108-2670
(816) 283-7061

Region 8

Colorado, Montana, North Dakota, South Dakota, Utah, Wyoming
Federal Emergency Management Agency
Denver Federal Center
Building 710, Box 25267
Denver, CO 80225-0267
(303) 235-4812

Region 9

American Samoa, Arizona, California, Guam, Hawaii, Nevada,
Commonwealth of the Northern Mariana Islands, Federated States of
Micronesia, Republic of the Marshall Islands
  Federal Emergency Management Agency
  1111 Broadway
  Suite 1200
  Oakland, CA 94607-4052
  (510) 627-7100

Region 10

Alaska, Idaho, Oregon, Washington
  Federal Emergency Management Agency
  Federal Regional Center
  130 228th Street, S.W.
  Bothell, WA 98021-9796
  (206) 487-4604

Emergency Management Institute
16825 South Seton Avenue
Emmitsburg, MD 21727

National Emergency Training Center
16825 South Seton Avenue
Emmitsburg, MD 21727

Mount Weather Emergency Assistance Center
19844 Blue Ridge Mountain Road
State Route 601
Bluemont, VA 20135

United States Fire Administration
16825 South Seton Avenue
Emmitsburg, MD 21727

Descriptions of the Five Color-Coded DHS Threat Levels

Green	Blue	Yellow	Orange	Red
Low Condition	**Guarded Condition**	**Elevated Condition**	**High Condition**	**Severe Condition**
This condition is declared when there is a low risk of terrorist attacks. Federal agencies will ensure that personnel receive proper training on the Homeland Security Advisory System and specific pre-planned department or agency protective measures; and institutionalize a process to assure that all facilities and regulated sectors are regularly assessed for vulnerabilities to terrorist attacks,	This condition is declared when there is a general risk of terrorist attacks. In addition to the Protective Measures taken in the previous threat condition, federal departments and agencies will check communications with designated emergency response or command locations; review and update emergency response procedures; and provide the public with any information that	An elevated condition is declared when there is a significant risk of terrorist attacks. In addition to the protective measures taken in the previous threat conditions, federal departments and agencies will increase surveillance of critical locations, coordinate emergency plans as appropriate with nearby jurisdictions, assess whether the precise characteristics of the threat require	A high condition is declared when there is a high risk of terrorist attacks. In addition to the protective measures taken in the previous threat conditions, federal departments and agencies will coordinate necessary security efforts with federal, state, and local law enforcement agencies, national guard or other armed forces organizations; take additional precautions at public events (includ-	A severe condition reflects a severe risk of terrorist attacks. Under most circumstances, the protective measures for a severe condition are not intended to be sustained for long periods of time. In addition to the protective measures in the previous threat conditions, federal departments and agencies will increase or redirect personnel to address critical emergency needs; assign emer-

continued   *continued*   *continued*   *continued*   *continued*

continued	*continued*	*continued*	*continued*	*continued*
Green	**Blue**	**Yellow**	**Orange**	**Red**
Low Condition	**Guarded Condition**	**Elevated Condition**	**High Condition**	**Severe Condition**
and all reasonable measures are taken to mitigate these vulnerabilities.	would strengthen its ability to act appropriately.	the further refinement of preplanned protective measures; and implement, as appropriate, contingency and emergency response plans.	ing moves to alternative venues or cancellation), prepare to execute contingency procedures, and restrict access to essential personnel only.	gency response personnel and pre–position and mobilize specially trained teams or resources; monitor, redirect, or constrain transportation systems; and close public and government facilities.

References and Readings

BIOTERRORISM AND EMERGING DISEASES

Atlas RM. (1998). "The Medical Threat of Biological Weapons." *Critical Reviews in Microbiology*, 24:157-168

Blank S., Moskin LC., Zucker JR. (2003). "An Ounce of Prevention Is a Ton of Work: Mass Antibiotic Prophylaxis for Anthrax: New York City, 2001" *Emerging Infectious Diseases*, Vol.9 (6) June 2003.

Bravata DM, McDonald KM, Owens DK, et al. (April 2004). "Regionalization of Bioterrorism Preparedness and Response." Summary, *Evidence Report/Technology Assessment: Number 96.* AHRQ Publication Number 04-E016-1. Agency for Healthcare Research and Quality, Rockville, MD.

Center for Disease Control. (2003). "Notice to Readers: Guidelines for Maintaining and Managing the Vaccine Cold Chain." *Morbidity and Mortality Weekly Report*, 52(42):10023-1025.

Franz DR, Jahrling PB, Friedlander AM, et al. (1997) "Clinical Recognition and Management of Patients Exposed to Biological Warfare Agents." *J Am Med Assoc*, 278:399-411.

Henderson DA, Inglesby TV, O'Toole TO. (2002). *Bioterrorism: Guidelines for Medical and Public Health Management.* JAMA & Archives Journals, Chicago.

Journal of Public Health Management and Practice. (2001) Novick, L.F., Marr, J.S., eds. Public Health Issues in Disaster Preparedness: Focus on Bioterrorism. 1-150.

Meehan, P.J., Rosenstein, N.E.; Gillen, M.; Meyer, R.F., Kiefer, M.J., Deitchman, S., Besser, R.E., Ehrenberg, R.L., Edwards, K.M., Martinez, K.F. (2004). "Responding to Detection of Aerosolized *Bacillus anthracis* by Autonomous Detection Systems in the Workplace." Centers for Disease Control and Prevention. 53 RR07; 1-12, Atlanta, Ga.

Shapiro RL, Hatheway C, Becher J, Swerdlow DL. (1997) "Botulism Surveillance and Emergency Response." *J Am Med Assoc.* 278:433-435.

Walker, D. H., A. G. Barbour, et al. (1996). "Emerging Bacterial Zoonotic and Vector-borne Diseases: Ecological and Epidemiological Factors." *Journal of the American Medical Association,* 275(6):463-469.

Weinstein RS, Alibek K. (2003). *Biological and Chemical Terrorism: A Guide for Healthcare Providers and First Responders.* Thieme Medical Publishers, Inc., New York

Woodall J. (1998). "The Role of Computer Networking in Investigating Unusual Disease Outbreaks and Allegations of Biological and Toxin Weapons Use." *Critical Reviews in Microbiology,* 24:255-272.

Smallpox

Henderson DA, Inglesby TV, Bartlett JG, Ascher MS, et al. (1999). "Smallpox as a Biological Weapon." *J Am Med Assn,* 281:2127-2137.

Henderson DA. (1999). "Smallpox: Clinical and Epidemiologic Features." *Em Inf Dis,* 5:537-539.

O'Toole T. (1999). "Smallpox: An Attack Scenario." *Em Inf Dis,* 5:540-560.

Anthrax

Dixon TC, Meselson M, Guillemin J, Hanna PC. (1999). Anthrax, review article. *New Engl J Med,* 341:815-826.

Inglesby TV, Henderson DA, Bartlett JG, Ascher MS, et al. (1999). Anthrax as a Biological Weapon. *J Am Med Assn,* 281:1735-1736.

Mina B, Dym J, Kuepper F, et al. Fatal Inhalational Anthrax with Unknown Source of Exposure in a 61-year-old Women in New York City. (2002). *Journal of the American Medical Association*, 287(7):858-862.

Response

Campbell J, Francesconi S, Boyd J, Worth L, Moshier T. (1999). Environmental Air Sampling to Detect Biological Warfare Agents. *Military Med*, 164:541-542.

Department of Justice. (2003). Criminal and Epidemiological Investigation Handbook. Washington, D.C.

Holloway HC, Norwood AE, Fullerton CS, Engel CC, Ursano RJ. (1997). The Threat of Biological Weapons. Prophylaxis and Mitigation of Psychological and Social Consequences. *J Am Med Assoc*, 278:425-427.

Lederberg J. (1997). Infectious Disease and Biological Weapons. Prophylaxis and mitigation. *J Am Med Assoc*, 278:435-436.

Murray V., ed. (1990). Major Chemical Disasters—Medical Aspects of Management. *Royal Society of Medicine Services Limited*, New York

Pepe, P.E., Rinnert, K.J. (2002). "Bioterrorism and Medical Risk Management." *The International Lawyer*, 36(1):9-20.

Laboratory Issues

Atlas RM. Biological Weapons Pose Challenge for Microbiology Community. (1998). ASM News 64:383-389.

Belgrader P, Benett W, Hadley D., Richards J, Stratton P, Mariella R, Milanovich F. (1999). PCR detection of bacteria in seven minutes. *Science*, 284:449-450.

Engelthaler DM, Gage NL, Montenieri JA, Chu M, Carter LG. (1999). PCR Detection of Yersinia Pestis in Fleas: Comparison with Mouse Inoculation. *J Clin Micro*, 37:1980-1984.

McDade JE. (1999). Addressing the Potential Threat of Bioterrorism-value Added to an Improved Public Health Infrastructure. *Em Inf Dis*, 5;591-592.

Rowe CA, Tender LM, Feldstein MJ, Golden JP, Scrugg SB, MacCraith BD, Cras JJ, Ligler FS. (1999). Array Biosensor for Simultaneous Identification of Bacterial, Viral, and Protein Analytes. *Analytical Chemistry*, 71:3846-3852.

CASE STUDIES

Alson, R., Alexander, D., et al. (1993). "Analysis of Medical Treatment at a Field Hospital Following Hurricane Andrew, 1992." *Annals of Emergency Medicine*, 22(11):1721-1728.

Bel, N. (1993). "Triumph over Tragedy: Emergency Response to Hurricane Andrew." *Emergency,* 25(4):28-31, 66.

Bernstein RS, Baxter PJ, Falk H, Ing R, Foster L, Frost F. (1986). "Immediate public health concerns and actions in volcanic eruptions: lessons from Mount St. Helens eruptions, May 18-October 18, 1980." *American Journal of Public Health,* 76(3 Suppl):25-37.

Brewer, R.D., Morris, P.D., et al. (1994). "Hurricane-related Emergency Department Visits in an Inland Area: An Analysis of the Public Health Impact of Hurricane Hugo in North Carolina." *Annals of Emergency Medicine*, 23(4):731-736.

Carr SJ, Leahy SM, London S, Sidhu S, Vogt J. (1996). "The Public Health Response to the Los Angeles, 1994 Earthquake." *American Journal of Public Health*, 86(4):589-590.

Centers for Disease Control (1986). "Hurricanes and Hospital Emergency-room Visits—Mississippi, Rhode Island, Connecticut." *Morbidity and Mortality Weekly Report*, 34(51& 52):765-770.

Centers for Disease Control (1991). "Tornado disaster—Illinois, 1990." *Morbidity and Mortality Weekly Report*, 40(2):33-36.

Centers for Disease Control (1992). "Rapid Health Needs Assessment Following Hurricane Andrew—Florida and Louisiana, 1992." *Morbidity and Mortality Weekly Report*, 41(37):685-688.

Centers for Disease Control and Prevention (1992). "Tornado Disaster— Kansas 1991." MMWR *Morbidity and Mortality Weekly Report*, 41(10):181-3, Mar 13.

Centers for Disease Control and Prevention. (2001). "Injury and Illness Among New York City Fire Department Rescue Workers After Responding to the World Trade Center Attacks." *MMWR Morbid Mortal Wkly Rep Special issue*, 51:1-20.

Center for Disease Control (1993). "Comprehensive Assessment of Health Needs 2 Months after Hurricane Andrew—Dade County, Florida." *Morbidity and Mortality Weekly Report*, 42(22):434-437.

Center for Disease Control (1993). "Injuries and Illnesses Related to Hurricane Andrew—Louisiana, 1992." *Morbidity and Mortality Weekly Report*, 42(13):242-251.

Centers for Disease Control (1993). "Morbidity Surveillance Following the Midwest Flood—Missouri, 1993." *Journal of the American Medical Association*, 270(18):2164.

Centers for Disease Control (1993). "Public Health Consequences of a Flood Disaster—Iowa, 1993." *Morbidity and Mortality Weekly Report*, 42: 653-656.

Centers for Disease Control (1994). "Rapid Assessment of Vectorborne Diseases during the Midwest Flood, United States, 1993." *Morbidity and Mortality Weekly Report*, 43(26):481-483.

Centers for Disease Control (1996). "Surveillance for Injuries and Illnesses and Rapid Health Needs Assessment Following Hurricanes Marilyn and Opal, September-October 1995." *Morbidity and Mortality Weekly Report*, 45(4):81-85.

Centers for Disease Control and Prevention. (1998). "Community Needs Assessment and Morbidity Surveillance Following an Ice Storm—Maine, January 1998." *MMWR Morbid Mortal Wkly Rep*, 47:361-364.

Centers for Disease Control and Prevention (2002). "Rapid Assessment of Injuries Among Survivors of the Terrorist Attack on the World Trade Center—New York City, September 2001," 51(01):1 January 11.

Centers for Disease Control and Prevention (2002). Needs Assessment Following Hurricane Georges—Dominican Republic, 1998. 48(05):93 February 12.

Centers for Disease Control and Prevention (2002). "Tropical Storm Allison Rapid Needs Assessment—Houston, Texas, June 2001." 51(17):365 May 3.

Centers for Disease Control and Prevention (2002). "Morbidity and Mortality Associated With Hurricane Floyd—North Carolina, September–October 1999." 49(17):369 May 05.

Centers for Disease Control and Prevention (2002). "Psychological and Emotional Effects of the September 11 Attacks on the World Trade Center—Connecticut, New Jersey, and New York 2001." 51(35):784 September 06.

Centers for Disease Control and Prevention (2002). "Community Needs Assessment of Lower Manhattan Residents Following the World Trade Center Attacks—Manhattan, New York City, 2001." 51(SP):10 September 11.

Centers for Disease Control and Prevention (2002). "Impact of September 11 Attacks on Workers in the Vicinity of the World Trade Center—New York City." 51(SP):8 September 11.

Centers for Disease Control and Prevention (2002). "Use of Respiratory Protection Among Responders at the World Trade Center Site—New York City, September 2001." 51(SP)6 September 11.

Centers for Disease Control and Prevention (2002). "Notice to Readers: New York City Department of Health Response to Terrorist Attack, September 11, 2001." 50(38):821 September 28.

Centers for Disease Control and Prevention (2003). "Cholera Epidemic after Increased Civil Conflict—Monrovia, Liberia. June–September 2003." 52(45):1093: November 14.

Combs, D.L., Parrish, R.G., et al. (1996). "Deaths Related to Hurricane Andrew in Florida and Louisiana, 1992." *International Journal of Epidemiology,* 25(3):537-544.

Durkin, M.E., Thiel, C.C. Jr., et al. (1991). "Injuries and Emergency Medical Response in the Loma Prieta Earthquake." *Bulletin of the Seismological Society of America,* 81:2143-2166.

Erikson, K. (1976). *Everything in Its Path: Destruction of Community in the Buffalo Creek Flood.* New York: Simon & Schuster.

Gautam K. "Organizational Problems Faced by the Missouri DOH in Providing Disaster Relief During the 1993 Floods." *Journal of Public Health Management & Practice*, 4(4):79-86.

Green, B.L., Grace, M.C., Lindy, J.D., Gleser, G.C., Leonard, A.C., Kramer, T.L. (1990a) Buffalo Creek Survivors in the Second Decade: Comparison with Unexposed and Non-litigant Groups. *Journal of Applied Social Psychology*, 20:1033-1050.

Grace, M.C., Green, B.L., Lindy, J.D., Leonard, A.C. (1993). The Buffalo Creek Disaster: A 14-year Follow-up. In: J.P. Wilson, B. Raphael, eds. *The International Handbook of Traumatic Stress Syndromes*. New York: Plenum Press, pp. 441-449.

Haynes, B. E., C. Freeman, et al. (1992). "Medical Response to Catastrophic Events: California's Planning and the Loma Prieta Earthquake." *Annals of Emergency Medicine*, 21(4):368-374.

Hogan, D.E., Waeckerle, J.F., et al. (1999). "Emergency Department Impact of the Oklahoma City Terrorist Bombing." *Annals of Emergency Medicine*, 34(2):160-167.

Jarret, J.C., Hagebak, B., et al. (1995). "Lessons from the Georgia Floods." *Public Health Reports*, 110:684-689.

Johnson, W.P., Lanza, C.V. (1993). "After Hurricane Andrew: An EMS Perspective." *Prehospital and Disaster Medicine*, 8(2):169-171.

Kerns, D.E., Anderson, P.B. (1990). "EMS response to a major aircraft incident: Sioux City, Iowa." *Prehospital and Disaster Medicine*, 5(2):159-166.

Landesman, L.Y. (2001). "A Department of Health Learns about Its Role in Emergency Public Health." In: Rowitz, L., ed. *Public Health Leadership: Putting Principles into Practice*. Gaithersburg, MD: Aspen Publishers, pp. 150-153.

McNabb, S.J.N., Kelso, K.Y., et al. (1995). "Hurricane Andrew-related Injuries and Illnesses, Louisiana, 1992." *Southern Medical Journal*, 88:6.

Noji, E.K., Kelen, G.D., Armenian, H.K., et al. (1990). "The 1988 Earthquake in Armenia: A Case Study." *Annals of Emergency Medicine*, pp 75-81.

Siders C, Jacobson R. (1998). "Flood Disaster Preparedness: A Retrospective from Grand Forks, South Dakota." *Journal of Healthcare Risk Management,* 18(2):33-40.

Whitman S, Good G, Donoghue ER, Benbow N, Shou W, Mou, S. (1997). "Mortality in Chicago Attributed to the July 1995 Heat Wave." *American Journal of Public Health,* 87(9):1515-1518.

COMMUNICATION

Best of Supplement to Government Technology. (2002) page 12- October.

American Medical Association, Ad Hoc Committee of Health Literacy for the Council of Scientific Affairs. (1999). Health literacy: Report of the Council of Scientific Affairs. *Journal of the American Medical Association,* 281(6):552-557.

Bennett P. Understanding responses to risk: Some basic findings. In: Bennett P, Calman K, eds. (1999). *Risk communication and public health.* Oxford: Oxford University Press; 319.

Chess C, Hance BJ, Sandman PM. (1988). *Improving Dialogue with Communities: A Short Guide to Government Risk Communication.* New Jersey Department of Environmental Protection.

Churchill RE. (1997). Effective Media Relations. In: Noji E.K., ed. *The Public Health Consequences of Disasters.* New York: Oxford University Press.

Covello V. (2003). Best Practices in Public Health Risk and Crisis Communication. *Journal of Health Communications,* 8(Suppl 1):5-8.

Covello V. (1992). Risk Communication, Trust, and Credibility. *Health and Environmental Digest,* 6(1):1-4 (April).

Ferguson EW, et al. (1995). Telemedicine for National and International Disaster Response. *Journal of Medical Systems,* 19(2):121-123

Fischhoff B, Lichtenstein S, Slovic P, Keeney D. 1981. *Acceptable Risk.* Cambridge, Massachusetts: Cambridge University Press.

Koplan J. (2003). Communication during public health emergencies. *Journal of Health Communication,* 8(Suppl 1):144-145.

Martchenke J, Rusteen J, Pointer JE (1995). "Prehospital Communications During the Loma Prieta Earthquake." *Prehospital and Disaster Medicine*, 10(4):225-31.

Mebane F, Temin S, Parvanta C. (2001). Communicating anthrax in 2001: A Comparison of CDC Information and Print Media AAccounts. *Journal of Health Communications*, 8(Suppl 1):50-82.

Morrisey G, Sechrest T. (1987). *Effective Business and Technical Presentation (Third Edition)*. New York: Addison-Wesley Publishing Co., Inc.

Mullin S. (2002). "Communicating Risk: Closing the Gap Between Perception and Reality." *Journal of Urban Health*, 79(3):296-297.

Parrott R. (1995). *Designing health messages: Approaches from communication theory and public health practice*. Thousand Oaks, CA: Sage Publications.

Pidgeon N, Henwood K, Maguire B. (1999). Public Health Communication and the Social Amplification of Risks: Present Knowledge and Future Prospects. In: Bennett P, Calman K, eds. *Risk communication and public health*. Oxford: Oxford University Press.

Prue C, Lackey C, Swenarski L, Gantt J. (2003). Communication monitoring: Shaping CDC's Emergency Risk Communication Efforts. *Journal of Health Communications*, 8(Suppl 1):35-49.

Payne J, Schulte S. (2003). Mass Media, Public Health, and Achieving Health Literacy. *Journal of Health Communication*, 8(Suppl 1):124-125.

Pollard W. (2003). Public Perceptions of Information Sources Concerning Bioterrorism Before and After Anthrax Attacks: An Analysis of National Survey Data. *Journal of Health Communication*, 8(Suppl 1):93-103.

Renn O. (1991). Risk Communication the Amplification of Risk. In: Kasperson R, Stallen P, eds. *Communicating Risks to the Public*. Dordrecht: Kluwer.

Stephenson R, Anderson PS. (1997). Disasters and the Information Technology Revolution. *Disasters*, 21(4):305-344.

Wray, R.J., Kreuter, M.W., Jacobsen, J., Clements, B., Evans, R.G. (2004). "Theoretical Perspectives on Public Communication Preparedness for Terrorist Attacks." Landesman LY, ed. *Family and Community Health*, 27(3):232-241.

CURRICULUM

Gebbie, KM (1999) "The Public Health Workforce: Key to Public Health Infrastructure." *American Journal of Public Health,* 89(5):660-1.

Landesman L.Y. (1993). "The Availability of Disaster Preparation Courses at US Schools of Public Health." *American Journal of Public Health,* 83(10):1494-5.

Landesman, L.Y., ed. (2001) Disaster Preparedness in Schools of Public Health: A Curriculum for the New Century, Association of Schools of Public Health, Public Health Foundation

Pesik, N., Keim, M., et al. (1999). "Do emergency medicine residency programs provide adequate training for bioterrorism?" *Annals of Emergency Medicine,* 34(2):173-176.

Qureshi, K.A., Gershon, R.R.M., Merrill, J.A., et al. (2004). "Effectiveness of an Emergency Preparedness Training Program for Public Health Nurses in New York City." Landesman, L.Y., ed. *Family and Community Health,* 27(3):242-249.

CYCLONE

Friedman, E. (1994). "Coping with calamity: How Well does Health Care Disaster Planning Work?" *JAMA,* 272(23):1875-1879.

Malilay, J. (1997). "Tropical Cyclones." In: Noji, E.K., ed. *The Public Health Consequences of Disasters.* New-York, Oxford: Oxford University Press. pp. 287-301.

DISASTERS AND THE DISABLED

Bondi, N. (2001). Few Regulations Exist For Evacuation Plans, iCan News Service (ican.com), http://www.ican.com/news/fullpage.cfm?articleid=CC0AC2E5-D0B2-44B9-B145CB76A126365E.

Cabrillo College, Emergency Response Management—Assisting People with Disabilities http://www.cabrillo.cc.ca.us/busserv/purchasing/emergency/16.htm

California Department of Rehabilitation. (1997). "Disaster Preparedness for Persons with Disabilities: Improving California's Response: A Report," Sacramento.

Cameron, C. (no date). Emergency Planning for People with Disabilities and Other Special Needs, http://www.disabilitypreparedness.com/emergency_planning_for_people_wi.htm.

Community Emergency Response Team—Los Angeles, Lifts and Carries, (2001). http://www.cert-la.com/liftcarry/Liftcarry.htm.

FEMA & United States Fire Administration, Emergency Procedures For Employees With Disabilities. In: Office Occupancies, Pub. No. FA154, June 1995, (ican.com), http://www.ican.com/news/fullpage.cfm?articleid=5C02D127-AA19-4B92-986031A11BC8CDD6&cx=independence.get_independent, 2002.

Fernandez, LS, Byard D, et al. (2002). Frail Elderly as Disaster Victims: Emergency Management Strategies. *Prehosp Disast Med,* 17(2):67-74.

Guide on the Special Needs of People with Disabilities for Emergency Managers, Planners & Responders, Emergency Preparedness Initiative, (2002) National Organization on Disability.

Kailes, J.I. (2001). Disaster Preparedness for People with Disabilities, http://www.jik.com/disaster.html.

United States Access Board, Evacuation Planning, (2002). http://www.access-board.gov/news/evacplanning.htm.

United States Access Board, Procedures & Technologies for People with Disabilities, Final Report of a State of the Art Review with Recommendations for Action, ATBCB (1988).

United States Access Board, Resources on Emergency Evacuation and Disaster Preparedness, (2001) http://www.access-board.gov/evac.htm.

DISASTERS, GENERAL

Dynes, R.R., Tierney, K.J., eds. (1994). *Disasters, Collective Behavior, and Social Organization.* Newark: University of Delaware Press.

EARTHQUAKE

Alexander, D. (1996). "The Health Effects of Earthquakes in the Mid-1990s." *Disasters,* 20(3):231-247.

Bissell, R.A., Pinet, P., Nelson, M., Levy, M. (2004). "Evidence of the Effectiveness of Health Sector Preparedness in Disaster Response: The Example of Four Earthquakes." Landesman, L.Y. ed. *Family and Community Health,* 27(3):193-203

Frankel, D.H. (1994). "Public Health Assessment after Earthquake." *Lancet,* 343:347-348.

Freeman, C. (1990). "Casualty Estimation and State Medical/health Response to Disasters." in California Emergency Medical Services Authority (ed.), *Workshop on modelling earthquake casualties for planning and response model definition and user output requirements.* pp.18-36. Sacramento: California Emergency Medical Services Authority.

Friedman, E. (1994). "Coping with Calamity: How Well Does Health Care Disaster Planning Work?" *JAMA,* 272(23):1875-1879.

Guha-Sapir, D. (1991) "Rapid assessment of Health Needs in Mass Emergencies: Review of Current Concepts and Methods." *Wld. Hlth. Statist. Quart.* 44(3):171-181.

Guha-Sapir, D. (1993). "Health effects of earthquakes and volcanoes: epidemiological and policy issues." *Disasters,* 17(3):255-262.

Noji, E.K. (1997). "Earthquakes." In: Noji, E.K., ed. *The Public Health Consequences of Disasters.* pp.135-178. New York, Oxford: Oxford University Press.

ENVIRONMENTAL CONTROL

Boyce J.M., Pittet D. (ed.) (2002). "Guideline for Hand Hygiene in Health Care Settings: Recommendations of the Healthcare Infection Control Practice Advisory Committee of the HICPA/SHEA/APIC/Hand Hygiene Task Force" Centers for Disease Control and Prevention, Atlanta.

California Association of Environmental Health Administrators (CAEHA). (1998). *Disaster Field Manual for Environmental Health Specialist.* Carmichael, California.

Claudio L, Garg A., Landrigan PJ. (2003). "Addressing Environmental Health Concerns." In: *Terrorism and Public Health.* Levy BS, Sidel VW, eds. New York: Oxford University Press, Inc.

Diaz, JH. (2004). "The Public Health Impact of Global Climate Change." Landesman, L.Y., ed. *Family and Community Health,* 27(3):218-229.

Federal Emergency Management Agency, United States Fire Administration, National Fire Academy and United States Department of Justice, Office of Justice. (May 2000). *Emergency Response to Terrorism Job Aid.* Washington, D.C.

Esrey S, et al. (1991). "Effects of Improved Water Supply and Sanitation on Ascariasis, Diarrhoea, Dracunculiasis, Hookwork Infection, Schistosomiasis, and Trachoma." *Bull. WHO,* 69(5):609-21.

Hatch D, et al. (1994). "Epidemic cholera during refugee resettlement in Malawi." *Int. J. of Epi.* 1994;22(6):1292-99.

Melosi MV. (1980). *Pollution and Reform in American Cities, 1870-1930.* Univ. of Texas Press, Austin.

National Institute for Occupational Safety and Health (NIOSH), Centers for Disease Control and Prevention (CDC). (2003) Filtration and Air-Cleaning Systems to Protect Building Environments from Airborne Chemical, Biological, or Radiological Attacks. Department of Health and Human Services, DHHS (NIOSH) Publication No. 2003-136.

National Institute for Occupational Safety and Health (NIOSH), Centers for Disease Control and Prevention (CDC). (2002) Guidance for Protecting Building Environments from Airborne Chemical, Biological, or Radiological Attacks. Department of Health and Human Services, DHHS (NIOSH) Publication No. 2002-139.

NFPA 1600 (2004 Edition) Standard on Disaster/Emergency Management and Business Continuity Programs. Quincy, MA.

OSHA 29 CFR 1910.38 Employee Emergency Plans and Fire Protection Plans.

OSHA 29 CFR 1910.120 Hazardous Waste Operations and Emergency Response Standard (HazWoper)

Peterson AE, Roberts L, Toole M, Peterson DE. (1998). "Soap Use Effect on Diarrhea: Nyamithuthu Refugee Camp." *Int. J. of Epi,* 1998;27: 520-524.

Spears, M.C., and Gregoire M., Spears M. (2003). Foodservice Organizations: A Managerial and Systems Approach, Fifth Edition, Pearson Education.

Westphal, R.G. (2004). "Commentary on "The Public Health Impact of Global Climate Change." Landesman, L.Y., ed. *Family and Community Health,* 27(3):230.

Wisner B, Adams J, eds. (2002). *Control Measures for Ensuring Food Safety from Environmental Health in Emergencies and Disasters.* World Health Organization. Geneva.

EPIDEMIC

Manderson, L., Aaby, P. (1992). "An Epidemic in the Field? Rapid Assessment Procedures and Health Research." *Soc. Sci. Med.* 35(7):839-850.

Mohamed, J. (1999). "Epidemics and Public Health in Early Colonial Somaliland." *Soc. Sci. Med.* 48:507-521.

Perrin, P. (1996). *War and Public Health: Handbook on War and Public Health.* Geneva: International Committee of the Red Cross.

Toole, M.J. (1994). "The rapid assessment of health problems in refugee and displaced populations." *Med. Glob. Surv,* 1(4):200-207.

Toole, M.J.(1997). "Communicable Diseases and Disease Control." In: Noji, E.K., ed. *The Public Health Consequences of Disasters.* New York, Oxford: Oxford University Press. pp.79-100.

Toole, M.J., Waldman, R. (1993). "Refugees and Displaced Persons: War, Hunger, and Public Health." *JAMA,* 270(5):600-605.

World Health Organization. (1999). *Rapid Health Assessment Protocols for Emergencies.* World Health Organization. Geneva: WHO.

EVALUATION METHODS APPLIED TO EMERGENCIES AND DISASTERS

Bissell R, Pretto E, Angus D, et al (1994). "Post Preparedness Medical Disaster Response In Costa Rica." *Prehospital and Disaster Medicine,* 9(2).

Cayton C, Herrmann N, Cole L, et al. (1978). "Assessing the Validity of EMS data." *Journal of the American College of Emergency Physicians,* 7:11.

Cayton C, Murphy J. (1986). "Evaluation." In: Schwartz G, Safar P, Stone I, et al. *Principles and Practices of Emergency Medicine,* ed 2. Philadelphia, WB Saunders, p. 634.

De Boer J. (1997). Tools for Evaluating Disasters: Preliminary Results of Some Hundreds of Disasters. *European Journal of Emergency Medicine,* 4:107-110.

Donabedian A. (1980). *The Definition of Quality and Approaches to Its Assessment.* Ann Arbor, MI: Health Administration Press.

Eisenberg M, Bergner J. (1979). "Paramedic Programs and Cardiac Mortality: Description of a Controlled Experiment." *Public Health Reports,* 94(1):80-84.

Gibson G. (1974). "Guidelines for Research and Evaluation of Emergency Medical Services." *Health Services Reports,* 89-99.

Klain M, Ricci E, Safar P, et al. (1989). "Disaster Reanimatology Potentials: A Structured Interview Study in Armenia, I: Methodology and Preliminary Results." *Pre-hospital and Disaster Medicine,* 4(2):135-154

Manni C, Magalini S (1989). "Disaster Medicine: A New Discipline or a New Approach?" *Pre-hospital and Disaster Medicine,* 4(2):167-70

McAuliffe W. (1979). "Measuring the Quality of Medical Care: Process Versus Outcome." *Mill Mem Fund Q,* 57:119.

Noji E.K. (1987). "Evaluation of the efficacy of disaster response." *United National Disaster Relief Organization News,* July/August, 11-13.

Quarantelli E.L., Taylor V. (1977). *Delivery of Emergency Medical Services Disasters.* Disaster Research Center, Columbus, OH, Ohio State University, 1977:18

Ricci E. (1985). "A model for evaluation of disaster management." *Prehospital and Disaster Medicine,* (Suppl 1).

Roy A, Looney G, Anderson G. (1979). "Prospective vs. Retrospective Data for Evaluating Emergency Care: A Research Methodology." *JACEP,* 8:141.

Succo W, Champion H, Stega M. (1984). *Trauma Care Evaluation.* Baltimore, University Park Press.

FAMINE

Seaman, J. (1994). "Population, Food Supply, and Famines: An Ecological or an Economic Dilemma?" In: Cartledge, B., ed. *Health and the Environment.* Oxford: Oxford University Press. pp. 29-45.

Sen, A. (1981). *Poverty and Famines: An Essay on Entitlement and Deprivation,* Oxford: Clarendon Press.

Toole, M.J. (1992). "Famine-affected, Refugee, and Displaced Populations: Recommendations for Public Health Issues." *MMWR,* 41(RR-13):1-366.

Toole, M.J., Waldman, R. (1993). "Refugees and Displaced Persons: War, Hunger, and Public Health." *JAMA,* 270(5):600-605.

Yip, R. (1997). "Famine." In: Noji, E.K., ed. *The Public Health Consequences of Disasters.* New York, Oxford: Oxford University Press. pp. 305-335.

Young, H. (1992). *Food Scarcity and Famine: Assessment and Response.* Oxford: Oxfam.

Zaman, M.S. (1991). "Famine: Causes and Health Consequences." In: World Health Organization and United Nations Institute for Training and Research (ed.), *The challenge of African disasters.* New York: UNITAR. pp. 77-107.

FLOOD

Ali, H.M., Homeida, M.M.A. (1991). "Flood Disaster Impact on Health and Nutritional Status of the Population—Khartoum, Sudan." In:

Abu Sin, M.E., *Disaster Prevention and Management in Sudan*. Khartoum: University of Khartoum. pp. 82-104.

Malilay, J. (1997). "Floods." In: Noji, E.K. ed. *The Public Health Consequences of Disasters*. New York, Oxford: Oxford University Press. pp. 287-301.

GEOGRAPHIC INFORMATION SYSTEMS (GIS)

Amdahl G. (2001). *Disaster Response: GIS for Public Safety*. ESRI Press, Redlands, CA.

Cromley, EK, McLafferty SL. (2002). *GIS and Public Health*. New York, The Guilford Press.

Greene RW. (2002). *Confronting Catastrophe: A GIS Handbook*. ESRI Press, Redlands, CA.

Kennedy H, ed. (2001). *Dictionary of GIS Terminology*. ESRI Press, Redlands, CA.

Lang L. (2000). *GIS for Health Organizations*. ESRI Press, Redlands, CA.

HOSPITAL PREPAREDNESS

Delaney, KA. (2002). "Impact of the Threat of Biological and Chemical Terrorism on Public Safety-Net Hospitals," *The International Lawyer*, 36(1):21-28.

Joint Commission on Accreditation of Healthcare Organizations (2003). Health Care at the Crossroads: Strategies for Creating and Sustaining Community-Wide Emergency Preparedness Systems. Ill.

Landesman, LY, ed. (1997). *Emergency Preparedness in the Healthcare Environment*. Joint Commission of Healthcare Organizations, Oakbrook, Ill.

Landesman LY, Markowitz SB, Rosenberg SN. (1994). "Hospital Preparedness for Chemical Accidents: The Effect of Environmental Legislation on Health Care Services." *Prehospital and Disaster Medicine*, 9(3):154-9, Jul-Sept.

Landesman LY. (1994). "*Hospital Preparedness for Chemical Accidents*" Plant, Technology & Safety Management Series, The Joint Commission on Accreditation of Healthcare Organizations, Oakbrook, Ill. Number 3:39-44.

Landesman LY, Leonard R. (1993). "SARA Three Years Later: Physician Knowledge and Actions in Hospital Preparedness." *The Intl Journal of Prehospital and Disaster Medicine*, Jan-Mar 39-44.

Lewis CP, Aghababiam R. (1996) Disaster Planning, Part 1: "Overview of Hospital and Emergency Department Planning for Internal and External Disasters." *Disaster Medicine*, 14(2):439-452.

Peters MS. (1996). "Hospitals Respond to Water Loss During the Midwest Floods of 1993: Preparedness and Improvisation." *Journal of Emergency Medicine*, 14(3):34-50.

Salinas C, Salinas C, Kurata J. (1998). "The Effects of the Northridge Earthquake on the Pattern of Emergency Department Care." *American Journal of Emergency Medicine*, 16(3):254-6.

Simon HK, Stegelman M, Button T. (1998). "A Prospective Evaluation of Pediatric Emergency Care During the 1996 Summer Olympic Games in Atlanta, Georgia." *Pediatric Emergency Care*, 14(1):1-3.

INFORMATION SYSTEMS

University of California San Francisco—Stamford Evidence-Based Practice Center. (2002) *Bioterrorism Preparedness and Response: Use of Information Technologies and Decision Support Systems.* Agency for Healthcare Research and Quality Publication No. 02-E028, Rockville, MD.

Butler DL, Anderson PS. (1992) "The Use of Wide Area Computer Networks in Disaster Management and the Implications for Hospital/Medical Networks." *Annals of the New York Academy of Sciences*, 670:202-10, 1992 Dec 17.

O'Carroll PW, Friede A, Noji EK, Lillibridge SR, Fries DJ, Atchison CG. (1995). "The Rapid Implementation of a Statewide Emergency Health Information System During the 1993 Iowa Flood." *American Journal of Public Health*, 85(4):564-7.

van Bemmel JH, Musen MA, eds. (1997). *Handbook of Medical Informatics.* Houten, the Netherlands: Bohn Stafleu Van Loghum.

LEGAL

Gostin, L. (2000) Public Health Law: Power, Duty, Restraint. U of California Press. Berkeley. Milbank Memorial Fund.

Gostin, L.O. (2002) "Public Health Law In An Age of Terrorism: Rethinking Individual Rights and Common Goods" *Health Affairs,* 21(6): Nov/Dec.

Martin, W. (2004). "Legal and Public Policy Responses of States to Bioterrorism." *American Journal of Public Health,* 94(7):1093-1095

Misrahi, JJ, Foster, JA, Shaw, FE, Cetron, MS. (2004). "HHS/CDC Legal Response to SARS Outbreak," *Emerging Infectious Diseases.* 10(2); http://www.cdc.gov/ncidod/eid/vol10no2/03-0721.htm (accessed 6/20/04).

Public Assistance Applicant Handbook. (1999). Federal Emergency Management Agency. FEMA 323.

Public Assistance Guide. (1999). Federal Emergency Management Agency. FEMA 322.

Public Assistance Policy Reference Manual. (2004). Federal Emergency Management Agency. 9500 Series.

MANAGEMENT

Bouzarth W, Mariano J, Smith J. (1986) "Disaster preparedness." In: Schwartz G, Safar P, Stone I, et al. *Principles and Practice of Emergency Medicine,* ed 2. Philadelphia, WB Saunders.

Carter WN. (1992). *Disaster Management.* Manila, Philippines: Asian Development Bank, 1992.

Dove D, Del Guerico L, Stahl W, et al. (1982). "A Metropolitan Airport Disaster Plan—Coordination of a Multi-hospital Response to Provide On-site Resuscitation and Stabilization Before Evacuation." *J. Trauma,* 22:550.

Drabek, TE. (1991). *Emergency Management: Principles and Practice for Local Government.* Washington, DC: International City Management Association, pp. 213-218.

de Ville de Goyet, C. (1993). "Post disaster relief: The supply–management challenge." *Disasters,* 17(2): 169-176.

Federal Emergency Management Agency (1999). *The Federal Response Plan.* Washington, DC: Federal Emergency Management Agency. April. FEMA 9230.1-PL

Heath SE, et al. (1997). "Integration of Veterinarians into the Official Response to Disasters." *Journal of the American Veterinarian Medical Association,* 210 (February 1).

Henderson, AK, Lillibridge, SR, et al. (1994). "Disaster medical assistance teams: Providing health care to a community struck by Hurricane Iniki." *Annals of Emergency Medicine,* 23(4):726-730.

Landesman LY, Malilay J, Bissell RA, Becker SM, Roberts L, Ascher M. (2001). "Roles and Responsibilities of Public Health in Disaster Preparedness and Response." In: Novick LF, Mays GP, eds. *Public Health Administration: Principles for Population-Based Management,* (646-708), Gaithersburg, Maryland, Aspen Publishers.

Leaning, J, Briggs, SM, Chen, LC, eds. (1999). *Humanitarian Crises: The Medical and Public Health Response.* Cambridge, MA: Harvard University Press.

Leviton, LC, Needleman, CE, Shapiro, MA. (1998). *Confronting Public Health Risks: A Decision Maker's Guide.* Thousand Oaks, CA: Sage Publications.

Logue, JN. (1996). Disasters, the Environment, and Public Health: Improving our Response. *American Journal of Public Health,* 86(9):1207-1210.

Noji, EK. (1995). 26. Natural Disaster Management. *Management of Wilderness and Environmental Emergencies.* P. S. Auerbach. St. Louis, Mosby-Yearbook: 644-663.

Pan American Health Organization (2000). *Natural Disasters: Protecting the Public's Health.* Scientific Publication No. 575, Washington, DC, Pan American Health Organization.

Phreaner, D, Jacoby I, et al. (1994). "Disaster Preparedness of Home Health Care Agencies in San Diego County." *Journal of Emergency Medicine,* 12(6):811-818.

Sadler A, Sadler B, Webb J. (1997). *Emergency Medical Care: The Neglected Public Service.* Cambridge, MA: Ballinger Publishing Co.

Schultz CH, Koenig KL, Noji E. (1996). "A Medical Disaster Response to Reduce Immediate Mortality after an Earthquake." *New England Journal of Medicine,* 334(7):438-444.

Schwartz L. (1986). "Field intervention medicine." In: Schwartz G, Safar P, Stone I, et al. *Principles and Practices of Emergency Medicine.* ed 2. Philadelphia: WB Saunders, p. 593.

MENTAL HEALTH

American Psychiatric Association. (2000). *Diagnostic and Statistical Manual of Mental Disorders.* Fourth Edition (DSM-IV-TR). Washington, DC: American Psychiatric Association.

American Psychiatric Association (1988). *Post-traumatic Stress Disorder (brochure).* Washington, DC: APA Joint Commission on Public Affairs and the Division of Public Affairs.

Armenian, HK. (2002). "Risk Factors For Depression in the Survivors of the 1988 Earthquake in Armenia." *Journal of Urban Health,* 79(3):373-382.

Austin, LS, ed. (1992). *Responding to Disaster: A Guide for Mental Health Professionals.* Washington, DC: American Psychiatric Press.

Baum, A, Fleming, R, Davidson, LM. (1983). "Natural disaster and technological catastrophe." *Environment and Behavior,* 15(3):333-354.

Black, D, Newman, M, Harris-Hendriks, J, Mezey, G, eds. (1997). *Psychological Trauma: A Developmental Approach.* London: Royal College of Psychiatrists.

Bracht, N, ed. (1990). *Health Promotion at the Community Level.* Newbury Park, CA: Sage.

Breslau N, Davis GC, Andreski P, et al. (1991). "Traumatic events and posttraumatic stress disorder in an urban population of young adults." *Arch Gen Psychiatry,* 48:216-222.

Carll, EK, ed. (1996). *Developing a Comprehensive Disaster and Crisis Response Program for Mental Health: Guidelines and Procedures.* Albany, NY: New York State Psychological Association (NYSPA) Disaster/Crisis Network.

DeGirolamo, G, McFarlane, AC. (1996). "The epidemiology of PTSD: A comprehensive review of the international literature." In: A.J. Marsella, M.J. Friedman, E.T. Gerrity, R.M. Scurfield, eds. *Ethnocultural Aspects of Post-traumatic Stress Disorder: Issues, Research, and Clinical Applications.* Washington, DC: American Psychological Association, pp. 33-85.

Erikson, K. (1995). *A New Species of Trouble: The Human Experience of Modern Disasters.* New York: W.W. Norton.

Everly, Jr., GS., Mitchell, JT. (1997). *Critical Incident Stress Management: A New Era and Standard of Care in Crisis Intervention.* Ellicott City, MD: Chevron Publishing Corporation.

Farberow, NL, Gordon, NS. (1981, 1995). *Manual for Child Health Workers in Major Disasters.* Washington, DC: Center for Mental Health Services, Substance Abuse and Mental Health Services Administration, U.S. Public Health Service.

Field Manual for Mental Health and Human Service Workers in Major Disasters (2000). Department of Health and Human Services, Substance Abuse and Mental Health Services Administration, Center for Mental Health Services.

Foa EB, Davidson JR, Frances A, et al. (1999). The Expert Consensus Guidelines Series: Treatment of Posttraumatic Stress Disorder. *J Clin Psychiatry,* 60(S16):1-76

Friedman, MJ, Marsella, AJ. (1996). "Post-traumatic Stress Disorder: An overview of the concept." In: A.J. Marsella, M.J. Friedman, E.T. Gerrity, R.M. Scurfield, eds. *Ethnocultural Aspects of Post-traumatic Stress Disorder: Issues, Research, and Clinical Applications.* Washington, DC: American Psychological Association, pp. 11-32.

Fritz, C.E. (1996). *Disasters and Mental Health: Therapeutic Principles Drawn from Disaster Studies.* (Historical and Comparative Disaster Series #10). Newark, DE: Disaster Research Center, University of Delaware.

Fullerton, CS, Ursano, RJ. (1997a). Post-traumatic Responses in Spouse/ Significant Others of Disaster Workers. In: C.S. Fullerton, R.J. Ursano, eds. *Post-traumatic Stress Disorder: Acute and Long-Term Responses to Trauma and Disaster.* Washington, DC: American Psychiatric Press, pp. 59-75.

Fullerton, CS, Ursano, RJ. (1997b). "The Other Side of Chaos: Understanding the Patterns of Post-traumatic Responses. In: C.S. Fullerton, R.J. Ursano, eds. *Post-traumatic Stress Disorder: Acute and Long-Term Responses to Trauma and Disaster.* Washington, DC: American Psychiatric Press, pp. 3-18.

Galea S, Ahern J, Resnick H, et al. (2002). Psychological Sequelae of the September 11 Terrorist Attacks in New York City. *N Engl J Med,* 346:982-987.

Galea, S, Resnick, H, Ahern, J, Gold, J, et al. (2002). "Posttraumatic Stress Disorder in Manhattan, New York City, after the September 11th Terrorist Attacks." *Journal of Urban Health,* 79(3):340-353.

Gerrity, ET, Flynn, BW. (1997). "Mental Health Consequences of Disasters." In: Noji, E.K., ed. *Public Health Consequences of Disasters.* Oxford: Oxford University Press, pp. 101-121.

Gerrity, ET, Steinglass, P. (1994). Relocation stress following natural disasters. In: R.J. Ursano, B.G. McCaughey, C.S. Fullerton, eds. *Individual and Community Responses to Trauma and Disaster: The Structure of Human Chaos.* Cambridge: Cambridge University Press, pp. 220-247.

Green, B.L. (1996). "Cross-national and Ethnocultural Issues in Disaster Research. In: A.J. Marsella, M.J. Friedman, E.T. Gerrity, R.M. Scurfield, eds. *Ethnocultural Aspects of Post-traumatic Stress Disorder: Issues, Research, and Clinical Applications.* Washington, DC: American Psychological Association, pp. 341-361.

Green, B.L., Solomon, S.D. (1995). The Mental Health Impact of Natural and Technological Disasters. In: J.R. Freedy, S.E. Hobfoll, eds., *Traumatic Stress: From Theory to Practice.* New York: Plenum Press, pp. 163-180.

Gusman, F.D., Stewart, J., Young, B.H., Riney, S.J., Abueg, F.R., Blake, D.D. (1996). A Multicultural Approach and Developmental Framework for Treating Trauma. In: A.J. Marsella, M.J. Friedman, E.T. Gerrity, R.M. Scurfield, eds. *Ethnocultural Aspects of Post-traumatic Stress Disorder: Issues, Research, and Clinical Applications.* Washington, DC: American Psychological Association, pp. 439-457.

Hartsough, D.M., Myers, D.G. (1985, 1995). *Disaster Work and Mental Health: Prevention and Control of Stress Among Workers.* Washington, DC: Center for Mental Health Services, Substance Abuse and Mental Health Services Administration, U.S. Public Health Service.

Havenaar, J.M., Cwikel, J.G., Bromet, E.J., eds. (2002). *Toxic Turmoil: Psychological and Societal Consequences of Ecological Disasters.* New York. Kluwer Academic/Plenum Publishers.

Herman, D., Felton, C., Susser, E. (2002). "Mental Health Needs in New York State Following the September 11th Attacks." *Journal of Urban Health,* 79(3):322-331.

Hodgkinson, P.E., Stewart, M. (1998). *Coping with Catastrophe: A Handbook of Post-Disaster Psychosocial Aftercare.* Second edition. London: Routledge.

Hoffman, K.J., Sasaki, J.E. (1997). "Comorbidity of Substance Abuse and PTSD." In: C.S. Fullerton, R.J. Ursano, eds., *Post-traumatic Stress Disorder: Acute and Long-Term Responses to Trauma and Disaster.* Washington, DC: American Psychiatric Press, pp. 159-174.

Jack, K., Glied, S. (2002). "The Public Costs of Mental Health Response: Lessons From the New York City Post-9/11 Needs Assessment." *Journal of Urban Health,* 79(3):332-339.

Kasperson, R.E., Kasperson, J.X. (1996). The social amplification and attenuation of risk. *Annals of the American Academy of Political and Social Science,* 545, 95-105.

Kleber, R.J., Brom, D. (1992). *Coping with Trauma: Theory, Prevention and Treatment.* Amsterdam: Swets & Zeitlinger.

Kliman, J., Kern, R., Kliman, A. (1982). "Natural and Human-made Disasters: Some Therapeutic and Epidemiological Implications for Crisis Intervention." In: U. Reuveni, R.V. Speck, J.L. Speck, eds. *Thera-*

peutic Intervention: Healing Strategies for Human Systems. New York: Human Sciences Press.

Lystad, M., ed. (1988). *Mental Health Response to Mass Emergencies: Theory and Practice.* New York: Brunner/Mazel Publishers.

Marsella, A.J., Friedman, M.J., Gerrity, E.T., Scurfield, R.M., eds. (1996). *Ethnocultural Aspects of Post-traumatic Stress Disorder: Issues, Research, and Clinical applications.* Washington, DC: American Psychological Association.

McFarlane, A.C. (1995). "Helping the Victims of Disasters." In: J.R. Freedy, S.E. Hobfoll, eds. *Traumatic Stress: From Theory to Practice.* New York: Plenum Press, pp. 287-314.

McKnight, J.L., Kretzmann, J.P. (1990). *Mapping Community Capacity.* Evanston, IL: Center for Urban Affairs and Policy Research, Northwestern University.

Mega, L.T., McCammon, S.L. (1992). "Tornado in Eastern North Carolina: Outreach to School and Community." In: L.S. Austin, ed. *Responding to Disaster: A Guide for Mental Health Professionals.* Washington, DC: American Psychiatric Press, pp. 211-230.

Mental health intervention for disasters. National Center for Post-Traumatic Stress Disorders. http://www.ncptsd.org/facts/disasters/fs_treatment_disaster.html

Mitchell, J.T., Everly, Jr., G.S. (1997). *Critical Incident Stress Debriefing: An Operations Manual for the Prevention of Traumatic Stress Among Emergency Service and Disaster Workers (Second Edition, Revised).* Ellicott City, MD: Chevron Publishing Corporation.

Myers, D. (1994). *Disaster Response and Recovery: A Handbook for Mental Health Professionals.* Rockville, MD, U.S. Department of Health and Human Services, Public Health Service, Substance Abuse and Mental Health Services Administration, Center for Mental Health Services.

Norris, F.H., Thompson, M.P. (1995). "Applying Community Psychology to the Prevention of Trauma and Traumatic Life Events." In: J.R. Freedy, S.E. Hobfoll, eds. *Traumatic Stress: From Theory to Practice.* New York: Plenum Press, pp. 49-71.

O'Brien, L.S. (1998). *Traumatic Events and Mental Health.* Cambridge: Cambridge University Press.

Pfefferbaum B., et al. (2000). "Posttraumatic Stress Two Years after the Oklahoma Bombing in Youths Geographically Distant from the Explosion" *Psychiatry,* Winter;6(4):358-70

Quarantelli, E.L., ed. (1998). *What is a Disaster? Perspectives on the Question.* London: Routledge.

Raphael, B., Wilson, J.P. (1993). "Theoretical and Intervention Considerations in Working with Victims of Disaster." In: J.P. Wilson, B. Raphael, eds. *International Handbook of Traumatic Stress Syndromes,* New York: Plenum Press.

Responding to the Needs of People with Serious and Persistent Mental Illness in Times of Disaster (1996). Washington, DC: Emergency Services and Disaster Relief Branch, Center for Mental Health Services, Substance Abuse and Mental Health Services Administration.

Schlenger W.E., Caddell J.M., Ebert L., Jordan B.K., Rourke, K.M., Wilson, D. Thalji L, Dennis J.M., Fairbank J.A., Kulka R.A. (2002). "Psychological Reactions to Terrorist Attacks: Findings From the National Study of Americans' Reactions to September 11," *JAMA,* Vol 288(5):581-588.

Streeter, C.L., Murty, S.A., eds. (1996). *Research on Social Work and Disasters.* New York: The Haworth Press.

Stuber J, Fairbrother G, Galea S, et al. (2002). "Determinants of Counseling for Children in Manhattan after the September 11 attacks." *Psychiatric Services,* 53:815-822.

Terr, L.C. (1992). "Large-group Preventive Techniques for Use after Disaster." In: L.S. Austin, ed. (1992). *Responding to Disaster: A Guide for Mental Health Professionals.* Washington, DC: American Psychiatric Press, pp. 81-99.

Training Manual for Mental Health and Human Service Workers in Major Disasters. http://www.mentalhealth.org/publications/allpubs/ADM90-538/tmpreface.asp

Ursano, R.J., McCaughey, B.G., Fullerton, C.S., eds. (1994). *Individual and Community Responses to Trauma and Disaster: The Structure of Human Chaos.* Cambridge: Cambridge University Press.

Van der Kolk, B.A., McFarlane, A.C., Weisaeth, L., eds. (1996). *Traumatic Stress: The Effects of Overwhelming Experience on Mind, Body, and Society.* New York: The Guilford Press.

Van Ommeren, M., Saxena, S. (2004). *Mental Health of Populations Exposed to Biological and Chemical Weapons.* World Health Organization, Geneva.

Weisaeth, L. (1993). "Disasters: Psychological and Psychiatric Aspects." In: L. Goldberger, S. Breznitz, eds., *Handbook of Stress: Theoretical and Clinical Aspects.* Second edition. New York: The Free Press.

Yehuda, R., ed. (1998). *Psychological Trauma.* Washington, DC: American Psychiatric Press.

Young, B.H., Ford, J.D., Ruzek, J.I., Friedman, M.J., Gusman, F.D. (1998). *Disaster Mental Health Services: A Guidebook for Clinicians and Administrators.* Menlo Park, CA: National Center for Post-Traumatic Stress Disorder.

MEDICAL CARE DELIVERY

Pointer, J.E., Michaelis, J., et al. (1992). "The 1989 Loma Prieta Earthquake: Impact on Hospital Patient Care." *Annals of Emergency Medicine,* 21(10):1228-1233.

Quinn, B., Baker, R., et al. (1994). "Hurricane Andrew and a Pediatric Emergency Department." *Annals of Emergency Medicine,* 23(4):737-741.

Sabatino, F. (1992). "Hurricane Andrew: South Florida hospitals shared Resources and Energy to Cope with the Storm's Devastation." *Hospitals, JAHA,* 26-30.

Scott, S., Constantine, L.M. (1990). "When Natural Disaster Strikes: With Careful Planning Pharmacists Can Continue to Provide Essential Services to Survivors in the Aftermath of a Disaster." *American Pharmacy,* NS30(11):27-31.

MORBIDITY AND MORTALITY

Burkle FM, ed. (1984). *Disaster Medicine.* New Hyde Park, NY: Medical Examination Publishing.

McNabb SJ, Kelso KY, Wilson SA, McFarland L, Farley TA. (1995). "Hurricane Andrew-related Injuries and Illnesses, Louisiana 1992." *Southern Medical Journal,* 88(6):615-8.

Noji, E. K. (1993). "Analysis of Medical Needs during Disasters Caused by Tropical Cyclones: Anticipated Injury Patterns." *Journals of Tropical Medicine and Hygiene,* 96:370-376.

Noji, E.K., Armenian, H.K., et al. (1993). "Issues of Rescue and Medical Care Following the 1988 Armenian Earthquake." *International Journal of Epidemiology,* 22(6):1070-1076.

Saylor LF, Gordon JE. (1957). "The Medical Component of Natural Disasters." *A. J. Med Sci,* 1957;234:342-362.

NATURAL HAZARDS

White, G.F. (1974). *Natural Hazards: Local, National, Global.* New York, Oxford, London, Toronto: Oxford University Press.

White, G.F., Haas, J.E. (1975). *Assessment of Research on Natural Hazards.* Cambridge, Massachusetts, London: The MIT Press.

Zebrowski, E. Jr. (1997). *Perils of a Restless Planet: Scientific Perspectives on Natural Disasters.* Cambridge, England: Cambridge University Press.

NUTRITION

World Health Organization (WHO). (2000). *The Management of Nutrition in Major Emergencies.* United Nations High Commissioner for Refugees, International Federation of Red Cross and Red Crescent Societies, and World Food Programme, Geneva, Switzerland.

PEDIATRICS

Markenson, D., Redlener I. (2003). *Pediatric Preparedness for Disasters and Terrorism: A National Consensus Conference, Executive Summary.* National Center for Disaster Preparedness, Mailman School of Public Health at Columbia University, New York, New York.

PLANNING

Auf der Heidi, E. (1996). "Disaster Planning, Part II: Disaster Problems, Issues, and Challenges Identified in the Research Literature." *Emerg. Med. Clin. North Am.* 14(2, May), 453-480.

Auf def Heide, E. (1994). "Designing a Disaster Plan: Important Questions." *Plant, Technology & Safety Management Series (Joint Commission on Accreditation of Healthcare Organizations)* 3 (Special Issue: Disaster Preparedness: Facing the real crisis): 7-18.

Auf der Heide, E. (1996). *Community Medical Disaster Planning and Evaluation Guide.* American College of Emergency Physicians, Dallas

Centers for Disease Control and Prevention. (1999). "Public Health Performance Assessment—Emergency Preparedness." October.

Centers for Disease Control, "Pandemic Influenza: A Planning Guide for State and Local Officials." (Draft 2.1).

Dynes, R.R. (1994). "Community Emergency Planning: False Assumptions and Inappropriate Analogies." *International Journal of Mass Emergencies and Disasters,* 12(2 August):141-158.

Fong, F., Schrader, D.C. (1996). "Radiation disasters and emergency department preparedness." *Emergency Medicine Clinics of North America,* 14(2):349-370.

Gibbs, M., Lachenmeyer, J.R., et al. (1996). "Effects of the AVIANCA air-crash on disaster workers." *International Journal of Mass Emergencies and Disasters,* 14(1):23-32.

Landesman, L.Y. (2004). "Foreward: Does Preparedness Make a Difference." Landesman, L.Y., ed. *Family and Community Health,* 27(3):186.

Lindell, M.K., Perry, R.W. (1992). *"Behavioral Foundations of Community Emergency Planning."* Hemisphere Publishing Corporation, Philadelphia. pp. 34-36.

Quarantelli, E.L. (1991). *Converting Disaster Scholarship into Effective Disaster Planning and Managing: Possibilities and Limitations.* Newark, DE, Disaster Research Center, University of Delaware

Waeckerle, J.F. (1991). "Review Article: Disaster Planning and Response." *New England Journal of Medicine,* 324(12): 815-821.

PUBLIC HEALTH

Lechat, M.F. (1979). "Disasters and Public Health." *Bulletin of the World Health Organization,* 57(1): 11-17.

Noji, E., ed. (1997). *The Public Health Consequences of Disaster.* Oxford University Press, New York.

Rosen, G. (1993). *A History of Public Health.* Johns Hopkins Univ. Press. 1993.

Sidel VW, Onel E, Geiger HJ, Leaning J, Foege WH. (1992). "Public Health Responses to Natural and Human-made Disasters." In: Last JM, Wallace RB, eds. Maxcy Rosenau-Last Public health and preventive medicine. Connecticut: Appleton & Lange. 1992:1173-1186.

RADIATION

Armed Forces Radiobiology Research Institute http://www.afrri.usuhs. mil

Centers for Disease Control and Prevention, Public Health Emergency Preparedness and Response. http://www.cdc.gov/nceh/radiationi response.htm

Centers for Disease Control "Acute Radiation Syndrome CDC Fact Sheet for Physicians." http://www.cdc.gov/nceh/radiation/factsheets/AcuteRadSvndrome.pdf

Chemical Casualty Care Division USAMRICD. 2000. Medical Management of Chemical Casualties Handbook, Third edition. U.S. Army Medical Research Institute of Chemical Defense (USAMRICD).

Aberdeen Proving Ground: Aberdeen, MD. http://ccc.apgea.army. mil/products/handbooks/RedHandbook/001TitlePage.htm

Disaster Preparedness for Radiology Professionals Response to Radiological Terrorism American College of Radiology. (2002). http:// www.acr.org/dyna/?doc=departments/educ/disaster_prep/dp_ primer.html

Food and Drug Administration guideline, "Potassium Iodide as a Thyroid Blocking Agent in Radiation Emergencies." http://www.fda. gov/cder/guidance/4825fnl.htm.

New York State Department of Health Bureau of Environmental Radiation Protection Potassium Iodide Fact Sheet. BERP@health.state .nv.us

The Radiation Emergency Assistance Center/Training Site (REAC/TS). http://www.orau.gov/reacts/

"Terrorism with Ionizing Radiation General Guidance: Pocket Guide", Office of Public Health and Environmental Hazards, Department of Veterans Affairs, April 2002. http://www.oqp.med.va.gov/cpg/cpg. htm; http://www.cs.amedd.armv.mil/qmo.

National Council on Radiation Protection and Measurement (NCRP) Report No. 138 "Management of Terrorist Events Involving Radioactive Material." http://www.ncrp.com.

RAPID NEEDS ASSESSMENT

Brown V, Jacquier G, Coulombier D, Balandine S, Belanger F, Legros D. (2001). "Rapid Assessment of Population Size by Area Sampling in Disaster Situations." *Disasters,* 25(2):164-71.

Guha-Sapir, D. (1991). "Rapid Assessment of Health Needs in Mass Emergencies: Review of Current Concepts and Methods." *World Health Statistics Quarterly,* 44:171-181.

Hlady, W.G., Quenemoen, L.E., et al. (1994). "Use of a Modified Cluster Sampling Method to Perform Rapid Needs Assessment after Hurricane Andrew." *Annals of Emergency Medicine,* 24(4): 719-725.

Lillibridge, S.R., Noji, E.K., et al. (1993). "Disaster Assessment: The Emergency Health Evaluation of a Population Affected by a Disaster." *Annals of Emergency Medicine,* 22(11): 1715-1720.

International Federation of the Red Cross and Red Crescent Societies. (1993). *"Vulnerability and Capacity Assessment."* Geneva: International Federation of Red Cross and Red Crescent Societies.

International Federation of the Red Cross and Red Crescent Societies. (1993). *"Vulnerability and Capacity Assessment."* Geneva: International Federation of Red Cross and Red Crescent Societies.

Malilay J, Flanders WD, Brogan D. (1996). "A Modified Cluster-sampling Method for Post-disaster Rapid Assessment of Needs." *Bull World Hlth Org,* 1996;74:399-406.

World Health Organization. (1999). *Rapid Health Assessment Protocols for Emergencies.* Geneva, WHO.

Yahmed SB, Koob P. (1996). "Health Sector Approach to Vulnerability Reduction and Emergency Preparedness." *World Health Statistics Quarterly,* 1996;49:172-178.

RECOVERY

Ball, N. (1997). "Demobilizing and Reintegrating Soldiers: Lessons from Africa," pp. 85-105, In: *Rebuilding Societies After Civil War. Critical Roles for International Assistance.* Kumar K., ed. Boulder and London: Lynne Rienner Publishers.

Berke Philip R, Kartez J, Wenger D.(1993) "Recovery after Disaster: Achieving Sustainable Development, Mitigation and Equity." *Disasters,* 17 (3): 93-109.

Cohen, R. (1995). *Refugee and Internally Displaced Women: A Development Perspective.* The Brookings Institution-Refugee Policy Group Project on Internal Displacement.

Cuny, F. (1983). *Disasters and Development.* Oxford University Press.

Eadie, C. (1996). "Kobe Eight Months After: Images of the 'Interim City.'" *Earthquake Engineering Research Institute Special Report.* www.eeri.org/Reconn/Kobe8/KobeEight3.html.

Felton, C. (2002). "Project Liberty: A Public Health Response to New Yorkers' Mental Health Needs Arising From the World Trade Center Terrorist Atacks." *Journal of Urban Health,* 79(3):429-433.

Krug, E.G., Kresnow M.-J., Peddicord J.P., Dahlberg L.L., Powell K.E., Crosby A.E. Annest J.L. (1998). "Suicide after Natural Disasters." *NEJM,* 338 (6):373-8.

McDonnell, S., Troiano, R.P., Barker, N., Noji, E., Hlady, G.W., Hopkins, R. (1995). "Evaluation of Long-term Community Recovery from Hurricane Andrew: Sources of Assistance Received by Population Sub-groups." *Disasters,* 19(4): 338-347.

Moore, S., Daniel, M., Linnan, L., Campbell, M., Benedict, S., and Meier, A. (2004). "After Hurricane Floyd Passed: Investigating the Social Determinants of Disaster Preparedness and Recovery." Landesman L.Y., ed. *Family and Community Health.* 27(3). 204-217.

Shrivastava, P. (1996). "Long-term Recovery from the Bhopal Crisis." In: Mitchell, J.K., ed. *The Long Road to Recovery: Community Responses to Industrial Disaster.* Tokyo: United Nations University Press. pp. 121-147.

Operations Evaluation Department. (1994) "Financing disaster reconstruction: The Popayan earthquake." *OED Precis,* #68. www.world bank.org/html/oed/pr068.htm.

Tokyo Guidelines for Trauma and Reconstruction: Draft conclusions and recommendations. Newsletter of The Japan Foundation Center for Global Partnership (CGP), (Winter 1998). Vol 18. www.cgp.org/cgplink/vol16/articlesvol16a.html

Wickramanayake, E., Shook, G.A. (1995). "Rehabilitation planning for flood affected areas of Thailand: Experience from Phipun District." *Disasters,* 19 (4): 348-355.

RISK ASSESSMENT

Malilay J, Henderson A, McGeehin M, Flanders WD. (1997). "Estimating health risks from natural hazards using risk assessment and epidemiology." *Risk Analysis,* 1997;17:363-368.

SURVEILLANCE

Disaster surveillance

Glass RI, Noji EK. (1992). "Epidemiologic Surveillance Following Disasters." In: Halperin W, Baker EL, eds. *Public health surveillance.* New York: Van Nostrand Reinhold. 1992:195-205.

Lechat MF. (1993-4). "Accident and disaster epidemiology." *Public Health Reviews,* 21(3-4):243-53.

Lee LE, Fonseca V, Brett KM, et al. (1993). "Active Morbidity Surveillance after Hurricane Andrew, Florida, 1992." *JAMA,* 1993;270:591-594.

Legome, E., A. Robbins, et al. (1995). "Injuries Associated with Floods: The Need for an International Reporting Scheme." *Disasters,* 19(1): 50-54.

Lore, E.L., Fonseca, V., et al. (1993). "Active Morbidity Surveillance after Hurricane Andrew-Florida, 1992." *Journal of the American Medical Association,* 270(5): 591-594.

Noji, E.K. (1997). "The Use of Epidemiologic Methods in Disasters." In: Noji, E.K., ed. *The Public Health Consequences of Disasters.* New York: Oxford University Press, 21-36.

Western KA.(1982). *Epidemiologic Surveillance after Natural Disasters.* Washington, D.C.: Pan American Health Organization, 1982: (scientific publication no. 420).

Wetterhall SF, Noji EK. (1997). "Surveillance and Epidemiology." In: Noji EK, ed. *The Public Health Consequences of Disasters.* New York: Oxford University Press. 37-64.

General surveillance

Halperin W, Baker EL Jr, Monson RR, eds.(1992). *Public Health Surveillance.* New York: Van Nostrand Reinhold. 238 pp.

Klauke DN, Buehler JW, Thacker SB, et al. (1988). "Guidelines for Evaluating Surveillance Systems." *MMWR,* 1988;37(S-5):1-18.

Langmuir AD. (1971). "Evolution of the concept of surveillance in the United States." *Proc Roy Soc Med,* 64:9-12.

Thacker SB, Berkelman RL. (1988). "Public Health Surveillance in the United States." *Epidemiol Rev,* 10:164-190.

Thacker SB, Berkelman RL, Stroup DF. (1989). "The Science of Public Health Surveillance." *J Public Health Policy,* 10:187-203.

Thacker SB, Choi K, Brachman PS. (1983). "The Surveillance of Infectious diseases." *JAMA,* 249:1181-1185.

Environmental public health surveillance

Deutsch PV, Adler J, Richter ED. (1992). "Sentinel Markers for Industrial Disasters." *Israel Journal of Medical Sciences,* 28(8-9):526-33.

Thacker SB, Stroup DF. (1994). "Future Directions of Comprehensive Public Health Surveillance and Health Information Systems in the United States." *Am J Epidemiol,* 140:1-15.

Thacker SB, Stroup DF, Parrish RG, Anderson HA. (1996). "Surveillance in Environmental Public Health: Issues, Systems, and Sources." *Am J Public Health,* 86:633-638.

Surveillance after specific disasters

Centers for Disease Control and Prevention. (1996). "Deaths Associated with Hurricanes Marilyn and Opal United States, September-October 1995." *MMWR Morb Mortal Wkly Rep,* 45:32-38.

Centers for Disease Control and Prevention. (1996). "Surveillance for Injuries and Illnesses and Rapid Health-needs Assessment Following Hurricanes Marilyn and Opal, September-October 1995." *MMWR Morb Mortal Wkly Rep,* 45:81-85.

Centers for Disease Control and Prevention. (1997). "Tornado Associated Fatalities Arkansas, 1997." *MMWR Morb Mortal Wkly Rep,* 46:412-416.

Centers for Disease Control and Prevention. (1994). "Coccidioidomycosis following the Northridge Earthquake California, 1994." *MMWR Morb Mortal Wkly Rep,* 43:194-195.

Centers for Disease Control and Prevention. (1990). "Surveillance of Shelters after Hurricane Hugo." *MMWR Morb Mortal Wkly Rep*, 39:41-47.

Centers for Disease Control and Prevention. (1998). "Community Needs Assessment and Morbidity Surveillance Following an Ice Storm Maine, January 1998." *MMWR Morb Mortal Wkly Rep*, 47:351-354.

Centers for Disease Control and Prevention. (1993) "Rapid Assessment of Vectorborne Diseases during the Midwest Flood—United States." *MMWR Morbidity and Mortality Weekly Report*, 43(26):481-3, 1994 Jul 8.

Centers for Disease Control and Prevention. (1992) "Rapid Assessment Following Hurricane Andrew B Florida and Louisiana, 1992." *MMWR Morbidity and Mortality Weekly Report*, 41(38):719, Sep 25.

Malilay J, Guido MR, Ramirez AV, Noji E, Sinks T. (1996). "Public Health Surveillance after a Volcanic Eruption: Lessons from Cerro Negro, Nicaragua, 1992." *Bulletin of PAHO*, 30(3):218-226.

OCarroll PW, Friede A, Noji EK, Lillibridge SR, Fries DJ, Atchison CG. (1995). "The Rapid Implementation of a Statewide Emergency Health Information System During the 1993 Iowa Flood." *Am J Public Health*, 85:564-567.

TECHNOLOGICAL DISASTERS

Baum, A. (1987). "Toxins, Technology, Disasters." In: G.R. VandenBos B.K. Bryant, eds., *Cataclysms, Crises, and Catastrophes: Psychology in Action*. Washington, DC: American Psychological Association.

Becker, S.M. (1997). "Psychosocial Assistance after Environmental Accidents: A Policy Perspective." *Environmental Health Perspectives*, 105(S6):1557-1563.

Bromet, E.J., Parkinson, D.K., Dunn, L.O. (1990). "Long-term Mental Health Consequences of the Accident at Three Mile Island." *International Journal of Mental Health*, 19, 48-60.

Cuthbertson, B.H., Nigg, J.M. (1987). "Technological Disaster and the Nontherapeutic Community: A Question of True Victimization." *Environment and Behavior*, 19(4):462-483.

Edelstein, M.R. (1988). *Contaminated Communities: The Social and Psychological Impacts of Residential Toxic Exposure.* Boulder, CO: Westview.

Edelstein, M.R., Wandersman, A. (1987). "Community Dynamics in Coping with Toxic Contaminants." In: I. Altman, A. Wandersman, eds., *Neighborhood and Community Environments.* Vol. 9, *Series Human Behavior and Environment: Advances in Theory and Research.* New York: Plenum Press.

Haavenaar, J.M., Rumyantzeva, G.M., van den Brink, W., Poelijoe, N.W., van den Bout, J., van Engeland, H., Koeter, M.W.J. (1997). Long-term Mental Healths Effects of the Chernobyl Disaster: An Epidemiologic Survey of Two Former Soviet Regions. *American Journal of Psychiatry,* 154, 1605-1607.

FRC (1996). Annex III: "The Role of the Red Cross and Red Crescent Societies in Response to Technological Disasters." *International Review of the Red Cross,* 310, 55-130.

Leonard, RB. (1993). "Hazardous materials accidents: Initial scene assessment and patient care." *Aviation, Space and Environmental Medicine,* June, 646-661.

Levitin, H.W., Siegelson, H.J. (1996). "Hazardous Materials: Disaster Medical Planning and Response." *Emergency Medicine Clinics of North America,* 14(2): 327-348.

Levy K, Hirsch, EF, Aghababian RV, Segall A, Vanderschmidt H. (1999). "Radiation Accident Preparedness: Report of a Training Program Involving the United States, Eastern Europe, and the Newly Independent States." *American Journal of Public Health.* 89(7):115-6.

Kroll-Smith, J.S., Couch, S.R. (1993). "Technological Hazards: Social Responses as Traumatic Stressors." In: J.P. Wilson, B. Raphael, eds. (1993). *The International Handbook of Traumatic Stress Syndromes.* New York: Plenum Press, pp. 79-91.

Lillibridge, S.R. (1997). *Industrial Disasters.* In: Noji, E.K., ed. *The Public Health Consequences of Disasters.* New York: Oxford University Press, pp. 354-372.

Quarantelli, E.L. (1993). "The Environmental Disasters of the Future Will be More and Worse but the Prospect is not Hopeless. *Disaster Prevention and Management,* 2, 11-25.

WORKER SAFETY

Lippy B. (2003). "Protecting the Health and Safety of Rescue and Recovery Workers." In: Levy, B.S., Sidel, V.W., eds. *Terrorism and Public Health: A Balanced Approach to Strengthening Systems and Protecting People.* New York: Oxford University Press, Inc.

National Institute for Occupational Safety and Health. (2004). "Protecting Emergency Responders, Volume 3 Safety Management in Disaster and Terrorism Response" DHHS (NIOSH) Publication No. 2004-144. RAND Publication No. MG-170. Cincinnati, OH and Santa Monica, CA.

http://www.osha-slc.gov/SLTC/smallbusiness/sec10.html

VOLCANOES

Baxter. P.J. "Volcanoes." In: Noji E.K., ed. *The Public Health Consequences of Disasters.* New York: Oxford University Press; 1997.

http://pubs.usgs.gov/gip/volc/eruptions.html

http://www.learner.org/exhibits/volcanoes/entry.html

http://volcanoes.usgs.gov/

http://volcanoes.usgs.gov/Products/Warn/warn.html

Index

assessments, 40
disaster preparedness, response and recovery, 305–312
education for, 41
emergencies, 37
evaluation, 43
functional model of response, 37
laws for, 37
personnel, 36
planning, 38
planning with GIS, 108
prevention, 38–39
recovery, 42–43
recovery and reconstruction, 263–270
response, 40, 271–277
role and responsibility, 33–43
structure and organization of, 45–89
surveillance, 42
types of data sets, 107
Public health preparedness program, key elements of, 345
Public health surveillance, 93
post-impact, 95–96, 96t
syndromic, 99
Public notice templates, 177
Public utilities, 124
Public works/highway department, 60t
Pulsenet, 101

Q
Q fever, 236
Quarantine, 234, 260

R
Rabies, 29t
Radio Amateur Civil Emergency Service (RACES), 145–146
Radiological power plants, 118
Radio networks, 143–144
Rapid health assessment, 115–129
Recovery, 149
Recovery and reconstruction, 263–270
Regional Emergency Management Plan (REMP), 182
Reimbursement, 88
Residential care facilities, 159
Response plan, bioterrorism, 237–238
Richter magnitude, 10
Richter Scale, 117
Risk assessment, 115–129, 362
modeling in, 122

S
S. aureus, 177
Safe Drinking Water Act, 174–175
Saffir-Simpson Hurricane Scale, 6t, 117
Salmonellosis, 29t, 177, 237, 365
Salvation Army, 146
Sanitation, 46, 54, 95, 123, 124, 126, 165–168, 341
Satellite communications, 144–145
Schools/day care, 108
Search and rescue, 155–156, 264, 275
Secretary's Command Center (SCC), 52
Security, 241
information technology, 373–377
Septic tanks, 172–174
Service animals, 227
Severe weather watches and warnings, definitions, 17t
Shelter, 108, 126, 134–135, 158, 165, 181–182, 218–219
Shigella dysenteriae, 181, 237, 365
Signage, tactile and audible, 223–224
Siple and Passel Index, 3
Sleep disturbances/insomnia, 192–194
Smallpox, 29t, 235–236, 238t
Snowfall, heavy, 3–4
Social environment, 269–270
Social unrest/war, 112t–113t
Social withdrawal, 192
Somatization, 192
Spatial Data Transfer Standard (SFTS), 109
Special needs persons, 158, 192
Special needs shelters, 266–267
supportive care in, 268–269
Splash exposures, 186
Stafford Disaster Relief and Emergency Assistance Act, 48–50, 88, 93, 160, 200
Staphylococcus enterotoxin, 237
State and local response, 71
State Coordinating Officer (SCO), 49
State Emergency Management Office (SEMO), 63
Strategic National Stockpile (SNS), 63, 239
Streptococcus, 177, 365
Stress
disaster-related, 190–191
environmental exposure, 199t
Submarine landslides, earthquake and, 10–11
Substance Abuse and Mental Health